Dungeons & Dragons®

Monster Manual® 2

ROLEPLAYING GAME SUPPLEMENT

Rob Heinsoo • Stephen Schubert

CREDITS

Design
Rob Heinsoo (lead), Eytan Bernstein,
Greg Bilsland, Jesse Decker, N. Eric Heath,
Peter Lee, Chris Sims, Owen K.C. Stephens

Additional Design
Logan Bonner, Greg Gorden Chris Lindsay,
Mike Mearls, Matthew Sernett, Greg Stolze,

Development
Stephen Schubert (lead),
Peter Lee, Peter Schaefer

Additional Development
Stephen Radney-MacFarland

Editing
Julia Martin (lead),
Greg Bilsland, Jeremy Crawford,
Paul Grasshoff, Scott Fitzgerald Gray,
M. Alexander Jurkat, Jessica Kristine,
Bill McQuillan, Jeff Morgenroth

Managing Editing
Torah Cottrill, Kim Mohan

Director of D&D R&D and Book Publishing
Bill Slavicsek

D&D Creative Manager
Christopher Perkins

Senior Art Director
Jon Schindehette

D&D Design Manager
James Wyatt

D&D Development and Editing Manager
Andy Collins

Art Director
Mari Kolkowsky

Graphic Designer
Bob Jordan

Cover Illustration
Jesper Ejsing (front), Ralph Horsley (back)

Interior Illustrations
Dave Allsop, Zoltan Boros & Gabor Szikszai, Christopher Burdett, Chippy, Brian Despain, Steve Ellis, Wayne England, Jason Engle, Adam Gillespie, Tomás Giorello, Lars Grant-West, Des Hanley, Ralph Horsley, Andrew Hou, Jeremy Jarvis, Todd Lockwood, Warren Mahy, Jim Nelson, William O'Connor, Steve Prescott, Vinod Rams, Chris Seaman, Matias Tapia, Mark Tedin, Francis Tsai, Brian Valenzuela, Franz Vohwinkel, Eva Widermann, Eric Williams, Sam Wood, Ben Wootten

D&D Brand Team
Liz Schuh, Scott Rouse, Kierin Chase, Sara Girard, Martin Durham

Publishing Production Specialist
Erin Dorries

Prepress Manager
Jefferson Dunlap

Imaging Technician
Ashley Brock

Production Manager
Cynda Callaway

Game rules based on the original DUNGEONS & DRAGONS® rules created by **E. Gary Gygax** and **Dave Arneson**, and the later editions by **David "Zeb" Cook** (2nd Edition); **Jonathan Tweet, Monte Cook, Skip Williams, Richard Baker,** and **Peter Adkison** (3rd Edition); and **Rob Heinsoo, Andy Collins,** and **James Wyatt** (4th Edition).

620-23966720-001 EN
9 8 7 6 5 4 3 2 1
First Printing:
May 2009
ISBN: 978-0-7869-5101-7

U.S., CANADA, ASIA, PACIFIC,
& LATIN AMERICA
Wizards of the Coast LLC
P.O. Box 707
Renton WA 98057-0707
+1-800-324-6496

EUROPEAN HEADQUARTERS
Hasbro UK Ltd
Caswell Way
Newport, Gwent NP9 0YH
GREAT BRITAIN
Please keep this address for your records

WIZARDS OF THE COAST, BELGIUM
Industrialaan 1
1702 Groot-Bijgaarden
Belgium
+32.070.233.277

VISIT OUR WEBSITE AT WWW.WIZARDS.COM/DND

CONTENTS

ALPHABETICAL LISTING OF MONSTERS

MONSTERS A TO Z

THE SECOND compendium of monsters for the DUNGEONS & DRAGONS® game, *Monster Manual*® 2 is filled with a new assortment of creatures designed to challenge and terrify adventurers of all levels.

The monsters in these pages offer threats of every level and include brand new monsters, such as firbolgs and djinns, as well as new versions of familiar monsters like giants and demons. *Monster Manual 2* also introduces the metallic dragons, which join their chromatic kin in the game.

The rest of this introduction explains how to read a monster's statistics block and assumes you're familiar with the power and combat rules in the *Player's Handbook*®. The glossary, starting on page 216, defines many of the terms used in the book, and the list of monsters by level, starting on page 221, is meant to assist you in tailoring encounters for your player characters (PCs).

THE STATISTICS BLOCK

A monster's statistics are presented in a format meant to be used in play. A typical statistics block is formatted as follows.

Monster Name	**Level and Role**
Size, origin, and type (keywords)	XP value

Initiative modifier   **Senses** Perception modifier; special senses
Aura name (keywords) aura size; effect.
HP maximum; **Bloodied** value
Regeneration
AC; **Fortitude, Reflex, Will**
Immune effects; **Resist** effects; **Vulnerable** effects
Saving Throws modifier
Speed
Action Points
[Power icon] **Power name** (action; requirement; recharge) ✦
　　Keywords
　　Range and area; targets; attack bonus vs. defense; effect on a hit. *Miss:* Result (if any). Other effects.
Alignment　　　　**Languages**
Skills skill modifiers
Str score (modifier)　**Dex** score (modifier)　**Wis** score (modifier)
Con score (modifier)　**Int** score (modifier)　　**Cha** score (modifier)
Equipment armor, shield, weapons, other equipment

Level and Role

A monster's level and role are tools for the DM to use when building an encounter. Chapter 4 of the *Dungeon Master's Guide* explains how to use these tools.

Level: A monster's level summarizes how tough it is in an encounter. Level determines most of the monster's statistics as well as the experience point (XP) award the PCs earn for defeating it (*Dungeon Master's Guide*, pages 56–57).

Role: A monster's role describes its preferred combat tactics, much as a character class's role suggests tactics for PCs. Monster roles are artillery, brute, controller, lurker, skirmisher, and soldier (*Dungeon Master's Guide*, pages 54–55).

A monster might have a second role: elite, solo, or minion. Elite monsters and solo monsters are tougher than standard monsters, and minions are weaker. For the purpose of encounter building, an elite monster counts as two standard monsters of its level, a solo monster counts as five, and four minions count as one.

In addition, a monster might have the leader subrole, indicating that it grants some sort of boon to its allies, such as a beneficial aura.

Size

A creature's size determines its space as well as its reach.

Monster Size	Space	Reach
Tiny	1/2 × 1/2	0
Small	1 × 1	1
Medium	1 × 1	1
Large	2 × 2	1 or 2
Huge	3 × 3	2 or 3
Gargantuan	4 × 4 or larger	3 or 4

Space: This is the area (measured in squares) that a creature occupies on the battle grid.

Reach: If a creature's reach is greater than 1, the reach is noted in any melee power the creature has that uses that reach. Even if a creature's reach is greater than 1, the creature can't make opportunity attacks against targets that aren't adjacent to it unless it has threatening reach.

A creature that has reach 0 cannot normally make melee attacks outside its own space.

Origin

A monster's origin summarizes its place in the D&D cosmology. Origins are aberrant, elemental, fey, immortal, natural, and shadow. See the glossary for information about each origin.

Type

A creature's type summarizes some basic things about its appearance and behavior. Types are animate, beast, humanoid, and magical beast. See the glossary for information about each type.

Keywords

Some monsters have keywords that further define them. These keywords represent groups of monsters, such as angel, demon, devil, dragon, and undead. See the glossary for definitions of a monster's keywords.

Senses

Every monster has a Perception modifier. Some monsters also have special senses, such as darkvision or tremorsense, which are noted in the "Senses" entry.

Aura

If a monster has an aura, that is noted near the top of its statistics block. An aura is a continuous effect that emanates from the monster. See the glossary for more about auras.

Regeneration

Some monsters have regeneration. At the start of each of its turns, a monster that has regeneration regains a specific number of hit points, as long as the monster has at least 1 hit point.

The regeneration of some monsters can be suppressed by certain types of damage or by specific circumstances, and some creatures can use regeneration only under specific circumstances (for example, only while bloodied).

Speed

If a monster has alternative movement modes, such as fly, climb, or swim, that fact is noted in its speed entry.

Action Points

Elite and solo monsters have action points they can spend to take extra actions, just as PCs do. Unlike PCs, a monster can spend more than 1 action point in an encounter, but only 1 per round.

Powers

A monster's powers are presented so that its basic attacks appear first, followed by its other powers.

Type

Each power has an icon that represents its type: melee (✦), ranged (✦), close (✦), or area (✦). If a power doesn't have an icon, it's a personal power.

A basic attack has a circle around its icon: melee basic attack ⊕ or ranged basic attack ⊛.

Action

If a power requires an action to use, that fact is noted in the power's description. An immediate action's trigger is noted right after the action type. Some powers don't require an action to use; they simply occur in response to a trigger.

Requirement

Some powers are usable only if a precondition is met. For example, a power might be usable only while a monster is bloodied or only if it is wielding a specific weapon. A requirement is noted after a power's action type, if any.

Recharge

A monster power is at-will, encounter, or daily, or it recharges in certain circumstances.

Recharge ⚀ ⚁ ⚂ ⚃ ⚄ : The power has a random chance of recharging during each round of combat. At the start of each of the monster's turns, roll a d6. If the roll is one of the die results shown in the power description, the monster regains the use of that power. The power also recharges after a short rest.

Recharges when . . . : The power recharges in a specific circumstance, such as when the monster is first bloodied during an encounter. The power also recharges after a short rest.

Range and Area

A melee power has a range of 1, unless otherwise noted. Ranged powers specify a range, and area powers and close powers specify a range and an area of effect.

Targets

Some monster powers specify targets. An area attack or a close attack targets each creature within its area of effect, unless otherwise noted.

Attack

Unless an attack power hits automatically, its description includes an attack notation, which specifies the monster's attack bonus for that power and which defense it targets.

Hit: The effect of a power hitting is specified after the attack notation.

Miss: Some attack powers have an effect on a miss (indicated by *Miss*).

Effect: Some attack powers have an effect whether or not the attack hits (indicated by *Effect*).

Effects

Monster powers include many of the same effects that appear in PC powers, such as aftereffects, conditions, damage of various types, ongoing damage, and secondary attacks.

A power's effects are instantaneous, unless otherwise noted. The effects of some powers can be sustained (indicated by *Sustain* and then whatever action is required to sustain the effect).

Alignment

A monster's most typical alignment is noted in its statistics block. Chapter 2 of the *Player's Handbook* contains information on the various alignments.

Languages

A statistics block gives the languages that a monster typically can speak and understand. An individual monster might know additional languages, like Common or the languages of its companions. See the *Dungeon Master's Guide*, page 171, for more information about the languages of the D&D world.

Skills

The skills section of a monster's statistics block includes only trained skills or skills for which the monster has an unusual modifier. A monster's Perception modifier isn't repeated here.

Ability Scores

A monster's six ability scores are included toward the bottom of its statistics block. Following each score in parentheses is the adjusted ability score modifier, including one-half the monster's level, which is useful whenever the monster needs to make an untrained skill check or an ability check.

Equipment

A monster's "Equipment" entry notes the weapons and implements the creature uses. If a character gains a monster's equipment, he or she can use it as normal equipment. A character does not gain the powers that a monster uses through its equipment.

Healing Surges

Monsters have healing surges. However, few monsters have powers that let them spend healing surges. The number of healing surges a monster has is based on its level: 1-10, one healing surge; 11-20, two healing surges; 21 or higher, three healing surges.

Because they rarely come into play, healing surges are not included in a monster's statistics block.

ANGELS ARE DIVINE SERVANTS OF THE GODS. Although common in the Astral Sea, they can be found anywhere acting on behalf of a deity or other force whose goals align with their calling.

ANGEL OF AUTHORITY

AN ANGEL OF AUTHORITY IS THE MOUTHPIECE of a deity. This angel governs other angels and servants of a deity in and out of combat.

Angel of Authority		Level 22 Controller (Leader)
Large immortal humanoid (angel)		XP 4,150

Initiative +17 **Senses** Perception +18
HP 203; **Bloodied** 101
AC 36; **Fortitude** 32, **Reflex** 34, **Will** 35
Immune fear; **Resist** 15 radiant
Speed 8, fly 12 (hover)

⊕ **Quarterstaff** (standard; at-will) ✦ **Radiant, Weapon**
  Reach 2; +27 vs. AC; 1d10 + 8 damage plus 1d10 radiant damage.

⌁ **Lightning Bolt** (standard; at-will) ✦ **Lightning**
  Ranged 10; +26 vs. Fortitude; 2d10 + 8 lightning damage, and the target is dazed until the end of the angel of authority's next turn.

⟵ **Majestic Rally** (standard; recharge ⚄ ⚅) ✦ **Radiant, Thunder**
  Close burst 5; targets enemies; +26 vs. Will; 1d10 + 8 radiant damage plus 1d10 thunder damage, and the target is weakened (save ends). *Miss:* Half damage. *Effect:* Any angel within the burst gains a +2 bonus to attack rolls until the end of the angel of authority's next turn.

Angelic Presence (while not bloodied)
  Any attack against the angel of authority takes a -2 penalty to the attack roll.

Alignment Unaligned   **Languages** Supernal
Skills Insight +23, Religion +23
Str 20 (+16)	**Dex** 22 (+17)	**Wis** 25 (+18)
Con 19 (+15)	**Int** 24 (+18)	**Cha** 27 (+19)
Equipment plate armor, quarterstaff

ANGEL OF AUTHORITY TACTICS
An angel of authority stays behind the lines, raining down *lightning bolts* and bolstering allies with *majestic rally* whenever possible.

ANGEL OF AUTHORITY LORE
  Religion DC 24: An angel of authority is the herald of a particular deity. The angel handles the most important tasks concerning the protection and well-being of the deity's dominion.

ENCOUNTER GROUPS
An angel of authority leads angels of protection, vengeance, supremacy, battle, and valor. It also administers or directs other servants of a deity who are not angels.

Level 22 Encounter (XP 21,400)
✦ 1 angel of authority (level 22 controller)
✦ 2 angels of vengeance (level 19 elite brute, *MM* 17)
✦ 6 angels of light (level 23 minion)

ANGEL OF RETRIEVAL

WHEN DEITIES REQUIRE THE RECOVERY of a stolen object or a kidnapped creature, they send a squad of divine beings that includes an expert tracker: the angel of retrieval.

Angel of Retrieval	Level 22 Artillery
Large immortal humanoid (angel)	XP 4,150

Initiative +20   **Senses** Perception +22; blindsight
HP 162; **Bloodied** 81
AC 34; **Fortitude** 33, **Reflex** 35, **Will** 33
Immune fear; **Resist** 15 radiant
Speed 8, fly 12 (hover), teleport 5

⊕ **Short Sword** (standard; at-will) ✦ **Radiant, Weapon**
  Reach 2; +27 vs. AC; 2d6 + 6 radiant damage.

⊙ **Angelic Bow** (standard; at-will) ✦ **Radiant, Weapon**
  Ranged 20/40; +27 vs. AC; 2d8 + 9 radiant damage, and each enemy adjacent to the target takes 10 radiant damage.

⸸ **Isolating Displacement** (standard; at-will) ✦ **Radiant, Teleportation**
  Reach 2; +27 vs. Reflex; 2d8 + 10 radiant damage, and the angel of retrieval teleports the target 5 squares. The angel then teleports to a space adjacent to the target. The angel can choose to deal no damage with this attack. *Miss:* The angel teleports 5 squares.

❖ **Clear the Way** (standard; recharge ⚄ ⚅) ✦ **Radiant**
  Area burst 3 within 10; +27 vs. Fortitude; 3d8 + 9 radiant damage, and the angel of retrieval slides the target 3 squares. *Miss:* Half damage, and the angel slides the target 1 square.

Hunt the Guilty (minor; encounter)
  The angel of retrieval chooses one enemy within 10 squares of it. Until the end of the encounter, the angel's attacks deal 1d10 extra damage against that creature.

Alignment Unaligned   **Languages** Supernal
Skills Arcana +28, Intimidate +29
Str 22 (+17)	**Dex** 28 (+20)	**Wis** 23 (+17)
Con 24 (+18)	**Int** 23 (+17)	**Cha** 24 (+18)
Equipment plate armor, longbow, short sword

ANGEL OF RETRIEVAL TACTICS
An angel of retrieval is often dispatched to capture a person or a thing. The angel uses *hunt the guilty* on the individual to be captured or the one holding an item to be recovered. The angel uses *clear the way* to give its allies more space to maneuver. Otherwise, the angel prefers to fight from a distance with its *angelic bow*.

(Left to right) angel of authority, angel of light, and angel of supremacy

ANGEL OF RETRIEVAL LORE

Religion DC 24: An angel of retrieval is best described as a bounty hunter from the Astral Sea. These angels are trained in rituals that allow them to hunt down creatures, such as Observe Creature (*Player's Handbook*, page 309) and Planar Portal (*Player's Handbook*, page 311).

ENCOUNTER GROUPS

An angel of retrieval is assisted by other angels in interplanar hunting parties.

Level 23 Encounter (XP 21,400)
✦ 1 angel of retrieval (level 22 artillery)
✦ 2 angels of supremacy (level 24 soldier)
✦ 12 angel of valor legionnaires (level 21 minion, *MM* 16)

ANGEL OF LIGHT

MADE PURELY OF DIVINE ENERGY, an angel of light exists as a brilliant embodiment of a deity's subconscious.

Angel of Light	Level 23 Minion Skirmisher
Medium immortal humanoid (angel)	XP 1,275

Initiative +19   **Senses** Perception +19
HP 1; a missed attack never damages a minion; see also *death burst*.
AC 37; **Fortitude** 34, **Reflex** 34, **Will** 36
Immune fear; **Resist** 15 radiant
Speed 8, fly 12 (hover)
⊕ **Angelic Glaive** (standard; at-will) ✦ **Weapon**
    Reach 2; +28 vs. AC; 15 damage.
⬳ **Death Burst** (when the angel of light drops to 0 hit points) ✦ **Radiant**
    The angel of light explodes in a burst of radiant light: close burst 10; targets enemies; +26 vs. Fortitude. *Effect:* Angels in the burst gain 10 temporary hit points.
Alignment Unaligned   **Languages** Supernal
Str 18 (+15)   **Dex** 23 (+17)   **Wis** 27 (+19)
Con 23 (+17)   **Int** 15 (+13)   **Cha** 23 (+17)
Equipment glaive

ANGEL OF LIGHT TACTICS

A squad of angels of light spreads out and tries to attack as many targets as possible. They never retreat from battle.

Angel of Light Lore

Religion DC 24: An angel of light is the bound form of a deity's subconscious thoughts, appearing in the Astral Sea as a mote of pure energy until given direction by more powerful angels. The thought that originally formed it drives its actions eternally.

Religion DC 29: Although directed by a deity's thoughts, angels of light can act independently to see those thoughts enacted. There have even been rare occasions when angels of light acted in ways contrary to their creators' ethos in zealous attempts to see those ideas made real.

Encounter Groups

Angels of light are found with other angels or as members of a larger group enforcing a deity's will.

Level 22 Encounter (XP 24,550)
+ 1 angel of supremacy (level 24 soldier)
+ 8 angels of light (level 23 minion)
+ 1 marut concordant (level 22 elite controller, MM 85)

Angel of Supremacy

ANGELS OF SUPREMACY ARE THE STRONGEST of the angelic fighters.

Angel of Supremacy	Level 24 Soldier
Large immortal humanoid (angel)	XP 6,050

Initiative +19   **Senses** Perception +18
HP 226; **Bloodied** 113
AC 40; **Fortitude** 38, **Reflex** 36, **Will** 35
Immune fear; **Resist** 15 radiant
Speed 8, fly 12 (hover)
⊕ **Spear** (standard; at-will) ✦ **Thunder, Weapon**
    Reach 3; +31 vs. AC; 1d10 + 9 damage plus 1d10 thunder damage.
↗ **Light of Justice** (standard; encounter) ✦ **Radiant**
    Ranged 10; +29 vs. Fortitude; 2d10 + 9 radiant damage. *Effect:* The target is marked until the end of the encounter.
↗ **Summons to Justice** (minor 1/round; at-will)
    Ranged sight; targets creatures marked by the angel of supremacy; no attack roll; the angel of supremacy pulls the target 1 square.
↶ **Astral Brilliance** (standard; encounter) ✦ **Radiant, Zone**
    Close burst 3; +29 vs. Reflex; 2d10 + 9 radiant damage. *Effect:* The burst creates a zone of radiance that lasts until the end of the encounter. The angel of supremacy's spear attack deals 1d10 extra radiant damage while the angel is within the zone.
Angelic Presence (while not bloodied)
    Any attack against the angel of supremacy takes a -2 penalty to the attack roll.
Threatening Reach
    An angel of supremacy can make opportunity attacks against all enemies in reach.
Alignment Unaligned   **Languages** Supernal
Skills Intimidate +21
Str 29 (+21)   **Dex** 21 (+17)   **Wis** 22 (+18)
Con 26 (+20)   **Int** 25 (+19)   **Cha** 19 (+16)
Equipment plate armor, heavy shield, spear

Angel of Supremacy Tactics

An angel of supremacy positions itself at a chokepoint or other tactically important location and uses *astral brilliance*. It targets a melee combatant with *summons to justice*, bringing the target within reach of its spear and the radiant zone.

Angel of Supremacy Lore

Religion DC 24: Angels of supremacy guard the homes of gods and protect the gods' favored mortal servants. They are also the backbone of strike force groups for a deity.

Encounter Groups

An angel of supremacy is the vanguard of any strike force sent by the gods.

Level 24 Encounter (XP 30,350)
+ 3 angels of supremacy (level 24 soldier)
+ 1 deva fallen star (level 26 artillery)
+ 1 tormenting ghost (level 21 controller, MM 117)

ARCHANGEL

The highest of all angels are the Archangels, powerful beings from the Astral Sea. An archangel is the ultimate authority in an astral dominion with the exception of the actual deity.

    The archangel template can be applied to any angel.

Archangel	Elite Controller
(angel)	XP Elite

Saving Throws +2
Action Point 1
Hit Points +8 per level + Constitution score
Powers
‡ **Avenging Strike** (when an ally within 5 squares of the archangel drops to 0 hit points; at-will)
    The archangel shifts 2 squares and makes a melee basic attack as a free action.
↶ **Overwhelming Presence** (standard; encounter) ✦ **Radiant**
    Close burst 5, targets enemies; level + 4 vs. Will; 1d8 + Wisdom modifier radiant damage, and the target is stunned until the end of the archangel's next turn.

ANKHEG

Loathsome insects with a taste for bipedal prey, ankhegs burst from hiding to seize the unwary. An ankheg moves with great stealth, but might be detected by the faint whiff of acid dripping from its twitching mandibles.

Ankheg	Level 3 Elite Lurker
Large natural beast	XP 300

Initiative +10   **Senses** Perception +9; tremorsense 5
HP 100; **Bloodied** 50
AC 17; **Fortitude** 14, **Reflex** 16, **Will** 14
Resist 5 acid
Saving Throws +2
Speed 8, burrow 4 (tunneling)
Action Points 1
⊕ **Claw** (standard; at-will)
    +8 vs. AC; 1d8 + 5 damage.
✦ **Mandible Grab** (standard; usable only while the ankheg does not
    have a creature grabbed; at-will)
    +8 vs. AC; 1d8 + 5 damage, and the target is grabbed; see also
    mandible carry.
✦ **Gnaw and Scuttle** (minor; at-will) ✦ **Acid**
    Targets a creature grabbed by the ankheg; +8 vs. AC; 1d8 + 2
    damage, and ongoing 5 acid damage (save ends). The ankheg
    then shifts 2 squares and pulls the target to space adjacent to
    its new location.
↩ **Acid Spray** (standard; recharges when first bloodied) ✦ **Acid**
    Close blast 3; +8 vs. Reflex; 1d8 + 5 acid damage, and the target
    is slowed and takes ongoing 5 acid damage (save ends both).
Mandible Carry
    An ankheg can move at normal speed while carrying a creature
    that is Medium or smaller.
Alignment Unaligned   **Languages** –
Skills Stealth +11

Str 15 (+3)	Dex 20 (+6)	Wis 16 (+4)
Con 18 (+5)	Int 2 (–3)	Cha 4 (–2)

Ankheg Broodling	Level 1 Minion Brute
Small natural beast	XP 25

Initiative +3   **Senses** Perception +1; tremorsense 5
HP 1; a missed attack never damages a minion.
AC 15; **Fortitude** 12, **Reflex** 14, **Will** 12
Resist 5 acid
Speed 6, burrow 2 (tunneling)
⊕ **Claw** (standard; at-will)
    +5 vs. AC; 4 damage.
✦ **Mandible Rip** (standard; at-will) ✦ **Acid**
    +4 vs. AC; 6 damage. If the ankheg broodling makes a critical
    hit against a target, each creature adjacent to that target takes 3
    acid damage.
Brood Swarm
    An ankheg broodling gains a +4 bonus to attack rolls against
    targets that are grabbed by any ankheg.
Alignment Unaligned   **Languages** –
Skills Stealth +8

Str 10 (+0)	Dex 16 (+3)	Wis 12 (+1)
Con 13 (+1)	Int 1 (–5)	Cha 2 (–4)

ANKHEG TACTICS

Adult ankhegs strike quickly, attempting to grab and carry away a vulnerable target. An ankheg broodling remains in hiding until an adult ankheg has brought a grabbed victim near.

ANKHEG LORE

Nature DC 10: Ankhegs dig mazelike networks of tunnels, which might contain other monsters that have claimed part of the tunnel network as their own.

Nature DC 15: Ankhegs are found in nesting pairs, their broodlings rarely emerging from the safety of their tunnels.

ENCOUNTER GROUPS

Ankhegs are normally encountered as pairs. Broodlings are occasionally controlled by giant ants after the ant hives drive away or kill the adult ankhegs.

Level 4 Encounter (XP 950)
✦ 2 ankhegs (level 3 elite lurker)
✦ 6 ankheg broodlings (level 1 minion)
✦ 1 rage drake (level 5 brute, *MM* 92)

WAVES OF SINGLE-MINDED GIANT ANTS can strip the landscape bare for miles, overcoming any foe with sheer numbers. They have been known to reduce towns to bare earth.

HIVE WORKER

WEAKEST OF THE GIANT ANTS, workers exist to fulfill the functional needs of the hive, providing little help in battle other than their swarming numbers.

Hive Worker	Level 1 Minion Skirmisher
Medium natural beast	XP 25

Initiative +0 · Senses Perception −1; low-light vision, tremorsense 10

HP 1; a missed attack never damages a minion.

AC 15; **Fortitude** 13, **Reflex** 13, **Will** 10

Speed 6, climb 6, burrow 2 (tunneling)

⊕ **Bite** (standard; at-will)
+6 vs. AC; 4 damage.

Hive Worker Frenzy (free, when any giant ant within 10 squares of the hive worker is reduced to 0 hit points; at-will)
The hive worker shifts 2 squares.

Alignment Unaligned	Languages —	
Str 17 (+3)	**Dex** 15 (+2)	**Wis** 9 (−1)
Con 14 (+2)	**Int** 2 (−4)	**Cha** 4 (−3)

HIVE WORKER TACTICS

A hive worker shows little initiative. It attacks any adjacent creature other than those of its own hive, or moves to attack any creature that is in combat with a member of its hive.

HIVE WARRIOR

A HIVE WARRIOR ACTS AS AN EXPLORER and guardian for the workers during their forays outside the hive.

Hive Warrior	Level 2 Skirmisher
Medium natural beast	XP 125

Initiative +6 · Senses Perception +0; low-light vision, tremorsense 10

HP 36; **Bloodied** 18

AC 16; **Fortitude** 14, **Reflex** 15, **Will** 11

Speed 8, climb 8

⊕ **Piercing Bite** (standard; at-will) ✦ Acid
+7 vs. AC; 1d8 + 4 damage. The hive warrior's attack deals 1d10 extra acid damage to any target that already has ongoing acid damage.

Hive Warrior Frenzy (free, when any giant ant within 10 squares of the hive warrior drops to 0 hit points; at-will)
The warrior is no longer marked or cursed, and it shifts 2 squares.

Alignment Unaligned	Languages —	
Str 14 (+3)	**Dex** 17 (+4)	**Wis** 9 (+0)
Con 12 (+2)	**Int** 2 (−3)	**Cha** 4 (−2)

HIVE SOLDIER

HIVE SOLDIERS REMAIN NEAR THE HIVE unless driven to conquest by the queen.

Hive Soldier	Level 3 Soldier
Medium natural beast	XP 150

Initiative +6 · Senses Perception +0; low-light vision, tremorsense 10

HP 46; **Bloodied** 23; see also *death convulsion*

AC 18; **Fortitude** 16, **Reflex** 15, **Will** 12

Speed 6, climb 6

⊕ **Grasping Mandibles** (standard; usable only while the hive soldier does not have a creature grabbed; at-will)
+10 vs. AC; 1d8 + 3 damage, and the target is grabbed.

↓ **Acid Sting** (standard; at-will) ✦ Acid
Targets a creature grabbed by the hive soldier; +10 vs. AC; 1d6 + 3 acid damage, and ongoing 5 acid damage (save ends).

↩ **Death Convulsion** (when the hive soldier drops to 0 hit points)
Close burst 1; targets enemies; +8 vs. Reflex; the target is knocked prone.

Hive Soldier Frenzy (when any giant ant within 10 squares of the hive soldier drops to 0 hit points; at-will)
The soldier gains a +2 bonus to attack rolls until the end of its next turn.

Alignment Unaligned	Languages —	
Str 17 (+4)	**Dex** 15 (+3)	**Wis** 9 (+0)
Con 14 (+3)	**Int** 2 (−3)	**Cha** 4 (−2)

WINGED DRONE

WINGED DRONES FLOOD FROM THE HIVE during mating season, spreading far and wide on iridescent wings.

Winged Drone	Level 4 Skirmisher
Medium natural beast	XP 175

Initiative +6 · Senses Perception +2; low-light vision, tremorsense 10

HP 55; **Bloodied** 27

AC 18; **Fortitude** 15, **Reflex** 17, **Will** 12

Speed 8, climb 8, fly 8

⊕ **Acid Sting** (standard; at-will) ✦ Acid
+9 vs. AC; 1d6 + 2 acid damage, and ongoing 5 acid damage (save ends).

↓ **Hive Drone Frenzy** (free, when any giant ant within 10 squares of the winged drone drops to 0 hit points; at-will)
The drone shifts 2 squares and uses *acid sting*.

↓ **Flyby Attack** (standard; at-will)
The winged drone flies 8 squares and makes one acid sting at any point during that movement. The drone doesn't provoke opportunity attacks when moving away from the target of the attack.

↩ **Shredding Wings** (standard; usable only while bloodied; encounter)
Close blast 2; +8 vs. AC; 3d6 + 4 damage, and the winged drone loses its fly speed until the end of the encounter.

Alignment Unaligned	Languages —	
Str 14 (+4)	**Dex** 18 (+6)	**Wis** 11 (+2)
Con 15 (+4)	**Int** 2 (−2)	**Cha** 4 (−1)

HIVE QUEEN

IN ADDITION TO BIRTHING FUTURE GENERATIONS, the hive queen directs the activities of her brood with a ruthless and single-minded purpose.

Hive Queen	Level 5 Elite Controller (Leader)
Large natural beast	XP 400

Initiative +6   **Senses** Perception +2; low-light vision, tremorsense 10

In the Presence of the Queen aura 10; each giant ant within the aura gains a +2 bonus to attack rolls and damage rolls.

HP 132; **Bloodied** 66

AC 19; **Fortitude** 19, **Reflex** 16, **Will** 17

Immune fear

Speed 6, climb 2

Saving Throws +2

Action Points 1

⊕ **Bite** (standard; at-will)
+10 vs. AC; 1d10 + 4 damage.

⊕ **Kick** (minor; at-will)
Reach 2; +9 vs. Reflex; 3 damage, and the hive queen pushes the target 3 squares.

⸸ **Hive Queen Frenzy** (free, when any giant ant within 10 squares of the hive queen drops to 0 hit points; at-will)
The queen shifts 2 squares and uses *kick*.

⬳ **Acidic Cloud** (standard; encounter) ✦ **Acid, Zone**
Close burst 4; the burst creates a zone of caustic gas that lasts until the end of the encounter. Any enemy that starts its turn within the zone takes 2 acid damage for each giant ant within the zone. The zone is centered on the hive queen and moves with her.

❈ **Acidic Blast** (standard; recharge ⚃ ⚅ ⚇) ✦ **Acid**
Area burst 3 within 10; targets enemies; +7 vs. Will; 1d6 + 2 acid damage, and the target is dazed (save ends). *Miss:* Half damage.

Call to Arms (when first bloodied; encounter)
Four new giant ant hive workers appear and act to defend their queen. Each ant appears within 5 squares of the hive queen, and acts on the queen's initiative count.

Alignment Unaligned   **Languages** –

Str 13 (+3)	Dex 12 (+3)	Wis 11 (+2)
Con 18 (+6)	Int 2 (−2)	Cha 15 (+4)

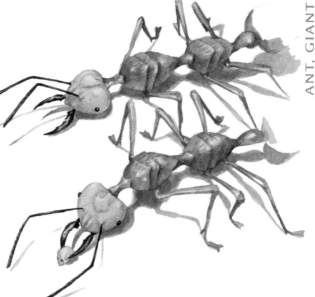

HIVE QUEEN TACTICS

A hive queen aims her *kick* carefully, pushing enemies into groups for an *acidic blast* attack or into swarming clusters of her brood. In a desperate situation, she calls a strategic retreat, sacrificing warriors without concern while leading soldiers and drones to a more advantageous location. If the entire brood is eliminated, the queen fights to the death.

GIANT ANT LORE

Nature DC 7: Giant ants live in hives consisting of hundreds of members. The majority of these ants are workers, but they all fight to defend the hive.

Nature DC 12: Although they are not intelligent, giant ants use teamwork and simple yet effective tactics. Giant ants possess a social organization rivaling that of the most efficient humanoids.

Nature DC 17: Giant ants communicate with nearby members of the hive by using a complex combination of pheromones. These pheromones are highly acidic, and the ants use them to damage foes.

ENCOUNTER GROUPS

Giant ants are encountered with others of their hive, since they generally consider anything else to be food.

Level 1 Encounter (XP 500)
✦ 1 hive soldier (level 3 soldier)
✦ 2 hive warriors (level 2 skirmisher)
✦ 4 hive workers (level 1 minion)

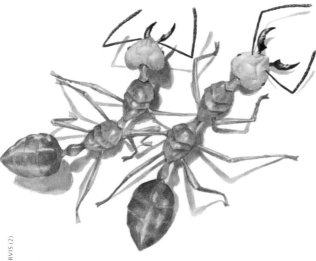

ARCHON

Primordials crafted archons to be soldiers in the cataclysmic war against the immortals of the Astral Sea. Now, they act as servitors and mercenaries for powerful forces within the Elemental Chaos, such as giants, efreets, and demons. These creatures of energy exert little will of their own, instead furthering the goals and ambitions of their masters. The few archons that are independent prowl the Elemental Chaos, attacking creatures without elemental origins.

Earth Archon Ground Rager

An earth archon ground rager is drawn to regions of geologic activity, such as volcanoes, fault zones, sink holes, or areas prone to landslides.

Earth Archon Ground Rager		Level 14 Controller
Medium elemental humanoid (earth)		XP 1,000

Initiative +9   **Senses** Perception +13; tremorsense 20
Earth Liquefaction aura 5; each creature without the earth
    keyword that ends its turn within the aura and did not move
    during its turn is slowed until the end of its next turn.
HP 143; **Bloodied** 71
AC 28; **Fortitude** 27, **Reflex** 25, **Will** 26
Immune disease, petrification, poison
Speed 6 (earth walk)
(⊕) **Slam** (standard; at-will)
    +19 vs. AC; 2d8 + 6 damage.
(↗) **Raging Earth** (standard; at-will) ✦ **Thunder**
    Ranged 20; +17 (+20 against slowed creatures) vs. Reflex; 1d8 +
    6 thunder damage, and the target is immobilized (save ends).
(↓) **Shove** (standard; at-will)
    +19 vs. AC; 1d10+6 damage, and the target is pushed 4 squares
    and knocked prone.
(✳) **Ground Eruption** (standard; recharge ⚄ ⚅) ✦ **Thunder**
    Area burst 1 within 10 ; +18 vs. Reflex; 2d8 + 6 thunder
    damage, and the target is knocked prone. *Miss:* Half damage,
    and the target is knocked prone.

Alignment Chaotic evil	**Languages** Primordial	
Str 20 (+12)	**Dex** 14 (+9)	**Wis** 23 (+13)
Con 23 (+13)	**Int** 19 (+11)	**Cha** 17 (+10)

Equipment chainmail

Earth Archon Seismic Striker

A seismic striker forms the foundation of an archon army in the Elemental Chaos. It sometimes acts as a guard for stone giants.

Earth Archon Seismic Striker		Level 16 Soldier
Medium elemental humanoid (earth)		XP 1,400

Initiative +16   **Senses** Perception +13; tremorsense 20
HP 160; **Bloodied** 80
AC 32; **Fortitude** 29, **Reflex** 28, **Will** 27
Immune disease, petrification, poison
Speed 6 (earth walk)
(⊕) **War Pick** (standard; at-will) ✦ **Thunder, Weapon**
    +23 vs. AC; 2d8 + 7 damage plus 1d8 thunder damage (crit 4d8
    + 23 damage plus 8 thunder damage).
(↗) **Stone Javelin** (standard; at-will) ✦ **Weapon**
    Ranged 10/20; +23 vs. AC; 1d10 + 7 damage, and the target is
    marked until the end of the earth archon seismic striker's next
    turn.
(↞) **Seismic Stomp** (standard; recharge ⚅) ✦ **Thunder**
    Close burst 3; +21 vs. Fortitude; 2d10 + 7 thunder damage, and
    the target is knocked prone. *Miss:* Half damage, and the target is
    knocked prone.
Ground Strike ✦ **Thunder**
    An earth archon seismic striker's attack deals an extra 1d8
    thunder damage against any prone enemy.
Combat Superiority
    An earth archon seismic striker gains a +5 bonus to opportunity
    attack rolls and immobilizes a creature that it hits with an
    opportunity attack.

Alignment Chaotic evil	**Languages** Primordial	
Str 18 (+12)	**Dex** 22 (+14)	**Wis** 21 (+13)
Con 24 (+15)	**Int** 15 (+10)	**Cha** 17 (+11)

Equipment plate armor, heavy shield, war pick, 5 javelins

Earth Archon Rumbler

Earth archon rumblers serve as shock troops in the armies of the Elemental Chaos, crushing any enemies too slow to flee.

Earth Archon Rumbler		Level 17 Brute
Medium elemental humanoid (earth)		XP 1,600

Initiative +12   **Senses** Perception +13; tremorsense 20
HP 204; **Bloodied** 102
AC 29; **Fortitude** 31, **Reflex** 28, **Will** 29
Immune disease, petrification, poison
Speed 6 (earth walk)
(⊕) **Stone Warhammer** (standard; at-will) ✦ **Weapon**
    +20 vs. AC; 2d10 + 9 damage.
(↞) **Avalanche Strike** (standard; at-will)
    Close burst 2; +18 vs. Reflex; 1d10 + 9 damage, and the target
    is knocked prone.
Thundering Might ✦ **Thunder**
    An earth archon rumbler's attack deals 2d8 extra thunder
    damage if the rumbler is adjacent to more than one enemy.

Alignment Chaotic evil	**Languages** Primordial	
Str 24 (+15)	**Dex** 18 (+12)	**Wis** 21 (+13)
Con 24 (+15)	**Int** 15 (+10)	**Cha** 17 (+11)

Equipment warhammer

(Left to right) earth archon seismic striker, ground rager, and rumbler

EARTH ARCHON LORE

Arcana DC 13: Earth archons prefer a slow, inexorable advance toward conquest, and they are excellent strategists. They prefer to take, hold, and fortify positions, unlike the rapid and destructive blazes of fire archons. In this regard earth archons are similar to ice archons and work well with them.

Arana DC 20: The greatest fortress of earth archons in the Elemental Chaos is Thrak-Harda, ruled by a stone titan named King Brakkamul. This sprawling fortification guards a huge gem called the Diamond of Despair.

Arcana DC 25: Rumors say that the fortifications around the Diamond of Despair are intended to protect others from it rather than to protect it from thieves. What danger it presents is a matter of speculation, and the Diamond has long been an obsession of the dao, mysterious cousins of the djinns and efreets.

ENCOUNTER GROUPS

Earth archons can be found with any type of elemental creature, eager to crush any enemy in their path.

Level 14 Encounter (XP 5,200)

✦ 1 earth archon ground rager (level 14 controller)
✦ 1 earth archon seismic striker (level 16 soldier)
✦ 2 fire archon emberguards (level 12 brute, *MM* 18)
✦ 1 ice archon hailscourge (level 16 artillery, *MM* 20)

Level 18 Encounter (XP 10,400)

✦ 1 cambion hellfire magus (level 18 artillery, *MM* 39)
✦ 1 earth archon ground rager (level 14 controller)
✦ 3 earth archon seismic strikers (level 16 soldier)
✦ 2 earth archon rumblers (level 17 brute)

STORM ARCHON SQUALLSHIELD

As tempestuous as a hurricane, a storm archon squallshield is always spoiling for a fight. It serves as versatile infantry to more powerful elemental lords, and goes out of its way to cause panic and suffering.

(Left to right) storm archon lightning walker, tempest weaver, and squallshield

Storm Archon Squallshield	Level 17 Soldier
Medium elemental humanoid (air, water)	XP 1,600

Initiative +15   **Senses** Perception +15
Rain Wall aura 1; each enemy that starts its turn within the aura must make a DC 22 Athletics check or Acrobatics check. An enemy that fails the check is knocked prone.
HP 168; **Bloodied** 84
AC 33; **Fortitude** 30, **Reflex** 30, **Will** 26
Immune disease, poison; **Resist** 15 lightning, 15 thunder
Speed fly 8 (hover)
ⓐ **Longsword** (standard; at-will) ✦ **Weapon**
    +23 vs. AC; 2d8 + 7 damage, and the target is marked until the end of the storm archon squallshield's next turn.
⟡ **Snarling Lightning** (standard; recharge ⚄ ⚅) ✦ **Lightning**
    Ranged 10; +21 vs. Reflex; 2d8 + 7 lightning damage, and the target is marked (save ends). Each enemy adjacent to the target takes half damage and is marked (save ends).
Pursuing Storm (move; recharge ⚄ ⚅) ✦ **Teleportation**
    The storm archon squallshield teleports 7 squares to a space adjacent to a creature it has marked. The target grants combat advantage to the squallshield until the end of the squallshield's turn.
Mark of the Tempest
    When a storm archon squallshield hits a creature marked by it with a ranged or melee attack, that creature is slowed (save ends).
Alignment Chaotic evil	**Languages** Primordial
Str 19 (+12)	**Dex** 20 (+13)	**Wis** 15 (+10)
Con 24 (+15)	**Int** 17 (+11)	**Cha** 17 (+11)

Equipment plate armor, light shield, longsword

STORM ARCHON SQUALLSHIELD TACTICS

A squallshield focuses its attacks on a weak target. It marks the foe from range using *snarling lightning* and then teleports next to it using *pursuing storm*. The squallshield then attacks with its longsword, keeping the target marked until the squallshield's other abilities recharge.

STORM ARCHON LIGHTNING WALKER

A LIGHTNING WALKER CRACKLES with intensity and arrogance, flashing across the battlefield faster than the eye can blink.

Storm Archon Lightning Walker	Level 18 Skirmisher
Medium elemental humanoid (air, water)	XP 2,000

Initiative +18   **Senses** Perception +16
HP 171; **Bloodied** 85
AC 32; **Fortitude** 29, **Reflex** 32, **Will** 29
Immune disease, poison; **Resist** 15 lightning, 15 thunder
Speed fly 8 (hover)
ⓐ **Spear** (standard; at-will) ✦ **Teleportation, Weapon**
    +23 vs. AC; 2d8 + 4 damage, and the storm archon lightning walker teleports the target 2 squares. *Effect:* The lightning walker teleports 2 squares.

+ Booming Retort (immediate reaction, when an enemy enters a square adjacent to the storm archon lightning walker; recharge ⚅ ⚄ ⚃) ✦ **Lightning, Thunder**
The triggering enemy takes ongoing 5 lightning and thunder damage (save ends), and the lightning walker shifts 2 squares.

↙ Lightning Pulse (standard; encounter) ✦ **Lightning, Teleportation**
Close burst 2; targets enemies; +21 vs. Reflex; 3d6 + 6 lightning damage. *Effect:* The storm archon lightning walker teleports 10 squares.

Alignment Chaotic evil	Languages Primordial	
Str 17 (+12)	Dex 24 (+16)	Wis 15 (+11)
Con 19 (+13)	Int 15 (+11)	Cha 18 (+13)
Equipment scale armor, spear		

STORM ARCHON
LIGHTNING WALKER TACTICS

A lightning walker is in constant motion on the battlefield, vanishing in a flash after every attack and reappearing a short distance away. The archon reserves *lightning pulse* for situations when it finds itself surrounded or flanked.

STORM ARCHON
TEMPEST WEAVER

RIDING THE TURBULENT WINDS and storms raging across the Elemental Chaos, a tempest weaver hurls down lightning at its foes with capricious zeal.

Storm Archon Tempest Weaver		Level 21 Artillery
Medium elemental humanoid (air, water)		XP 3,200

Initiative +12   Senses Perception +14
HP 155; **Bloodied** 77
AC 33 (35 with *defensive squall*); **Fortitude** 32, **Reflex** 33 (35 with *defensive squall*), **Will** 33
Immune disease, poison; **Resist** 15 lightning, 15 thunder
Speed 6, fly 8 (hover)

Ⓟ **Storm Touch** (standard; at-will) ✦ **Lightning**
+26 vs. Fortitude; 2d10 + 4 lightning damage.

⤢ **Resounding Bolt** (standard; at-will) ✦ **Lightning, Thunder**
Ranged 10; +26 vs. Fortitude; 1d10 + 5 thunder damage, and ongoing 10 lightning damage (save ends).

↙ **Lightning Blast** (standard; recharges when first bloodied) ✦ **Lightning**
Close burst 2; +24 vs. Reflex; 2d8 + 5 lightning damage, and the target is blinded until the end of the storm archon tempest weaver's next turn.

✳ **Heart of the Tempest** (standard; encounter) ✦ **Lightning, Thunder**
Area burst 3 within 20; targets enemies; +24 vs. Reflex; the target slides 3 squares, takes ongoing 10 lightning damage and ongoing 10 thunder damage, and is restrained (save ends all).

Defensive Squall
A storm archon tempest weaver gains a +2 bonus to its AC and Reflex against ranged attacks.

Alignment Chaotic evil	Languages Primordial	
Skills Intimidate +20		
Str 14 (+12)	Dex 15 (+12)	Wis 18 (+14)
Con 23 (+16)	Int 25 (+17)	Cha 25 (+16)
Equipment robes		

STORM ARCHON
TEMPEST WEAVER TACTICS

Unlike most artillery, a tempest weaver is willing to move close in combat. It begins with *heart of the tempest*, incapacitating as many creatures as possible and rearranging the battlefield to its advantage before closing in to use *storm touch*. The tempest weaver then withdraws, using its fly speed to put distance between itself and attackers.

STORM ARCHON LORE

Arcana DC 16: Storm archons live in floating storm cities that cruise through the Elemental Chaos. Always on the move, these cities drift overhead, indifferent to what happens beneath them. However, storm archons strike without provocation if they grow bored.

Arcana DC 24: Storm archons can be found in the company of storm giants, especially during the howling black tempests that rise up from the Abyss. Storm archons and storm giants ride these evil winds as they swirl through the layers of the Elemental Chaos, spilling out into planes beyond to cause tornadoes and hurricanes.

Arcana DC 29: Storm archons and storm giants are at their worst when they ride a black tempest's winds. While flying upon a tempest, they can attract demons to follow or fight alongside them.

ENCOUNTER GROUPS

Teams of storm archons patrol their masters' domains within the Elemental Chaos. Storm archons often serve storm giants and their elemental comrades.

Level 18 Encounter (XP 10,400)
✦ 2 storm archon squallshields (level 17 soldier)
✦ 2 storm archon lightning walkers (level 18 skirmisher)
✦ 1 storm archon tempest weaver (level 21 artillery)

Level 18 Encounter (XP 11,600)
✦ 2 fire archon blazesteels (level 19 soldier, *MM* 19)
✦ 1 ice archon frostshaper (level 20 controller, *MM* 21)
✦ 2 storm archon lightning walkers (level 18 skirmisher)

Level 22 Encounter (XP 20,750)
✦ 2 storm archon tempest weavers (level 21 artillery)
✦ 1 storm giant (level 24 controller, *MM* 24)
✦ 1 thunderhawk (level 22 elite soldier, *MM* 221)

Water Archon Shoal Reaver

A SHOAL REAVER IS A MERCILESS RAIDER, happy to dispatch any creatures in its way. It savages enemies with ruthless strikes of its trident, pulling them to the water's edge.

Water Archon Shoal Reaver	Level 13 Brute
Medium elemental humanoid (aquatic, water)	XP 800

Initiative +8   **Senses** Perception +7
HP 159; **Bloodied** 79
AC 25; **Fortitude** 27, **Reflex** 25, **Will** 24
Immune disease, forced movement, poison; **Resist** 10 acid;
  Vulnerable cold (a water archon shoal reaver that takes cold damage is slowed until the end of its next turn)
Saving Throws +2 against immobilized, restrained, and slowed
Speed 5, swim 7
ⓘ **Trident** (standard; at-will) ✦ **Weapon**
  +16 vs. AC; 3d8 + 3 damage, and the target takes a –2 penalty to AC until the end of its next turn.
↗ **Water Harpoon** (standard; recharge ⚄ ⚅)
  Ranged 5; +16 vs. AC; 4d8 + 5 damage, and the water archon shoal reaver pulls the target adjacent to it.
↩ **Whirlpool of Tines** (standard; recharges when first bloodied)
  Close burst 1; targets enemies; +16 vs. AC; 2d8 + 5 damage, and the target takes 2 damage for each square it moves on its turn (save ends). *Miss:* Half damage, and the target takes 1 damage for each square it moves on its turn (save ends).
Alignment Chaotic evil   **Languages** Primordial
Str 18 (+10)   **Dex** 15 (+8)   **Wis** 13 (+7)
Con 19 (+10)   **Int** 12 (+7)   **Cha** 10 (+6)
Equipment scale armor, trident

Water Archon Shoal Reaver Tactics

A shoal reaver uses its swim speed to its advantage, assaulting enemies who venture into the water. Additionally, its liquid body allows the creature to move freely onto land. It employs *water harpoon* to draw enemies close before using *whirlpool of tines*, which it uses against at least two targets at a time.

Water Archon Tide Strider

TACITURN AND VIOLENT, a tide strider does its talking with the end of its deadly spear.

Water Archon Tide Strider	Level 15 Skirmisher
Medium elemental humanoid (aquatic, water)	XP 1,200

Initiative +13   **Senses** Perception +9
Body Torrent aura 1; each enemy within the aura that hits or misses the water archon tide strider with an attack is pushed 1 square.
HP 144; **Bloodied** 72
AC 29; **Fortitude** 27, **Reflex** 28, **Will** 26
Immune disease, forced movement, poison; **Resist** 10 acid;
  Vulnerable cold (a water archon tide strider that takes cold damage is slowed until the end of its next turn)
Saving Throws +2 against immobilized, restrained, and slowed
Speed 6, swim 8
ⓘ **Greatspear** (standard; at-will) ✦ **Weapon**
  Reach 2; +20 vs. AC; 2d10 + 4 damage.
⸸ **Way of Water** (standard; recharge ⚅)
  The water archon tide strider shifts 6 squares and makes one greatspear attack against each enemy within reach at any point during the move.
Combat Advantage
  Hits from a water archon tide strider's melee attacks knock prone any target that is granting combat advantage to it.
Alignment Chaotic evil   **Languages** Primordial
Str 17 (+10)   **Dex** 19 (+11)   **Wis** 14 (+9)
Con 16 (+10)   **Int** 15 (+9)   **Cha** 14 (+9)
Equipment scale armor, greatspear

Water Archon Tide Strider Tactics

A tide strider waits until its allies engage an enemy before attacking. It uses *way of water* at each opportunity, using combat advantage to knock prone as many enemies as possible.

Water Archon Waveshaper

MANIPULATING THE OCEAN with gestures of its war fans, a waveshaper works tirelessly to see the world drowned by the churning waters of the Elemental Chaos.

Water Archon Waveshaper	Level 16 Controller (Leader)
Medium elemental humanoid (aquatic, water)	XP 1,400

Initiative +10   **Senses** Perception +12
HP 157; **Bloodied** 78
AC 30; **Fortitude** 28, **Reflex** 27, **Will** 30
Immune disease, forced movement, poison; **Resist** 10 acid;
  Vulnerable cold (a water archon waveshaper that takes cold damage is slowed until the end of its next turn)
Saving Throws +2 against immobilized, restrained, and slowed
Speed 6, swim 8
ⓘ **Waveshape** (standard; at-will)
  +20 vs. Reflex; 2d6 + 5 damage, and the target is pushed 1 square and knocked prone.
↗ **Dizzying Whirlpool** (standard; at-will)
  Ranged 10; +19 vs. Fortitude; 2d8 + 7 damage, and the target cannot charge or shift (save ends).
✳ **Geyser** (standard; recharge ⚄ ⚅)
  Area burst 2 within 10; +19 vs. Reflex; 2d8 + 4 damage, and the target is knocked prone and cannot use immediate actions until the end of its next turn.
Ocean Call (minor; recharges when bloodied)
  Each ally that is within 10 squares of the water archon waveshaper and that has the water keyword or the aquatic keyword shifts 3 squares as a free action and gains 10 temporary hit points.
Alignment Chaotic evil   **Languages** Primordial
Skills Intimidate +16
Str 14 (+10)   **Dex** 19 (+12)   **Wis** 25 (+15)
Con 21 (+13)   **Int** 15 (+10)   **Cha** 17 (+11)
Equipment robes, 2 war fans

(Left to right) water archon waveshaper, shoal reaver, and tide strider

WATER ARCHON WAVESHAPER TACTICS

A waveshaper is content to linger at the edge of battle, just within the limits of its ranged powers. From this location, the waveshaper alternates between using *dizzying whirlpool* and *geyser*, using the first while the second recharges. A waveshaper uses *ocean call* early in combat, once its allies have engaged their enemies.

WATER ARCHON LORE

Arcana DC 18: Water archons don't limit themselves to seas. They use rivers and streams as highways, setting up outposts in swamps or lakes. Water archons prefer to remain near water, but use land-based attacks as a surprise tactic.

Arcana DC 23: Water archons prowl waterways in great ships of water crafted by waveshapers. These strange aquatic masses have a semisolid state that allows them to rise and submerge as the water archons wish. These ships have given water archons a reputation as planar pirates.

ENCOUNTER GROUPS

Water archons typically find themselves in the service of masters as mercurial and destructive as the sea itself. They are loyal as long as they are not sent too far from water and are given frequent opportunities to spread misery and woe.

Level 12 Encounter (XP 3,500)
+ 1 human pirate captain (level 10 soldier)
+ 2 windfiend furies (level 12 controller)
+ 2 water archon shoal reavers (level 13 brute)

Level 14 Encounter (XP 5,200)
+ 1 aboleth slime mage (level 17 artillery, *MM* 8)
+ 3 water archon shoal reavers (level 13 brute)
+ 1 water archon waveshaper (level 15 controller)

BARGHEST

SAVAGE GOBLIN SHAPESHIFTERS, barghests seek power and influence through violence and treachery. Barghests can adopt the forms of a variety of creatures, including bugbears, hobgoblins, and wolves.

BARGHEST SAVAGER

THIS BUGBEAR BARGHEST lives for battle. A barghest savager tries to incite bugbears, goblins, and hobgoblins to violence, and often leads raiding parties in slaughter and pillage.

Barghest Savager	Level 4 Brute
Medium natural humanoid (shapechanger)	XP 175

Initiative +4   **Senses** Perception +9; low-light vision
HP 63; **Bloodied** 31
AC 16; **Fortitude** 17, **Reflex** 15, **Will** 15
Speed 6 (8 in wolf form)
ⓟ **Bite** (standard; usable only in wolf form; at-will)
+7 vs. AC; 2d8 + 4 damage.
ⓟ **Battleaxe** (standard; usable only in bugbear form; at-will) ✦ **Weapon**
+7 vs. AC; 1d10 + 6 damage.
↯ **Jump Strike** (standard; recharge ⚄ ⚅)
The barghest savager shifts 3 squares before and after the attack: +7 vs. AC; 3d8 + 5 damage.
↯ **Power Feed** (standard; usable only in wolf form; encounter) ✦ **Psychic, Reliable**
+5 vs. Will; 2d6 + 5 psychic damage, and the barghest savager gains one use of an at-will or encounter attack power that it has seen the target use during this encounter.
The savager must use the gained power while in its bugbear form and before the end of the encounter. The attack bonus for the power is +7 vs. AC and +5 vs. any other defense.

Change Shape (minor 1/round; at-will) ✦ **Polymorph**
A barghest savager can alter its physical form to appear as a wolf or a bugbear (see Change Shape, MM 280).
Alignment Evil	**Languages** Common, Goblin

Skills Stealth +9

Str 18 (+6)		
Con 13 (+3)	**Dex** 15 (+4)	**Wis** 14 (+4)
	Int 12 (+3)	**Cha** 11 (+2)

Equipment battleaxe

BARGHEST SAVAGER TACTICS

Rare is a savager that doesn't charge headlong into battle; subtlety is for other beasts. It uses *jump strike* to hit defenders, then bounds away toward a party's strikers and controllers to feed upon a useful power.

BARGHEST BATTLE LORD

A BATTLE LORD GAINS ITS NAME from its propensity for taking control of the flow of combat, earning respect and fear from friend and foe alike.

Barghest Battle Lord	Level 7 Controller
Medium natural humanoid (shapechanger)	XP 300

Initiative +5   **Senses** Perception +12; low-light vision
HP 82; **Bloodied** 41
AC 21; **Fortitude** 19, **Reflex** 19, **Will** 19
Resist 5 psychic
Speed 6 (8 in wolf form)
ⓟ **Bite** (standard; usable only in wolf form; at-will)
+12 vs. AC; 2d6 + 4 damage, and the target is knocked prone.
ⓟ **Greatsword** (standard; usable only in hobgoblin form; at-will) ✦ **Weapon**
+12 vs. AC; 1d10 + 5 damage, and the barghest battle lord is invisible to the target until the end of the battle lord's next turn.
ⓐ **Psychic Howl** (standard; at-will) ✦ **Fear, Psychic**
Ranged 10; +11 vs. Will; 1d8 + 5 psychic damage, and the target is dazed until the end of the barghest battle lord's next turn.
Aftereffect: The target takes a –2 penalty to attack rolls (save ends).

Barghest savager in bugbear form and in wolf form

CHIPPY

Barghest battle lord in hobgoblin form and in wolf form

⟵ **Life Feed** (standard; usable only in wolf form; encounter) ✦
Healing, Necrotic
Close blast 5; +11 vs. Fortitude; 1d8 + 1 necrotic damage, and
ongoing 5 necrotic damage (save ends). When a target takes the
ongoing damage, the barghest battle lord regains 5 hit points.

Change Shape (minor 1/round; at-will) ✦ **Polymorph**
A barghest battle lord can alter its physical form to appear as a
wolf or a hobgoblin (see Change Shape, *MM* 280).

Get Some Distance (immediate reaction, when hit by a melee
attack; encounter)
The barghest battle lord shifts 2 squares.

Alignment Evil	**Languages** Common, Goblin	
Skills Intimidate +11		
Str 16 (+6)	**Dex** 15 (+5)	**Wis** 18 (+7)
Con 18 (+7)	**Int** 19 (+7)	**Cha** 16 (+6)
Equipment greatsword		

BARGHEST BATTLE LORD TACTICS

A barghest battle lord keeps its distance, preferring to let other creatures rush into melee. It allows
itself to be surrounded in order to use *life feed* to best
effect, afterward putting distance between itself and
enemies.

BARGHEST LORE

Nature DC 7: Although barghests are shapeshifters of the goblin race, they can also be found with
other evil creatures. Barghests are born at random
among goblins, which is viewed by parents as a bless-
ing from Bane.

Nature DC 12: Barghests gain energy by feeding
on their foes' will. Some steal powers; others use their
foes' strength to heal their own wounds.

Nature DC 17: Barghests have unusual features
that indicate their special nature even in goblin
form; a shock of white hair or a discolored eye is a
common sign.

ENCOUNTER GROUPS

Barghests can be found terrorizing prey alongside
all types of goblins, which they almost always lead
through brute force or intimidation.

Level 3 Encounter (XP 825)
✦ 1 barghest savager (level 4 brute)
✦ 2 goblin sharpshooters (level 2 artillery, *MM* 137)
✦ 4 goblin warriors (level 1 skirmisher, *MM* 137)

Level 6 Encounter (XP 1,350)
✦ 1 barghest battle lord (level 7 controller)
✦ 2 barghest savagers (level 4 brute)
✦ 2 bugbear stranglers (level 6 lurker, *MM* 136)
✦ 1 hobgoblin commander (level 5 soldier, *MM* 140)

BEHIR

THE BEHIR IS A MULTILEGGED SERPENTINE HORROR known for its fearsome lightning-spitting attack. Clever and voracious predators, behirs are deadly hunters from the time they are hatched.

BEHIR

SHREWD AND DEADLY, a behir is capable of running down prey and swallowing it whole. A quick-witted opponent could try to reason with—or bribe—a behir before becoming its next meal.

Behir	Level 14 Solo Soldier
Huge natural magical beast	XP 5,000

Initiative see *lightning reflexes* **Senses** Perception +12; tremorsense 10

Lightning Storm aura 5; an enemy that starts its turn in the aura takes 5 lightning damage.

HP 564; **Bloodied** 282

AC 30; **Fortitude** 27, **Reflex** 26, **Will** 26

Resist 15 lightning

Saving Throws +5

Speed 7, climb 5

Action Points 2

⊕ **Claw** (standard; at-will)
Reach 3; +21 vs. AC; 2d8 + 6 damage.

↯ **Bite** (standard; at-will) ✦ **Lightning**
Reach 3; +21 vs. AC; 1d8 + 6 damage plus 1d8 lightning damage.

↯ **Devour** (standard; recharges when no creature is affected by this power)
Reach 3; +19 vs. Reflex; 2d8 + 6 damage, and a Medium or smaller target is swallowed. A swallowed target is grabbed and restrained. A swallowed creature has line of sight and line of effect only to the behir, and no creature has line of sight or line of effect to it. A creature that escapes the grab is no longer swallowed and appears in a space adjacent to the behir. A behir can move normally while it has a target grabbed in this way. When the behir dies, the target can escape as a move action, appearing in the behir's former space. *Sustain Minor:* The behir sustains the grab, and the target takes 15 damage.

↤ **Lightning Breath** (standard; recharge ⚅ ⚅) ✦ **Lightning**
Close blast 5; +17 vs. Reflex; 3d10 + 6 lightning damage and the target is dazed. *Miss:* Half damage.

↤ **Thunderleg Stomp** (standard; at-will)
Close burst 3; +17 vs. Fortitude; 1d8 + 6 damage, and the target is knocked prone.

Lightning Reflexes
The behir acts three times in a round, on initiative counts 30, 20, and 10. It cannot delay or ready actions. On each turn, it has a standard action instead of the normal allotment of actions. It can use one immediate action between each pair of turns.

Alignment Unaligned	**Languages** Common, Draconic

Str 23 (+13)	**Dex** 20 (+12)	**Wis** 21 (+12)
Con 21 (+12)	**Int** 7 (+5)	**Cha** 13 (+8)

BEHIR TACTICS

A behir begins combat by attacking a weak-looking target with *devour*, even if that means provoking opportunity attacks when moving past other foes. While sustaining *devour*, it uses *lightning breath* and *thunderleg stomp* to target multiple foes, falling back on bite and claw attacks if pressed in melee.

BEHIR BOLTER WHELP

ALTHOUGH SMALL IN COMPARISON with adult behirs, a behir bolter whelp is large and fast enough to easily capture and consume the creatures it preys upon.

Behir Bolter Whelp	Level 8 Solo Soldier
Large natural magical beast	XP 1,750

Initiative see *lightning reflexes* **Senses** Perception +7; tremorsense 10

HP 352; **Bloodied** 176

AC 24; **Fortitude** 19, **Reflex** 21, **Will** 19

Resist 10 lightning

Saving Throws +5

Speed 8, climb 5

Action Points 2

⊕ **Claw** (standard; at-will)
Reach 2; +15 vs. AC; 2d6 + 5 damage.

↯ **Bite** (standard; at-will) ✦ **Lightning**
Reach 2; +15 vs. AC; 1d6 + 5 damage plus 1d6 lightning damage.

↯ **Knockdown Rush** (minor; recharge ⚁ ⚂ ⚃)
The behir bolter whelp charges and makes the following attack: +16 vs. AC; 1d12 + 6 damage, and the target is knocked prone.

↯ **Rip-Claw Response** (immediate reaction, when hit by a melee attack; at-will)
The behir bolter whelp makes a claw attack against the triggering creature.

↤ **Lightning Shock** (standard; recharge ⚄ ⚅ and when first bloodied) ✦ **Lightning**
Close burst 2; +13 vs. Reflex; 2d10 + 7 lightning damage. *Miss:* Half damage.

Lightning Reflexes
The behir bolter whelp acts three times in a round, on initiative counts 20, 15, and 5. It cannot delay or ready actions. On each turn, it has a standard action instead of the normal allotment of actions. It can use one immediate action between each pair of turns.

Alignment Unaligned	**Languages** Common, Draconic

Str 17 (+7)	**Dex** 20 (+9)	**Wis** 17 (+7)
Con 16 (+7)	**Int** 7 (+2)	**Cha** 11 (+4)

BEHIR BOLTER WHELP TACTICS

A bolter whelp moves swiftly into melee and focuses on a single lightly armored foe. It uses *knockdown rush* before making bite and claw attacks, and it uses *jumping shock* and *rip-claw response* against foes that move between it and its chosen target.

BEHIR STORMSTEED

TRAINED AS MOUNTS BY STORM GIANTS, behir stormsteeds focus their lightning breath into constant streams of arcing electricity that they cling to and climb upon with their many legs.

Behir Stormsteed	Level 24 Soldier
Huge natural magical beast	XP 6,050

Initiative +21   **Senses** Perception +18; tremorsense 10
HP 229; **Bloodied** 114
AC 40; **Fortitude** 38, **Reflex** 36, **Will** 35
Resist 15 lightning
Speed 8, fly 8 (hover)

(†) **Bite** (standard; at-will) ✦ **Lightning**
> Reach 2; +31 vs. AC; 1d8 + 9 damage plus 1d8 lightning damage, and each creature within 3 squares of the target takes 5 lightning damage.

(↙) **Lightning Breath** (standard; recharge ▣ ▣ ▣) ✦ **Lightning**
> Close burst 3; two creatures in burst; +29 vs. Reflex; 1d10 + 9 lightning damage and the target is slowed until the end of the target's next turn.

Ride the Lightning (while mounted by a friendly rider of 24th level or higher; at-will) ✦ **Mount**
> The behir stormsteed can use its bite or lightning breath once per turn as a minor action. In addition, the rider gains a +2 bonus to attacks with lightning powers.

Alignment Unaligned   **Languages** Common, Draconic
Str 27 (+20)   **Dex** 25 (+19)   **Wis** 23 (+18)
Con 29 (+21)   **Int** 7 (+10)   **Cha** 15 (+14)

BEHIR STORMSTEED TACTICS

A stormsteed works with its rider to charge at tight groups of enemies, using its attacks to spread damage among as many targets as possible.

BEHIR LORE

Nature DC 11: A behir is a cunning predator that spends its life apart from others of its kind. Behirs eject their young from their lairs shortly after birth, forcing them to fight to survive.

Nature DC 18: Despite its bestial nature, a behir is surprisingly intelligent. By virtue of their ability to speak and understand Common, behirs are sought out by creatures looking to entice one of these predators into their service. Such negotiations end badly if the behir's terms are not met.

Nature DC 23: Stormsteeds can ride the lightning they generate, allowing them to fly through the air and even hover. They are allies and mounts of storm giants.

ENCOUNTER GROUPS

Behirs most often hunt and live alone. However, they are clever enough to work with other creatures when necessary, and even to recruit weaker creatures to serve them.

Level 10 Encounter (2,500 XP)
✦ 1 behir bolter whelp (level 8 solo soldier)
✦ 3 bugbear wardancers (level 6 skirmisher)

Level 17 Encounter (8,200 XP)
✦ 1 behir (level 14 solo soldier)
✦ 1 medusa shroud of zehir (level 18 skirmisher, MM 187)
✦ 1 yuan-ti malison incanter (level 15 artillery, MM 269)

WAYNE ENGLAND

With their deadly eye rays and voracious nature, beholders are among the most powerful and most feared of monsters.

BEHOLDER GAUTH

The gauth is the least among beholderkind, but it uses the reputation of its more fearsome kin to gain power over weaker creatures.

Beholder Gauth		Level 5 Elite Artillery
Medium aberrant magical beast		XP 400

Initiative +4　　**Senses** Perception +10; all-around vision, darkvision

HP 102; **Bloodied** 51

AC 17; **Fortitude** 16, **Reflex** 18, **Will** 19

Saving Throws +2

Speed fly 6 (hover)

Action Points 1

⊕ **Bite** (standard; at-will)

　+12 vs. AC; 2d4 damage.

⊙ **Central Eye** (minor; at-will)

　Ranged 5; +10 vs. Will; the target is immobilized until the end of the beholder gauth's next turn.

⌁ **Eye Rays** (standard; at-will) ✦ see text

　The beholder gauth uses two *eye ray* powers chosen from the list below. Each *eye ray* must target a different creature. Using *eye rays* does not provoke opportunity attacks.

　1—Fire Ray (Fire): Ranged 8; +10 vs. Reflex; 2d6 + 4 fire damage.

　2—Exhaustion Ray (Necrotic): Ranged 8; +10 vs. Fortitude; 1d8 + 4 necrotic damage, and the target is weakened (save ends).

　3—Sleep Ray (Sleep): Ranged 8; +10 vs. Fortitude; the target is slowed (save ends). *First Failed Saving Throw:* The target is knocked unconscious (save ends).

　4—Telekinesis Ray: Ranged 8; +10 vs. Fortitude; the beholder gauth slides the target 4 squares.

Alignment Evil	**Languages** Deep Speech	
Str 12 (+3)	**Dex** 15 (+4)	**Wis** 16 (+5)
Con 15 (+4)	**Int** 18 (+6)	**Cha** 20 (+7)

GAUTH TACTICS

The gauth relies on allies and servants to keep enemies away while it attacks with its *eye rays*. If confronted by a strong melee combatant, it uses its *telekinesis ray* to push the creature within range of its allies. Spellcasters and ranged combatants are taken out of the fight with the gauth's *sleep ray* or immobilized by its *central eye*.

GAUTH LORE

Dungeoneering DC 12: Though less powerful than its other beholder kin, a gauth possesses deadly *eye rays* and a hunger for power.

Dungeoneering DC 17: A gauth is a cowardly creature that relies on allies and slaves for protection. It is perfectly willing to sacrifice those allies to save its own life.

BEHOLDER EYE OF FROST

The eye of frost is a heartless predator that hunts in frozen lands of ice and snow. More so than other types of beholders, the eye of frost lives for the twisted pleasures of the moment, seldom concerning itself with long-term plans.

Beholder Eye of Frost		Level 14 Elite Artillery
Large aberrant magical beast		XP 2,000

Initiative +12　　**Senses** Perception +16; all-around vision, darkvision

HP 222; **Bloodied** 111; see also *ice armor*

AC 26 (28 with *ice armor*); **Fortitude** 26 (28 with *ice armor*), **Reflex** 26, **Will** 27

Resist 15 cold

Saving Throws +2

Speed fly 4 (hover)

Action Points 1

⊕ **Bite** (standard; at-will)

　+21 vs. AC; 2d6 damage.

⊙ **Central Eye** (minor 1/round; at-will)

　Ranged 8; +20 vs. Reflex; the target is weakened (save ends). If the target takes cold damage while weakened by this power, it is immobilized until no longer weakened.

⌁ **Eyes of the Beholder** (free, when an enemy starts its turn within 5 squares of the beholder eye of frost; at-will)

　The eye of frost uses *eye ray* against the triggering enemy. While the eye of frost is bloodied, a creature it hits also gains vulnerable 5 cold until the end of the eye of frost's next turn.

⌁ **Eye Rays** (standard; at-will) ✦ see text

　The beholder eye of frost uses one *eye ray* power chosen from the list below. Using *eye rays* does not provoke opportunity attacks.

　1—Freeze Ray (Cold): Ranged 10; +19 vs. Reflex; 2d8 + 7 cold damage.

　2—Telekinesis Ray: Ranged 10; +19 vs. Fortitude; the eye of frost slides the target 6 squares.

　3—Ice Ray (Cold): Ranged 10; +19 vs. Reflex; 1d8 + 6 cold damage, and the target takes ongoing 5 cold damage and is immobilized (save ends both).

Ice Armor (when first bloodied; encounter)

　The beholder eye of frost's AC and Fortitude increase by 2 until the end of the encounter.

Alignment Evil	**Languages** Deep Speech	
Str 13 (+8)	**Dex** 21 (+12)	**Wis** 18 (+11)
Con 21 (+12)	**Int** 12 (+8)	**Cha** 23 (+13)

BEHOLDER EYE OF CHAOS

THE EYE OF CHAOS IS A SINGULAR ENGINE of destruction, eschewing tactics and reason in favor of sowing a maximum amount of mayhem and ruin.

Beholder Eye of Chaos	Level 25 Elite Artillery
Large aberrant magical beast	XP 14,000

Initiative +20   **Senses** Perception +16; all-around vision, darkvision

HP 364; **Bloodied** 182; see also *ripple of chaos*

AC 37; **Fortitude** 37, **Reflex** 37, **Will** 38

Saving Throws +2

Speed fly 8 (hover)

Action Points 1

ⓐ **Bite** (standard; at-will)

  +32 vs. AC; 2d6 + 7 damage.

↗ **Central Eye** (minor 1/round; at-will)

  Ranged 20; +30 vs. Fortitude, and the target cannot use encounter attack powers or daily attack powers until the end of the beholder eye of chaos's next turn.

↗ **Eyes of the Beholder** (free, when an enemy starts its turn within 5 squares of the beholder eye of chaos; at-will)

  The eye of chaos uses *eye ray* against the triggering enemy.

↗ **Eye Rays** (standard; at-will) ✦ see text

  The beholder eye of chaos uses one *eye ray* power chosen from the list below. Using *eye rays* does not provoke opportunity attacks.

  1—Telekinesis Ray: Ranged 10; +30 vs. Fortitude; 3d8 + 7 damage, and the eye of chaos slides the target 6 squares.

  2—Blinding Ray: Ranged 10; +30 vs. Reflex; 3d8 + 7 damage, and the target is blinded (save ends).

  3—Confounding Ray (Charm, Psychic): Ranged 10; +30 vs. Will; 3d8 + 7 psychic damage, the eye of chaos slides the target 6 squares, and the target is dazed (save ends).

  4—Maddening Ray (Charm, Psychic): Ranged 10; +30 vs. Will; 3d8 + 7 psychic damage, and the target is dominated until the end of the eye of chaos's next turn.

  5—Fear Ray (Fear, Psychic): Ranged 10; +30 vs. Will; 3d8 + 7 psychic damage, and the target moves its speed away from the eye of chaos by the safest route possible.

  6—Teleporting Ray (Teleportation): Ranged 10; +30 vs. Reflex; 3d8 + 7 damage, and the eye of chaos teleports the target 10 squares.

↗ **Ripple of Chaos** (when first bloodied; encounter)

  Each enemy within 5 squares of the beholder eye of chaos is targeted by a random *eye ray* power as a free action. The eye of chaos then teleports 6 squares as a free action.

Alignment Chaotic evil	**Languages** Deep Speech	
Str 18 (+16)	**Dex** 26 (+20)	**Wis** 18 (+16)
Con 26 (+20)	**Int** 21 (+17)	**Cha** 28 (+21)

EYE OF FROST TACTICS

Each round, the eye of frost targets the nearest foe with its *central eye* followed by an *eye ray*. It uses *ice ray* to immobilize melee foes, employing its *telekinesis ray* to slide targets within range of its *eyes of the beholder* effect.

EYE OF FROST LORE

Dungeoneering DC 18: An eye of frost prefers to dwell in cold lands within the world and the Elemental Chaos, drifting high above the frozen landscape to spy prey from afar.

Dungeoneering DC 23: Ice archons, frost giants, and oni employ eyes of frost as hunters and guardians. These sadistic beholders often chafe under the command of such creatures, but they obey as long as their masters sate their appetite for cruelty.

Eye of Chaos Tactics

The eye of chaos targets a random creature with its *central eye* each round while targeting another creature with one of its *eye rays*. When bloodied, it uses *ripple of chaos* to attack the closest targets, then teleports to an easily defended location.

Eye of Chaos Lore

Dungeoneering DC 26: Eyes of chaos are associated with demons and other creatures of the Elemental Chaos, although they ally themselves with any creature if doing so advances their ruinous goals. Like a demon, an eye of chaos seeks to sow destruction and discord, but its plans are far more complex.

Dungeoneering DC 31: Eyes of chaos arose from an ancient beholder eye tyrant that sought to tap the power of the shard of pure evil that created the Abyss. Although it never found the shard, this eye tyrant returned from the Abyss possessed of great power that warped it physically and mentally. None can say what secret goals drive the eyes of chaos, but their actions more often align with the interests of demons than with those of other beholders.

Beholder Ultimate Tyrant

The most horrible of all beholders, ultimate tyrants emerge from the Far Realm to spread dark madness in their wake.

Beholder Ultimate Tyrant	Level 29 Solo Artillery
Huge aberrant magical beast	XP 75,000

Initiative +20   **Senses** Perception +27; all-around vision, darkvision
HP 1,080; **Bloodied** 540; see also *spasmodic rays*
AC 41; **Fortitude** 38, **Reflex** 40, **Will** 42
Immune petrification
Saving Throws +5
Speed fly 8 (hover)
Action Points 2

⊕ **Bite** (standard; at-will)
+36 vs. AC; 3d8 + 10 damage.

↗ **Central Eye** (minor 1/round; at-will)
Ranged 30; +34 vs. Fortitude; the target is dazed and slowed (save ends both). *First Failed Saving Throw:* The target is stunned (save ends). *Miss:* The target is slowed (save ends).

↗ **Eyes of the Beholder** (free, when an enemy starts its turn within 5 squares of the beholder; at-will)
The ultimate tyrant uses *eye ray* against the triggering enemy.

⤺ **Spasmodic Rays** (when first bloodied and again when the beholder ultimate tyrant drops to 0 hit points)
The ultimate tyrant uses a random *eye ray* attack against each enemy within 10 squares.

✳ **Eye Ray** (standard; at-will) ✦ see text
The beholder ultimate tyrant uses two *eye ray* powers chosen from the list below. The origin square of each area burst must be centered on a different enemy. Using *eye ray* does not provoke opportunity attacks.
1—Madness Ray (Charm, Psychic): Area burst 1 within 10; +32 vs. Will; 2d8 + 7 psychic damage, and the target must make a basic attack against its nearest ally as a free action.
2—Unraveling Ray: Area burst 1 within 10; +32 vs. Fortitude; 2d6 + 7 damage, and the target takes ongoing 10 damage (save ends). *First Failed Saving Throw:* The target takes 1d10 damage. *Second Failed Saving Throw:* The target takes 2d10 damage. *Third Failed Saving Throw:* The target takes 3d10 damage, and the ongoing damage from this power ends.
3—Withering Ray (Necrotic): Area burst 1 within 10; +32 vs. Fortitude; 2d8 + 7 damage, and the target takes ongoing 10 necrotic damage (save ends). *First Failed Saving Throw:* The target is weakened (save ends).
4—Burning Ray (Fire): Area burst 1 within 10; +32 vs. Reflex; 2d6 + 7 fire damage, and the target takes a -2 penalty to attack rolls and ongoing 10 fire damage (save ends both).
5—Telekinesis Ray: Area burst 1 within 10; +32 vs. Fortitude; the beholder slides the target 8 squares, and the target is knocked prone.
6—Frost Ray (Cold): Area burst 1 within 10; +32 vs. Reflex; 2d8 + 7 cold damage, and the target takes a -2 penalty to saving throws until the end of the beholder's next turn.
7—Petrifying Ray: Area burst 1 within 10; +32 vs. Fortitude; the target is slowed (save ends). *First Failed Saving Throw:* The target is immobilized instead of slowed (save ends). *Second Failed Saving Throw:* The target is petrified.
8—Disintegrate Ray: Area burst 1 within 10; +32 vs. Fortitude; 2d10 + 7 damage, and the target takes ongoing 15 damage (save ends). *Aftereffect:* Ongoing 10 damage (save ends).

9—Ray of Attraction: Area burst 1 within 10; +32 vs. Reflex; the target takes a -5 penalty to all defenses, and at the start of the target's turn the beholder pulls it 2 squares (save ends both). *Aftereffect:* The target takes a -2 penalty to all defenses (save ends).

10—Ray of Repulsion: Area burst 1 within 10; +32 vs. Reflex; the target takes a -2 penalty to Reflex, and at the start of the target's turn the ultimate tyrant pushes it 6 squares (save ends both). *Aftereffect:* The target is pushed 3 squares at the start of its turn (save ends).

Antimagic Field

A beholder ultimate tyrant takes no damage from zone effects.

Alignment Evil	Languages Deep Speech	
Str 22 (+20)	Dex 22 (+20)	Wis 27 (+22)
Con 30 (+24)	Int 34 (+26)	Cha 38 (+28)

ULTIMATE TYRANT TACTICS

The ultimate tyrant focuses its *central eye* attacks on the strongest-looking melee combatants, hoping to keep them out of the fray. It hovers above foes on the ground, keeping out of melee as it assaults the closest targets with its *eye ray* powers. However, it stays near enemies in order to maximize the effect of its *spasmodic rays*.

ULTIMATE TYRANT LORE

Dungeoneering DC 28: The ultimate tyrant is the pinnacle of beholderkind. These creatures originate in the Far Realm, drawing power from the madness of that unknowable place.

Dungeoneering DC 33: Ultimate tyrants command the allegiance of lesser beholders. Even the willful and unpredictable eye of chaos bows to the leadership of an ultimate tyrant.

ENCOUNTER GROUPS

Beholders command a wide range of forces, typically consisting of servants willing to stand between them and their foes. Many beholders recruit flying creatures to their service, creating a deadly airborne strike force.

Level 5 Encounter (1,100 XP)
✦ 1 beholder gauth (level 5 elite artillery)
✦ 2 barghest savagers (level 4 brute)
✦ 1 goblin underboss (level 4 elite controller, *MM* 138)

Level 13 Encounter (4,000 XP)
✦ 1 beholder eye of frost (level 14 elite artillery)
✦ 1 oni mage (level 10 elite lurker, *MM* 201)
✦ 2 wyverns (level 10 skirmisher, *MM* 268)

Level 24 Encounter (34,750 XP)
✦ 1 beholder eye of chaos (level 25 elite artillery)
✦ 1 chaos hydra (level 22 solo brute)

Level 29 Encounter (89,000 XP)
✦ 1 beholder ultimate tyrant (level 29 solo artillery)
✦ 2 slaughterstone hammerers (level 25 soldier)

Nasty and noisome, bullywugs turn any swamp they inhabit into a dismal echo of the land it once was, so much so that even they view their existence as innately askew. Bullywugs sense this "wrongness" as a heightened paranoia, a feeling that everyone is out to kill them. And it's true—creatures that attack a bullywug with extreme power or precision find themselves blessed by a moment of clarity and renewed strength, as if the natural world were thanking them.

Bullywug Mucker

Strong and stout, a bullywug mucker leaps into combat to knock foes prone.

Bullywug Mucker		Level 1 Brute
Medium natural humanoid (aquatic)		XP 100

Initiative +2   **Senses** Perception +0
Rancid Air (Poison) aura 2; each enemy that spends a healing
    surge within the aura is weakened until the end of its next turn.
HP 34; **Bloodied** 17
AC 12; **Fortitude** 12, **Reflex** 12, **Will** 10
Speed 6 (swamp walk), swim 4
⊕ **Spear** (standard; at-will) ✦ **Weapon**
    +4 vs. AC; 1d8 + 3 damage.
↯ **Bullywug Rush** (standard; usable only in place of a melee basic
    attack when charging; recharge ⚁ ⚃)
    +5 vs. Fortitude; 2d6 + 4 damage, and the target is knocked
    prone. *Miss:* The bullywug mucker takes 3 damage and is
    knocked prone.
Bully
    A bullywug mucker's attack deals 1d6 extra damage against
    prone targets.
Nature's Release ✦ Healing
    Any attacker who scores a critical hit against a bullywug mucker
    regains 3 hit points.
Alignment Chaotic evil   **Languages** Primordial
Skills Athletics +8

Str 16 (+3)	**Dex** 14 (+2)	**Wis** 10 (+0)
Con 14 (+2)	**Int** 6 (-2)	**Cha** 8 (-1)

Equipment leather armor, spear

Bullywug Twitcher

A BULLYWUG TWITCHER SPASMS around the battlefield erratically, making it hard to know where its javelins will land.

Bullywug Twitcher		Level 2 Skirmisher
Medium natural humanoid (aquatic)		XP 125

Initiative +7   **Senses** Perception +3
Rancid Air (Poison) aura 2; each enemy that spends a healing
    surge within the aura is weakened until the end of its next turn.
HP 34, **Bloodied** 17
AC 16; **Fortitude** 13, **Reflex** 14, **Will** 13
Speed 7 (swamp walk), swim 5
⊕ **Javelin** (standard; at-will) ✦ **Weapon**
    +6 vs. AC; 1d6 + 3 damage.
↣ **Javelin** (standard; at-will) ✦ **Weapon**
    Ranged 10/20; +8 vs. AC; 1d6 + 3 damage.
↯ **Spasmodic Hop** (standard; encounter) ✦ **Reliable, Weapon**
    Marks on the bullywug twitcher end, and it shifts 4 squares
    before the attack: +7 vs. AC; 2d6 + 3 damage, and the target
    takes a -4 penalty to attack rolls against the twitcher until the
    end of the twitcher's next turn.
Nature's Release ✦ Healing
    Any attacker who scores a critical hit against a bullywug
    twitcher regains 4 hit points.
Alignment Chaotic evil   **Languages** Primordial
Skills Athletics +8

Str 14 (+3)	**Dex** 18 (+5)	**Wis** 14 (+3)
Con 10 (+1)	**Int** 10 (+1)	**Cha** 8 (+0)

Equipment 5 javelins

Bullywug Croaker

Weak and flabby, a croaker belches foul gas in loud croaks.

Bullywug Croaker		Level 3 Minion Brute
Medium natural humanoid (aquatic)		XP 38

Initiative +3   **Senses** Perception +0
Rancid Air (Poison) aura 2; each enemy that spends a healing
    surge within the aura is weakened until the end of its next turn.
HP 1; a missed attack never damages a minion.
AC 14; **Fortitude** 12, **Reflex** 14, **Will** 12
Resist 5 poison
Speed 6 (swamp walk), swim 4
⊕ **Claw** (standard; at-will)
    +6 vs. AC; 7 damage.
↞ **Foul Croak** (standard; at-will) ✦ **Poison**
    Close blast 2; +4 vs. Fortitude; 4 poison damage.
Nature's Release ✦ Healing
    Any attacker who scores a critical hit against a bullywug croaker
    regains 3 hit points.
Alignment Chaotic evil   **Languages** Primordial
Skills Athletics +6

Str 10 (+1)	**Dex** 14 (+3)	**Wis** 10 (+1)
Con 14 (+3)	**Int** 6 (-1)	**Cha** 5 (-2)

Bullywug Mud Lord

A MUD LORD POSSESSES GREATER INTELLIGENCE than others of its kind. It prefers to keep out of harm's way, and has no compunctions about sacrificing underlings.

Bullywug Mud Lord — Level 3 Artillery
Medium natural humanoid (aquatic) · XP 150

Initiative +2 · **Senses** Perception +9

Rancid Air (Poison) aura 2; each enemy that spends a healing surge within the aura is weakened until the end of its next turn.

HP 39; **Bloodied** 19

AC 16; **Fortitude** 14, **Reflex** 14, **Will** 16

Speed 6 (swamp walk), swim 4

ⓣ **Quarterstaff** (standard; at-will) ✦ **Weapon**
+8 vs. AC; 1d8 + 1 damage.

⟵ **Electric Reflux** (standard; recharge ⚅⚅) ✦ **Cold, Lightning**
Close blast 3; +6 (+8 with *necessary sacrifices*) vs. Reflex; 2d6 + 4 cold and lightning damage, and the target is dazed until the end of the bullywug mud lord's next turn. *Miss:* Half damage.

❄ **Fiery Croak** (standard; at-will) ✦ **Fire, Thunder**
Area burst 1 within 20; +6 (+8 with *necessary sacrifices*) vs. Reflex; 1d10 + 4 fire and thunder damage.

Necessary Sacrifices
If a bullywug mud lord includes at least one ally in the area of its area or close attacks, each of its rolls with that attack gains a +2 power bonus.

Nature's Release ✦ **Healing**
Any attacker who scores a critical hit against a bullywug mud lord regains 5 hit points.

Alignment Chaotic evil · **Languages** Primordial
Skills Arcana +6, Nature +9
Str 12 (+2) · **Dex** 14 (+2) · **Wis** 16 (+4)
Con 15 (+3) · **Int** 11 (+1) · **Cha** 10 (+1)
Equipment quarterstaff

Bullywug Lore

Nature DC 10: Bullywugs say they were created by the original primordials, not by the gods. Their primitive societies are among the pettiest and most mindlessly destructive of all humanoid societies.

Nature DC 15: By amassing legacies of savagery, the cruelest bullywugs imagine that they will one day be reborn as slaads. Bullywug tribes that have exhausted a swamp's resources have been known to resort to cannibalism; others are cannibals by choice.

Encounter Groups

Bullywugs have a hard time teaming up with any other creatures, but when they do it is with the foul, the chaotic, and the feral.

Level 1 Encounter (XP 524)
✦ 1 bloodthorn vine (level 2 soldier)
✦ 2 bullywug croakers (level 3 minion)
✦ 2 bullywug muckers (level 1 brute)
✦ 1 bullywug twitcher (level 2 skirmisher)

Level 6 Encounter (XP 1,250)
✦ 1 bullywug mud lord (level 3 artillery)
✦ 3 bullywug twitchers (level 2 skirmisher)
✦ 3 ettercap fang guards (level 4 soldier)
✦ 1 ettercap webspinner (level 5 controller)

(Left to right) bullywug croaker, twitcher, mud lord, and mucker

CENTAUR

Part humanoid and part horse, centaurs are untamed warriors that revel in the glory of battle and the raw power of nature.

Centaur Hunter

A centaur hunter earns its name not from hunting game but from tracking and dispatching foes.

Centaur Hunter		Level 12 Artillery
Large fey humanoid		XP 700

Initiative +14 **Senses** Perception +14; low-light vision
HP 96; **Bloodied** 48
AC 25; **Fortitude** 24, **Reflex** 25, **Will** 23
Speed 8

⊕ **Bastard Sword** (standard; at-will) ✦ **Weapon**
+17 vs. AC; 1d10 + 4 damage, plus 1d6 damage when charging.

↯ **Quick Kick** (immediate reaction, when a creature moves into a space where it flanks the centaur hunter; at-will)
Targets the triggering creature; +17 vs. AC; 1d6 + 4 damage.

↗ **Lightning-Fast Shots** (standard; at-will) ✦ **Weapon**
Ranged 25/50; +19 vs. AC; 1d12 + 2 damage. *Effect:* Make the attack one more time against the same target or a different one.

↗ **Charger Arrow** (standard; at-will) ✦ **Weapon**
Ranged 25/50; +19 vs. Fortitude; 1d12 + 5 damage, and the target is pushed 3 squares and knocked prone.

↗ **Triple Shot** (standard; encounter) ✦ **Weapon**
Ranged 25/50; targets one, two, or three creatures; +19 vs. AC; 1d12 + 5 damage.

Close-Combat Archer
When making ranged attacks, a centaur hunter does not provoke opportunity attacks from the targets.

Alignment Unaligned **Languages** Elven
Skills Athletics +15, Nature +14
Str 18 (+10)	**Dex** 20 (+11)	**Wis** 16 (+9)
Con 18 (+10)	**Int** 10 (+6)	**Cha** 12 (+7)
Equipment bastard sword, longbow, 40 arrows

Centaur Ravager

A ravager delights in battle and is overcome by a mixture of ecstasy and rage when fighting.

Centaur Ravager		Level 12 Brute
Large fey humanoid		XP 700

Initiative +10 **Senses** Perception +9; low-light vision
HP 150; **Bloodied** 75; see also *brash retaliation*
AC 24; **Fortitude** 26, **Reflex** 24, **Will** 23
Speed 8

⊕ **Greatsword** (standard; at-will) ✦ **Weapon**
+15 vs. AC; 1d10 + 6 damage, plus 1d10 damage when charging.

↯ **Quick Kick** (immediate reaction, when a creature moves into a space where it flanks the centaur ravager; at-will)
Targets the triggering creature; +14 vs. AC; 1d6 + 6 damage.

↯ **Berserk Rush** (standard; recharges when first bloodied) ✦ **Weapon**
+15 vs. Fortitude; 2d10 + 6 damage (plus 1d10 damage when charging), and the target is pushed 2 squares and knocked prone. *Special:* When charging, the centaur ravager can use this power in place of a melee basic attack.

↯ **Brash Retaliation** (free, when first bloodied; encounter) ✦ **Weapon**
+15 vs. AC; 3d10 + 6 damage, and the centaur ravager pushes the target 2 squares.

Alignment Unaligned **Languages** Elven
Skills Athletics +17, Nature +14
Str 22 (+12)	**Dex** 18 (+10)	**Wis** 16 (+9)
Con 20 (+11)	**Int** 9 (+5)	**Cha** 10 (+6)
Equipment greatsword

Centaur Mystic

A centaur mystic advises its tribe about the ways of nature and about their duties to the spirits of their ancestors. It possesses magic power that stems from both the wilderness and the spirit realm.

Centaur Mystic		Level 13 Controller (Leader)
Large fey humanoid		XP 800

Initiative +8 **Senses** Perception +16; low-light vision
HP 132; **Bloodied** 66
AC 27; **Fortitude** 26, **Reflex** 24, **Will** 26
Speed 8

⊕ **Quarterstaff** (standard; at-will) ✦ **Weapon**
Reach 2; +16 vs. AC; 1d8 + 6 damage, plus 1d6 damage when charging.

↯ **Quick Kick** (immediate reaction, when a creature moves into a space where it flanks the centaur mystic; at-will)
Targets the triggering creature; +15 vs. AC; 1d6 + 4 damage.

↯ **Rootwhip Staff** (standard; at-will) ✦ **Weapon**
Reach 2; +15 vs. Reflex; 1d8 + 6 damage, the centaur mystic slides the target 3 squares, and the target is slowed (save ends).

↞ **Ancestral Chargers** (standard; recharges when a centaur within 10 squares of the centaur mystic drops to 0 hit points) ✦ **Psychic**
Close blast 5; targets enemies; +14 vs. Fortitude and Will (one attack roll against both defenses); 3d8 +5 psychic damage if the attack hits the target's Will; the target is pushed 2 squares and knocked prone if the attack hits the target's Fortitude.

- � **Biting Earth** (standard; recharges when first bloodied) ✦ **Zone**

  Area burst 2 within 10; the burst creates a zone of biting earth that lasts until the end of the centaur mystic's next turn. Any enemy that ends its turn within the zone is immobilized (save ends). As a free action, an enemy immobilized by the zone can take 3d8 damage to save against the effect. *Sustain Standard:* The zone persists, and the mystic can move it 3 squares.
- **Mystic Resonance** (minor; encounter) ✦ **Healing**

  The centaur mystic and each ally it can see regain 10 hit points and can make a saving throw against one effect.

Alignment Unaligned	**Languages** Elven	
Skills Athletics +15, Heal +16, Insight +16, Nature +16		
Str 18 (+10)	**Dex** 14 (+8)	**Wis** 21 (+11)
Con 20 (+11)	**Int** 16 (+9)	**Cha** 14 (+8)

Equipment leather armor, quarterstaff

CENTAUR FEY CHARGER

A FEY CHARGER BRINGS THE POWER OF STORMS to bear against its enemies.

Centaur Fey Charger		**Level 18 Soldier**
Large fey humanoid		XP 2,000

Initiative +15   **Senses** Perception +16; low-light vision
HP 172; **Bloodied** 86
AC 34; **Fortitude** 31, **Reflex** 29, **Will** 30
Speed 8

- ⊕ **Bastard Sword** (standard; at-will) ✦ **Weapon**

  +24 vs. AC; 1d10 + 6 damage, plus 1d6 damage when charging. *Effect:* The target is marked until the end of the centaur fey charger's next turn.
- ⊹ **Quick Kick** (immediate reaction, when a creature moves into a space where it flanks the centaur fey charger; at-will)

  Targets the triggering creature; +25 vs. AC; 1d6 + 6 damage.
- ⊹ **Storming Charge** (standard; usable only in place of a melee basic attack when charging; encounter) ✦ **Lightning, Thunder, Weapon**

  +24 vs. AC; 2d10 + 7 damage plus 2d6 lightning damage, and the centaur fey charger makes a secondary attack. *Secondary Attack:* Close burst 2 centered on the target; targets enemies; +21 vs. Fortitude; 1d8 + 6 thunder damage, and the target is knocked prone and marked until the end of the fey charger's next turn.
- ⊹ **Thunder Hooves** (immediate reaction, when a creature marked by the centaur fey charger makes an attack that does not include the centaur fey charger) ✦ **Thunder**

  Targets the triggering creature; +21 vs. Fortitude; 2d10 + 5 thunder damage.
- ⟐ **Stab of Lightning** (standard; at-will) ✦ **Lightning**

  Ranged 10; +23 vs. Reflex; 1d10 + 7 lightning damage.

Alignment Unaligned	**Languages** Elven	
Skills Athletics +20, Insight +16, Nature +16		
Str 23 (+15)	**Dex** 19 (+13)	**Wis** 14 (+11)
Con 20 (+14)	**Int** 11 (+9)	**Cha** 21 (+14)

Equipment chainmail, light shield, bastard sword

CENTAUR CAMPAIGNER

A CAMPAIGNER BRINGS DECADES of battle experience to each conflict, leading fellow centaurs with courage and skill.

Centaur Campaigner	**Level 25 Soldier (Leader)**
Large fey humanoid	XP 7,000

Initiative +20   **Senses** Perception +20; low-light vision
HP 230; **Bloodied** 115
AC 42; **Fortitude** 38, **Reflex** 36, **Will** 36
Speed 8; see also *light hoof* and *sky bound*

- ⊕ **Longsword** (standard; at-will) ✦ **Thunder, Weapon**

  +32 vs. AC; 2d8 + 8 damage, plus 2d8 thunder damage when charging.
- ⊹ **Quick Kick** (immediate reaction, when a creature moves into a space where it flanks the centaur campaigner; at-will)

  Targets the triggering creature; +30 vs. AC; 1d6 + 8 damage.
- ⬸ **Hoofed Tornado** (standard; recharges when first bloodied) ✦ **Thunder, Weapon**

  Close burst 1; targets enemies; +30 vs. AC; 3d8 + 8 damage plus 1d6 + 4 thunder damage, and the target is knocked prone. *Effect:* The target is marked until the end of the centaur campaigner's next turn.
- **Light Hoof**

  A centaur campaigner ignores difficult terrain.
- **Shock Trooper**

  When a centaur campaigner has more than one enemy adjacent to it, its melee attacks deal 1d6 extra damage.
- **Sky Bound** (free; at-will)

  The centaur campaigner gains a fly speed of 8 until the end of its turn. If the campaigner doesn't end its turn on the ground, it floats to the ground at the end of its turn without taking falling damage.
- **Three-Thunder Assault** (free, when the campaigner hits with a charge attack; encounter) ✦ **Thunder**

  Two allies within 10 squares of the centaur campaigner make charge attacks as free actions. Each ally's attack deals 6 extra thunder damage.

Alignment Unaligned	**Languages** Common, Elven	
Skills Athletics +23 Intimidate +23, Nature +20		
Str 26 (+20)	**Dex** 23 (+18)	**Wis** 16 (+15)
Con 22 (+18)	**Int** 12 (+13)	**Cha** 22 (+18)

Equipment plate armor, light shield, longsword

CENTAUR LORE

Nature DC 10: Centaurs are wild folk with a love of battle so powerful that they sell their combat services to other creatures, especially fey. Highly territorial, centaurs brook no trespass and challenge those who enter their lands. Their homes commonly include stretches of awe-inspiring steppes in the Feywild, bordered by rough hills or mountains. Worldly plains, particularly near elven lands, might also support a tribe of centaurs.

Centaurs build their villages among hills near water and in natural caves. They do so for protection and a good view of surrounding territory. Peaceful visitors to such settlements do well to loudly announce themselves and bring friendship offerings of food and strong drink, a common centaur custom.

(Left to right) centaur hunter, ravager, and mystic

Nature DC 16: Centaurs revere the wild forces represented by Kord and Melora, rather than those of the fey god Corellon. Thus, they love the wild, and they fiercely protect pure lands from despoiling interlopers and monsters. They see combat and athletic contests as paths to renown, and they do not fear death in battle. Their celebrations after successful battles, hunts, or births are unruly and long, full of boasting, sport, and drink.

As fierce as they are, centaurs are gentle to one another and to friends. They have a strong mystical tradition and wise leaders, most of which are female. Their laws are simple and very different from human standards. The punishment for serious crimes is banishment from the tribe. Such outlaws must leave the tribe's lands, and no other tribe member can raise hand or hoof to help them.

Nature DC 21: Devotion to Kord's creed and a spiritual connection to nature is physically manifest in these fey creatures; mystics among the centaurs develop amazing powers over the natural world. Centaurs devoted to battle, as well as centaur mages, develop power over lightning and thunder.

ENCOUNTER GROUPS

Centaurs have strong ties with elves, eladrin, gnomes, and satyrs. Many adventurous centaurs live among other fey and explore the wider cosmos. Fey chargers, for example, have been seen as "knights" in eladrin courts. Exiled centaurs do the same, although these outcasts are more likely to be evil. A few centaurs, often campaigners, venture far afield as mercenaries.

Level 23 Encounter (XP 25,500)
✦ 1 centaur campaigner (level 25 soldier)
✦ 2 fell wyverns (level 24 skirmisher)
✦ 2 eladrin ghaeles of winter (level 21 artillery, MM 103)

CENTIPEDE

THESE VORACIOUS NOCTURNAL PREDATORS thrive in dark conditions such as forest undergrowth and moist caves. Centipedes are quick and silent hunters that prey on any creature they are able to eat.

CENTIPEDE SWARM

ALTHOUGH EACH INDIVIDUAL IS JUST A FOOT LONG, when groups of centipedes swarm together they can kill and consume far larger targets.

Centipede Swarm		Level 2 Brute
Medium natural beast (swarm)		XP 125

Initiative +4   Senses Perception +1; darkvision
Swarm Attack aura 1; each enemy that starts its turn within the aura takes 3 damage plus 2 extra damage per centipede swarm adjacent to the enemy.
HP 44; Bloodied 22
AC 14; Fortitude 14, Reflex 15, Will 10
Resist half damage from melee and ranged attacks; Vulnerable 10 against close and area attacks
Speed 6, climb 6 (spider climb)
ⓐ **Swarm of Mandibles** (standard; at-will) ✦ **Poison**
    +4 vs. Reflex; 1d6 damage, and ongoing 5 poison damage (save ends); a creature already taking ongoing poison damage is also weakened (save ends). The centipede swarm's attack deals 1 extra damage for each centipede swarm adjacent to it.
Survival Instinct (immediate reaction, when hit by an area or close attack; at-will)
    The centipede swarm shifts 3 squares.

Alignment Unaligned	Languages –	
Skills Stealth +9		
Str 9 (+0)	Dex 17 (+4)	Wis 10 (+1)
Con 14 (+3)	Int 1 (-4)	Cha 6 (-1)

CENTIPEDE SCUTTLER

THIS ENORMOUS CENTIPEDE positions itself to ambush prey, sometimes clinging overhead or lurking in debris. It relentlessly pursues one target.

Centipede Scuttler		Level 4 Skirmisher
Medium natural beast		XP 175

Initiative +8   Senses Perception +2; darkvision
HP 51; Bloodied 25
AC 18; Fortitude 16, Reflex 18, Will 14
Speed 8, climb 8 (spider climb); see also *scuttle*
ⓐ **Bite** (standard; at-will) ✦ **Poison**
    +9 vs. AC; 1d6 + 2 damage, and ongoing 5 poison damage (save ends); a creature already taking ongoing poison damage is also weakened (save ends).
✦ **Feed** (standard; at-will)
    Targets a weakened creature; +9 vs. AC; 3d6 + 2 damage.
Scuttle (move; at-will)
    The centipede scuttler shifts 4 squares. When it shifts into an ally's space, that movement does not count toward the 4 squares the scuttler can shift.

Alignment Unaligned	Languages –	
Skills Stealth +11		
Str 14 (+4)	Dex 18 (+6)	Wis 10 (+2)
Con 11 (+2)	Int 2 (-2)	Cha 9 (+1)

CENTIPEDE LORE

Nature DC 10: Centipedes are plentiful in woodlands and caves, and their poison can drain a victim's strength.

Nature DC 15: Centipedes are sacred to Torog, and his worshipers keep them as pets.

ENCOUNTER GROUPS

Because they're wide-ranging and not smart, centipedes serve other forest and underground creatures as pets or guardians.

Level 4 Encounter (XP 800)
✦ 1 ankheg (level 3 elite lurker)
✦ 2 bloodthorn vines (level 2 soldier)
✦ 2 centipede swarms (level 2 brute)

Level 5 Encounter (XP 1,050)
✦ 2 centipede scuttlers (level 4 skirmisher)
✦ 1 gnoll huntmaster (level 5 artillery, *MM* 132)
✦ 2 gnoll marauders (level 6 brute, *MM* 132)

CHAOS SHARD

At the maelstrom that marks the boundaries of the Abyss, the raging energy of the Elemental Chaos merges with an all-pervasive evil. Where these forces coalesce, they give rise to chaos shards—intelligent and malevolent creatures of living crystal.

STORM SHARD

A storm shard pummels its foes with powerful blasts of thunder and lightning.

Storm Shard		Level 4 Artillery
Medium elemental magical beast		XP 175

Initiative +6   Senses Perception +4; darkvision
Static Storm (**Lightning, Thunder**) aura 2; each enemy that ends its turn within the aura takes 3 lightning and thunder damage. An immobilized enemy instead takes 5 lightning and thunder damage.
HP 44; **Bloodied** 22; see also *storm shatter*
AC 16; **Fortitude** 15, **Reflex** 17, **Will** 15
Immune disease, poison; **Resist** 5 variable (1/encounter)
Speed 3, fly 3 (hover)
⊕ **Thunder Strike** (standard; at-will) ✦ **Thunder**
  +9 vs. Fortitude; 1d6 + 4 thunder damage, and if the target is bloodied it is knocked prone.
⇗ **Shock Bolt** (standard; at-will) ✦ **Lightning**
  Ranged 10; +9 vs. Fortitude; 1d6 + 4 lightning damage, and if the target does not end its next turn at least 4 squares from where it started its turn, it takes 3d6 + 6 lightning damage.
↩ **Storm Shatter** (when the storm shard drops to 0 hit points) ✦ **Lightning, Thunder**
  Close burst 3; +9 vs. Fortitude; 2d6 lightning and thunder damage, and the target is pushed 3 squares and deafened (save ends).

Alignment Chaotic evil   **Languages** Abyssal
Str 15 (+4)	**Dex** 18 (+6)	**Wis** 14 (+4)
Con 14 (+4)	**Int** 7 (+0)	**Cha** 15 (+4)

DEATH SHARD

These eerily glowing shards drain the life from their enemies.

Death Shard		Level 8 Artillery
Medium elemental magical beast		XP 350

Initiative +9   Senses Perception +7; darkvision
Death Shadow (**Necrotic**) aura 2; each enemy that ends its turn within the aura takes 4 necrotic damage. A slowed enemy instead takes 6 necrotic damage.
HP 71; **Bloodied** 35
AC 20; **Fortitude** 19, **Reflex** 21, **Will** 19
Immune disease, poison; **Resist** 10 necrotic, 5 variable (1/encounter); see also *life to death*
Speed 3, fly 3 (hover)
⊕ **Razor Shard** (standard; at-will)
  +13 vs. Reflex; 1d10 + 4 damage.
⇗ **Death Bolt** (standard; at-will) ✦ **Necrotic**
  Ranged 10; +13 vs. Fortitude; 2d6 + 5 necrotic damage, and the target is slowed (save ends).
↩ **Critical Fracture** (immediate reaction, when an enemy scores a critical hit against the death shard; encounter) ✦ **Necrotic**
  Close burst 2; targets enemies; +13 vs. Fortitude; 1d8 + 5 necrotic damage, and the target is weakened until the end of its next turn.
Life to Death (whenever the death shard resists damage)
  The death shard's attacks deal 1d8 extra damage until the end of its next turn.

Alignment Chaotic evil   **Languages** Abyssal
Skills Stealth +14
Str 14 (+6)	**Dex** 20 (+9)	**Wis** 16 (+7)
Con 17 (+7)	**Int** 7 (+2)	**Cha** 14 (+6)

FLAME SHARD

Flame shards radiate heat and can target even distant creatures with gouts of fire.

Flame Shard		Level 12 Artillery
Medium elemental magical beast		XP 700

Initiative +10   Senses Perception +8; darkvision
Heat Wave (**Fire**) aura 2; each enemy that ends its turn within the aura takes 5 fire damage and takes a –2 penalty to saving throws against ongoing fire damage during its current turn.
HP 100; **Bloodied** 50; see also *flame shatter*
AC 24; **Fortitude** 25, **Reflex** 23, **Will** 23
Immune disease, poison; **Resist** 10 variable (2/encounter)
Speed 4, fly 4 (hover)
⊕ **Burning Shard** (standard; at-will) ✦ **Fire**
  +17 vs. Reflex; 1d8 + 5 fire damage.
↩ **Flame Shatter** (when the flame shard drops to 0 hit points) ✦ **Fire**
  Close burst 2; +17 vs. Reflex; 1d8 + 5 fire damage, and the target takes ongoing 5 fire damage (save ends).
✳ **Flame Burst** (standard; at-will) ✦ **Fire**
  Area burst 2 within 20; +17 vs. Reflex; 1d8 + 5 fire damage.

Alignment Chaotic evil   **Languages** Abyssal
Str 19 (+10)	**Dex** 19 (+10)	**Wis** 15 (+8)
Con 22 (+12)	**Int** 7 (+4)	**Cha** 18 (+10)

(Left to right) flame shard, death shard, storm shard, prismatic shard

PRISMATIC SHARD

MULTIHUED CRYSTALLINE SHAPES, prismatic shards dazzle their targets before killing them.

Prismatic Shard	Level 16 Artillery
Medium elemental magical beast	XP 1,400

Initiative +13   **Senses** Perception +9; darkvision
Prismatic Corona (Radiant) aura 2; each enemy that ends its turn
    within the aura takes 5 radiant damage and takes a -2 penalty
    to saving throws during its current turn.
HP 123; **Bloodied** 61; see also *prismatic shatter*
AC 28; **Fortitude** 27, **Reflex** 27, **Will** 29
Immune disease, poison, radiant; **Resist** 10 variable (4/encounter)
Speed 4, fly 4 (hover)
⊕ **Prism Flare** (standard; at-will) ✦ **Radiant**
    +21 vs. Reflex; 1d10 + 7 radiant damage.
↗ **Iridescent Bolt** (standard; at-will) ✦ **Radiant**
    Ranged 20; +21 vs. Will; 2d8 + 7 radiant damage, and the target
    is blinded until the end of the prismatic shard's next turn.
↢ **Flashing Colors** (minor; recharge ⚄ ⚅)
    Close burst 3; targets enemies; +21 vs. Will; the target is dazed
    (save ends).
↢ **Prismatic Shatter** (when the prismatic shard drops to 0 hit
    points) ✦ **Radiant**
    Close burst 2; +21 vs. Will; 2d8 + 7 radiant damage, and the
    target is blinded (save ends).
Alignment Chaotic evil   **Languages** Abyssal
Str 19 (+12)   **Dex** 20 (+13)   **Wis** 13 (+9)
Con 21 (+13)   **Int** 7 (+6)   **Cha** 24 (+15)

CHAOS SHARD LORE

Arcana DC 10: Chaos shards are sentient crystal creatures formed in the maelstrom where the deepest levels of the Elemental Chaos become the Abyss.

Arcana DC 16: Chaos shards exist due to the influence of the shard of pure evil from which the Abyss was created. Legends state that the most powerful of the chaos shards are splinters of this legendary crystalline fragment.

Arcana DC 21: Wizards and those that draw power from the Elemental Chaos sometimes capture chaos shards to use them as sources of power.

ENCOUNTER GROUPS

Chaos shards travel together in small clusters, sowing upheaval wherever they go. They are also highly sought after by arcane casters and creatures of the Elemental Chaos, which use them as powerful (if unpredictable) guardians.

Level 7 Encounter (XP 1,500)
✦ 2 death shards (level 8 artillery)
✦ 1 bloodseep demon (level 7 skirmisher)
✦ 2 evistros (level 6 brute, *MM* 54)

Level 17 Encounter (XP 8,200)
✦ 1 prismatic shard (level 16 artillery)
✦ 3 blue slaads (level 17 brute, *MM* 238)
✦ 1 green slaad (level 18 controller, *MM* 238)

COCKATRICE

This odd-looking creature terrifies even the bravest because of its ability to turn flesh into stone.

Cockatrice		Level 5 Skirmisher
Small natural beast		XP 200

Initiative +8   **Senses** Perception +2; low-light vision
HP 63; **Bloodied** 31
AC 19; **Fortitude** 17, **Reflex** 19, **Will** 15
Immune petrification
Speed 4, fly 6 (clumsy)

⊕ **Bite** (standard; at-will)
+10 vs. AC; 1d6 + 3 damage, and the cockatrice makes a secondary attack against the same target. *Secondary Attack:* +8 vs. Fortitude; the target is slowed (save ends). *First Failed Saving Throw:* The target is immobilized instead of slowed (save ends). *Second Failed Saving Throw:* The target is petrified.

↯ **Buffeting Wings** (immediate interrupt, when an enemy moves adjacent to the cockatrice; recharge ⚁ ⚄ ⚅)
The cockatrice uses its bite against the triggering enemy and then shifts 3 squares.

Alignment Unaligned   **Languages** —
Skills Stealth +11

Str 9 (+1)	**Dex** 18 (+6)	**Wis** 11 (+2)
Con 15 (+4)	**Int** 2 (-2)	**Cha** 4 (-1)

COCKATRICE TACTICS

Despite its fearsome reputation, a cockatrice is a cowardly foe. It engages one enemy at a time, using its *buffeting wings* to bite and then retreat.

COCKATRICE LORE

Nature DC 12: The lair of a cockatrice is filled with broken statues of previous victims, which include various wild animals. In the wild, the soft ground of a cockatrice's lair is filled with short tunnels and hollows that a cockatrice can use when attacked.

Nature DC 17: Feathers freshly plucked from a cockatrice can be mixed with mud to create a poultice that reverses petrification when spread over an affected creature. This method requires a DC 20 Heal check and 30 minutes, and it is successful only if the poultice is applied within twenty-four hours of the petrification. One cockatrice provides enough feathers to create a poultice for one petrified creature.

ENCOUNTER GROUPS

Reptilian and serpentine monsters such as yuan-ti, lizardfolk, and medusas sometimes keep cockatrices as pets or guardians.

Level 3 Encounter (XP 850)
✦ 2 cockatrices (level 5 skirmisher)
✦ 1 poisonscale collector (level 3 lurker)
✦ 2 poisonscale myrmidons (level 3 soldier)

COLOSSUS

A COLOSSUS EXISTS TO FULFILL the will of its creators, but the creators of the primordial colossi passed into myth long ago.

Primordial Colossus	Level 28 Elite Brute
Huge elemental animate (construct)	XP 26,000

Initiative +21 **Senses** Perception +22
Elemental Presence (Acid, Cold, Fire, Lightning, Thunder) aura 5; each creature that starts its turn within the aura takes 15 acid, cold, fire, lightning, and thunder damage.
HP 640; **Bloodied** 320
AC 40; **Fortitude** 44, **Reflex** 37, **Will** 38
Immune disease, fear, poison, sleep; **Resist** 15 variable (3/ encounter)
Saving Throws +2
Speed 10
Action Points 1
ⓐ **Slam** (standard; at-will)
    +29 vs. AC; 3d10 + 14 damage.
ⓒ **Colossal Slam** (standard; at-will) ✦ **Acid, Cold, Fire, Lightning, Thunder**
    Close blast 3; +29 vs. AC; 3d10 + 14 damage, and the primordial colossus can make a secondary attack. *Secondary Attack*: close blast 3; +28 vs. Fortitude; 3d8 acid, cold, fire, lightning, and thunder damage, and the target is knocked prone.
ⱡ **Reactive Kick** (immediate reaction, when an enemy moves adjacent to the primordial colossus; recharges when first bloodied) ✦ **Acid, Cold, Fire, Lightning, Thunder**
    Targets the triggering creature; +30 vs. Fortitude; 3d8 + 7 acid, cold, fire, lightning, and thunder damage, and the target is pushed 4 squares and knocked prone.
⤳ **Primordial Stone** (standard; at-will) ✦ **Acid, Cold, Fire, Lightning, Thunder**
    Ranged 20; +29 vs. Reflex; 3d6 + 14 damage, and the primordial colossus can make a secondary attack that is a burst 5 centered on the target. *Secondary Attack*: +28 vs. Fortitude; 3d8 acid, cold, fire, lightning, and thunder damage, and the secondary target is knocked prone.
Alignment Unaligned   **Languages** –

Str 38 (+28)	Dex 25 (+21)	Wis 27 (+22)
Con 30 (+24)	Int 3 (+10)	Cha 15 (+16)

COLOSSUS LORE

Arcana or Religion DC 28: Originally crafted by the primordials, primordial colossi now slumber in crumbling ruins or move freely throughout the planes, seeking to fulfill the orders of their long-gone masters. Some primordial colossi appear to be shattered statues, but rise in fury when approached.

Arcana or Religion DC 33: Most primordial colossi are as ageless as their original masters. However, these powerful guardians can also be created by the death or awakening of mighty elemental beings, from a buildup of arcane energy, or by the rituals of mighty wizards.

ENCOUNTER GROUPS

Though a primordial colossus can arise spontaneously, most of these creatures are found in the ancient ruins they were created to defend, fighting alongside other immortal guardians.

Level 26 Encounter (XP 45,100)
✦ 1 primordial colossus (level 28 elite brute)
✦ 2 great flameskulls (level 24 artillery, *MM* 109)
✦ 1 slaughterstone hammerer (level 25 soldier)

Level 27 Encounter (XP 61,000)
✦ 1 primordial colossus (level 28 elite brute)
✦ 1 primordial naga (level 25 solo artillery, *MM* 195)

COUATL

The ancient race of couatls has earned renown for selflessly opposing the evil of demons and the Abyss. However, the couatls' legendary virtue and benevolence can sometimes be occluded by their single-minded pursuit of their goals.

COUATL CLOUD SERPENT

A couatl cloud serpent attacks from above, hurling lightning at its foes.

Couatl Cloud Serpent	Level 18 Artillery
Large immortal magical beast (reptile)	XP 2,000

Initiative +13   **Senses** Perception +21
HP 135; **Bloodied** 67
AC 30; **Fortitude** 29, **Reflex** 30, **Will** 31
Saving Throws see *twist free*
Speed 6, fly 8 (hover)

ⓐ **Bite** (standard; at-will) ✦ **Poison, Radiant**
   Reach 2; +25 vs. AC; 1d6 + 4 poison and radiant damage, and ongoing 10 poison and radiant damage (save ends).

↓ **Hurtling Coils** (minor 1/round; at-will)
   Reach 2; +23 vs. Fortitude; the target is pushed 2 squares and knocked prone.

⤢ **Sky Bolt** (standard; at-will) ✦ **Lightning, Radiant**
   Ranged 20; +23 vs. Reflex; 2d10 + 6 lightning and radiant damage.

✳ **Snaking Arcs** (standard; recharges when first bloodied) ✦ **Lightning, Radiant**
   Area burst 3 within 20; targets enemies; +23 vs. Reflex; 2d8 + 6 lightning and radiant damage.

Radiant Absorption ✦ **Radiant**
   If a couatl cloud serpent takes radiant damage, its attacks deal 5 extra radiant damage until the end of its next turn.

Twist Free
   A couatl cloud serpent makes saving throws against immobilized and restrained conditions at the start of its turn as well as at the end of its turn. In addition, a cloud serpent can make saving throws against immobilized and restrained conditions that do not allow saving throws and would normally end at the end of its turn or at the end of an enemy's turn.

Alignment Unaligned   **Languages** Supernal
Skills Arcana +20, Diplomacy +19, Insight +21
Str 19 (+13)	**Dex** 18 (+13)	**Wis** 24 (+16)
Con 21 (+14)	**Int** 22 (+15)	**Cha** 20 (+14)

COUATL STAR SERPENT

A couatl star serpent rushes fearlessly into battle, constricting enemies in its coils.

Couatl Star Serpent	Level 15 Elite Controller (Leader)
Large immortal magical beast (reptile)	XP 2,400

Initiative +11   **Senses** Perception +18; low-light vision
HP 286; **Bloodied** 143
AC 29; **Fortitude** 27, **Reflex** 27, **Will** 28
Saving Throws +2; see also *twist free*
Speed 6, fly 8 (hover)
Action Points 1

ⓐ **Bite** (standard; at-will) ✦ **Poison, Radiant**
   Reach 2; +20 vs. AC; 1d6 + 5 poison and radiant damage, and the target takes ongoing 5 poison and radiant damage and is slowed (save ends both).

↓ **Couatl Radiance** (standard; encounter) ✦ **Fire, Healing, Radiant**
   The couatl star serpent gains insubstantial and phasing until the end of its turn, and moves 8 squares. The star serpent can move through enemies' spaces. If the star serpent moves through an ally's space, that ally regains 15 hit points and can spend a healing surge. If it passes through an enemy's space, the couatl makes an attack against that enemy: +19 vs. Will; 1d6 + 5 fire and radiant damage, and ongoing 10 fire and radiant damage (save ends). The star serpent can attack a target only once with each use of this power.

↓ **Righteous Coils** (minor 1/round; at-will)
   Reach 2; +19 vs. Fortitude; 1d6 + 5 damage, and the target is grabbed. A creature grabbed by the couatl star serpent grants combat advantage to the star serpent, and the star serpent can move the grabbed creature without needing to make a Strength attack.

↓ **Constrict** (minor 1/round; at-will)
   Reach 2; targets a creature grabbed by the couatl star serpent; +19 vs. Fortitude; 2d6 + 5 damage, and the target is dazed until the end of the couatl's next turn.

⇐ **Purifying Scream** (standard; encounter) ✦ **Psychic**
   Close burst 5; targets enemies; +18 vs. Will; 1d10 + 6 psychic damage, and the target is dazed (save ends). If the target is taking ongoing fire, poison, or radiant damage, it is also stunned until the end of the couatl star serpent's next turn.

Radiant Absorption ✦ **Radiant**
   If a couatl star serpent takes radiant damage, its attacks deal 5 extra radiant damage until the end of its next turn.

Twist Free
   A couatl star serpent makes saving throws against immobilized and restrained conditions at the start of its turn as well as at the end of its turn. In addition, a star serpent can make saving throws against immobilized and restrained conditions that do not allow saving throws and would normally end at the end of its turn or at the end of an enemy's turn.

Alignment Unaligned   **Languages** Supernal
Skills Arcana +17, Diplomacy +17, Insight +18
Str 20 (+12)	**Dex** 18 (+11)	**Wis** 22 (+13)
Con 15 (+9)	**Int** 20 (+12)	**Cha** 20 (+12)

COUATL LORE

Religion DC 11: Couatls are benevolent celestial serpents known for their hatred of demons and other forces of evil and chaos.

Religion DC 18: The couatls' benevolent reputation is only partly deserved. Although they are driven in their hatred of evil, couatls are single-minded in their dedication to their specific plans, whether protecting a village, propelling a chosen creature on a path of destiny, or preventing a planar breach. Creatures that stand opposed to a couatl's plans—knowingly or otherwise—can easily find themselves the object of the creature's wrath.

Religion DC 23: Couatls were supposedly born of the first light in the world. Ancient lore speaks of great couatls fighting in the war between the gods and the primordials, and of how these creatures bound mighty beings within the world or on other planes. Free couatls and their followers work to make sure such sites remain forever undisturbed.

ENCOUNTER GROUPS

Couatls most often ally with other creatures that share a desire to oppose malevolence or guard against ancient evil. However, a couatl might fight on the side of unaligned or even evil creatures if doing so works against a greater evil in the long term.

Level 14 Encounter (XP 5,600)
✦ 1 couatl star serpent (level 15 elite controller)
✦ 3 deva knights-errant (level 11 soldier)
✦ 1 phoelarch warrior (level 12 elite skirmisher)

Level 20 Encounter (XP 15,500)
✦ 2 couatl cloud serpents (level 18 artillery)
✦ 2 marut executioners (level 22 brute)
✦ 1 marut prosecutor (level 21 controller)

CROSSING BETWEEN WORLDS

A couatl can cross from any plane to the Astral Sea by taking 10 minutes to do so. It arrives at a random location or at a teleportation circle it knows. If it chooses to, it can make an Arcana check to leave a portal open behind it. Such a portal's duration is the same as if the couatl had created it using the Planar Portal ritual (*PH* 311).

CYCLOPSES SERVE MORE POWERFUL creatures as warriors and bodyguards. Their *evil eyes* are legendary.

CYCLOPS CRUSHER

CRUSHERS LOOM OVER THEIR VICTIMS, swinging their clubs with brutal glee.

Cyclops Crusher		Level 14 Brute
Large fey humanoid		XP 1,000

Initiative +12 **Senses** Perception +16; truesight 6
HP 171; **Bloodied** 85
AC 26; **Fortitude** 27, **Reflex** 26, **Will** 25
Speed 8
⊕ **Spiked Greatclub** (standard; at-will) ✦ **Weapon**
  Reach 2; +17 vs. AC; 2d10 + 8 damage.
➷ **Evil Eye** (minor 1/round; at-will)
  Ranged sight; targets a creature the cyclops crusher has hit with a melee attack during this round; the target takes a -2 penalty to attack rolls and all defenses until the end of the encounter or until the crusher uses *evil eye* against a different target.
↢ **Tremor Smash** (standard; recharge ⚅ ⚅) ✦ **Weapon**
  Close blast 2; +17 vs. AC; 2d12 + 8 damage, and the target is knocked prone.
Alignment Unaligned   **Languages** Elven
Skills Athletics +18
Str 23 (+13)   **Dex** 20 (+12)   **Wis** 19 (+11)
Con 21 (+12)   **Int** 10 (+7)   **Cha** 11 (+7)
Equipment scale armor, greatclub

CYCLOPS FEYBLADE

MORE SHREWD AND AGILE THAN CRUSHERS, feyblades are a lethal combination of strength, speed, and conceit.

Cyclops Feyblade		Level 21 Soldier
Large fey humanoid		XP 3,200

Initiative +18   **Senses** Perception +21; truesight 6
HP 200; **Bloodied** 100
AC 37; **Fortitude** 34, **Reflex** 32, **Will** 32
Speed 8
⊕ **Longsword** (standard; at-will) ✦ **Weapon**
  Reach 2; +28 vs. AC; 2d10 + 8 damage.
⤼ **Wildstep** (immediate interrupt, when the creature marked by the cyclops feyblade's *evil eye* makes an attack that does not include the feyblade; at-will)
  The feyblade teleports 10 squares to a space adjacent to the triggering creature and makes an attack: +28 vs. AC; 2d6 + 7 damage.
➷ **Evil Eye** (minor 1/round; at-will)
  Ranged 20; the target is marked until the end of the encounter or until the cyclops feyblade uses *evil eye* against a different target.
Alignment Unaligned   **Languages** Elven
Str 27 (+18)   **Dex** 23 (+16)   **Wis** 23 (+16)
Con 24 (+17)   **Int** 12 (+11)   **Cha** 13 (+11)
Equipment chainmail, longsword

CYCLOPS LORE

Arcana DC 20: Fomorians employ crushers as slave minders, and these brutal cyclopses take great pleasure in punishing those that step out of line.

Arcana DC 25: Cyclops feyblades are highly trained bodyguards that rarely engage in manual labor or menial tasks. They lord their favored position over other cyclopses whenever they can.

ENCOUNTER GROUPS

Cyclopses readily take orders from more powerful creatures such as firbolgs, fomorians, and drow.

Level 13 Encounter (XP 4,200)
✦ 2 cyclops crushers (level 14 brute)
✦ 2 eladrin bladesingers (level 11 skirmisher)
✦ 1 firbolg moon seer (level 14 controller)

CHIPPY

DARKMANTLE

STRANGE ÉMIGRÉS FROM THE SHADOWFELL, dark-mantles lurk in caverns, ruins, and other dark places. They feed by dropping on prey from above.

DARKMANTLE ENVELOPER TACTICS

A darkmantle enveloper waits for a group to approach. Once a few targets are near, it attacks with *shadowcry* and then immediately drops down to use *engulf* against a dazed foe.

DARKMANTLE LORE

Arcana DC 14: Darkmantles are strange preda-tors from the Shadowfell. The enveloper clings to the ceiling and drops upon prey, using its size to engulf a foe.

Arcana DC 19: Shadar-kai and cave dwellers use darkmantles as guard pets. Darkmantles possess at least as much intelligence as dogs.

ENCOUNTER GROUPS

Darkmantles often hunt in hanging packs. They are also used as living traps by numerous humanoid tribes.

Level 6 Encounter (XP 1,400)
✦ 2 darkmantle envelopers (level 8 lurker)
✦ 2 duergar shock troopers (level 6 brute)
✦ 1 duergar theurge (level 5 controller)

Darkmantle Enveloper	**Level 8 Lurker**
Large shadow magical beast	XP 350

Initiative +12   **Senses** Perception +7; blindsight 8, darkvision

Shadowy Field aura 5; bright light within the aura is reduced to dim light.

HP 76; **Bloodied** 38

AC 21; **Fortitude** 22, **Reflex** 20, **Will** 19

Vulnerable 5 radiant (a darkmantle enveloper that takes radiant damage cannot use *shadowy field* until the end of its next turn)

Speed 2, climb 2 (spider climb), fly 6; see also *darkjump*

⊕ **Tentacle Lash** (standard; at-will)
    +13 vs. AC; 2d6 + 5 damage.

✦ **Engulf** (standard; usable only while the darkmantle enveloper does not have a creature grabbed; at-will)
    +11 vs. Reflex; 2d6 + 5 damage, and the target is grabbed. The target is blinded until the grab ends. *Sustain Minor:* The enveloper sustains the grab, and the target takes 5 damage.

↞ **Shadowcry** (minor; encounter) ✦ **Thunder**
    Close burst 3; targets enemies; +11 vs. Fortitude; 1d4 + 3 thunder damage, and the target is dazed until the end of the darkmantle enveloper's next turn.

Darkjump (immediate reaction, when damaged by an attack; recharge ⚄ ⚅) ✦ **Teleportation**
    The darkmantle enveloper teleports 6 squares to a space that is in darkness or is illuminated by dim light. The enveloper becomes invisible, and its *shadowy field* aura is deactivated until the start of its next turn.

Alignment Unaligned   **Languages** –

Skills Stealth +13

Str 19 (+8)	**Dex** 19 (+8)	**Wis** 16 (+7)
Con 22 (+10)	**Int** 3 (+0)	**Cha** 5 (+1)

DEMOGORGON

Demogorgon, Prince of Demons, is a two-headed monstrosity who commands the fear and respect of deities, devils, demons, and primordials alike. His followers embrace wanton destruction, and his wars against Orcus and Graz'zt have raged across the Abyss for eons. Only Demogorgon's two competing minds keep his mad ambitions in check.

The Prince of Demons is cunning, cruel, envious, and ferocious even for a demon. He sees both sides of every problem and has plenty of attention to spare for his cosmos-spanning cult of sadism and destruction.

Demogorgon's worshipers include troglodytes, kuo-toa, and other humanoids that exult in mindless violence and destruction. In times of chaos, humans and others flock to Demogorgon's cult. Demogorgon's priests teach that through savagery, strength, and slaughter, followers thrive and multiply where others fade and die. When war wracks the land—particularly when hordes of monsters sweep over bastions of civilization, leaving them in ruin—Demogorgon's cult grows strong.

Although Demogorgon's cult is small, it leaves a terrible swath of destruction across the land. Demogorgon's cultists organize themselves into crude war bands, relying on battle madness and wrath to overpower their enemies. They wander from town to town, burning and looting everything in their paths. Like miniature aspects of their lord's wrath, they destroy all they see.

No commentary on Demogorgon is complete without mention of Dagon, a mighty demon lord who prowls the deepest waters of the Abyss. If Demogorgon is the machine of destruction, Dagon is the cool, calculating mind behind it, sowing chaos in subtle, intricate ways. Dagon, Lord of the Depths, is an oracle and sage among demons. Creatures of the Abyss, and those brave or foolish enough to seek his counsel, offer him powerful artifacts and favors in return for shares of his knowledge.

The rough alliance between Dagon's intellect and Demogorgon's brute strength makes their combined power formidable. Dagon whispers his knowledge into each of Demogorgon's heads—never both at the same time—thus playing a significant role in the tension between Demogorgon's two minds.

DEMOGORGON TACTICS

Demogorgon attempts to divide and conquer his enemies. He uses *inescapable grasp* to pull individuals toward him, rips into his chosen targets with his tentacle attack, and uses *Aameul's gaze* and *Hethradiah's gaze* to keep other enemies at bay. If sorely pressed, Demogorgon teleports away.

Demogorgon   **Level 34 Solo Controller**
Gargantuan elemental humanoid (aquatic, demon)   XP 195,000

Initiative +24   **Senses** Perception +28; darkvision
HP 1,260; **Bloodied** 630
AC 48; **Fortitude** 46, **Reflex** 43, **Will** 44
Resist 30 variable (3/encounter)
Saving Throws +5
Speed 8, teleport 10, swim 8
Action Points 2

⊕ **Tentacle Strike** (standard; at-will)
Reach 5; +39 vs. AC; 3d8 + 8 damage.

↢ **Forked Tail** (standard; at-will) ✦ **Necrotic**
Close blast 5; +35 vs. Reflex; 2d10 + 10 necrotic damage, and the target is weakened (save ends).

↢ **Tentacle Blast** (standard; at-will)
Close blast 5; +35 vs. Fortitude; 2d8 + 8 damage, and ongoing 15 damage (save ends). If Demogorgon's attack deals ongoing damage to a creature that is already taking ongoing damage, the ongoing damage increases by 5.

↗ **Inescapable Grasp** (standard; at-will) ✦ **Teleportation**
Ranged 50; +37 vs. Reflex; the target is teleported to a space within 5 squares of Demogorgon.

↢ **Aameul's Gaze** (minor 1/round; at-will) ✦ **Psychic, Gaze**
Close blast 5; targets enemies; +35 vs. Will; 2d10 + 10 psychic damage, and the target is dazed (save ends). If the target is already dazed, it is instead dominated (save ends).

↢ **Hethradiah's Gaze** (minor 1/round; at-will) ✦ **Psychic, Gaze**
Close blast 5; +35 vs. Will; 1d12 + 10 psychic damage, and the target uses an at-will attack power of Demogorgon's choice against a target of Demogorgon's choice as a free action.

↢ **Dual Aspects of Demogorgon** (standard; recharge ⚅) ✦ **Psychic**
Close blast 10; targets enemies; +35 vs. Will; 4d10 + 10 psychic damage, and the target is knocked unconscious (save ends).

↢ **Gaze of Abyssal Might** (free, when an enemy starts its turn within 10 squares of Demogorgon; at-will)
Close burst 10; targets the triggering creature; +37 vs. Will; the target is dazed until the end of its turn.

Double Actions
At the start of combat, Demogorgon makes two initiative checks. Each check corresponds to one of Demogorgon's heads—Aameul or Hethradiah—and Demogorgon takes a turn on both initiative counts. Demogorgon has a full set of actions on each of these turns, and Demogorgon's ability to take an immediate action refreshes on each turn. Each of Demogorgon's heads is unable to use the attack power named for the other head.

Dual Brain
At the end of each of his turns, Demogorgon saves against dazed and stunned conditions and charm effects.

Alignment Chaotic evil   **Languages** Abyssal, Common
Skills Arcana +27, Athletics +35, Diplomacy +33, Insight +28, Intimidate +33

| **Str** 36 (+30) | **Dex** 25 (+24) | **Wis** 23 (+23) |
| **Con** 35 (+29) | **Int** 30 (+27) | **Cha** 32 (+28) |

DEMOGORGON LORE

Arcana DC 22: Demogorgon's two heads are named Aameul and Hethradiah. Aameul prefers deception, and Hethradiah favors destruction. Originally, Demogorgon had one head and one mind. A mighty blow from the deity Amoth split him nearly in two before Demogorgon killed Amoth. After he healed, Demogorgon's head remained split. The two heads often disagree with one another but turn disagreement to their mutual advantage. For instance, one head struck an alliance with a powerful lich queen of the deep Shadowfell, and the other killed her to steal her powers.

Arcana DC 32: As comfortable in the seas as on the land, Demogorgon makes his home in a tropical region of the Abyss that is composed of dense jungles, deep oceans, and vast stretches of brine flats. The mightiest of the demon princes, Demogorgon commands creatures from places as as varied as the depths of the Underdark and the decadent palaces of civilization. Troglodytes worship him as a deity, sparking endless battles against their Torog-worshiping kin. Colonies of kuo-toas appeal to him for aid in reclaiming their once-great empire.

Arcana DC 37: Twins born to cultists or kidnapped and indoctrinated at a young age lead Demogorgon's mightiest cults. Each twin serves one of Demogorgon's two personalities. Invariably, such a cult falls to infighting as one high priest turns against the other, hindering many a foul plot.

Arcana DC 39: Temples to Demogorgon often reflect the dual nature of the Prince of Demons. Builders construct each temple symmetrically: One half is dedicated to Aameul, and the other to Hethradiah. Priests, warriors, petitioners, and other functionaries dwell in whichever side of the temple better fits their personalities. A grand cathedral unites the two halves at the center.

ASPECT OF DEMOGORGON

THE RITUAL FOR SUMMONING AN ASPECT of Demogorgon—a manifestation of Demogorgon's form and powers that is less potent than the Prince of Demons—involves "twinning" to represent Demogorgon's two personalities. A cultist might split a sacrifice in half down the center.

An aspect of Demogorgon acts more like one of the demon's heads than the other, being an unbalanced version of the demon. The aspect behaves like Demogorgon but does not commune with either of Demogorgon's minds. It melts into a puddle of venom when it completes the task for which it was summoned.

Aspect of Demogorgon	Level 25 Elite Controller
Huge elemental humanoid (aquatic, demon)	XP 14,000

Initiative +17   Senses Perception +25; darkvision
HP 476; Bloodied 238
AC 39; Fortitude 37, Reflex 36, Will 37
Resist 10 variable (3/encounter)
Saving Throws +2
Speed 6, teleport 6
Action Points 1

⊕ **Forked Tail** (standard; at-will) ✦ **Necrotic**
   Reach 5; +29 vs. Reflex; 2d8 + 5 necrotic damage, and the target is weakened (save ends).

↞ **Tentacle Blast** (standard; at-will)
   Close blast 3; +27 vs. Fortitude; 2d8 + 5 damage, and ongoing 10 damage (save ends). If the aspect of Demogorgon's attack deals ongoing damage to a creature that is already taking ongoing damage, the ongoing damage increases by 5.

↗ **Inescapable Grasp** (standard; at-will) ✦ **Psychic, Teleportation**
   Ranged 10; +31 vs. Reflex; the target is teleported to a space within 3 squares of the aspect of Demogorgon.

↞ **Dominating Glare** (standard; recharge ⚅) ✦ **Psychic**
   Close blast 5; targets enemies; +29 vs. Will; 1d10 + 5 psychic damage, and the target is dominated (save ends).

↞ **Gaze of Abyssal Might** (free, when an enemy starts its turn within 10 squares of the aspect of Demogorgon; at-will)
   Close burst 10; targets the triggering creature; roll a d20; on a roll of 10 or higher, the target is slowed until the end of its turn.

Double Actions
   At the start of combat, an aspect of Demogorgon makes two initiative checks. Each check corresponds to one of the aspect's heads—Aameul or Hethradiah—and the aspect takes a turn on both initiative counts. The aspect has a full set of actions on each of these turns, and the aspect's ability to take an immediate action refreshes on each turn.

Dual Brain
   At the end of its turn, an aspect of Demogorgon saves against dazed and stunned conditions and charm effects.

Alignment Chaotic evil   Languages Abyssal, Common
Skills Athletics +27, Intimidate +21
Str 31 (+22)   Dex 20 (+17)   Wis 18 (+16)
Con 30 (+22)   Int 28 (+21)   Cha 30 (+22)

ASPECT OF DEMOGORGON TACTICS

An aspect of Demogorgon uses tactics similar to those of the true demon lord. Lacking gaze attacks, it instead uses *dominating glare* to turn several enemies into allies and then focuses subsequent attacks on those who avoid the effect.

ASPECT OF DEMOGORGON LORE

Arcana DC 26: The dark ritual to summon Demogorgon requires a sacrifice of life. Only the most faithful—thus, the most demented—of his followers can successfully complete the ceremony.

Arcana DC 31: Mortals cannot summon Demogorgon, but an aspect of him answers the ritual's call. A temporary manifestation of power, the aspect has no psychic or spiritual connection to the demon lord.

DAGON

DAGON WAS THE FIRST DEMON LORD to appear in the Abyss. None can say whether the Chained God created the Abyss or opened the first passage to its depths. When the first primordials entered the Abyss, they found Dagon already lurking deep within its dark seas and hidden recesses.

Dagon	Level 32 Solo Soldier
Gargantuan elemental magical beast (aquatic, demon)	XP 135,000

Initiative +25 **Senses** Perception +28; darkvision

Eye of the Abyss aura 10; an enemy that starts its turn in the aura is pulled 5 squares.

HP 1,184; **Bloodied** 592

AC 48; **Fortitude** 44, **Reflex** 46, **Will** 42

Resist 10 variable (3/encounter)

Saving Throws +5

Speed 4, swim 8, teleport 8

Action Points 2

(+) **Tentacle Strike** (standard; at-will)

  Reach 5; +39 vs. AC; 3d8 + 8 damage and Dagon slides the target 2 squares.

✦ **Grasping Tentacles** (immediate interrupt, when an enemy attacks Dagon; at-will)

  Reach 5; targets the triggering enemy; +39 vs. AC; 1d10 + 10 damage, and the target is grabbed.

↢ **Claws of the Deep** (standard; at-will)

  Close burst 1; targets enemies; +35 vs. Reflex; 2d12 + 15 damage.

↢ **Doom Drone** (minor; recharge ⚄ ⚅) ✦ **Psychic**

  Close burst 10; targets enemies; +35 vs. Will; 2d6 + 8 psychic damage, Dagon pulls the target 5 squares, and the target is stunned (save ends).

↢ **Form of Madness** (minor; recharge ⚄ ⚅) ✦ **Psychic**

  Close burst 10; targets enemies; +35 vs. Will; 2d6 + 4 psychic damage, Dagon slides the target 5 squares, and the target is dazed (save ends).

↢ **Tentacle Blast** (standard; at-will)

  Close blast 5; +37 vs. AC; 3d8 + 8 damage, and Dagon slides the target 2 squares.

❋ **Abyssal Tides** (standard; at-will) ✦ **Force, Teleportation**

  Area burst 3 within 20; +35 vs. Reflex; 2d8 + 10 force damage, and the target is immobilized (save ends). *Effect:* Dagon teleports 5 squares.

Threatening Reach

  Dagon can make opportunity attacks against enemies within 5 squares of him.

Alignment Chaotic evil **Languages** Abyssal, Common

Skills Arcana +34, Diplomacy +30, History +34, Insight +28, Intimidate +28, Religion +34

Str 33 (+27)	Dex 25 (+23)	Wis 25 (+23)
Con 32 (+27)	Int 36 (+29)	Cha 28 (+25)

DAGON TACTICS

Dagon draws his enemies near in battle, particularly warlocks, clerics, and other spellcasters who avoid close fighting. Dozens of clawed tentacles constrict and tear unlucky captives to pieces. A calculating tactician, Dagon uses *wrath of the deep* to turn the area within 5 squares of him into a killing zone. Dagon uses *doom drone* and *abyssal tides* to keep his enemies within that area.

DAGON LORE

Arcana DC 20: Dagon, the oldest of the demon lords, possesses a treasure trove of lost secrets and blasphemous knowledge. He allied with Demogorgon soon after the Abyss formed, and since then the two demon princes have fought Orcus and Graz'zt for domination. Although Dagon sends fewer demons and followers into these battles than Demogorgon does, his knowledge of the Abyss and his keen mind allow their combined minion forces to outmaneuver their enemies.

Arcana DC 30: Dagon's cultists reside in isolated seaside towns and villages. He can call up storms and tidal waves to punish those who defy him and send great schools of fish to those who offer sacrifices to him. Villages prone to the cult descend into savagery, because Dagon demands greater and greater sacrifices of intelligent humanoids in return for his favors.

Arcana DC 35: Wizards and sages willing to trade their sanity for arcane lore seek Dagon's counsel. Arcane casters lead many of his cults. Shadow wars between clerics of Vecna and followers of Dagon are common.

Arcana DC 37: Dagon's temples are underwater, although they include air-filled chambers and caverns for his terrestrial followers. Powerful currents sweep petitioners through water-filled tunnels and deposit them in deep sea caves to allow them access to Dagon's temples.

Kazuul, Exarch of Demogorgon

As a champion of good who served Erathis, Kazuul carved a swath of order through savage lands. In time, though, Kazuul came to embrace destruction. He became a manifestation of the forces of chaos and carnage and joined Demogorgon's faithful. Kazuul turned his back on humanity entirely and accepted an investiture of demonic size and strength from the demon lord. Now an exarch of Demogorgon, he fights for Hethradiah, the aspect of Demogorgon dedicated to savagery.

Twice the size of a mortal human, Kazuul has a heavily armored body deformed by demonic musculature. Wielding a sword and an axe, he stalks the battlefields of the Abyss and beyond, herding an army of demons before him and leaving desolation and gore in his wake.

Kazuul	Level 28 Elite Soldier
Large elemental humanoid (demon)	XP 26,000

Initiative +20   **Senses** Perception +20; darkvision
HP 528; **Bloodied** 264
AC 44; **Fortitude** 40, **Reflex** 37, **Will** 40
Resist 10 variable (3/encounter)
Saving Throws +2
Speed 5, fly 5
Action Points 1

⊕ **Tooth of Grom** (standard; at-will) ✦ **Weapon**
Reach 2; +36 vs. AC; 1d10 + 10 damage, and the target makes a melee basic attack against a target of Kazuul's choice as a free action.

⊕ **World Splitter** (standard; at-will) ✦ **Weapon**
Reach 2; +35 vs. AC; 1d12 + 10 damage, and the target takes a –4 penalty to AC (save ends).

⸸ **Wrath of Kazuul** (standard; at-will)
Kazuul makes a *tooth of Grom* attack and a *world splitter* attack.

⬅ **Vortex of Blades** (standard; recharge ⚄ ⚅) ✦ **Weapon**
Close burst 3; targets enemies; +33 vs. Reflex; 2d10 + 10 damage, and the target is stunned (save ends).

⬅ **Word of Doom** (standard; encounter)
Close burst 3; +33 vs. Will; 6d6 + 15 damage, and Kazuul can score a critical hit against the target on an attack roll of 15-20 (save ends).

✳ **Abyssal Flames** (standard; at-will) ✦ **Fire**
Area burst 3 within 20; +33 vs. Reflex; 4d6 + 8 fire damage.

Threatening Reach
Kazuul can make opportunity attacks against enemies within 2 squares of him.

Alignment Chaotic evil   **Languages** Abyssal, Common
Skills Athletics +29, Insight +25, Nature +25, Religion +24
Str 33 (+25)   **Dex** 19 (+18)   **Wis** 22 (+20)
Con 32 (+25)   **Int** 20 (+19)   **Cha** 25 (+21)
Equipment plate mail, Tooth of Grom (longsword), World Splitter (battleaxe)

Kazuul Tactics

Kazuul throws himself into the fray like a madman, shrieking a battle cry and launching himself at the nearest enemy. Only the sight of a powerful magic weapon can lure him from his battle madness. If one of Kazuul's enemies uses a 28th-level or higher magic weapon, he focuses all his attacks on that enemy.

Kazuul once owned the mighty blade Gorgorin the Shatterer but lost it in battle against Hainard, exarch of Pelor and leader of that deity's White Guard. Kazuul burns with desire to find a worthy replacement or to recover Gorgorin.

Kazuul Lore

Arcana DC 28: Kazuul bears two weapons taken from exarchs. One, the Tooth of Grom, is a longsword forged from the tooth of a slain fire titan lord. Kazuul claimed the other weapon, a battleaxe called World Splitter, from Clangeddin Silverbeard, who still harbors a grudge for its loss.

In battle, Kazuul seeks out the enemy who bears the mightiest weapon. He loves nothing more than pulling such armaments from his enemies' shattered corpses.

Arcana DC 33: An ancient prophecy uncovered by the eladrin sage Ellannia proclaims that when Kazuul reclaims the sword Gorgorin, he will use it to slay Demogorgon and will then displace Yeenoghu as lord of the gnolls. The prophecy has spawned infighting and attempts to wrest it from its hiding places in the Feywild and in the world.

Thrarak, Exarch of Demogorgon

Demogorgon's claim to the title "Prince of Demons" has long been disputed, but no being has defeated him to claim that name. He has fought dozens of would-be conquerors, both fellow demon lords and primordials eager to regain their lost might. One such enemy was Storralk, a primordial of stone and earth that fell upon Demogorgon soon after Demogorgon's battle with Amoth split Demogorgon's head in two.

Storralk, failing to recognize Demogorgon's rise to power, foolishly challenged the demon lord to a battle. The shock waves of that cataclysmic battle were felt in the depths of the Abyss and across the Astral Sea.

Demogorgon tore his enemy to pieces. So great was Demogorgon's wrath that he used a powerful ritual given to him by Dagon to extend Storralk's agony. With that ritual, he called forth ettins from the blood Storralk spilled that day. Each ettin carries with it a small shard of Storralk. Every time an ettin feels pain, Storralk's quivering, flayed corpse writhes with agony in his tomb beneath Demogorgon's throne.

Thrarak was one of the first ettins. She remained in Demogorgon's lair, currying favor at first by alternately tending to Storralk's wounds and sawing through the whimpering primordial's flesh. Today, she is the Flayed Maiden, a two-headed agent of vengeance dispatched by Aameul to visit agony upon Demogorgon's hated enemies. She breaks her enemies' minds and bodies, leaving their gibbering husks as a warning to those who would dare cross the Prince of Demons.

THRARAK LORE

Arcana DC 26: Thrarak seeks out those among Demogorgon's enemies who have the potential to become threats, such as adventurers beginning on their paths of destiny. She hunts them across the planes, killing them before they can challenge the Prince of Demons.

Arcana DC 31: According to legend, Thrarak possesses the key to freeing Storralk, the primordial of earth and stone trapped beneath Demogorgon's throne. If Thrarak is slain and her heart burned upon Demogorgon's throne, Storralk will break free of the endless torment he has suffered in Demogorgon's realm. In a battle against Demogorgon, the primordial could prove a powerful ally.

Thrarak	Level 26 Elite Brute
Large elemental humanoid (giant)	XP 18,000

Initiative +18   **Senses** Perception +25; darkvision
HP 596; **Bloodied** 298
AC 38; **Fortitude** 38, **Reflex** 35, **Will** 37
Saving Throws +2
Speed 8
Action Points 1

⊕ **Lash of Ruin** (standard; requires a whip; at-will) ✦ **Weapon**
Reach 3; +28 vs. Reflex; 4d4 + 11 damage, and the target is knocked prone. Also, the target is dazed until the end of Thrarak's next turn.

↞ **Howl of Madness** (standard; encounter) ✦ **Psychic**
Close blast 5; +28 vs. Will; 1d8 + 12 psychic damage, Thrarak slides the target 3 squares, and the target makes a melee basic attack against a target of Thrarak's choice as a free action.

↞ **Lashing Flurry** (standard; requires a whip; recharge ⚅ ⚄) ✦ **Weapon**
Close burst 3; +28 vs. Reflex; 2d4 + 11 damage, and the target is dazed (save ends).

Double Actions
At the start of combat, Thrarak makes two initiative checks. Each check corresponds to one of her heads, and Thrarak takes a turn on both initiative counts. Thrarak has a full set of actions on each of her turns, and her ability to take an immediate action refreshes on each turn.

Dual Brain
At the end of each of her turns, Thrarak saves against dazed and stunned conditions and charm effects.

Alignment Chaotic evil   **Languages** Abyssal, Common, Giant
Skills Athletics +28
Str 31 (+23)   **Dex** 21 (+18)   **Wis** 24 (+20)
Con 28 (+22)   **Int** 16 (+16)   **Cha** 26 (+21)
Equipment 2 whips

THRARAK TACTICS

As the exarch of Aameul, the head of Demogorgon that uses deception to destroy its enemies, Thrarak fights using a seemingly random strategy. She shrieks strange oaths and curses containing cryptic riddles, cosmic truths, and forgotten lore.

If on a mission for Demogorgon, Thrarak pursues her designated target with relentless fury. She forgoes attacking so that she can move close to her enemy, even at the risk of taking opportunity attacks. If not on a mission for Demogorgon, she selects an enemy at random and focuses all her attacks on that enemy, despite any attempts by other enemies to distract her.

ABYSSAL MARAUDER

DEMOGORGON'S ABYSSAL MARAUDERS swoop upon isolated villages and towns, slaughtering inhabitants, carrying off treasure, and burning buildings to the ground. Marauders roam land and sea. On land, they travel in loose war bands. Seaborne marauders use poorly maintained ships that they barely know how to handle. Pirate captains recruit marauders as shock troops, though only a powerful sea prince—or one who supplies plenty of loot and rum—can keep them in check between battles.

Abyssal Marauder		Level 6 Skirmisher
Medium natural humanoid, human		XP 250

Initiative +8   **Senses** Perception +3
HP 69; **Bloodied** 34
AC 20; **Fortitude** 18, **Reflex** 18, **Will** 17
Speed 6
⊕ **Longspear** (standard; at-will) ✦ **Weapon**
   Reach 2; +11 vs. AC; 1d8 + 6 damage, and the abyssal marauder shifts 1 square.
⊗ **Throwing Axe** (standard; at-will) ✦ **Weapon**
   Ranged 5/10; +11 vs. AC; 1d6 + 6 damage, and the abyssal marauder shifts 1 square.
↗↙ **Howling Charge** (standard; encounter)
   The abyssal marauder makes a throwing axe attack and then charges the target of that attack.
Death Fury
   While bloodied, an abyssal marauder can make two longspear attacks as a standard action, each with a -2 penalty to the attack roll. The marauder cannot use its throwing axe or *howling charge* while it is bloodied.
Alignment Chaotic evil   **Languages** Common
Skills Acrobatics +11, Athletics +11
| **Str** 16 (+6) | **Dex** 16 (+6) | **Wis** 11 (+3) |
| **Con** 13 (+4) | **Int** 9 (+2) | **Cha** 10 (+3) |
Equipment leather armor, longspear, 2 throwing axes

ABYSSAL MARAUDER TACTICS

In battle, the abyssal marauder dances through enemies' ranks, shifting to dart out of reach after attacking. Marauders fight alongside shrieking cultists, using their comrades as living barriers. While the cultists' axes rise and fall, marauders dart in to soften up or finish off the enemy.

ABYSSAL MARAUDER LORE

Arcana DC 12: Selfish and wrathful, abyssal marauders pledge themselves to Demogorgon and adopt his savagery, becoming his thralls.

Arcana DC 17: Abyssal marauders roam land and sea. On land, they travel in war bands. On the sea, they inexpertly sail ramshackle ships from town to town. Pirate captains recruit marauders to aid in maritime battles, luring them with promises of loot and mayhem.

BERSERKER PRELATE OF DEMOGORGON

PRELATES LEAD THE CULT in prayers to Demogorgon, begging the Prince of Demons to bring forth the raging beasts that lurk within their hearts.

Berserker Prelate	Level 8 Controller (Leader)
of Demogorgon	
Medium natural humanoid, human	XP 350

Initiative +4   **Senses** Perception +5
HP 86; **Bloodied** 43
AC 22; **Fortitude** 20, **Reflex** 18, **Will** 20
Speed 5
⊕ **Greatclub** (standard; at-will) ✦ **Weapon**
   +13 vs. AC; 1d10 + 7 damage, and the berserker prelate of Demogorgon pushes the target 1 square.
⊗ **Abyssal Bolt** (standard; at-will)
   Ranged 10; +12 vs. Will; 1d8 + 4 damage, and the berserker prelate of Demogorgon slides the target 2 squares.
↩ **Bloodletter's Call** (standard; recharge ⚄ ⚅) ✦ **Psychic**
   Close burst 3; targets enemies; +10 vs. Will; 2d6 + 5 psychic damage, and the target is dazed until the end of the berserker prelate of Demogorgon's next turn. *Effect:* Any ally within the burst gains a +2 bonus to attack rolls until the end of its next turn.
Death Fury (minor; usable only while bloodied; encounter)
   Until the end of the encounter, the berserker prelate of Demogorgon can make two greatclub attacks as a standard action, each with a -2 penalty to the attack roll. The prelate cannot use *abyssal bolt* or *bloodletter's call* until the end of the encounter.
Alignment Chaotic evil   **Languages** Common
Skills Diplomacy +12, Religion +11
| **Str** 17 (+7) | **Dex** 11 (+4) | **Wis** 12 (+5) |
| **Con** 14 (+6) | **Int** 14 (+6) | **Cha** 17 (+7) |
Equipment hide armor, greatclub, symbol of Demogorgon

BERSERKER PRELATE OF DEMOGORGON TACTICS

Berserker prelates of Demogorgon lead the faithful into battle, fighting at the front. Other demon worshipers might prefer to sacrifice their followers to preserve their own lives, but Demogorgon's prelates exult in destruction.

At the start of a fight, a prelate uses its *abyssal bolt* attack to force enemies apart. *Bloodletter's call* bogs enemies down and improves the cult's attacks. Once bloodied, the prelate wades amid enemies and uses *death fury*, committing, at that point, to victory or death in Demogorgon's name.

BERSERKER PRELATE OF DEMOGORGON LORE

Nature DC 14: Berserker prelates of Demogorgon are mad prophets that lapse into trancelike states, babble about visions, and make pronouncements. They lead cults of Demogorgon or act as spiritual mascots.

(Left to right) shrieking cultist of Demogorgon, abyssal marauder, and berserker prelate of Demogorgon

Nature DC 19: Prelates believe that, like Demogorgon, they each possess two distinct minds. One mind is a set of shackles that restrains the other wild, impulsive mind, which exults in destruction and terror.

Doom Flayer

Doom flayers gain access to Dagon's secrets by offering sacrifices to him and dedicating their lives to acquiring more knowledge to fuel his sprawling plots. They provide arcane support in battle and lend their cunning to channel cultists' brute strength.

Doom Flayer	Level 8 Artillery
Medium natural humanoid, human	XP 350

Initiative +5   **Senses** Perception +11
HP 65; **Bloodied** 32
AC 20; **Fortitude** 18, **Reflex** 20, **Will** 21
Speed 6
⊕ **Dagger** (standard; at-will) ✦ **Weapon**
   +13 vs. AC; 1d4 + 3 damage.
⌁ **Force Lash** (standard; at-will) ✦ **Force, Implement**
   Ranged 10; +12 vs. Reflex; 1d6 + 6 force damage, and the target is slowed until the end of the doom flayer's next turn.
⌁ **Grasping Tentacles** (standard; recharge ⚄ ⚅) ✦ **Implement**
   Ranged 10; +12 vs. Fortitude; 1d8 + 4 damage, and the target is immobilized (save ends). Until the target saves, any ally of the target that starts its turn adjacent to the target is slowed (save ends).
⌁ **Doom Foretold** (minor; encounter)
   Ranged 10; the target grants combat advantage until the end of the doom flayer's next turn.
✳ **Churning Vortex** (standard; encounter) ✦ **Implement**
   Area burst 1 within 10; +10 vs. Reflex; 2d8 + 5 damage, the doom flayer slides the target 1 square, and the target is knocked prone. *Miss:* Half damage.

Alignment Chaotic evil	**Languages** Abyssal, Common, Giant

Skills Arcana +13, History +13
Str 8 (+3)	**Dex** 12 (+5)	**Wis** 15 (+6)
Con 11 (+4)	**Int** 19 (+8)	**Cha** 16 (+7)

Equipment robes, dagger, staff, mask of Dagon

Doom Flayer Tactics

Doom flayers use *force lash* and *grasping tentacles* to slow or immobilize enemies while allies such as abyssal marauders sweep in to attack and then shift away. A doom flayer saves *doom foretold* for a particularly dangerous enemy.

Doom Flayer Lore

   Nature DC 14: A doom flayer is a mage who worships Dagon and hopes to learn his secrets.
   Nature DC 19: A doom flayer gains an advantage over its enemy with spells that reveal disturbing images of a potential future.

CHIPPY

Shrieking Cultist of Demogorgon

Demogorgon's cultists desire only to loot, slay, and destroy. Revolutions, war, famine, and other troubles bolster the cult's ranks, because Demogorgon's prelates preach that the best way to avoid suffering is to be among the predators and brutal killers who dole it out.

Shrieking Cultist of Demogorgon	Level 7 Brute
Medium natural humanoid, human	XP 300

Initiative +3   **Senses** Perception +4
HP 94; **Bloodied** 47
AC 18; **Fortitude** 19, **Reflex** 17, **Will** 18
Speed 5

ⓣ **Greataxe** (standard; at-will) ✦ **Weapon**
+10 vs. AC; 1d12 + 6 damage (crit 1d12 + 18).

ⓡ **Javelin** (standard; at-will) ✦ **Weapon**
Ranged 10/20; +10 vs. AC; 1d6 + 6 damage.

⟵ **Death Wrath** (standard; encounter) ✦ **Zone**
Close burst 1; +10 vs. AC; 1d12 + 6 damage. *Effect:* The burst creates a zone of horrible noise centered on the shrieking cultist of Demogorgon that lasts until the end of the cultist's next turn. When the cultist moves, the zone moves with it, remaining centered on it. Any enemy that starts its turn in the zone takes 5 damage.

⟵ **Howl of Fury** (standard; encounter) ✦ **Psychic**
Close blast 3; +8 vs. Will; 1d8 + 4 psychic damage, and the target is immobilized until the end of the shrieking cultist of Demogorgon's next turn.

Alignment Chaotic evil   **Languages** Common
Skills Athletics +11, Intimidate +8
Str 17 (+6)   **Dex** 11 (+3)   **Wis** 13 (+4)
Con 14 (+5)   **Int** 8 (+2)   **Cha** 10 (+3)
Equipment chainmail, greataxe, 3 javelins

Shrieking Cultist of Demogorgon Tactics

Demogorgon's shrieking cultists fight with the vengeful fury of the damned. As part of their indoctrination, they embrace nihilistic violence and rage. In battle, they shriek like wild animals with *howl of fury* and hack at their nearest enemies with greataxes and *death wrath.*

Shrieking Cultist of Demogorgon Lore

Nature DC 14: Shrieking cultists of Demogorgon give themselves over to the savage rage of Hethradiah, one of Demogorgon's heads. They howl like maniacs in battle and paint themselves in blood.

Nature DC 19: Shrieking cultists yell and scream incoherently, but when many of them gather, anyone already on the path to madness might sense a demonic song buried in the cacophony.

Encounter Groups

Demogorgon's cultists gather in small raiding parties that range far and wide. They rally in large numbers only when resisted by a town's fortifications.

Level 7 Encounter (XP 1,500)
✦ 1 abyssal marauder (level 6 skirmisher)
✦ 1 berserker prelate of Demogorgon (level 8 controller)
✦ 2 shrieking cultists of Demogorgon (level 7 brute)
✦ 1 tiefling darkblade (level 7 lurker, *MM* 250)

Level 7 Encounter (XP 1,650)
✦ 1 doom flayer (level 8 artillery)
✦ 2 troglodyte thrashers (level 7 brute)
✦ 2 abyssal marauders (level 6 skirmishers)
✦ 1 gnaw demon (level 5 skirmisher)

Level 24 Encounter (XP 34,400)
✦ 1 aspect of Demogorgon (level 25 elite controller)
✦ 2 glabrezus (level 23 elite brute, *MM* 54)

Level 25 Encounter (XP 35,300)
✦ Thrarak (level 26 elite brute)
✦ 1 abyssal rotfiend (level 26 controller)
✦ 2 nycademons (level 22 skirmisher)

Level 27 Encounter (XP 60,100)
✦ 1 kazuul (level 28 elite soldier)
✦ 1 marilith (level 24 elite skirmisher, *MM* 57)
✦ 1 balor (level 27 elite brute, *MM* 53)

Level 35 Encounter (XP 239,000)
✦ 2 balors (level 27 elite brute, *MM* 53)
✦ Demogorgon (level 34 solo controller)

DEMON

DEMONS ARE AMONG THE OLDEST CREATURES in the universe. At the birth of the Abyss—the profane and terrifying realm in which demons dwell—only a few demons existed. These demon princes were weapons of unfettered destruction, intended for no other purpose than to bring the universe under the heel of the Chained God. As the Abyss grew, its evil spread into other elemental creatures, creating demons of infinite variety and dreadful power. Demons are scourges of the universe, antagonists of creation and order.

ABYSSAL EVISCERATOR

ABYSSAL EVISERATORS TEAR INTO ENEMIES, ripping out their guts in a frenzy of slaughter.

ABYSSAL EVISCERATOR LORE

Arcana DC 18: The dimwitted eviscerators often end up under the control of powerful, malign individuals who use them as guardians and muscle.

Abyssal Eviscerator		Level 14 Brute
Medium elemental humanoid (demon)		XP 1,000

Initiative +10 **Senses** Perception +9
HP 173; **Bloodied** 86
AC 26; **Fortitude** 28, **Reflex** 25, **Will** 24
Resist 15 variable (2/encounter)
Speed 6
⊕ **Claw** (standard; at-will)
  +17 vs. AC; 2d10 + 6 damage.
↓ **Grab** (standard; at-will)
  +15 vs. Reflex; 2d6 + 6 damage, and the target is grabbed.
↓ **Eviscerating Talons** (minor 1/round, 3/round while bloodied; at-will)
  Targets a creature grabbed by the abyssal eviscerator; no attack roll; 6 damage.
Alignment Chaotic evil   **Languages** Abyssal
Skills Athletics +18

Str 23 (+13)	Dex 17 (+10)	Wis 15 (+9)
Con 23 (+13)	Int 7 (+5)	Cha 11 (+7)

ENCOUNTER GROUPS

Other demons understand that a hard-to-control eviscerator is still a powerful weapon.

Level 13 Encounter (XP 4,900)
✦ 3 abyssal eviscerators (level 14 brute)
✦ 1 arctide runespiral demon (level 12 artillery)
✦ 1 immolith (level 15 controller, *MM* 56)

(Left to right) abyssal eviscerator and bloodseep demon

Abyssal Rotfiend

Abyssal rotfiends are demons of despair and madness, dark souls wrapped in stitched-together demon and devil skins.

Abyssal Rotfiend	**Level 26 Controller**
Large elemental humanoid (demon, undead)	XP 9,000

Initiative +20 **Senses** Perception +20; truesight 20
Abyssal Fields aura 5; each enemy within the aura cannot teleport.
HP 245; **Bloodied** 122
AC 40; **Fortitude** 38, **Reflex** 36, **Will** 40
Immune fear; **Resist** 20 fire, 10 necrotic, 20 variable (3/encounter)
Speed 6, fly 6 (hover)
Skullsplitter (standard; at-will) ✦ **Psychic**
Reach 2; +28 vs. Reflex; 3d8 + 8 psychic damage, or 2d8 + 8 psychic damage against a bloodied target.
Conjure Abscess (standard; at-will) ✦ **Psychic**
Ranged 10; +29 vs. Fortitude; 2d8 + 8 psychic damage, and if the target moves more than 2 squares on its turn, it takes 2d8 extra damage (save ends). If the abyssal rotfiend is bloodied, the target takes the damage for moving 1 or more squares.
Floating Despair (standard; encounter) ✦ **Psychic, Zone**
Area burst 2 within 10; the burst creates a zone of dark miasma that lasts until the end of the abyssal rotfiend's next turn. Any enemy that starts its turn within the zone takes 10 psychic damage and grants combat advantage to the rotfiend until the end of its next turn. *Sustain Minor:* The zone persists, and the rotfiend can move it 5 squares.
Alignment Chaotic evil **Languages** Abyssal, Common
Str 26 (+21) **Dex** 25 (+20) **Wis** 25 (+20)
Con 29 (+22) **Int** 20 (+18) **Cha** 32 (+24)

Abyssal Rotfiend Tactics

The abyssal rotfiend unleashes *floating despair,* moving the zone around the battlefield to affect as many enemies as possible. It uses its aura and *conjure abscess* on creatures inside its *floating despair* zone, hindering their escape. The rotfiend relishes inflicting pain on as many targets as possible, and so it prefers to attack uninjured or unbloodied targets over those that are bloodied or injured.

Abyssal Rotfiend Lore

Arcana DC 26: Abyssal rotfiends are demonic undead contained by demon and devil flesh. The spirit within a rotfiend is often a demon soul, although it can come from any evil creature.

Arcana DC 31: Orcus chains abyssal rotfiends in the halls of Everlost, using them as guardians against intruders that can teleport.

Encounter Groups

The abyssal rotfiend favors demonic allies that are maneuverable enough to get between it and dangerous adversaries.

Level 24 Encounter (XP 31,300)
✦ 1 abyssal rotfiend (level 26 controller)
✦ 1 glabrezu (level 23 elite brute, *MM* 54)
✦ 1 marilith (level 24 elite skirmisher, *MM* 57)

Bebilith

Originating in the web-strewn realm of Lolth, the spiderlike bebiliths crawl through the Abyss and other planes, hunting and killing for the joy of it.

Bebilith	**Level 18 Solo Brute**
Huge elemental magical beast (demon)	XP 10,000

Initiative see *dangersense* **Senses** Perception +14; darkvision, tremorsense 20
Spectral Death Web aura 3; each enemy within the aura that is hit by an attack loses all resistances until the end of its next turn.
HP 696; **Bloodied** 348
AC 30; **Fortitude** 30, **Reflex** 31, **Will** 29
Resist 20 fire, 20 variable (2/encounter)
Saving Throws +5
Speed 12, climb 12 (spider climb)
Action Points 2
Reaving Claw (standard; at-will)
Reach 3; +21 vs. AC; 2d10 + 6 damage, and the target takes a cumulative -1 penalty to AC each time it is hit until the end of the encounter.
Flashing Claws (standard; at-will)
The bebilith makes two *reaving claw* attacks against two different targets.
Venomous Bite (standard; usable only while bloodied; recharge ⚅) ✦ **Poison**
+21 vs. AC; 2d8 + 6 damage, and ongoing 10 poison damage (save ends).

RALPH HORSLEY

Flaming Web (minor; recharge ⚅ ⚃) ✦ **Fire**

Close blast 5; +19 vs. Reflex; 2d8 + 10 fire damage, and the target is slowed and takes ongoing 10 fire damage (save ends both). *First Failed Saving Throw:* The target is restrained instead of slowed and takes ongoing 15 fire damage (save ends both).

Hunter's Reflexes (immediate reaction, when an enemy moves into an adjacent space; recharge ⚅ ⚃)

The bebilith shifts 4 squares. This shift can move through enemies' spaces.

Dangersense

The bebilith acts two times in a round, on initiative counts 20 and 10. It cannot delay or ready actions. On each turn, it has a standard action instead of its normal allotment of actions. It can use one immediate action between each pair of turns.

Alignment Chaotic evil	**Languages** Abyssal	
Str 22 (+15)	**Dex** 25 (+16)	**Wis** 20 (+14)
Con 22 (+15)	**Int** 5 (+6)	**Cha** 19 (+13)

Bebilith Tactics

A bebilith moves around constantly during combat, slowing foes with the burning strands of its *flaming web*.

Bebilith Lore

Arcana DC 20: Bebiliths often serve Lolth, but their limited intellect makes them poor participants in drow schemes. Drow summon these demons as engines of destruction or entrap them for use as guardians.

Encounter Groups

Lolth is fond of bebiliths, so they're often found among drow and other denizens of the Demonweb Pits.

Level 20 Encounter (XP 14,200)

✦ 1 bebilith (level 18 solo brute)
✦ 3 drider shadowspinners (level 14 skirmisher, MM 93)
✦ 1 drow priest (level 15 controller, MM 95)

Bloodseep Demon

The bloodseep demon's poison blood weeps and spurts from its translucent, cracking body, hastening the death of its enemies while healing its allies.

Bloodseep Demon	**Level 7 Skirmisher (Leader)**	
Medium elemental humanoid (demon)		XP 300

Initiative +9   **Senses** Perception +8; darkvision

Weeping Poison (Healing, Poison) aura 2; each enemy that starts its turn within the aura takes 5 poison damage. While the bloodseep demon is bloodied, any demon that starts its turn within the aura regains 5 hit points.

HP 79; **Bloodied** 39

AC 21; **Fortitude** 18, **Reflex** 20, **Will** 19

Resist 10 variable (1/encounter)

Speed 7, teleport 3

ⓜ **Claw** (standard; at-will) ✦ **Poison**

+12 vs. AC; 2d4 + 5 damage, and ongoing 5 poison damage (save ends).

† **Poison Portal Strike** (standard; recharge ⚄ ⚅ ⚃) ✦ **Teleportation**

The bloodseep demon teleports 5 squares and makes a claw attack. If the attack hits, the bloodseep demon teleports 5 squares.

⟵ **Poison Blast** (minor; encounter) ✦ **Healing, Poison**

Close blast 5; targets enemies; +10 vs. Fortitude; 1d4 + 5 poison damage. *Effect:* Each demon in the blast regains 1d4 + 5 hit points.

Alignment Chaotic evil	**Languages** Abyssal, Common	
Str 15 (+5)	**Dex** 19 (+7)	**Wis** 11 (+3)
Con 15 (+5)	**Int** 11 (+3)	**Cha** 17 (+6)

Bloodseep Demon Tactics

The bloodseep demon teleports near other demons so that its aura can affect them. It uses *poison blast* or its claw attack on enemies, but allows allies to do most of the damage while it heals them.

Bloodseep Demon Lore

Arcana DC 14: Bloodseep demons like to weaken their foes before facing them in combat, such as by tainting enemy food sources.

Encounter Groups

Bloodseep demons prefer grouping with other demons, particularly those that enjoy standing toe-to-toe with enemies.

Level 7 Encounter (XP 1,500)

✦ 2 barlguras (level 8 brute, MM 53)
✦ 1 bloodseep demon (level 7 skirmisher)
✦ 2 evistros (level 6 brute, MM 54)

DRETCH

FOUL-SMELLING DRETCHES prefer to attack in large numbers and overwhelm their foes.

Dretch	Level 2 Brute
Small elemental humanoid (demon)	XP 125

Initiative +3   **Senses** Perception +1; darkvision
Sickening Miasma: aura 1; each enemy within the aura takes 1 damage whenever it takes a standard action or a move action. Multiple *sickening miasma* auras deal cumulative damage, up to 5 damage.
HP 44; **Bloodied** 22; see also *vile death*
AC 14; **Fortitude** 14, **Reflex** 13, **Will** 11
Resist 10 variable (1/encounter)
Speed 5
⊕ **Savage Claws** (standard; at-will)
  +5 vs. AC; 2d6 + 2 damage.
↯ **Frenzy of Claws** (free, when first bloodied; encounter)
  The dretch attacks one or two creatures with *savage claws*.
⟳ **Vile Death** (when the dretch drops to 0 hit points) ✦ **Poison, Zone**
  Close burst 1; the burst creates a zone of poison centered on the dretch that lasts until what would be the start of the dretch's next turn. Any nondemon that enters the zone or starts its turn there takes 5 poison damage.

Alignment Chaotic evil   **Languages** Abyssal
Str 17 (+4)   **Dex** 14 (+3)   **Wis** 11 (+1)
Con 14 (+3)   **Int** 5 (-2)   **Cha** 7 (-1)

DRETCH TACTICS

Dretches attack as a gang to combine their *sickening miasma* auras. Although they are incapable of inventing any other tactics, they can be effectively directed by a leader.

DRETCH LORE

Arcana DC 10: Quarrelsome and stupid, dretches can be tricked into fighting one another if no leader is present.

ENCOUNTER GROUPS

Demons of greater power and intelligence often use dretches as the first wave of an attack, both to see what their enemies are capable of and for the sheer amusement of watching the dretches meet their doom.

Level 7 Encounter (XP 1,700)
✦ 1 bloodseep demon (level 7 skirmisher)
✦ 8 dretches (level 2 brute)
✦ 2 gnaw demons (level 5 skirmisher)

GNAW DEMON

GNAW DEMONS CONSUME EVERYTHING they can get their hands on. Although they can subsist on inanimate objects, they prefer living flesh.

Gnaw Demon	Level 5 Skirmisher
Small elemental humanoid (demon)	XP 200

Initiative +2   **Senses** Perception +3; darkvision
Ankle Biter aura 1; each enemy that starts its turn within the aura takes a –2 penalty to speed until the end of its turn.
HP 66; **Bloodied** 33
AC 19; **Fortitude** 19, **Reflex** 14, **Will** 16
Resist 10 variable (1/encounter)
Speed 3, fly 5 (clumsy)
⊕ **Bite** (standard; at-will)
  +10 vs. AC; 1d8 + 6 damage.
Abyssal Hunger
  A gnaw demon's melee attacks deal 1d8 extra damage against a bloodied target.
Hungry Teleport (move; at-will) ✦ **Teleportation**
  The gnaw demon teleports 10 squares into a square adjacent to a bloodied enemy.
Pain-Induced Teleport (free, when first bloodied; encounter) ✦ **Teleportation**
  The gnaw demon teleports 10 squares.

Alignment Chaotic evil   **Languages** Abyssal
Skills Stealth +5
Str 15 (+4)   **Dex** 7 (+0)   **Wis** 12 (+3)
Con 18 (+6)   **Int** 9 (+1)   **Cha** 9 (+1)

GNAW DEMON TACTICS

Slow and clumsy, gnaw demons keep to the edge of the battlefield until an enemy becomes bloodied. Then they use *hungry teleport* to close with that enemy and attack it.

GNAW DEMON LORE

Arcana DC 12: Gnaw demons are cowardly demons that usually choose escape over destruction. Fleeing gnaw demons can become distracted by a weak target, so chasing them down is often as simple as locating their next likely victim.

KAZRITH TACTICS

The kazrith lurks underground and uses tremorsense to locate its enemies. Once it has chosen a target, it surfaces and attacks, using *acidic retreat* after the attack. It waits for the acid to run its course and then resurfaces to finish off the victim.

KAZRITH LORE

Arcana DC 22: Kazrith demons are water-dwelling predators of the planes. They lurk in lakes, rivers, and waterways, waiting for unwary prey to pass by. Kazriths can also burrow. Acid sprays from a kazrith's pores, aiding the demon's ability to burrow and leaving a fountain of acid in its wake.

ENCOUNTER GROUPS

Gnaw demons work on the promise of food.

Level 6 Encounter (XP 1,250)
✦ 1 gnoll demonic scourge (level 8 brute, *MM* 132)
✦ 1 gnoll fang of Yeenoghu (level 7 skirmisher)
✦ 3 gnaw demons (level 5 skirmisher)

KAZRITH

KAZRITHS PROWL THE MURKY DEPTHS of lakes, underground waterways, and flooded tunnels.

Kazrith		Level 20 Lurker
Medium elemental magical beast (demon, water)		XP 2,800

Initiative +22　　　**Senses** Perception +19; tremorsense 20
HP 146; **Bloodied** 73; see also *acidic seepage*
AC 34; **Fortitude** 32, **Reflex** 34, **Will** 30
Immune acid; **Resist** 20 variable (2/encounter)
Speed 6, burrow 6 (tunneling), swim 8

⊕ **Bite** (standard; at-will) ✦ **Acid**
　　+25 vs. AC; 2d6 + 4 damage, and ongoing 5 acid damage (save ends).

⬳ **Acidic Retreat** (standard; recharge ⚄ ⚅) ✦ **Acid**
　　Close burst 2; +23 vs. Reflex; 1d6 + 4 damage, and ongoing 10 acid damage (save ends). *Effect:* The kazrith burrows its speed.

Acidic Seepage (usable only while bloodied) ✦ **Acid**
　　The kazrith gains a +4 bonus to its burrow speed, and at the start of its turn creatures adjacent to it take 10 acid damage.

Slippery
　　A kazrith makes saving throws against immobilized, restrained, and slowed conditions at the start of its turn as well as at the end of its turn.

Alignment Chaotic evil　　**Languages** Abyssal, Primordial
Skills Stealth +23
Str 22 (+16)　　**Dex** 26 (+18)　　**Wis** 19 (+14)
Con 20 (+15)　　**Int** 14 (+12)　　**Cha** 12 (+11)

Kazrith and rupture demon

Arcana DC 25: Kazriths travel between bodies of water by creating vast networks of interconnecting flooded tunnels. These networks lie close to the surface so that the kazriths can sense prey overhead. Although most kazriths dwell in the Elemental Chaos, they sometimes find natural gates leading into the world.

ENCOUNTER GROUPS

Kazriths are often found among other sinister aquatic monsters.

Level 18 Encounter (XP 10,200)
✦ 1 aboleth lasher (level 17 brute, *MM* 8)
✦ 4 aboleth servitors (level 16 minion, *MM* 9)
✦ 1 aboleth slime mage (level 17 artillery, *MM* 8)
✦ 2 kazriths (level 20 lurker)

NEEDLE DEMON

NEEDLE DEMONS TURN ENEMIES against one another by making them believe that their closest friends have betrayed them. Needle demons wreak havoc and destruction throughout the Abyss and take any opportunity to bring that chaos to the mortal realms.

Needle Demon		Level 12 Controller
Medium elemental humanoid (demon)		XP 700

Initiative +10   **Senses** Perception +9; darkvision
HP 123; **Bloodied** 61
AC 26; **Fortitude** 23, **Reflex** 23, **Will** 25
Resist 15 variable (2/encounter)
Speed 6
⊕ **Claws** (standard; at-will)
  +17 vs. AC; 2d6 + 5 damage.
↯ **Claws of Betrayal** (standard; requires combat advantage against each target; at-will)
  The needle demon makes two claw attacks. If both attacks hit the same target, the target takes ongoing 10 damage (save ends).
↯ **Tail Whip** (immediate reaction, when an enemy moves into a square adjacent to the needle demon; at-will)
  +17 vs. AC; 1d6 + 2 damage.
⬁ **Rage of the Betrayed** (standard; recharge ⚄⚅) ✦ **Charm**
  Close blast 5; targets enemies; +16 vs. Will; the target is dominated (save ends).
Alignment Chaotic evil   **Languages** Abyssal
Skills Bluff +17, Insight +14, Intimidate +17
Str 16 (+9)   **Dex** 19 (+10)   **Wis** 17 (+9)
Con 19 (+10)   **Int** 14 (+8)   **Cha** 22 (+12)

NEEDLE DEMON TACTICS

A needle demon uses *rage of the betrayed* on as many targets as possible. It then moves around and looks for opportunities to attack with *claws of betrayal*. If *rage of the betrayed* recharges, the needle demon might save its next use for escaping from a hopeless fight.

NEEDLE DEMON LORE

Arcana DC 16: Needle demons possess greater cunning than most give them credit for, and they are more patient than many other demons. This craftiness often puts needle demons in the role of advisors to more powerful demons and even as the true powers behind manipulated puppets. However, their hunger for watching foes fight one another often gets the better of them, and they are rarely capable of more than simple deceptions.

ENCOUNTER GROUPS

Needle demons will join any cause that brings destruction and bloodshed, but it is never long before they turn on their allies.

Level 9 Encounter (XP 2,100)
✦ 1 cacklefiend hyena (level 7 brute, *MM* 166)
✦ 1 gnoll demonic scourge (level 8 brute, *MM* 132)
✦ 3 gnoll claw fighters (level 6 skirmisher, *MM* 132)
✦ 1 needle demon (level 12 controller)

Level 12 Encounter (XP 3,300)
✦ 1 drow arachnomancer (level 13 artillery, *MM* 94)
✦ 3 mezzodemons (level 11 soldier, *MM* 58)
✦ 1 needle demon (level 12 controller)

NELDRAZU

NELDRAZUS HIDE IN THE SHADOWS on the edge of a battle, then charge in to snatch enemies away. Once a neldrazu gets its target alone, it tears into it with its four savage claws.

Neldrazu		Level 8 Lurker
Large elemental humanoid (demon)		XP 350

Initiative +13   **Senses** Perception +7; darkvision
HP 71; **Bloodied** 35; see also *bloodied abduction*
AC 22; **Fortitude** 20, **Reflex** 21, **Will** 19
Resist 10 variable (1/encounter)
Speed 8, climb 6 (spider climb)
⊕ **Slashing Claw** (standard; at-will)
  Reach 2; +13 vs. AC; 2d6 + 5 damage.
↯ **Abduct** (move; recharge ⚅ ⚄⚅) ✦ **Teleportation**
  Reach 2; +11 vs. Reflex; targets enemies only; the neldrazu teleports the target 10 squares, and the neldrazu teleports to a space adjacent to the target. *Miss:* The neldrazu teleports 10 squares.
↯ **Flaying Claws** (standard; usable when only one enemy is within 5 squares of the neldrazu; at-will)
  Reach 2; +13 vs. AC; 4d6 + 5 damage, and ongoing 5 damage (save ends).
Bloodied Abduction (free, when first bloodied; encounter) ✦ **Teleportation**
  The neldrazu teleports an enemy adjacent to it 5 squares, and the neldrazu teleports to a space adjacent to the creature.
Alignment Chaotic evil   **Languages** Abyssal
Skills Stealth +14
Str 15 (+6)   **Dex** 20 (+9)   **Wis** 16 (+7)
Con 17 (+7)   **Int** 7 (+2)   **Cha** 11 (+4)

(Left to right) neldrazu, needle demon, and nycademon

NELDRAZU TACTICS

The neldrazu looks for a lightly armored enemy and uses *abduct* to bring it among the neldrazu's allies. Once the enemy is isolated, the neldrazu tears it apart with *flaying claws*. If attacking in groups, neldrazus teleport in different directions, spreading out their enemies as much as possible.

NELDRAZU LORE

Arcana DC 14: Although difficult to control, neldrazus make excellent abductors for slavers or kidnappers that don't mind if their goods are slightly damaged.

ENCOUNTER GROUPS

Neldrazus are usually encountered with other demons, but take any opportunity to wreak havoc. They prefer being near places where they can keep their victims isolated, such as narrow ledges, steep slopes, or pit traps.

Level 7 Encounter (XP 1,650)
- ✦ 2 barlguras (level 8 brute, *MM* 53)
- ✦ 2 neldrazus (level 8 lurker)
- ✦ 1 tiefling heretic (level 6 artillery, *MM* 250)

NYCADEMON

RIPPLING WITH MUSCLES AND THICK TENDONS, nycademons are winged terrors that soar over the charred landscape of the Abyss, searching for prey on the open expanses. These predators harry ground creatures for amusement, lifting their hapless victims high into the air and dropping them.

Nycademon	Level 22 Skirmisher
Large elemental humanoid (demon)	XP 4,150

Initiative +21   **Senses** Perception +17
HP 210; **Bloodied** 105
AC 35; **Fortitude** 35, **Reflex** 35, **Will** 32
Resist 20 variable (2/encounter)
Speed 6, fly 6 (hover)
⊕ **Wicked Axe** (standard; at-will)
     Reach 2; +27 vs. AC; 2d8 + 5 damage (crit 3d8 + 21), and ongoing 5 damage (save ends).
† **Wicked Edges** (standard; at-will)
     The nycademon makes two *wicked axe* attacks.
† **Snatch** (standard; at-will)
     Before or after the attack, the nycademon flies 6 squares. Reach 2; +25 vs. Fortitude; the target is grabbed.
Strong Flyer
     When a nycademon moves a grabbed target, it does not have to make a Strength attack. While bloodied, a nycademon can fly at full speed instead of half speed when moving a grabbed target.
Alignment Chaotic evil   **Languages** Abyssal, Common
Skills Intimidate +21
Str 25 (+18)   **Dex** 26 (+19)   **Wis** 13 (+12)
Con 26 (+19)   **Int** 8 (+10)   **Cha** 21 (+16)
Equipment 2 greataxes

Nycademon Tactics

A nycademon snatches a target and then flies into the air, attacking the target with *wicked edges* until the creature escapes. If the creature proves particularly dangerous, the nycademon drops the enemy from a high altitude and returns to the battle to grab new prey.

Nycademon Lore

Arcana DC 24: Nycademons are nicknamed "sky demons" for their tendency to swoop down and grab their enemies, carrying them high into the sky and releasing them to fall to their deaths.

Arcana DC 29: Nycademons put great stock in their physical superiority over their foes. This belief makes them overconfident when facing enemies that don't immediately show signs of power and hesitant when facing enemies that show great strength.

Encounter Groups

Nycademons are mercenary enough to work with almost any creature in the short term, but their superiority complexes soon infuriate most allies.

Level 21 Encounter (XP 17,250)
✦ 1 goristro (level 19 elite brute, *MM* 55)
✦ 3 nycademons (level 22 skirmisher)
✦ 1 rot harbinger (level 22 artillery, *MM* 223)

Pod Demon

THE DISGUSTING AND DEMENTED pod demon creates spawn that it uses to corner and terrorize other creatures.

Pod Demon	Level 15 Elite Artillery
Large elemental humanoid (demon)	XP 2,400

Initiative +12   **Senses** Perception +10; darkvision
HP 176; **Bloodied** 88
AC 27; **Fortitude** 25, **Reflex** 27, **Will** 29
Resist 15 variable (2/encounter)
Saving Throws +2
Speed 8
Action Points 1

⊕ **Slam** (standard; at-will) ✦ **Poison**
+20 vs. AC; 1d6 + 5 damage, and ongoing 5 poison damage (save ends).

↗ **Detonate Minion** (minor 1/round; recharge ⚄ ⚅) ✦ **Poison**
Ranged 10; targets one podspawn; the podspawn explodes, dropping to 0 hit points and dealing 1d8 + 3 poison damage to each creature adjacent to the podspawn.

↞ **Spew Podspawn** (standard; at-will) ✦ **Acid**
Close blast 3; +18 vs. Reflex; 2d6 + 5 acid damage.

↞ **Generate Podspawn** (standard; recharges when first bloodied) ✦ **Poison**
Close burst 2; +18 vs. Reflex; 3d6 + 5 poison damage. *Effect:* If the pod demon has fewer than four podspawn, it spawns podspawn into unoccupied squares within the burst, bringing its total number of minions to four.

❋ **Fling Podspawn** (standard; at-will) ✦ **Acid**
Area burst 1 within 10; +18 vs. Reflex; 2d6 + 5 acid damage.

Combat Advantage
A pod demon's attack deals 2d6 extra damage to any target granting combat advantage to it.

Spawn
If a pod demon has fewer than four podspawn at the start of its turn, it spawns one podspawn within 2 squares of it.

Transfer Essence (move; at-will)
The pod demon swaps positions with a podspawn within 10 squares of it.

Alignment Evil	**Languages** Abyssal, Common	
Str 17 (+10)	**Dex** 20 (+12)	**Wis** 16 (+10)
Con 21 (+12)	**Int** 12 (+8)	**Cha** 24 (+14)

Podspawn	Level 15 Minion Skirmisher
Small elemental humanoid (demon)	XP 300 or 0 if encountered with pod demon

Initiative +14 **Senses** Perception +6; darkvision
HP 1; a missed attack never damages a minion.
AC 29; **Fortitude** 28, **Reflex** 28, **Will** 25
Resist The podspawn shares any resistances that its pod demon progenitor has.
Speed 8
⊕ **Corroding Slime** (standard; at-will) ✦ **Acid**
  +20 vs. AC; 12 acid damage.
Dangerous Proximity
  Any enemy adjacent to a podspawn grants combat advantage to it.
Alignment Evil   **Languages** Abyssal, Common
Str 13 (+8)   **Dex** 20 (+12)   **Wis** 8 (+6)
Con 21 (+12)   **Int** 5 (+4)   **Cha** 15 (+9)

POD DEMON TACTICS

A pod demon prefers to enter combat with four minions. It sends minions out to grant combat advantage to itself and its allies. Then it uses *detonate minion* before creating more minions, always attempting to have four minions alive at a time.

POD DEMON LORE

Arcana DC 18: Pod demons are demons of madness that spawn tiny versions of themselves from their backs. A pod demon can psychically transfer its consciousness to any of its spawn, transforming that spawn's body into a new pod demon while its former body shrinks to podspawn form.

Arcana DC 23: The madness that possesses pod demons seems related to the Chained God, and some pod demons carry or wrap themselves in chains as a symbol of their allegiance.

ENCOUNTER GROUPS

Pod demons work with any demon that promises them the chance to terrorize the weak and fearful with their podspawn.

Level 16 Encounter (XP 7,200)
✦ 1 immolith (level 15 controller, *MM* 56)
✦ 1 pod demon (level 15 elite artillery)
✦ 4 podspawn (level 15 minion skirmisher)
✦ 2 red slaads (level 15 soldier, *MM* 238)

RUNESPIRAL DEMON

ARCANE RUNES ARE CUT DEEP into the thick shells of runespiral demons, channeling deadly energy from deep within the Abyss.

Runespiral Demon	Level 5 Artillery
Small elemental magical beast (demon)	XP 200

Initiative +6   **Senses** Perception +5
HP 51; **Bloodied** 25; see also *bloodied shock*
AC 17; **Fortitude** 16, **Reflex** 18, **Will** 17
Resist 10 variable (1/encounter)
Speed 7
⊕ **Bite** (standard; at-will)
  +10 vs. AC; 1d4 + 4 damage.
↯ **Arcane Arc** (immediate interrupt, when an enemy moves adjacent to the runespiral demon; at-will) ✦ **Lightning**
  +10 vs. Reflex; 1d6 + 4 lightning damage.
⤳ **Focused Strike** (standard; at-will) ✦ **Lightning**
  Ranged 10; +10 vs. Reflex; 2d6 + 4 lightning damage.
⬰ **Bloodied Shock** (free, when first bloodied; encounter) ✦ **Lightning**
  Close burst 1; +8 vs. Reflex; 1d6 + 4 lightning damage, and the target is dazed (save ends).
⁙ **Lightning Burst** (standard; at-will) ✦ **Lightning**
  Area burst 2 within 10; +8 vs. Reflex; 1d6 + 4 lightning damage. The attack deals 1 extra lightning damage for each creature in the burst.
Alignment Chaotic evil   **Languages** Abyssal
Str 13 (+3)   **Dex** 19 (+6)   **Wis** 16 (+5)
Con 15 (+4)   **Int** 5 (-1)   **Cha** 12 (+3)

Arctide Runespiral Demon	Level 12 Artillery
Large elemental magical beast (demon)	XP 700

Initiative +12   **Senses** Perception +10
HP 97; **Bloodied** 48; see also *bloodied shock*
AC 24; **Fortitude** 23, **Reflex** 25, **Will** 23
Resist 15 variable (2/encounter)
Speed 7
⊕ **Bite** (standard; at-will)
    +17 vs. AC; 1d6 + 5 damage.
† **Arcane Arc** (immediate interrupt, when an enemy moves
    adjacent to the arctide runespiral demon; at-will) ✦ **Lightning**
    +17 vs. Reflex; 1d8 + 5 lightning damage.
⤳ **Focused Strike** (standard; at-will) ✦ **Lightning**
    Ranged 10; +19 vs. Reflex; 2d8 + 5 lightning damage.
⬳ **Bloodied Shock** (free, when first bloodied; encounter) ✦
    Lightning
    Close burst 1; +15 vs. Reflex; 1d8 + 5 lightning damage, and the
    target is dazed (save ends).
❊ **Charged Lightning Burst** (standard; at-will) ✦ **Lightning**
    Area burst 2 within 10; +15 vs. Reflex; 1d8 + 5 lightning
    damage. The attack deals 1 extra lightning damage for each
    creature in the burst. Each ally damaged by the attack gains
    a +1 bonus to any recharge rolls at the start of its next turn.
    If the bonus causes a recharge roll to exceed 6, the result is
    considered 6.
Alignment Chaotic evil   **Languages** Abyssal
Str 15 (+8)   **Dex** 23 (+12)   **Wis** 19 (+10)
Con 19 (+10)   **Int** 7 (+4)   **Cha** 12 (+7)

RUNESPIRAL DEMON TACTICS

A runespiral demon circles the periphery of a battlefield while attacking with *focused strike* and *charged
lightning burst*. It shifts away from opponents to get the
most out of *arcane arc*.

RUNESPIRAL DEMON LORE

    Arcana DC 16: A runespiral demon has a thick
shell carved deeply with arcane runes that give it
mastery over lightning energy.
    Arcana DC 21: Although lightning-powered
runespiral demons are the most common, those using
other types of energy exist, each bearing a different
style of runes.

ENCOUNTER GROUPS

Other demons muster runespiral demons to their
cause with a mixture of threats and promises of
carnage.

Level 5 Encounter (XP 1,200)
✦ 2 evistros (level 6 brute, *MM* 54)
✦ 1 human hexer (level 7 controller)
✦ 2 runespiral demons (level 5 artillery)

RUPTURE DEMON

SYMBIOTIC DEMONS COMPOSED OF EVIL SLUDGE, rupture
demons slink through all layers of the Abyss, following behind more powerful demons and consuming
the remains of their kills.

Rupture Demon	Level 5 Minion Soldier
Small elemental magical beast (demon)	XP 50

Initiative +8   **Senses** Perception +4; low-light vision
HP 1; a missed attack never damages a minion; see also *demonic
    infestation*.
AC 20; **Fortitude** 16, **Reflex** 18, **Will** 16
Speed 6, spider climb 3
⊕ **Slimy Extrusion** (standard; at-will)
    +12 vs. AC; 5 damage.
† **Enveloping Embrace** (standard; encounter)
    No attack roll; the target is restrained (save ends), and the
    rupture demon drops to 0 hit points.
Demonic Infestation (when the rupture demon drops to 0 hit
    points) ✦ **Healing**
    The rupture demon erupts in a gory explosion of ichor and
    tentacles that latch on to a demon within 5 squares of the
    rupture demon and of level 10 or lower. That demon regains
    5 hit points and gains a +2 bonus to melee damage rolls until
    the end of the encounter. This bonus is cumulative with other
    demonic infestation bonuses (maximum +10).
Alignment Chaotic evil   **Languages** Abyssal
Str 15 (+4)   **Dex** 18 (+6)   **Wis** 15 (+4)
Con 11 (+2)   **Int** 4 (-1)   **Cha** 4 (-1)

RUPTURE DEMON TACTICS

A rupture demon possesses little sense of self and
virtually no sense of self-preservation. It wades into
melee, attacking any creatures that attack it. It uses
enveloping embrace when it causes maximum destruction or when a more powerful or intelligent demon
demands it.

RUPTURE DEMON LORE

    Arcana DC 12: Rupture demons are oily demons
made of liquefied evil. Barely sentient, rupture
demons never work for themselves or have their own
plans. In any place where a rupture demon is found,
it's certain that a more powerful demon lurks nearby.
    Arcana DC 17: Rupture demons are the weakest
spawns of Juiblex, the demon lord of ooze and slime.
Sages speculate that the rupture demons' aiding of
other demons through their deaths must be part of
some scheme by the enigmatic demon lord.

ENCOUNTER GROUPS

As servitors of Juiblex, rupture demons are found
among other slimes and oozes.

Level 6 Encounter (XP 1,250)
✦ 1 black pudding (level 8 elite brute)
✦ 1 evistro (level 6 brute, *MM* 54)
✦ 6 rupture demons (level 5 minion soldier)

YOCHLOL

YOCHLOLS ARE THE HANDMAIDENS OF LOLTH, feared by drow and other creatures as the Spider Queen's spies. These horrific fiends combine the subtle cruelty of drow with the savagery of demons.

Yochlol Tempter	Level 17 Controller
Medium elemental humanoid (demon, shapechanger)	XP 1,600

Initiative +14 **Senses** Perception +18; darkvision
HP 158; **Bloodied** 79
AC 31; **Fortitude** 27, **Reflex** 29, **Will** 30
Resist 10 poison
Speed 6, climb 8 (spider climb)
Demon Form Powers
 The yochlol tempter has the following powers in demon form.
⊕ **Tentacle** (standard; at-will)
 Reach 2; +22 vs. AC; 1d4 + 4 damage.
⨎ **Amorphous Flurry** (standard; at-will)
 The yochlol tempter makes four tentacle attacks. A target hit by two or more tentacle attacks takes a -4 penalty to Will (save ends).
✳ **Maddening Web** (standard; recharge ⚅ ⚄ ⚃ while bloodied)
 ✦ **Psychic**
 Area burst 2 within 10; targets enemies; +21 vs. Reflex; the target is immobilized and takes ongoing 5 psychic damage (save ends both).
Drow Shape (minor; at-will) ✦ **Polymorph**
 A yochlol tempter can alter its physical form to take on the appearance of a unique female drow.
Drow Form Powers
 The yochlol tempter has the following powers in drow form.
⊕ **Spider Touch** (standard; at-will) ✦ **Poison**
 +21 vs. Reflex; 1d6 + 5 damage, and ongoing 10 poison damage (save ends).
⊙ **Venom Bolt** (standard; at-will) ✦ **Poison**
 Ranged 10; +21 vs. Reflex; 1d6 + 5 damage, and the target is slowed and takes ongoing 5 poison damage (save ends both).
⌁ **Seductive Glare** (minor 1/round; recharges when the target saves) ✦ **Charm, Reliable**
 Ranged 10; +23 vs. Will; the target is dazed (save ends). *First Failed Saving Throw:* The target is stunned (save ends). *Second Failed Saving Throw:* The target is dominated (save ends).
Demon Shape (minor; at-will) ✦ **Polymorph**
 A yochlol tempter can alter its physical form to resume its demon form.

Alignment Chaotic evil	**Languages** Abyssal, Common, Elven

Skills Bluff +20, Intimidate +20, Religion +17, Stealth +19

Str 18 (+12)	**Dex** 23 (+14)	**Wis** 21 (+13)
Con 14 (+10)	**Int** 19 (+12)	**Cha** 24 (+15)

YOCHLOL TACTICS

Typically starting a fight in drow form, a yochlol shifts between its forms in battle, and it uses *venom bolt* and *spider touch* to weaken its enemies. When pressed into melee, it adopts its true form and unleashes *amorphous flurry*. If the flurry reduces a foe's Will, it shifts back into drow form to use *seductive glare*.

YOCHLOL LORE

Arcana DC 13: Yochlols are among the most favored of Lolth's servants, and the Spider Queen sends her handmaidens to attend priests that have gained her favor.

Arcana DC 20: A yochlol can adopt two forms. In its true form, it is a strange, oozelike creature similar to a heap of filth, with several tentacles and a red, baleful eye. In its other form, it appears as an attractive female drow.

Arcana DC 25: Yochlols are so skilled at infiltrating drow society that they might operate undetected for years at a time, even attaining positions of great power.

ENCOUNTER GROUPS

Yochlols work within drow societies, driving Lolth's mortal servants to commit horrific acts of cruelty and evil in the Spider Queen's name. They can usually be found in the company of Lolth's priests and templars.

Level 16 Encounter (XP 7,600)
✦ 2 drow arachnomancers (level 13 artillery, *MM* 94)
✦ 1 drow blademaster (level 13 elite skirmisher, *MM* 94)
✦ 1 drow priest (level 15 controller, *MM* 95)
✦ 2 yochlol tempters (level 17 controller)

DEVA

In ages long past, benevolent angels took it upon themselves to descend to the world in mortal form. Now their spirits are perpetually reincarnated as mortal devas, creatures driven to bring light to the world–or corrupted by material influences to oppose the goals of their kind.

DEVA KNIGHT-ERRANT

A deva knight-errant travels the world as a champion of holy causes. A knight-errant might prove a worthy ally to a party of adventurers. However, a holy champion can be a deadly adversary if the party's motives are less than pure.

Deva Knight-Errant	Level 11 Soldier (Leader)
Medium immortal humanoid	XP 600

Initiative +7 **Senses** Perception +8
HP 111; **Bloodied** 55
AC 27; **Fortitude** 24, **Reflex** 22, **Will** 22 (+1 to all defenses against bloodied enemies)
Resist 10 necrotic, 10 radiant
Speed 5
⊕ **Broadsword** (standard; at-will) ✦ **Weapon**
+18 vs. AC; 2d10 + 2 damage, and the target is marked until the end of the deva knight-errant's next turn.
⇂ **Rejuvenating Smite** (standard; recharges after hitting with a broadsword attack) ✦ **Healing, Weapon**
+18 vs. AC; 2d10 + 2 damage, and the deva knight-errant regains hit points equal to half the damage dealt.
⇐ **Martyr's Cry** (standard; recharge ⚅) ✦ **Implement, Psychic**
Close burst 3; targets enemies; +16 vs. Will; 2d6 + 4 psychic damage, and the target is marked (save ends).
Inner Radiance ✦ **Radiant**
Any attack a deva knight-errant makes can instead deal radiant damage. In addition, a knight-errant can take a -2 penalty to an attack roll to deal 4 extra radiant damage on the attack.
Health Transfer (minor; encounter) ✦ **Healing**
The deva knight-errant takes up to 25 damage, and one ally within 10 squares of it regains the same number of hit points. The knight-errant can then transfer one condition from the ally to itself.
Memory of a Thousand Lifetimes (free, when the deva knight-errant makes an attack roll, a skill check, or an ability check and dislikes the result; encounter)
The knight-errant adds 1d6 to the triggering roll.
Alignment Good **Languages** Common
Skills History +16, Insight +14, Religion +16
Str 21 (+10)	**Dex** 10 (+5)	**Wis** 16 (+8)
Con 15 (+7)	**Int** 18 (+9)	**Cha** 18 (+9)
Equipment plate armor, heavy shield, broadsword, holy symbol

DEVA ZEALOT

Deva zealots wield their belief as well as their weapons in the battle against evil.

Deva Zealot	Level 14 Skirmisher
Medium immortal humanoid	XP 1,000

Initiative +15 **Senses** Perception +15
HP 135; **Bloodied** 67
AC 28; **Fortitude** 25, **Reflex** 27, **Will** 25 (+1 to all defenses against bloodied enemies)
Resist 10 necrotic, 10 radiant
Speed 6
⊕ **Falchion** (standard; at-will) ✦ **Radiant, Weapon**
+19 vs. AC; 4d4 + 5 damage (crit 8d4 + 21) plus 1d6 radiant damage.
⇂ **Path of Virtue** (standard; encounter)
The deva zealot shifts half its speed and makes one falchion attack against each enemy within reach during the move.
Dazzling Soul (minor; recharge ⚃ ⚄ ⚅)
The deva zealot gains concealment until the start of its next turn, and any other square within 6 squares of the zealot is illuminated by bright light. Any square within 12 squares of the zealot is illuminated by dim light.
Radiant Retribution (free, when an enemy hits the deva zealot on the zealot's turn; at-will) ✦ **Radiant**
The triggering enemy takes half the attack's damage as radiant damage.
Memory of a Thousand Lifetimes (free, when the deva zealot makes an attack roll, a skill check, or an ability check and dislikes the result; encounter)
The zealot adds 1d6 to the triggering roll.
Skirmish ✦ **Radiant**
If a deva zealot ends its move at least 4 squares from the square where it started the move, its attacks deal 1d6 extra radiant damage until the start of its next turn.
Alignment Unaligned **Languages** Common
Skills Acrobatics +18, Religion +16, Stealth +18
Str 20 (+12)	**Dex** 22 (+13)	**Wis** 16 (+10)
Con 15 (+9)	**Int** 14 (+9)	**Cha** 20 (+12)
Equipment leather armor, falchion

DEVA FALLEN STAR

A deva fallen star manipulates the field of battle, reshaping fate to suit its corrupt plans.

Deva Fallen Star	Level 26 Artillery
Medium immortal humanoid	XP 9,000

Initiative +15 **Senses** Perception +19
HP 188; **Bloodied** 94; see also *vile rebirth*
AC 38; **Fortitude** 37, **Reflex** 37, **Will** 38 (+1 to all defenses against bloodied enemies)
Resist 15 necrotic, 15 radiant
Speed 6, fly 8 (clumsy)
⊕ **Rebuking Rod** (standard; at-will) ✦ **Implement, Psychic, Radiant**
+31 vs. Will; 2d8 + 8 psychic and radiant damage, and the deva fallen star makes a secondary attack against the target. *Secondary Attack:* +31 vs. Fortitude; the fallen star gains total concealment against the target (save ends).

(Left to right) deva zealot, deva knight-errant, and deva fallen star

↗ **Fateful Transposition** (immediate interrupt, when an enemy attacks the deva fallen star; encounter) ✦ **Teleportation**
Ranged 10; +31 vs. Will; the target swaps positions with the deva fallen star. The triggering enemy's attack deals half damage to the fallen star, and the target takes damage equal to half the attack's damage.

↗ **Forgetting Ray** (standard; at-will) ✦ **Charm, Psychic**
Ranged 20; +31 vs. Reflex; 3d6 + 8 psychic damage, and the target can use only basic attacks and at-will powers during its next turn.

☀ **Soul Scourge** (standard; recharges when first bloodied) ✦ **Necrotic, Radiant**
Area burst 2 within 15; targets enemies; +31 vs. Will; 1d6 + 8 radiant damage, and the target takes ongoing 15 necrotic damage (save ends).

Fate Manipulation (free; recharges when first bloodied)
The deva fallen star adds 1d8 to or subtracts 1d8 from an attack roll, ability check, or saving throw made by itself or any creature within 10 squares of it.

Vile Rebirth (when the deva fallen star is reduced to 0 hit points by non-necrotic damage) ✦ **Healing**
The fallen star does not die and instead remains at 0 hit points until the start of its next turn, when it regains 25 hit points, loses resistance to radiant damage, and gains the undead keyword. This power recharges, and the triggering damage type changes to nonradiant damage.

Alignment Evil		**Languages** Common, Supernal
Skills Arcana +26, History +28, Insight +19, Religion +28		
Str 14 (+15)	**Dex** 15 (+15)	**Wis** 12 (+14)
Con 26 (+21)	**Int** 26 (+21)	**Cha** 29 (+22)
Equipment robes, rod		

DEVA LORE

Religion DC 16: A deva transforms spontaneously from bodiless soul to physical form, awakening as an adult already in possession of the skills required to defend the world against evil. With strong ties to fate, devas take the role of born heroes, leaders—or villains.

Religion DC 21: The life cycle of the deva parallels that of the rakshasa (MM 217)—a spirit constantly reincarnating to mortal form. When a deva gives in to iniquity to become a fallen star, its soul is corrupted. If it dies in that state, it returns to combat as an undead; if finally slain by radiant damage, it carries its wickedness into its next life and becomes a rakshasa—a fate that even evil devas revile.

ENCOUNTER GROUPS

Deva zealots and knights-errant are most often found leading or assisting creatures dedicated to a worthy cause. However, evil devas can create alliances with even the foulest creatures.

Level 27 Encounter (XP 58,000)
✦ 2 deva fallen stars (level 26 artillery)
✦ 2 efreet karadjins (level 28 soldier, MM 100)
✦ 2 efreet pyresingers (level 25 controller, MM 99)

Devils rebelled against the gods and were banished to the Nine Hells, where they forever bicker and plot. Devious and nefarious, devils find no scheme too convoluted.

ASSASSIN DEVIL

Murder looms large as a tactic in the plots of devils, and for the purpose of murder, they have no better tool than the assassin devil. Shrouded in a cloak of shadows, this devil is a consummate killer.

Assassin Devil	Level 24 Lurker
Medium immortal humanoid (devil)	XP 6,050

Initiative +25　　**Senses** Perception +23; darkvision
HP 167; **Bloodied** 83
AC 38; **Fortitude** 34, **Reflex** 38, **Will** 36
Resist 25 fire
Speed 12
⊕ **Shadow Sword** (standard; at-will) ✦ **Necrotic, Weapon**
　+27 vs. Fortitude; 3d6 + 5 necrotic damage, and ongoing 5 damage (save ends).
✣ **Shadow Net** (standard; recharges when the assassin devil uses *shadow cloak*) ✦ **Necrotic**
　Area burst 2 within 10; +26 vs. Reflex; the target is restrained, is weakened, and takes ongoing 10 necrotic damage (save ends all). While a target is affected by *shadow net*, the assassin devil cannot use its *shadow cloak* power.
Dangerous Shadows
　An assassin devil's *shadow sword* attack deals 4d6 extra necrotic damage against any target granting combat advantage to it.
Shadow Cloak (standard; recharges when no creatures are affected by *shadow net*) ✦ **Illusion**
　The assassin devil is invisible until it hits or misses with an attack.
Alignment Evil	**Languages** Common, Supernal
Skills Stealth +27
| **Str** 21 (+17) | **Dex** 28 (+21) | **Wis** 25 (+19) |
| **Con** 17 (+15) | **Int** 17 (+15) | **Cha** 13 (+13) |
Equipment leather armor, sword

ASSASSIN DEVIL TACTICS

An assassin devil uses *shadow net* on as many enemies as it can, and then attacks with *shadow sword* amplified by *dangerous shadows*. When too many unrestrained enemies threaten it, an assassin devil uses its *shadow cloak* to hide and position itself for another *shadow net* attack.

ASSASSIN DEVIL LORE

　Religion DC 24: Rarely the masterminds of any plot, assassin devils fulfill the evil will of others, taking great pride in their lethal occupation.
　Religion DC 29: Many assassin devils report directly to Asmodeus, covertly feeding him the secrets of their patrons. Devils that discover this treachery rarely respond with accusations and attacks. Instead, they attempt to dispose of the treacherous servants or manipulate them into giving Asmodeus favorable information.

ENCOUNTER GROUPS

Assassin devils prefer to work alone because other devils get in their way. When they face a tough opponent, they rely on war devils and other melee combatants to distract the enemy while they move in for the kill.

Level 22 Encounter (XP 23,200)
✦ 2 assassin devils (level 24 lurker)
✦ 1 human diabolist (level 20 artillery)
✦ 2 war devils (level 22 brute, *MM* 67)

ERINYES

Furies of vengeance and rage, erinyes exist for battle. Although they are not the most powerful warriors in the Nine Hells, their combat skills inspire allies.

Erinyes	Level 13 Soldier (Leader)
Medium immortal humanoid (devil)	XP 800

Initiative +10　　**Senses** Perception +9; darkvision
Blade Shield aura 3; each ally within the aura gains a +2 bonus to AC.
HP 131; **Bloodied** 65; see also *bloody spiral*
AC 29; **Fortitude** 25, **Reflex** 23, **Will** 23
Speed 5
⊕ **Compelling Strike** (standard; at-will) ✦ **Weapon**
　+20 vs. AC; 2d10 + 3 damage, and one ally within 5 squares of the erinyes gains 8 temporary hit points.
↓ **Flitting Blade** (standard; at-will) ✦ **Weapon**
　Targets one, two, or three creatures; +18 vs. AC; 1d10 + 3 damage.
⬗ **Bloody Spiral** (immediate reaction, when first bloodied; encounter) ✦ **Weapon**
　Close burst 1; +18 vs. Reflex; 5 damage, and the target is knocked prone. If two or more enemies are knocked prone, each ally within 5 squares of the erinyes gains 10 temporary hit points.
Devastating Opportunist
　An erinyes gains a +3 bonus to attack rolls when making opportunity attacks, and if an opportunity attack hits, it shifts 1 square as a free action.
Alignment Evil	**Languages** Supernal
Skills Diplomacy +15, Endurance +15, Intimidate +15
| **Str** 22 (+12) | **Dex** 19 (+10) | **Wis** 16 (+9) |
| **Con** 19 (+10) | **Int** 14 (+8) | **Cha** 18 (+10) |
Equipment plate armor, light shield, bastard sword

ERINYES TACTICS

An erinyes starts combat with a *compelling strike*. It then attempts to engage as many foes as possible using *flitting blade*. When an ally loses its temporary hit points, the erinyes switches back to *compelling strike*. Multiple erinyes aid one another with positioning, opting to hem in and engage a group of foes rather than moving to flank them.

(Left to right) infernal armor animus, erinyes, and shocktroop devil

Erinyes Lore

Religion DC 18: Masters of sword and shield, erinyes inspire allies with the carnage they inflict. Mortal warriors have been known to sell their souls to train with these demons.

Religion DC 23: Erinyes act as arbiters of justice among the devils and on behalf of their interests. Those who break a contract with infernal powers should not be surprised to find a host of erinyes on their heels.

Encounter Groups

Groups led by erinyes frequently include bearded devils, chain devils, legion devil hellguards, and a wide variety of mortal creatures.

Level 12 Encounter (XP 3,550)
✦ 3 erinyes (level 13 soldier)
✦ 2 chain devils (level 11 skirmisher, *MM* 62)
✦ 5 legion devil hellguards (level 11 minion, *MM* 64)

Gorechain Devil

THESE SHAMBLING HULKS career through the hells and the world's hellish charnel fields, wrapping their soon-to-be-dead foes in gore-encrusted spiked chains and controlling them like puppets.

Gorechain Devil	Level 12 Elite Brute
Large immortal humanoid (devil)	XP 1,400

Initiative +10   **Senses** Perception +8
Grasping Chains aura 3; any enemy that starts its turn within the aura must make a DC 21 Athletics check or Acrobatics check in order to leave the aura. If the check fails, the enemy cannot attempt to leave the aura again until the start of its next turn.
HP 298; **Bloodied** 149
AC 24; **Fortitude** 23, **Reflex** 21, **Will** 21
Resist 10 fire
Saving Throws +2
Speed 5
Action Points 1
⊕ **Gorechain Strike** (standard; at-will) ✦ **Weapon**
    Reach 3; +15 vs. AC; 2d12 + 4 damage.
↯ **Gorechain Flail** (standard; recharge ⚅)
    The gorechain devil makes a *gorechain strike* attack against each enemy within reach.
↯ **Gorechain Takeover** (standard; recharge ⚄ ⚅) ✦ **Charm**
    Reach 3; +15 vs. Fortitude; 3d6 + 5 damage, and the target is dominated (save ends). The dominated condition ends if the target is more than 3 squares away from the gorechain devil at the start of the target's turn.
Alignment Evil	**Languages** Supernal	
Str 22 (+12)	**Dex** 19 (+10)	**Wis** 15 (+8)
Con 19 (+10)	**Int** 15 (+8)	**Cha** 13 (+7)

Gorechain Devil Tactics

Gorechain devils aim *gorechain takeover* attacks at the strongest-looking targets while concentrating their other attacks on enemies that look like controllers or leaders.

GORECHAIN DEVIL LORE

Religion DC 16: Larger and more powerful than chain devils, gorechain devils use their chains to control their foes.

Religion DC 21: Chain devils act as jailers among devils; gorechain devils behave more like bounty hunters.

ENCOUNTER GROUPS

Gorechain devils are more likely than other devils to consort with undead.

Level 12 Encounter (XP 3,800)
- 2 gorechain devils (level 12 elite brute)
- 1 skeleton tomb guardian (level 10 brute, *MM* 235)
- 1 skull lord (level 10 artillery, *MM* 236)

INFERNAL ARMOR ANIMUS

THROUGH AN EVIL RITUAL, a devil can invest a suit of armor with a mortal soul. The tortured spirit within provides military support for its devil overlords. When its physical form is ruined, the soul bursts free, only to be consumed by the nearest devil.

Although it doesn't speak, an infernal armor animus understands Common and Supernal.

Infernal Armor Animus	Level 3 Minion Soldier
Medium immortal animate (devil, undead)	XP 38

Initiative +5   **Senses** Perception +1; darkvision
Bloodlust aura 2; each nonminion devil within the aura gains a +1 bonus to damage rolls. Multiple *bloodlust* auras grant a cumulative bonus.
HP 1; a missed attack never damages a minion; see also *essence transference*.
AC 19; **Fortitude** 16, **Reflex** 15, **Will** 14
Resist 5 fire
Speed 6
ⓐ **Short Sword** (standard; at-will) ✦ **Weapon**
+8 vs. AC; 5 damage.
Essence Transference (when the infernal armor animus drops to 0 hit points) ✦ **Healing**
The nearest nonminion devil within 5 squares of the animus regains 15 hit points.

Alignment Evil	**Languages** —	
Str 19 (+5)	**Dex** 14 (+3)	**Wis** 10 (+1)
Con 15 (+3)	**Int** 8 (+0)	**Cha** 11 (+1)

Equipment heavy shield, short sword

INFERNAL ARMOR ANIMUS TACTICS

Infernal armor animuses hurl themselves into the fray, flanking foes when possible and moving to keep as many powerful devils in their auras as they can.

INFERNAL ARMOR ANIMUS LORE

Religion DC 10: Infernal armor animuses are mortal souls bound to suits of armor to serve as caches of life energy for devils.

Religion DC 15: When it dies, an infernal armor animus heals a nearby devil, so it is often the best tactic to destroy all animuses before attacking other devils.

ENCOUNTER GROUPS

Infernal armor animuses are most effective when massed with more powerful devils.

Level 5 Encounter (XP 1,054)
- 8 infernal armor animuses (level 3 minion soldier)
- 2 spined devils (level 6 skirmisher, *MM* 66)
- 1 tiefling heretic (level 6 artillery, *MM* 250)

MISFORTUNE DEVIL

THE MISFORTUNE DEVIL GATHERS SOULS for the Nine Hells by enticing mortals. It lures mortals into taking increasingly larger risks–risks that ultimately lead to the moment when the devil owns the mortals' souls.

Misfortune Devil	Level 15 Artillery
Medium immortal humanoid (devil)	XP 1,200

Initiative +10   **Senses** Perception +12; darkvision, truesight 10
HP 115; **Bloodied** 57
AC 27; **Fortitude** 26, **Reflex** 28, **Will** 27
Speed 6, fly 6 (hover)
ⓐ **Lucky Maneuver** (standard; at-will) ✦ **Psychic, Teleportation**
+18 vs. Will; 1d8 + 7 psychic damage, and the misfortune devil teleports 4 squares.
↗ **Ray of Distortion** (standard; recharge ⚄ ⚅)
Ranged 20; +18 vs. Reflex; 4d8 + 7 damage. The target can choose to take 5 damage and redirect the damage of this attack to the ally with the most current hit points. The full damage is then rerolled and applied to that ally.
Roll the Bones (immediate interrupt, when the misfortune devil is hit by a melee or ranged attack; encounter)
The triggering attack targets a creature of the devil's choice within 5 squares of the devil.

Alignment Evil	**Languages** Supernal, Common	
Skills Bluff +20, Diplomacy +20, Insight +22, Intimidate +20		
Str 14 (+9)	**Dex** 17 (+10)	**Wis** 20 (+12)
Con 19 (+11)	**Int** 23 (+13)	**Cha** 16 (+10)

MISFORTUNE DEVIL TACTICS

The misfortune devil lets its allies engage first and then moves to the safest spot within range, attacking foes with *ray of distortion*. It saves *roll the bones* for a dangerous or hampering attack, particularly one scoring a critical hit.

(Left to right) misfortune devil, withering devil, gorechain devil, and assassin devil

MISFORTUNE DEVIL LORE

Religion DC 18: Misfortune devils encourage others to take unreasonable risks by preying on their inner desires. They delight in promoting addictive habits and exhorting the passionate into folly.

Religion DC 23: Misfortune devils enjoy using their silver tongues to trick others into making poor decisions. If the physical appearance of a misfortunate devil would frighten away a prospective mark, it uses underlings to deliver the message, or magic to disguise itself in the form of a trusted friend.

ENCOUNTER GROUPS

Misfortune devils tend to attach themselves to legions of devils on some infernal errand, hoping to warp probability in Hell's favor.

Level 13 Encounter (XP 4,750)
✦ 2 erinyes (level 13 soldier)
✦ 5 legion devil hellguards (level 11 minion, *MM* 64)
✦ 2 misfortune devils (level 15 artillery)

SHOCKTROOP DEVIL

SHOCKTROOP DEVILS SLAM INTO ENEMY RANKS like metal battering rams, delivering brutal attacks that throw their enemies off balance.

Shocktroop Devil		Level 16 Soldier
Large immortal humanoid (devil)		XP 1,400
Initiative +15	**Senses** Perception +9; darkvision	
HP 155; **Bloodied** 77		
AC 33; **Fortitude** 27, **Reflex** 26, **Will** 26; see also *Asmodeus's shield*		
Speed 6, fly 8		

⊕ **Sword and Shield** (standard; at-will) ✦ **Weapon**
    Reach 2; +23 vs. AC; 2d8 + 6 damage, and the shocktroop devil makes a secondary attack. *Secondary Attack:* Reach 2; +20 vs. Fortitude; the target is pushed 2 squares and dazed until the end of the shocktroop devil's next turn.

⨮ **Shocktroop Attack** (standard; recharges when the shocktroop devil has full hit points)
    The devil makes three *sword and shield* attacks, each against a different target.

Asmodeus's Shield
    While a shocktroop devil is not bloodied, it gains a +2 bonus to all defenses against divine attack powers. While bloodied, it takes a –2 penalty to all defenses against divine attack powers.

Alignment Evil	**Languages** Common, Supernal	
Str 22 (+14)	**Dex** 20 (+13)	**Wis** 13 (+9)
Con 19 (+12)	**Int** 10 (+8)	**Cha** 20 (+13)

Equipment plate armor, heavy shield, longsword

Shocktroop Devil Tactics

The shocktroop devil starts combat with its *shocktroop* attack, using sword and shield whenever possible to daze and push enemies out of the way. Later in a fight, if shocktroop devils have forces to screen for them and the fight appears to be going against them, they might retreat. They then rest, regroup, and make a new lightning-fast assault.

Shocktroop Devil Lore

Religion DC 20: Shocktroop devils are front-line soldiers for hell's armies. They break up enemy charges, shatter enemy formations, and can single-handedly slaughter a great number of the enemy.

Religion DC 25: It is important to hurt shock-troop devils as quickly as possible. A shocktroop devil fighting at full strength is a terrible foe.

Encounter Groups

Shocktroop devils work for anyone who promises incessant battle and threatens rigid discipline.

Level 16 Encounter (XP 7,000)
+ 1 bone devil (level 17 controller, *MM* 62)
+ 1 misfortune devil (level 15 artillery)
+ 3 shocktroop devils (level 16 soldier)

Withering Devil

WITHERING DEVILS HARVEST SOULS for the Nine Hells by sapping the vitality out of all that they meet. By tempting or tricking mortals into apathy and depression, withering devils cause famine, plague, and strife.

Withering Devil	Level 14 Controller
Medium immortal humanoid (devil)	XP 1,000

Initiative +8   **Senses** Perception +8; darkvision
Aura of Exhaustion (Charm) aura 3; each enemy within the aura is weakened.
HP 138; **Bloodied** 69
Resist 15 fire
AC 28; **Fortitude** 24, **Reflex** 25, **Will** 26
Speed 6
ⓘ **Staff of Weariness** (standard; at-will) ✦ **Weapon**
  +19 vs. AC; 2d8 + 6 damage.
➣ **Draining Ray** (standard; at-will) ✦ **Psychic**
  Ranged 20; +18 vs. Reflex; 2d8 + 6 psychic damage, and the target is immobilized until the end of the withering devil's next turn.
➣ **Gaze of Apathy** (minor; recharge ⚄ ⚅) ✦ **Charm, Gaze**
  Ranged 10; +17 vs. Will; the target is slowed (save ends).
Alignment Evil   **Languages** Common, Supernal
Skills Bluff +18, Insight +13
Str 11 (+7)   **Dex** 12 (+8)   **Wis** 13 (+8)
Con 18 (+11)   **Int** 20 (+12)   **Cha** 23 (+13)
Equipment quarterstaff

Withering Devil Tactics

A withering devil uses its *draining ray* on ranged attackers, and then it closes the distance to keep such attackers within its aura. Withering devils position themselves near enemy melee combatants in order to affect them with *aura of exhaustion*.

Withering Devil Lore

Religion DC 18: Withering devils tempt and trick others into not caring for each other or their duties. They destroy individuals and groups by encouraging apathy and the lack of empathy.

Religion DC 23: Although their natural appearance is hideous, withering devils show extraordinary aptitude at disguising themselves as other humanoids. Some find and use magic to aid these attempts, but a heavy cloak and a dark room can prove just as effective.

Encounter Groups

Withering devils cooperate with those that have similar goals, but won't hesitate to abandon their allies if the situation looks grim.

Level 13 Encounter (XP 4,000)
+ 2 bearded devils (level 13 soldier, *MM* 60)
+ 4 legion devil hellguards (level 11 minion, *MM* 56)
+ 1 withering devil (level 14 controller)
+ 1 yuan-ti malison sharp-eyes (level 13 artillery, *MM* 269)

Level 15 Encounter (XP 6,600)
+ 1 shadow snake (level 16 skirmisher, *MM* 240)
+ 3 yuan-ti abominations (level 14 soldier, *MM* 270)
+ 1 yuan-ti malison incanter (level 15 artillery, *MM* 269)
+ 1 withering devil (level 14 controller)

DIMENSIONAL MARAUDER

THESE CLEVER, SKULKING PREDATORS travel the planes and the world in search of easy prey. They are especially fond of places where mortals gather.

Dimensional Marauder	Level 4 Lurker
Medium aberrant magical beast	XP 175

Initiative +10   **Senses** Perception +5; low-light vision
HP 45; **Bloodied** 22
AC 18; **Fortitude** 15, **Reflex** 17, **Will** 16
Vulnerable psychic; a dimensional marauder that takes psychic damage immediately ends *planephase form*.
Speed 7, teleport 3
⊕ **Bite** (standard; at-will)
    +9 vs. AC; 2d6 + 3 damage.
↯ **Reality Warp** (standard; usable only while insubstantial; at-will)
    ✦ **Teleportation**
    +7 vs. Reflex; 1d10 + 4 damage, and the dimensional marauder teleports the target 3 squares. The marauder then teleports 3 squares into a space adjacent to the target.
Planar Evasion (immediate reaction, when the dimensional marauder is hit by a melee attack; recharge ⚁ ⚂ ⚃) ✦ **Teleportation**
    The marauder teleports 3 squares.
Planephase Form (standard; at-will)
    The dimensional marauder partially phases into another plane, gaining insubstantial and phasing until the end of its next turn or until it hits or misses with an attack. *Sustain Minor:* The effect persists.

Alignment Unaligned	**Languages** Deep Speech	
Skills Stealth +11		
Str 11 (+2)	**Dex** 18 (+6)	**Wis** 16 (+5)
Con 15 (+4)	**Int** 4 (–1)	**Cha** 12 (+3)

DIMENSIONAL MARAUDER TACTICS

Dimensional marauders are cowardly creatures that prefer to lie in ambush or stalk foes from the shadows. A dimensional marauder waits until adversaries are engaged in combat before moving in for opportunistic bite attacks. It enters *planephase form* when first hit in combat, then strikes with *reality warp* to isolate an opponent.

DIMENSIONAL MARAUDER LORE

Dungeoneering DC 17: Dimensional marauders have powers of teleportation and phasing. Some dimensional marauders seek easy prey, and can be found near cities and other areas of high population.

ENCOUNTER GROUPS

Many extraplanar civilizations use dimensional marauders as guards and hunters. However, these creatures' predatory instincts sometimes inspire them to jump into a battle simply because one side or the other looks weak.

Level 3 Encounter (XP 850)
✦ 2 dimensional marauders (level 4 lurker)
✦ 2 ettercap fang guards (level 4 soldier, *MM* 107)
✦ 1 gnome arcanist (level 3 controller, *MM* 134)

BRIAN DESPAIN

TIRELESS AND DRIVEN BY DARK COVENANTS, undead direguards possess powerful magic and the skills of battle retained from their past lives.

DIREGUARD LORE

Religion DC 16: A direguard is a skeletal undead imbued with powerful magic. Foul rituals transform willing warriors into direguards, but at a price. If a direguard does not meet a specific quota of killing, it is destroyed by the dark pact that grants its power.

Religion DC 21: Liches and death knights perform the ritual that turns a living ally into a direguard tied to their wills. A deathbringer might be assigned to kill a certain number of sentient beings, or an assassin to kill members of a specific race.

DIREGUARD DEATHBRINGER

THE SKELETAL DEATHBRINGER uses its blazing claws against its enemies as its force armor deflects attacks.

Direguard Deathbringer Level 8 Elite Artillery (Leader)	
Medium natural humanoid (undead)	XP 700

Initiative +7   **Senses** Perception +11; darkvision, truesight 10
Command Zone aura 4; each ally within the aura gains a +2 bonus to attack rolls.
HP 134; **Bloodied** 67; see also *force armor*
AC 20; **Fortitude** 20, **Reflex** 21, **Will** 22
Immune disease, poison
Saving Throws +2
Speed 7
Action Points 1
⊕ **Blazing Bone Claw** (standard; at-will) ✦ **Force**
+15 vs. AC; 1d6 + 9 force damage.
➹ **Force Blast** (standard; at-will) ✦ **Force**
Ranged 15; +13 vs. Reflex; 2d8 + 5 force damage, and the direguard deathbringer pushes the target 3 squares. *Miss:* The target is slowed until the end of the deathbringer's next turn.
➹ **Frightful Force** (standard; recharge ⚄ ⚅ ⚅)
The direguard deathbringer makes three *force blast* attacks, each against a different target.
↫ **Vile Command** (standard; recharge ⚄ ⚅)
Close blast 3; targets allies; the target shifts 2 squares and makes a basic attack as a free action.
Force Armor (when first bloodied; encounter)
The direguard deathbringer gains a +4 power bonus to AC and Reflex until it is hit by an attack.
Alignment Evil   **Languages** Common
Skills Bluff +12, Insight +11, Intimidate +12
Str 17 (+7)   **Dex** 17 (+7)   **Wis** 14 (+6)
Con 13 (+5)   **Int** 19 (+8)   **Cha** 20 (+9)

DIREGUARD ASSASSIN

A MYSTERIOUS FIGURE OF SMOKE AND SHADOW, the direguard assassin wields a glowing red blade.

Direguard Assassin	Level 11 Skirmisher
Medium natural humanoid (undead)	XP 600

Initiative +12   **Senses** Perception +14; darkvision, truesight 10
HP 111; **Bloodied** 55
AC 25; **Fortitude** 23, **Reflex** 24, **Will** 23
Immune disease, poison
Speed 8
⊕ **Force Blade** (standard; at-will) ✦ **Force**
+16 vs. AC; 2d6 + 6 force damage.
↫ **Dire Blades** (standard; encounter) ✦ **Force**
Close burst 1; +16 vs. AC; 2d6 + 6 force damage.
Mist Walk (immediate reaction, when missed by a melee attack; at-will)
The direguard assassin shifts 2 squares and gains insubstantial and phasing until the end of its next turn.
Mobile Assault
If a direguard assassin ends its move at least 4 squares from where it began its move, it gains a +2 bonus to melee attack rolls until the end of its turn.
Alignment Evil   **Languages** Common
Skills Stealth +15
Str 18 (+9)   **Dex** 21 (+10)   **Wis** 18 (+9)
Con 15 (+7)   **Int** 16 (+8)   **Cha** 17 (+8)

DJINN

Ingenious engineers of the fabulous, djinns work with that most transitory of elements—air—to create effects more enduring than the life spans of many worldly empires. Carving gigantic floating cities from the Elemental Chaos, djinns build shining palaces gleaming with treasures beyond mortal imagination.

Allying with the primordials in the struggle against the gods, the djinns paid a high price for their defeat. Many are still imprisoned in towers, mirrors, lamps, and other lowly relics, and the few that roam free in the world possess only a fraction of their former power.

DJINN THUNDERER

This elemental shakes the battle with blasts of thunder, brandishing a jeweled scepter.

Djinn Thunderer	Level 20 Artillery
Large elemental humanoid (air)	XP 2,800

Initiative +16   **Senses** Perception +16; blindsight 10
HP 146; **Bloodied** 73
AC 32; **Fortitude** 34, **Reflex** 32, **Will** 32
Immune disease, poison; **Resist** 15 thunder
Speed 6, fly 8 (hover)
Action Points see *rage of storms*
⊕ **Scepter** (standard; at-will) ✦ **Weapon**
   Reach 2; +27 vs. AC; 3d8 + 2 damage.
↩ **Rage of Storms** (free, when a critical hit damages the djinn thunderer; encounter) ✦ **Thunder**
   Close burst 2; +25 vs. Reflex; 3d8 + 12 thunder damage, and the thunderer pushes the target 5 squares. *Effect:* The thunderer gains 1 action point.
❄ **Imperious Thunder** (standard; encounter) ✦ **Thunder**
   Area burst 2 within 20; +25 vs. Reflex; 2d8 + 9 thunder damage, and the target takes ongoing 10 thunder damage (save ends). *Miss:* The target takes ongoing 10 thunder damage (save ends).
❄ **Thunderburst** (standard; at-will) ✦ **Thunder**
   Area burst 2 within 20; +25 vs. Fortitude; 2d8 + 9 thunder damage, and the target is dazed until the end of the djinn thunderer's next turn.
Zephyr Step (minor; recharge ⚁) ✦ **Teleportation**
   The djinn thunderer teleports 20 squares.
Alignment Unaligned   **Languages** Common, Primordial
Skills Insight +21
Str 26 (+18)   **Dex** 23 (+16)   **Wis** 23 (+16)
Con 20 (+15)   **Int** 21 (+15)   **Cha** 19 (+14)
Equipment scepter (mace)

DJINN THUNDERER TACTICS

Djinn thunderers have little stomach for melee, preferring to use *thunderburst* and *imperious thunder* from the edge of the fray. If pressed, a thunderer makes a scepter attack, then uses *zephyr step* to escape to the other side of the battlefield.

Djinn Stormsword

A djinn stormsword defends other djinns, pulling enemies inexorably toward its deadly scimitar.

Djinn Stormsword	Level 24 Soldier
Large elemental humanoid (air)	XP 6,050

Initiative +21   **Senses** Perception +19; blindsight 10
HP 222; **Bloodied** 111
AC 40; **Fortitude** 38, **Reflex** 36, **Will** 36
Immune disease, poison; **Resist** 15 lightning, 15 thunder
Speed 6, fly 8 (hover)
⊕ **Scimitar** (standard; at-will) ✦ **Weapon**
     Reach 2; +31 vs. AC; 3d10 + 3 damage (crit 9d10 + 33), and the target is marked until the end of the djinn stormsword's next turn.
➹ **Come to Me** (minor 1/round; at-will)
     Ranged 5; +27 vs. Fortitude; the djinn stormsword pulls the target 5 squares.
➹ **Spinning Vortex** (standard; recharge ⚅) ✦ **Cold, Thunder**
     Ranged 5; +27 vs. Reflex; 4d12 + 8 cold and thunder damage, and the target is immobilized (save ends).
↢ **Whirlwind Dervish** (standard; recharges when the djinn stormsword is struck by a critical hit) ✦ **Lightning, Thunder**
     Close burst 2; +29 vs. AC; 4d8 + 12 lightning and thunder damage.
Alignment Unaligned   **Languages** Common, Primordial
Skills Bluff +22, Insight +24
Str 28 (+21)   **Dex** 25 (+19)   **Wis** 25 (+19)
Con 22 (+18)   **Int** 19 (+16)   **Cha** 20 (+17)
Equipment scimitar

Djinn Windbow

A djinn windbow fires arrows of whirling winds at its enemies.

Djinn Windbow	Level 22 Skirmisher
Large elemental humanoid (air)	XP 4,150

Initiative +21   **Senses** Perception +15; blindsight 10
HP 204; **Bloodied** 102
AC 36; **Fortitude** 33, **Reflex** 34, **Will** 33
Immune disease, poison; **Resist** 15 thunder
Speed 6, fly 8 (hover)
Action Points see blowback
⊕ **Slash of Thunder** (standard; at-will) ✦ **Thunder**
     Reach 2; +27 vs. AC; 2d8 + 10 thunder damage.
➲ **Windbow** (standard; at-will) ✦ **Weapon**
     Ranged 10/20; +27 vs. AC; 3d8 + 6 damage.
↢ **Blowback** (free, when a critical hit damages the djinn windbow; encounter) ✦ **Thunder**
     Close burst 2; +25 vs. Reflex; 4d8 + 8 thunder damage, and the windbow pushes the target 5 squares. *Effect:* The windbow gains 1 action point.
➹ **Brutal Zephyr** (standard; recharge ⚄ ⚅) ✦ **Thunder**
     Ranged 30; +25 vs. Reflex; 2d8 + 13 thunder damage. *Miss:* The djinn windbow chooses another target within 10 squares of the first target, and rerolls the attack against the new target. If the second attack misses, the power ends.
Alignment Unaligned   **Languages** Common, Primordial
Skills Bluff +23, Insight +20
Str 24 (+18)   **Dex** 27 (+19)   **Wis** 19 (+15)
Con 20 (+16)   **Int** 22 (+17)   **Cha** 24 (+18)
Equipment longbow, 20 arrows

DJINN STORMSWORD TACTICS

Protection of artillery and controllers is the djinn stormsword's first priority. A stormsword uses *come to me* every round to keep targets away from its allies, punishing foes with *spinning vortex* and scimitar attacks.

DJINN SKYLORD

A DJINN SKYLORD DIRECTS ITS ALLIES in combat, confusing its enemies with powerful storms.

Djinn Skylord	Level 25 Controller (Leader)
Large elemental humanoid (air)	XP 7,000

Initiative +17   **Senses** Perception +21; blindsight 10
HP 236; **Bloodied** 118
AC 39; **Fortitude** 38, **Reflex** 36, **Will** 36
Immune disease, poison; **Resist** 15 thunder
Speed 6, fly 8 (hover)

⊕ **Storm Staff** (standard; at-will) ✦ **Weapon**
Reach 2; +30 vs. AC; 3d10 + 4 damage, and the djinn skylord either shifts 2 squares or makes an extra recharge roll for *storm shout*.

↗ **Elemental Command** (minor 1/round; at-will)
Ranged 10; no attack roll; the djinn skylord slides the target 1 square.

↗ **Mystic Hail** (standard; at-will) ✦ **Psychic**
Ranged 20; +29 vs. Will; 2d8 + 8 psychic damage, and the target grants combat advantage to the djinn skylord until the target uses a standard action to clear its head of the *mystic hail*.

↤ **Sandstorm** (standard; encounter) ✦ **Psychic, Zone**
Close burst 5; +29 vs. Will; 4d8 + 8 damage. *Effect:* The burst creates a zone of swirling sand that lasts until the end of the djinn skylord's next turn. Each ally within the zone gains concealment. Each enemy that starts its turn within the zone is dazed until the start of its next turn. *Sustain Minor:* The zone persists.

↤ **Storm Shout** (standard; recharge ⚄ ⚅) ✦ **Thunder**
Close blast 5; +29 vs. Will; 3d10 + 10 thunder damage, and the target is pushed 3 squares and knocked prone.

Alignment Unaligned	**Languages** Common, Primordial

Skills Diplomacy +24, Insight +21

Str 23 (+18)	Dex 20 (+17)	Wis 18 (+16)
Con 28 (+21)	Int 25 (+19)	Cha 25 (+19)

Equipment quarterstaff

DJINN SKYLORD TACTICS

A djinn skylord tries to seize advantageous ground for its allies, swooping to the center of the battlefield and blasting foes with *sandstorm*. From the edge of the zone, it uses *mystic hail* and *elemental command* until it needs to defend itself with *storm shout*.

DJINN LORE

Arcana DC 24: Djinns are native to the Elemental Chaos, but as punishment for their role in the war against the gods, they were scattered after their defeat. Many djinns were imprisoned in worldly objects or had their powers severely curtailed.

Arcana DC 29: Those djinns that are free seek to regain their lost might and reclaim the relics and outposts of their old empires, many of which now lie in the world. Characters who aid a djinn in a quest to reclaim a cloud palace or locate an artifact can expect great reward. Creatures that oppose the ambition of the djinns are certain to earn their eternal enmity.

ENCOUNTER GROUPS

Djinns prefer to ally with their own kind, but they can often be found in the company of other creatures of the air. A djinn has no interest in leading other creatures, and all djinns rankle at the thought of taking orders from lesser beings. As a result, any alliance with a djinn is short-lived at best.

Level 22 Encounter (21,400 XP)
✦ 1 djinn stormsword (level 24 soldier)
✦ 2 djinn thunderers (level 20 artillery)
✦ 1 djinn windbow (level 22 skirmisher)
✦ 2 rimefire griffons (level 20 skirmisher, *MM* 147)

Level 26 Encounter (54,950 XP)
✦ 1 djinn skylord (level 25 controller)
✦ 1 djinn thunderer (level 20 artillery)
✦ 3 djinn stormswords (level 24 soldier)
✦ 3 storm gorgons (level 26 skirmisher, *MM* 143)

DRAGON

Dragons are widely renowned as some of the most powerful monsters in the world. Metallic dragons give fealty to Bahamut in his role as the Platinum Dragon. However, even the most equitable of these great creatures do not hesitate to use their might to crush opponents.

Despite their relatively benign nature, many metallic dragons engage in cruelty. All metallic dragons are fierce when protecting their treasures.

Metallic Dragon Lore

Nature DC 15: Metallic dragons love learned discourse, but they also have a keen sense of insight and are quick to sense deception. Those who seek to rob or deceive a metallic dragon are shown no mercy.

Nature DC 20: Metallic dragons can be found in a wide range of climes and locales, preferring to sequester themselves inside ancient sites of great learning. They are as likely to be found in the heart of a living city as in some ancient ruin.

Nature DC 25: Metallic dragons do not make pacts with other groups of creatures, but an individual dragon is very likely to have gathered a wide variety of lesser creatures around it. Metallic dragons treat such creatures as students and wards rather than as slaves. In return, these creatures act as the dragons' servants and guards, and are deeply loyal to their dragon lieges.

Metallic Dragon Encounters

Many metallic dragons guard great works of magic or items of historical significance. As a dragon ages and grows in power, it gathers more precious objects. A metallic dragon is often found with a large number of lesser creatures, which help protect the dragon's lair and the treasures the dragon guards.

ADAMANTINE DRAGON

ADAMANTINE DRAGONS ARE TACTICIANS that supplement their melee abilities with blasts of thunderous power. They can be found anywhere, but prefer to lair in huge underground caverns.

ADAMANTINE DRAGON TACTICS

An adamantine dragon favors frontal assaults against a single target that it can take down quickly. When working with a group of allies, an adamantine dragon doesn't hesitate to bear the brunt of enemies' attacks. When fighting alone, an adamantine dragon attempts to isolate weaker foes first and finish them off quickly.

Young Adamantine Dragon	Level 7 Solo Soldier
Large natural magical beast (dragon)	XP 1,500

Initiative +8   **Senses** Perception +10; darkvision
HP 332; **Bloodied** 166; see also *bloodied breath*
AC 23; **Fortitude** 22, **Reflex** 20, **Will** 19
Resist 15 thunder
Saving Throws +5
Speed 6, fly 8 (hover), overland flight 10
Action Points 2

⊕ **Bite** (standard; at-will)
Reach 2; +12 vs. Reflex; 1d10 + 6 damage.

⊕ **Claw** (standard; at-will)
Reach 2; +12 vs. Reflex ; 1d8 + 6 damage.

✦ **Double Attack** (standard; at-will)
The young adamantine dragon makes two claw attacks.

✦ **Wing Buffet** (immediate reaction, when an enemy enters or leaves an adjacent square; at-will)
Reach 2; +12 vs. Fortitude; 1d8 + 3 damage, and the target is knocked prone.

⟵ **Breath Weapon** (standard; recharge ⚄ ⚅) ✦ **Thunder**
Close blast 5; +10 vs. Fortitude; 2d6 + 3 thunder damage, and the target is knocked prone. *Miss:* Half damage. *Effect:* At the start of the young adamantine dragon's next turn, it gives a thunderous roar: close burst 3; no attack roll; 10 thunder damage.

⟵ **Bloodied Breath** (free, when first bloodied; encounter)
Breath weapon recharges, and the young adamantine dragon uses it.

⟵ **Frightful Presence** (standard; encounter) ✦ **Fear**
Close burst 5; targets enemies; +12 vs. Will; the target is stunned until the end of the young adamantine dragon's next turn. *Aftereffect:* The target takes a -2 penalty to attack rolls (save ends).

Alignment Unaligned   **Languages** Common, Draconic
Skills Insight +10, Intimidate +9

Str 20 (+8)	**Dex** 17 (+6)	**Wis** 14 (+5)
Con 19 (+7)	**Int** 11 (+3)	**Cha** 12 (+4)

Adult Adamantine Dragon	Level 14 Solo Soldier
Large natural magical beast (dragon)	XP 5,000

Initiative +14   **Senses** Perception +16; darkvision
HP 564; **Bloodied** 282; see also *bloodied breath*
AC 30; **Fortitude** 28, **Reflex** 27, **Will** 26
Resist 20 thunder
Saving Throws +5
Speed 8, fly 10 (hover), overland flight 15
Action Points 2

⊕ **Bite** (standard; at-will)
Reach 2; +19 vs. Reflex; 2d6 + 6 damage, and ongoing 5 damage (save ends).

⊕ **Claw** (standard; at-will)
Reach 2; +19 vs. Reflex; 1d10 + 6 damage.

✦ **Draconic Fury** (standard; at-will)
The adult adamantine dragon makes three claw attacks and then makes a bite attack against a different target.

✦ **Wing Buffet** (immediate reaction, when an enemy enters or leaves an adjacent square; at-will)
Reach 2; +19 vs. Fortitude; 1d8 + 6 damage, and the target is knocked prone.

⟵ **Breath Weapon** (standard; recharge ⚄ ⚅) ✦ **Thunder**
Close blast 5; +17 vs. Fortitude; 2d10 + 6 thunder damage, and the target is knocked prone. *Miss:* Half damage. *Effect:* At the start of the adult adamantine dragon's next turn, it gives a thunderous roar: close burst 3; no attack roll; 15 thunder damage.

⟵ **Bloodied Breath** (free, when first bloodied; encounter)
Breath weapon recharges, and the adult adamantine dragon uses it.

⟵ **Frightful Presence** (standard; encounter) ✦ **Fear**
Close burst 5; targets enemies; +17 vs. Will; the target is stunned until the end of the adult adamantine dragon's next turn. *Aftereffect:* The target takes a -2 penalty to attack rolls (save ends).

Alignment Unaligned   **Languages** Common, Draconic
Skills Insight +15, Intimidate +13

Str 23 (+13)	**Dex** 21 (+12)	**Wis** 18 (+11)
Con 21 (+12)	**Int** 11 (+7)	**Cha** 12 (+8)

Elder Adamantine Dragon	Level 21 Solo Soldier
Huge natural magical beast (dragon)	XP 16,000

Initiative +17   **Senses** Perception +19; darkvision
HP 796; **Bloodied** 398; see also *bloodied breath*
AC 37; **Fortitude** 36, **Reflex** 33, **Will** 32
Resist 25 thunder
Saving Throws +5
Speed 8, fly 10 (hover), overland flight 15
Action Points 2

⊕ **Bite** (standard; at-will)
Reach 2; +26 vs. Reflex; 2d8 + 8 damage, and ongoing 10 damage (save ends).

⊕ **Claw** (standard; at-will)
Reach 2; +26 vs. Reflex; 1d12 + 8 damage.

↯ **Draconic Fury** (standard; at-will)
The elder adamantine dragon makes four claw attacks and then makes a bite attack against a different target.

↯ **Wing Buffet** (immediate reaction, when an enemy enters or leaves an adjacent square; at-will)
Reach 2; +26 vs. Fortitude; 1d10 + 8 damage, and the target is knocked prone.

⤳ **Painful Resonance** (minor; recharge ⚅) ✦ **Thunder**
Ranged 20; +26 vs. Fortitude; the target takes ongoing 10 thunder damage and is dazed (save ends both).

⬳ **Breath Weapon** (standard; recharge ⚄ ⚅) ✦ **Thunder**
Close blast 5; +24 vs. Fortitude; 3d12 + 6 thunder damage, and the target is knocked prone. *Miss:* Half damage. *Effect:* At the start of the elder adamantine dragon's next turn, it gives a thunderous roar: close burst 3; no attack roll; 15 thunder damage.

⬳ **Bloodied Breath** (free, when first bloodied; encounter)
Breath weapon recharges, and the elder adamantine dragon uses it.

⬳ **Frightful Presence** (standard; encounter) ✦ **Fear**
Close burst 10; targets enemies; +24 vs. Will; the target is stunned until the end of the elder adamantine dragon's next turn. *Aftereffect:* The target takes a -2 penalty to attack rolls (save ends).

Alignment Unaligned   **Languages** Common, Draconic
Skills Insight +19, Intimidate +17

Str 26 (+18)	Dex 21 (+15)	Wis 18 (+14)
Con 23 (+16)	Int 13 (+11)	Cha 14 (+12)

ADAMANTINE DRAGON LORE

Nature DC 20: The teeth and claws of adamantine dragons can slice through the thickest armor. Adamantine dragons breathe powerful blasts of thunder energy that produce powerful aftershocks.

Nature DC 25: Haughty and imperious, adamantine dragons assume leadership of any creatures in their territory. They demand loyalty, tribute, and respect, and in return they take the responsibility of protecting their charges seriously.

Ancient Adamantine Dragon	Level 28 Solo Soldier
Gargantuan natural magical beast (dragon)	XP 65,000

Initiative +21   **Senses** Perception +24; darkvision
HP 1,020; **Bloodied** 510; see also *bloodied breath*
AC 44; **Fortitude** 42, **Reflex** 38, **Will** 38
Resist 30 thunder; see also *bloodied resilience*
Saving Throws +5
Speed 8, fly 12 (hover), overland flight 15
Action Points 2

⊕ **Bite** (standard; at-will)
Reach 4; +33 vs. Reflex; 2d10 + 9 damage, and ongoing 15 damage (save ends).

⊕ **Claw** (standard; at-will)
Reach 4; +33 vs. Reflex; 2d8 + 9 damage.

↯ **Draconic Fury** (standard; at-will)
The ancient adamantine dragon makes four claw attacks and then makes a bite attack against a different target.

↯ **Wing Buffet** (immediate reaction, when an enemy enters or leaves an adjacent square; at-will)
Reach 2; +33 vs. Fortitude; 2d8 + 9 damage, and the target is knocked prone.

⤳ **Painful Resonance** (minor; recharge ⚅) ✦ **Thunder**
Ranged 20; +33 vs. Fortitude; the target takes ongoing 15 thunder damage and is dazed (save ends both).

⬳ **Breath Weapon** (standard; recharge ⚄ ⚅) ✦ **Thunder**
Close blast 5; +31 vs. Reflex; 4d12 + 6 thunder damage, and the target is knocked prone. *Miss:* Half damage. *Effect:* At the start of the ancient adamantine dragon's next turn, it gives a thunderous roar: close burst 5; no attack roll; 20 thunder damage.

⬳ **Bloodied Breath** (free, when first bloodied; encounter)
Breath weapon recharges, and the ancient adamantine dragon uses it.

⬳ **Frightful Presence** (standard; encounter) ✦ **Fear**
Close burst 10; targets enemies; +31 vs. Will; the target is stunned until the end of the ancient adamantine dragon's next turn. *Aftereffect:* The target takes a -2 penalty to attack rolls (save ends).

Bloodied Resilience (while bloodied)
An ancient adamantine dragon gains resist 10 to all damage on the first attack that targets it in each round.

Alignment Unaligned   **Languages** Common, Draconic
Skills Insight +24, Intimidate +21

Str 28 (+23)	Dex 21 (+19)	Wis 20 (+19)
Con 23 (+20)	Int 15 (+16)	Cha 14 (+16)

ENCOUNTER GROUPS

Adamantine dragons gather allies that can best supplement their melee abilities. Tactically minded, they favor allies such as harpies, hags, and other creatures that can use magic to control their enemies' minds.

Level 15 Encounter (XP 6,400)
✦ 1 adult adamantine dragon (level 14 solo soldier)
✦ 2 banshrae warriors (level 12 skirmisher, MM 25)

COPPER DRAGON

THE MOST COVETOUS AND MISERLY of the metallic dragons, copper dragons are nonetheless social creatures. They breathe destructive blasts of acid and make their lairs in dry, rocky uplands and mountains.

COPPER DRAGON TACTICS

Copper dragons lair in locations that let them exploit their excellent mobility. A copper dragon favors repeated *flyby attacks* while maneuvering to make the greatest use of blocking terrain. It is careful to limit its exposure to ranged attacks, and uses its breath weapon against multiple foes. With the right terrain and careful positioning, a copper dragon can avoid most of its opponents' attacks.

COPPER DRAGON LORE

Nature DC 20: Copper dragons lair among dry hills and mountains. They are willing to engage in prolonged battles, harrying their prey over long periods of time.

Nature DC 25: A copper dragon is covetous by nature; despite its pleasant demeanor, it seldom leaves a situation without gaining some benefit. Copper dragons breathe streams of acid and are among the swiftest of all dragons.

ENCOUNTER GROUPS

Copper dragons recruit creatures as fast and agile as they are, allowing them to conduct running skirmishes against their enemies. Hippogriffs, kenkus, rocs, and sphinxes are often found with copper dragons. Copper dragons sometimes hire human and elf cavalry to help run down their enemies.

Level 8 Encounter (XP 1,850)
✦ 3 hippogriffs (level 5 skirmisher, *MM* 146)
✦ 1 young copper dragon (level 6 solo skirmisher)

Level 14 Encounter (XP 5,600)
✦ 1 adult copper dragon (level 13 solo skirmisher)
✦ 2 dragonborn raiders (level 13 skirmisher, *MM* 86)

Young Copper Dragon — Level 6 Solo Skirmisher
Large natural magical beast (dragon)   XP 1,250

Initiative +10   **Senses** Perception +10; darkvision
HP 296; **Bloodied** 148; see also *bloodied breath*
AC 20; **Fortitude** 18, **Reflex** 19, **Will** 16
Resist 15 acid
Saving Throws +5
Speed 8, fly 10 (hover), overland flight 15
Action Points 2

⊕ **Bite** (standard; at-will) ✦ **Acid**
The young copper dragon shifts 2 squares before and after making the attack. Reach 2; +11 vs. AC; 1d10 + 4 damage plus 1d6 acid damage.

⊕ **Claw** (standard; at-will)
Reach 2; +11 vs. AC; 1d8 + 4 damage.

† **Double Attack** (standard; at-will)
The young copper dragon makes two claw attacks and then shifts 2 squares.

† **Flyby Attack** (standard; at-will)
The young copper dragon flies 10 squares and makes one melee basic attack at any point during that movement. The dragon doesn't provoke opportunity attacks when moving away from the target.

† **Cutwing Step** (immediate reaction, when an enemy moves to a space where it flanks the young copper dragon; at-will)
Targets the triggering enemy; +11 vs. AC; 1d8 + 3 damage, and the copper dragon shifts 2 squares.

↞ **Breath Weapon** (standard; recharge ⚄ ⚅) ✦ **Acid**
Close blast 5; +7 vs. Reflex; 1d10 + 4 acid damage, and the target is slowed (save ends). *Miss:* Half damage.

↞ **Bloodied Breath** (free, when first bloodied; encounter)
Breath weapon recharges, and the young copper dragon uses it.

↞ **Frightful Presence** (standard; encounter) ✦ **Fear**
Close burst 5; targets enemies; +7 vs. Will; the target is stunned until the end of the young copper dragon's next turn. *Aftereffect:* The target takes a –2 penalty to attack rolls (save ends).

Alignment Unaligned   **Languages** Common, Draconic
Skills Acrobatics +13, Bluff +9, Insight +10
Str 16 (+6)   **Dex** 20 (+8)   **Wis** 14 (+5)
Con 18 (+7)   **Int** 12 (+4)   **Cha** 12 (+4)

Adult Copper Dragon — Level 13 Solo Skirmisher
Large natural magical beast (dragon)   XP 4,000

Initiative +15   **Senses** Perception +14; darkvision
HP 528; **Bloodied** 264; see also *bloodied breath*
AC 27; **Fortitude** 25, **Reflex** 27, **Will** 23
Resist 20 acid
Saving Throws +5
Speed 9, fly 12 (hover), overland flight 15
Action Points 2

⊕ **Bite** (standard; at-will) ✦ **Acid**
The adult copper dragon shifts 2 squares before and after making the attack. Reach 2; +18 vs. AC; 2d6 + 6 damage plus 2d6 acid damage.

⊕ **Claw** (standard; at-will)
Reach 2; +18 vs. AC; 1d10 + 6 damage.

† **Double Attack** (standard; at-will)
The adult copper dragon makes two claw attacks and then shifts 3 squares.

† **Flyby Attack** (standard; at-will)
The adult copper dragon flies 14 squares and makes one melee basic attack at any point during that movement. The dragon doesn't provoke opportunity attacks when moving away from the target.

† **Cutwing Step** (immediate reaction, when an enemy moves to a space where it flanks the adult copper dragon; at-will)
Targets the triggering enemy; +18 vs. AC; 1d10 + 6 damage, and the dragon shifts 2 squares.

↞ **Breath Weapon** (standard; recharge ⚄ ⚅) ✦ **Acid**
Close blast 5; +14 vs. Reflex; 2d10 + 6 acid damage, and the target is slowed (save ends). *Miss:* Half damage.

↞ **Bloodied Breath** (free, when first bloodied; encounter)
Breath weapon recharges, and the adult copper dragon uses it.

↞ **Frightful Presence** (standard; encounter) ✦ **Fear**
Close burst 5; targets enemies; +14 vs. Will; the target is stunned until the end of the adult copper dragon's next turn. *Aftereffect:* The target takes a –2 penalty to attack rolls (save ends).

Unfettered Wings
An adult copper dragon makes saving throws against immobilized, slowed, and restrained conditions at the start of its turn as well as at the end of its turn.

Alignment Unaligned   **Languages** Common, Draconic
Skills Acrobatics +18, Bluff +14, Insight +14
Str 18 (+10)   **Dex** 24 (+13)   **Wis** 16 (+9)
Con 20 (+11)   **Int** 14 (+8)   **Cha** 16 (+9)

Elder Copper Dragon — Level 20 Solo Skirmisher

Huge natural magical beast (dragon) — XP 14,000

Initiative +20 **Senses** Perception +19; darkvision
HP 760; **Bloodied** 380; see also *bloodied breath*
AC 34; **Fortitude** 32, **Reflex** 34, **Will** 31
Resist 25 acid
Saving Throws +5
Speed 10, fly 14 (hover), overland flight 18
Action Points 2

⊕ **Bite** (standard; at-will) ✦ **Acid**
Reach 2; +25 vs. AC; 2d8 + 8 damage plus 3d6 acid damage. The elder copper dragon shifts 2 squares before and after making the attack.

⊕ **Claw** (standard; at-will)
Reach 2; +25 vs. AC; 2d6 + 8 damage.

⫽ **Double Attack** (standard; at-will)
The elder copper dragon makes two claw attacks and then shifts 3 squares.

⫽ **Flyby Attack** (standard; at-will)
The elder copper dragon flies 14 squares and makes one melee basic attack at any point during that movement. The dragon doesn't provoke opportunity attacks when moving away from the target.

⫽ **Cutwing Step** (immediate reaction, when an enemy moves to a space where it flanks the elder copper dragon; at-will)
Targets the triggering enemy; +25 vs. AC; 2d6 + 8 damage, and the dragon shifts 3 squares.

⟻ **Breath Weapon** (standard; recharge ⚄ ⚅ ⚅) ✦ **Acid**
Close blast 5; +21 vs. Reflex; 3d10 + 6 acid damage, and the target is slowed (save ends). *Miss:* Half damage.

⟻ **Bloodied Breath** (free, when first bloodied; encounter)
Breath weapon recharges, and the elder copper dragon uses it.

⟻ **Frightful Presence** (standard; encounter) ✦ **Fear**
Close burst 10; targets enemies; +21 vs. Will; the target is stunned until the end of the elder copper dragon's next turn. *Aftereffect:* The target takes a -2 penalty to attack rolls (save ends).

Unfettered Wings
An elder copper dragon makes saving throws against immobilized, slowed, and restrained conditions at the start of its turn as well as at the end of its turn.

Alignment Unaligned **Languages** Common, Draconic
Skills Acrobatics +23, Bluff +20, Insight +19

| Str 20 (+15) | Dex 26 (+18) | Wis 18 (+14) |
| Con 22 (+16) | Int 16 (+13) | Cha 20 (+15) |

Ancient Copper Dragon — Level 27 Solo Skirmisher

Huge natural magical beast (dragon) — XP 55,000

Initiative +25 **Senses** Perception +22; darkvision
HP 1,000; **Bloodied** 500; see also *bloodied breath*
AC 41; **Fortitude** 39, **Reflex** 41, **Will** 37
Resist 30 acid
Saving Throws +5
Speed 10, fly 14 (hover), overland flight 18
Action Points 2

⊕ **Bite** (standard; at-will) ✦ **Acid**
The ancient copper dragon shifts 2 squares before and after making the attack. Reach 2; +32 vs. AC; 2d10 + 10 damage plus 4d6 acid damage.

⊕ **Claw** (standard; at-will)
Reach 2; +32 vs. AC; 2d8 + 9 damage.

⫽ **Double Attack** (standard; at-will)
The ancient copper dragon makes two claw attacks and then shifts 3 squares.

⫽ **Double Flyby Attack** (standard; at-will)
The ancient copper dragon flies 16 squares and makes a melee basic attack against each of two different targets at any point during that movement. The dragon doesn't provoke opportunity attacks when moving away from the targets.

⫽ **Cutwing Step** (immediate reaction, when an enemy moves to a space where it flanks the ancient copper dragon; at-will)
Targets the triggering enemy; +32 vs. AC; 2d8 + 9 damage, and the dragon shifts 4 squares.

⟻ **Breath Weapon** (standard; recharge ⚄ ⚅ ⚅) ✦ **Acid**
Close blast 5; +28 vs. Reflex; 4d10 + 8 acid damage, and the target is slowed (save ends). *Miss:* Half damage.

⟻ **Bloodied Breath** (free, when first bloodied; encounter)
Breath weapon recharges, and the ancient copper dragon uses it.

⟻ **Frightful Presence** (standard; encounter) ✦ **Fear**
Close burst 10; targets enemies; +28 vs. Will; the target is stunned until the end of the ancient copper dragon's next turn. *Aftereffect:* The target takes a -2 penalty to attack rolls (save ends).

Unfettered Wings
An ancient copper dragon makes saving throws against immobilized, slowed, and restrained conditions at the start of its turn as well as at the end of its turn.

Alignment Unaligned **Languages** Common, Draconic
Skills Acrobatics +28, Bluff +24, Insight +22

| Str 22 (+19) | Dex 30 (+23) | Wis 18 (+17) |
| Con 26 (+21) | Int 18 (+17) | Cha 22 (+19) |

Gold Dragon

GOLD DRAGONS BREATHE TORRENTS OF FLAME, and as they age, their scales grow bright with radiant energy. They lair in a variety of climes, favoring plains and rolling hills where they can easily survey the land. Gold dragons are renowned above all other children of Io, and few creatures dare to test the might of the oldest of them.

Gold Dragon Tactics

Gold dragons seek to control the flow of battle. A gold dragon opens battle by catching as many foes as possible with its *breath weapon,* then scattering them using *frightful presence.* Once its foes are separated, the gold dragon pounces on the weakest.

Gold Dragon Lore

Nature DC 20: Gold dragons often lair in plains or hills, but their terrain preference is secondary to the goal of influencing a society or protecting a magic secret. Gold dragons often assume leadership of a group of lesser creatures. Gold dragons breathe powerful gouts of flame.

Nature DC 25: Gold dragons are usually honest and forthright, but they show little interest in the concerns of other creatures. Societies led by a gold dragon sometimes find themselves at the mercy of its long-term plans.

Nature DC 30: Some gold dragons know a ritual that allows them to assume humanoid forms. A gold dragon divests itself of this disguise when threatened.

Encounter Groups

Gold dragons that have selfish or evil tendencies recruit minotaurs, ogres, and trolls as disposable shock troops. Other gold dragons might be defended by members of the societies they lead.

Level 10 Encounter (XP 2,700)
✦ 2 angels of valor (level 8 soldier, *MM* 16)
✦ 1 young gold dragon (level 9 solo controller)

Level 19 Encounter (XP 12,200)
✦ 1 adult gold dragon (level 17 solo controller)
✦ 3 savage minotaurs (level 16 brute, *MM* 191)

Young Gold Dragon — Level 9 Solo Controller
Large natural magical beast (dragon) — XP 2,000

Initiative +7 **Senses** Perception +12; darkvision
HP 380; **Bloodied** 190; see also *bloodied breath*
AC 23; **Fortitude** 21, **Reflex** 23, **Will** 21
Resist 15 fire
Saving Throws +5
Speed 8, fly 10 (hover), overland flight 15
Action Points 2

- ⊕ **Bite** (standard; at-will) ✦ **Fire**
  Reach 2; +14 vs. AC; 2d8 + 4 damage plus 2d6 fire damage.
- ⊕ **Claw** (standard; at-will)
  Reach 2; +14 vs. AC; 2d6 + 4 damage.
- ⊣ **Double Attack** (standard; at-will)
  The young gold dragon makes two claw attacks.
- ⊣ **Fiery Wing Riposte** (immediate reaction, when the young gold dragon is hit by a creature adjacent to it; at-will) ✦ **Fire**
  +13 vs. Fortitude; the target is pushed 5 squares and takes ongoing 5 fire damage (save ends).
- ⬳ **Breath Weapon** (standard; recharge ⚃ ⚄) ✦ **Fire**
  Close blast 5; +11 vs. Reflex; 2d6 + 5 fire damage, and the target is weakened (save ends). *Miss:* Half damage.
- ⬳ **Bloodied Breath** (free, when first bloodied; encounter)
  Breath weapon recharges, and the young gold dragon uses it.
- ⬳ **Frightful Presence** (standard; encounter) ✦ **Fear**
  Close burst 5; targets enemies; +11 vs. Will; the target is stunned until the end of the young gold dragon's next turn. *Aftereffect:* The target takes a -2 penalty to attack rolls (save ends).

Alignment Unaligned **Languages** Common, Draconic
Skills Arcana +15, Athletics +13, Diplomacy +13, Insight +12, Intimidate +13

Str 18 (+8)	Dex 16 (+7)	Wis 16 (+7)
Con 15 (+6)	Int 23 (+10)	Cha 18 (+8)

Adult Gold Dragon — Level 17 Solo Controller
Large natural magical beast (dragon) — XP 8,000

Initiative +12 **Senses** Perception +17; darkvision
HP 652; **Bloodied** 326; see also *bloodied breath*
AC 31; **Fortitude** 29, **Reflex** 31, **Will** 29
Resist 20 fire
Saving Throws +5
Speed 8, fly 10 (hover), overland flight 15
Action Points 2

- ⊕ **Bite** (standard; at-will) ✦ **Fire**
  Reach 2; +22 vs. AC; 2d8 + 7 damage plus 3d8 fire damage.
- ⊕ **Claw** (standard; at-will)
  Reach 2; +22 vs. AC; 2d8 + 7 damage.
- ⊣ **Double Attack** (standard; at-will)
  The adult gold dragon makes two claw attacks.
- ⊣ **Fiery Wing Riposte** (immediate reaction, when the adult gold dragon is hit by a creature adjacent to it; at-will) ✦ **Fire**
  +21 vs. Fortitude; the target is pushed 5 squares and takes ongoing 10 fire damage (save ends).
- ⬳ **Breath Weapon** (standard; recharge ⚁ ⚄ ⚅) ✦ **Fire**
  Close blast 5; +19 vs. Reflex; 2d8 + 7 fire damage, and the target is weakened (save ends). *Miss:* Half damage.
- ⬳ **Bloodied Breath** (free, when first bloodied; encounter)
  Breath weapon recharges, and the adult gold dragon uses it.
- ⬳ **Frightful Presence** (standard; encounter) ✦ **Fear**
  Close burst 5; targets enemies; +19 vs. Will; the target is stunned until the end of the adult gold dragon's next turn. *Aftereffect:* The target takes a -2 penalty to attack rolls (save ends).
- ❈ **Burning Tomb** (standard; recharge ⚅) ✦ **Fire, Zone**
  Area burst 1 within 20; +19 vs. Reflex; 2d8 + 8 damage, and the target is immobilized (save ends). *Effect:* The burst creates a zone of fire that lasts until the end of the adult gold dragon's next turn. Each creature that starts its turn within the zone takes 15 fire damage. *Sustain Minor:* The zone persists.

Alignment Unaligned **Languages** Common, Draconic
Skills Arcana +21, Athletics +20, Diplomacy +19, Insight +17, Intimidate +19

Str 25 (+15)	Dex 18 (+12)	Wis 18 (+12)
Con 19 (+12)	Int 26 (+16)	Cha 22 (+14)

Elder Gold Dragon — Level 24 Solo Controller
Huge natural magical beast (dragon) — XP 30,250

Initiative +18   **Senses** Perception +23; darkvision

Weakening Flames (Fire) aura 2; each enemy that enters or starts its turn in the aura chooses either to take 15 fire damage or to be weakened until the start of its next turn.

HP 888; **Bloodied** 444; see also *bloodied breath*

AC 38; **Fortitude** 36, **Reflex** 38, **Will** 36

Resist 25 fire

Saving Throws +5

Speed 8, fly 12 (hover), overland flight 15

Action Points 2

⊕ **Bite** (standard; at-will) ✦ **Fire**
  Reach 3; +29 vs. AC; 2d10 + 8 damage plus 3d10 fire damage.

⊕ **Claw** (standard; at-will)
  Reach 3; +29 vs. AC; 2d10 + 8 damage.

✦ **Double Attack** (standard; at-will)
  The elder gold dragon makes two claw attacks.

✦ **Fiery Wing Riposte** (immediate reaction, when the elder gold dragon is hit by a creature adjacent to it; at-will) ✦ **Fire**
  +28 vs. Fortitude; the target is pushed 5 squares and takes ongoing 10 fire damage (save ends).

↢ **Beguiling Glow** (minor; recharge ⚄ ⚅) ✦ **Charm**
  Close burst 8; targets enemies; +26 vs. Will; the target is pulled 5 squares and dazed (save ends).

↢ **Breath Weapon** (standard; recharge ⚃ ⚄ ⚅) ✦ **Fire**
  Close blast 5; +26 vs. Reflex; 3d8 + 8 fire damage, and the target is weakened (save ends). *Miss:* Half damage.

↢ **Bloodied Breath** (free, when first bloodied; encounter)
  Breath weapon recharges, and the elder gold dragon uses it.

↢ **Frightful Presence** (standard; encounter) ✦ **Fear**
  Close burst 10; targets enemies; +26 vs. Will; the target is stunned until the end of the elder gold dragon's next turn. *Aftereffect:* The target takes a -2 penalty to attack rolls (save ends).

⁂ **Burning Tomb** (standard; at-will) ✦ **Fire, Zone**
  Area burst 1 within 20; +26 vs. Reflex; 3d8 + 8 damage, and the target is immobilized (save ends). *Effect:* The burst creates a zone of fire that lasts until the end of the elder gold dragon's next turn. Each creature that starts its turn within the zone takes 15 fire damage. *Sustain Minor:* The zone persists.

Alignment Unaligned   **Languages** Common, Draconic

Skills Arcana +27, Athletics +25, Diplomacy +25, Insight +23, Intimidate +25

Str 27 (+20)	**Dex** 22 (+18)	**Wis** 23 (+18)
Con 22 (+18)	**Int** 30 (+22)	**Cha** 26 (+20)

Ancient Gold Dragon — Level 30 Solo Controller
Gargantuan natural magical beast (dragon) — XP 95,000

Initiative +22   **Senses** Perception +28; darkvision

Weakening Flames (Fire) aura 5; each enemy that enters the aura or starts its turn there chooses either to take 20 fire damage or to be weakened until the start of its next turn.

HP 1,088; **Bloodied** 544; see also *bloodied breath*

AC 44; **Fortitude** 42, **Reflex** 44, **Will** 42

Resist 30 fire

Saving Throws +5

Speed 8, fly 12 (hover), overland flight 15

Action Points 2

⊕ **Bite** (standard; at-will) ✦ **Fire**
  Reach 4; +35 vs. AC; 3d10 + 9 damage plus 4d10 fire damage.

⊕ **Claw** (standard; at-will)
  Reach 4; +35 vs. AC; 3d10 + 9 damage.

✦ **Triple Attack** (standard; at-will)
  The ancient gold dragon makes three claw attacks.

✦ **Fiery Wing Riposte** (immediate reaction, when the ancient gold dragon is hit by a creature adjacent to it; at-will) ✦ **Fire**
  +34 vs. Fortitude; the target is pushed 5 squares and takes ongoing 20 fire damage (save ends).

↢ **Ancient Radiance** (standard; recharge ⚅) ✦ **Radiant**
  Close burst 4; targets enemies; +32 vs. Fortitude; 3d10 + 9 radiant damage, and the target is dazed until the end of the ancient gold dragon's next turn. *Aftereffect:* The target gains vulnerable 10 radiant (save ends).

↢ **Beguiling Glow** (minor; recharge ⚄ ⚅) ✦ **Charm**
  Close burst 8; targets enemies; +32 vs. Will; the target is pulled 5 squares and dazed (save ends).

↢ **Breath Weapon** (standard; recharge ⚃ ⚄ ⚅) ✦ **Fire, Radiant**
  Close blast 5; +32 vs. Reflex; 4d8 + 9 fire and radiant damage, and the target is weakened (save ends). *Miss:* Half damage.

↢ **Bloodied Breath** (free, when first bloodied; encounter)
  Breath weapon recharges, and the ancient gold dragon uses it.

↢ **Frightful Presence** (standard; encounter) ✦ **Fear**
  Close burst 10; targets enemies; +32 vs. Will; the target is stunned until the end of the ancient gold dragon's next turn. *Aftereffect:* The target takes a -2 penalty to attack rolls (save ends).

⁂ **Burning Tomb** (standard; at-will) ✦ **Fire, Zone**
  Area burst 1 within 20; +32 vs. Reflex; 4d8 + 13 damage, and the target is immobilized (save ends). *Effect:* The burst creates a zone of fire that lasts until the end of the ancient gold dragon's next turn. Each creature that starts its turn within the zone takes 20 fire damage. *Sustain Minor:* The zone persists.

Alignment Unaligned   **Languages** Common, Draconic

Skills Arcana +33, Athletics +29, Diplomacy +29, History +33, Insight +28, Intimidate +29

Str 28 (+24)	**Dex** 24 (+22)	**Wis** 26 (+23)
Con 24 (+22)	**Int** 36 (+28)	**Cha** 28 (+24)

Iron Dragon

QUICK AND DECEPTIVE BY NATURE, iron dragons hunt from the shadows, striking when and where they choose. Iron dragons prefer to lair in regions of low hills and deep forests, or other environments that offer good concealment for a large predator.

Iron Dragon Tactics

Iron dragons prefer to strike from ambush. An iron dragon's lair features an extensive series of chambers, each with multiple entrances and exits. The dragon stations traps or minions in each of these chambers, waiting until its foes are distracted by more obvious threats before it strikes.

Iron Dragon Lore

Nature DC 20: Savage and surly, iron dragons are reclusive and prefer to strike from ambush. Iron dragons breathe blasts of lightning.

Nature DC 25: As iron dragons age, they become more impervious to attack. A battle with an older iron dragon promises to be a prolonged affair.

Encounter Groups

As befits their sly nature, iron dragons do not have allies so much as dupes. They lure dwarves, hobgoblins, minotaurs, and other greedy humanoids into working for them in return for a promise of easy loot. An iron dragon dispatches its "friends" to ambush intruders. Once the fighting starts, the dragon watches for a few moments. If its intercession can win the battle, it attacks. If its allies seem likely to be defeated, an iron dragon flees rather than risk its own hide.

Level 7 Encounter (XP 1,600)
+ 3 dwarf hammerers (level 5 soldier, *MM* 97)
+ 1 young iron dragon (level 5 solo lurker)

Level 13 Encounter (XP 4,000)
+ 1 adult iron dragon (level 11 solo lurker)
+ 2 minotaur warriors (level 10 soldier, *MM* 190)

Young Iron Dragon — Level 5 Solo Lurker
Large natural magical beast (dragon) — XP 1,000

Initiative +8 **Senses** Perception +8; darkvision
HP 268; **Bloodied** 134; see also *bloodied breath*
AC 19; **Fortitude** 19, **Reflex** 17, **Will** 16
Resist 15 lightning
Saving Throws +5
Speed 8, fly 8 (hover), overland flight 10
Action Points 2

⊕ **Bite** (standard; at-will) ✦ **Lightning**
Reach 2; +10 vs. AC; 2d8 + 4 damage plus 1d8 lightning damage.
⊕ **Claw** (standard; at-will)
Reach 2; +10 vs. AC; 1d10 + 4 damage.
⥋ **Double Attack** (standard; at-will)
The young iron dragon makes two claw attacks.
⥋ **Wing Block** (immediate interrupt, when the young iron dragon is hit by an attack; at-will)
The dragon gains resist 5 to all damage of the triggering attack, and it makes an attack: +10 vs. AC; 1d6 + 4 damage.
↞ **Breath Weapon** (standard; recharge ⚄ ⚅) ✦ **Lightning**
Close blast 5; +6 vs. Reflex; 2d6 + 4 lightning damage, and the young iron dragon pulls the target 3 squares. *Miss:* Half damage.
↞ **Bloodied Breath** (free, when first bloodied; encounter)
Breath weapon recharges, and the young iron dragon uses it.
↞ **Frightful Presence** (standard; encounter) ✦ **Fear**
Close burst 5; targets enemies; +6 vs. Will; the target is stunned until the end of the young iron dragon's next turn. *Aftereffect:* The target takes a -2 penalty to attack rolls (save ends).

Alignment Unaligned **Languages** Common, Draconic
Skills Acrobatics +9, Athletics +8, Stealth +9
Str 13 (+3) **Dex** 14 (+4) **Wis** 12 (+3)
Con 19 (+6) **Int** 12 (+3) **Cha** 11 (+2)

Adult Iron Dragon — Level 11 Solo Lurker
Large natural magical beast (dragon) — XP 3,000

Initiative +13 **Senses** Perception +14; darkvision
HP 472; **Bloodied** 236; see also *bloodied breath*
AC 25; **Fortitude** 25, **Reflex** 23, **Will** 23
Resist 20 lightning
Saving Throws +5
Speed 8, fly 8 (hover), overland flight 10
Action Points 2

⊕ **Bite** (standard; at-will) ✦ **Lightning**
Reach 2; +16 vs. AC; 2d6 + 5 damage plus 2d6 lightning damage.
⊕ **Claw** (standard; at-will)
Reach 2; +16 vs. AC; 1d10 + 5 damage.
⥋ **Double Attack** (standard; at-will)
The adult iron dragon makes two claw attacks.
⥋ **Wing Block** (immediate interrupt, when the adult iron dragon is hit by an attack; at-will)
The dragon gains resist 5 to all damage of the triggering attack, and it makes an attack: +16 vs. AC; 1d10 + 3 damage.
↞ **Breath Weapon** (standard; recharge ⚄ ⚅) ✦ **Lightning**
Close blast 5; +12 vs. Reflex; 3d6 + 6 lightning damage, and the adult iron dragon pulls the target 3 squares. *Miss:* Half damage.
↞ **Bloodied Breath** (free, when first bloodied; encounter)
Breath weapon recharges, and the adult iron dragon uses it.
↞ **Frightful Presence** (standard; encounter) ✦ **Fear**
Close burst 5; targets enemies; +12 vs. Will; the target is stunned until the end of the adult iron dragon's next turn. *Aftereffect:* The target takes a -2 penalty to attack rolls (save ends).

Alignment Unaligned **Languages** Common, Draconic
Skills Acrobatics +14, Athletics +13, Stealth +14
Str 16 (+8) **Dex** 18 (+9) **Wis** 19 (+9)
Con 22 (+11) **Int** 14 (+7) **Cha** 11 (+5)

Elder Iron Dragon — Level 19 Solo Lurker
Huge natural magical beast (dragon) — XP 12,000

Initiative +19 **Senses** Perception +20; darkvision
HP 740; **Bloodied** 370; see also *bloodied breath*
AC 33; **Fortitude** 32, **Reflex** 31, **Will** 31; see also *iron wing defense*
Resist 25 lightning
Saving Throws +5
Speed 9, fly 9 (hover), overland flight 12
Action Points 2

⊕ **Bite** (standard; at-will) ✦ **Lightning**
Reach 2; +24 vs. AC; 2d8 + 6 damage plus 4d6 lightning damage.
⊕ **Claw** (standard; at-will)
Reach 2; +24 vs. AC; 2d6 + 6 damage.
⥋ **Triple Attack** (standard; at-will)
The elder iron dragon makes three claw attacks.
⥋ **Wing Block** (immediate interrupt, when the elder iron dragon is hit by an attack; at-will)
The dragon gains resist 10 to all damage of the triggering attack, and it makes an attack: +24 vs. AC; 2d6 + 4 damage.
↞ **Breath Weapon** (standard; recharge ⚃ ⚄ ⚅) ✦ **Lightning**
Close blast 5; +20 vs. Reflex; 3d10 + 7 lightning damage, and the elder iron dragon pulls the target 3 squares. *Miss:* Half damage.
↞ **Bloodied Breath** (free, when first bloodied; encounter)
Breath weapon recharges, and the elder iron dragon uses it.
↞ **Frightful Presence** (standard; encounter) ✦ **Fear**
Close burst 10; targets enemies; +20 vs. Will; the target is stunned until the end of the elder iron dragon's next turn. *Aftereffect:* The target takes a -2 penalty to attack rolls (save ends).
Iron Wing Defense (minor; recharge ⚄ ⚅)
The elder iron dragon gains a +2 bonus to all defenses until the end of its next turn.

Alignment Unaligned **Languages** Common, Draconic
Skills Acrobatics +20, Athletics +18, Stealth +20
Str 19 (+13) **Dex** 23 (+15) **Wis** 23 (+15)
Con 25 (+16) **Int** 17 (+12) **Cha** 19 (+13)

Ancient Iron Dragon	Level 26 Solo Lurker
Gargantuan natural magical beast (dragon)	XP 45,000

Initiative +25 **Senses** Perception +28; darkvision
HP 992; **Bloodied** 496; see also *bloodied breath*
AC 40; **Fortitude** 40, **Reflex** 38, **Will** 38; see also *iron wing defense*
Resist 30 lightning
Saving Throws +5
Speed 9, fly 10 (hover), overland flight 15
Action Points 2

⊕ **Bite** (standard; at-will) ✦ **Lightning**
    Reach 2; +31 vs. AC; 3d8 + 9 damage plus 4d8 lightning damage.

⊕ **Claw** (standard; at-will)
    Reach 2; +31 vs. AC; 3d8 + 9 damage.

✦ **Triple Attack** (standard; at-will)
    The ancient iron dragon makes three claw attacks.

✦ **Predator's Response** (immediate reaction, when the ancient
    iron dragon is hit by a melee or close attack; at-will)
    The dragon makes a claw attack against any enemy adjacent to
    it and shifts 2 squares.

✦ **Wing Block** (immediate interrupt, when the ancient iron dragon
    is hit by an attack; at-will)
    The dragon gains resist 15 to all damage of the triggering
    attack, and it makes an attack: +31 vs. AC; 3d8 + 9 damage.

↢ **Breath Weapon** (standard; recharge ⚃ ⚄ ⚅) ✦ **Lightning**
    Close blast 5; +27 vs. Reflex; 4d10 + 11 lightning damage, and
    the ancient iron dragon pulls the target 3 squares. *Miss:* Half
    damage.

↢ **Bloodied Breath** (free, when first bloodied; encounter)
    Breath weapon recharges, and the ancient iron dragon uses it.

↢ **Frightful Presence** (standard; encounter) ✦ **Fear**
    Close burst 10; targets enemies; +27 vs. Will; the target is
    stunned until the end of the ancient iron dragon's next turn.
    Aftereffect: The target takes a -2 penalty to attack rolls (save
    ends).

↢ **Iron Wing Shroud** (minor; recharge ⚅)
    Close burst 3; +29 vs. AC; 2d10 + 9 damage. *Effect:* The dragon
    gains resist 15 to all damage until the start of its next turn, but
    cannot make attacks until the start of its next turn.

Iron Wing Defense (minor; recharge ⚄ ⚅)
    The ancient iron dragon gains a +2 bonus to all defenses until
    the end of its next turn.

Alignment Unaligned	**Languages** Common, Draconic

Skills Acrobatics +26, Athletics +26, Stealth +26

Str 26 (+21)	**Dex** 27 (+21)	**Wis** 30 (+23)
Con 32 (+24)	**Int** 23 (+19)	**Cha** 21 (+18)

SILVER DRAGON

SILVER DRAGONS ARE THE KNIGHTS-ERRANT of dragonkind, frequently traveling the world in order to be at the flashpoint of interesting conflicts. Although they breathe cones of icy destruction, they favor melee combat over the use of their breath weapon.

SILVER DRAGON TACTICS

Silver dragons are straightforward and enthusiastic combatants. They move directly to confront as many foes as possible, attacking with tooth, claw, and tail. As they age, silver dragons become even more capable of shaking off hindering effects, and are among the most formidable of the dragons in face-to-face confrontation.

SILVER DRAGON LORE

Nature DC 20: Silver dragons travel widely, but prefer to inhabit the cool heights of mountains or cloud castles. Silver dragons breathe blasts of cold, and they also have significant melee abilities.

Nature DC 25: Silver dragons are susceptible to flattery and are highly intolerant of aggression or arrogance in others. They are slower in the air than most other dragons.

ENCOUNTER GROUPS

A silver dragon prefers to be in the front line of a battle. A silver dragon's idealism and crusading temperament lead it to recruit allies who share its sensibilities. Dwarves, dragonborn, angels, devas, and any other creatures that place ideals above profit might be found fighting alongside silver dragons.

Level 10 Encounter (XP 2,100)
✦ 2 eladrin twilight incanters (level 8 controller, MM 102)
✦ 1 young silver dragon (level 8 solo brute)

Level 17 Encounter (XP 8,000)
✦ 1 adult silver dragon (level 15 solo brute)
✦ 2 deva zealots (level 14 skirmisher)

Young Silver Dragon — Level 8 Solo Brute
Large natural magical beast (dragon)   XP 1,750

Initiative +7   **Senses** Perception +10; darkvision
HP 376; **Bloodied** 188; see also *bloodied breath*
AC 20; **Fortitude** 22, **Reflex** 19, **Will** 18
Resist 15 cold
Saving Throws +5
Speed 6, fly 6 (hover), overland flight 10
Action Points 2

⊕ **Bite** (standard; at-will)
     Reach 2; +11 vs. AC; 2d8 + 5 damage.

⊕ **Claw** (standard; at-will)
     Reach 2; +11 vs. AC; 1d6 + 5 damage.

ϯ **Dragon Onslaught** (standard; at-will)
     The young silver dragon makes a claw attack against each enemy within reach.

ϯ **Wing Slice** (immediate reaction, when an enemy attacks the young silver dragon while flanking it; at-will)
     Reach 2; targets the triggering enemy and an enemy flanking with the triggering enemy; +11 vs. AC; 1d6 + 5 damage.

⟸ **Breath Weapon** (standard; recharge ⚄ ⚅) ✦ **Cold**
     Close blast 5; +7 vs. Reflex; 1d8 + 5 cold damage, and the target gains vulnerable 5 to all damage (save ends). *Miss:* Half damage.

⟸ **Bloodied Breath** (free, when first bloodied; encounter)
     Breath weapon recharges, and the young silver dragon uses it.

⟸ **Frightful Presence** (standard; encounter) ✦ **Fear**
     Close burst 5; targets enemies; +7 vs. Will; the target is stunned until the end of the young silver dragon's next turn. *Aftereffect:* The target takes a -2 penalty to attack rolls (save ends).

Alignment Unaligned   **Languages** Common, Draconic
Skills Athletics +16, Insight +10

| **Str** 24 (+11) | **Dex** 16 (+7) | **Wis** 12 (+5) |
| **Con** 22 (+10) | **Int** 12 (+5) | **Cha** 13 (+5) |

Adult Silver Dragon — Level 15 Solo Brute
Large natural magical beast (dragon)   XP 6,000

Initiative +10   **Senses** Perception +13; darkvision
HP 608; **Bloodied** 304; see also *bloodied breath*
AC 27; **Fortitude** 29, **Reflex** 26, **Will** 25
Resist 20 cold
Saving Throws +5
Speed 8, fly 8 (hover), overland flight 12
Action Points 2

⊕ **Bite** (standard; at-will)
     Reach 2; +18 vs. AC; 3d6 + 6 damage.

⊕ **Claw** (standard; at-will)
     Reach 2; +18 vs. AC; 2d6 + 6 damage.

ϯ **Dragon Onslaught** (standard; at-will)
     The adult silver dragon makes a claw attack against each enemy within reach. It also attacks one creature with a bite.

ϯ **Wing Slice** (immediate reaction, when an enemy attacks the adult silver dragon while flanking it; at-will)
     Reach 2; targets the triggering enemy and an enemy flanking with the triggering enemy; +18 vs. AC; 1d8 + 9 damage.

⟸ **Breath Weapon** (standard; recharge ⚄ ⚅) ✦ **Cold**
     Close blast 5; +14 vs. Reflex; 2d8 + 7 cold damage, and the target gains vulnerable 5 to all damage (save ends). *Miss:* Half damage.

⟸ **Bloodied Breath** (free, when first bloodied; encounter)
     Breath weapon recharges, and the adult silver dragon uses it.

⟸ **Frightful Presence** (standard; encounter) ✦ **Fear**
     Close burst 5; targets enemies; +14 vs. Will; the target is stunned until the end of the adult silver dragon's next turn. *Aftereffect:* The target takes a -2 penalty to attack rolls (save ends).

Threatening Reach
     An adult silver dragon can make opportunity attacks against all enemies within its reach (2 squares).

Alignment Unaligned   **Languages** Common, Draconic
Skills Athletics +21, Insight +13

| **Str** 28 (+16) | **Dex** 22 (+13) | **Wis** 12 (+8) |
| **Con** 24 (+14) | **Int** 12 (+8) | **Cha** 20 (+12) |

Elder Silver Dragon — Level 22 Solo Brute
Huge natural magical beast (dragon)   XP 20,750

Initiative +14   **Senses** Perception +18; darkvision
HP 840; **Bloodied** 420; see also *bloodied breath*
AC 34; **Fortitude** 36, **Reflex** 33, **Will** 32
Resist 25 cold
Saving Throws +5
Speed 8, fly 8 (hover), overland flight 15
Action Points 2

⊕ **Bite** (standard; at-will)
     Reach 2; +25 vs. AC; 3d8 + 8 damage.

⊕ **Claw** (standard; at-will)
     Reach 2; +25 vs. AC; 2d8 + 8 damage.

⟸ **Tail Slam** (standard; at-will)
     Close blast 5; +23 vs. AC; 4d6 + 8 damage, and the target is dazed (save ends).

ϯ **Furious Dragon Onslaught** (standard; at-will)
     The elder silver dragon makes a claw attack against each enemy within reach. It also attacks one creature with a bite.

ϯ **Wing Slice** (immediate reaction, when an enemy attacks the elder silver dragon while flanking it; at-will)
     Reach 2; targets the triggering enemy and an enemy flanking with the triggering enemy; +25 vs. AC; 2d8 + 8 damage.

⟸ **Breath Weapon** (standard; recharge ⚂ ⚄ ⚅) ✦ **Cold**
     Close blast 5; +21 vs. Reflex; 3d8 + 8 cold damage, and the target gains vulnerable 10 to all damage (save ends). *Miss:* Half damage.

⟸ **Bloodied Breath** (free, when first bloodied; encounter)
     Breath weapon recharges, and the elder silver dragon uses it.

⟸ **Frightful Presence** (standard; encounter) ✦ **Fear**
     Close burst 10; targets enemies; +21 vs. Will; the target is stunned until the end of the elder silver dragon's next turn. *Aftereffect:* The target takes a -2 penalty to attack rolls (save ends).

Threatening Reach
     An elder silver dragon can make opportunity attacks against all enemies within its reach (2 squares).

Unstoppable
     An elder silver dragon makes saving throws against ongoing damage at the start of its turn as well as at the end of its turn.

Alignment Unaligned   **Languages** Common, Draconic
Skills Athletics +26, Insight +18

| **Str** 30 (+21) | **Dex** 24 (+18) | **Wis** 14 (+13) |
| **Con** 26 (+19) | **Int** 14 (+13) | **Cha** 22 (+17) |

Ancient Silver Dragon **Level 29 Solo Brute**
Gargantuan natural magical beast (dragon) XP 75,000

Initiative +17 **Senses** Perception +21; darkvision
HP 1,072; **Bloodied** 536; see also *bloodied breath*
AC 41; **Fortitude** 43, **Reflex** 40, **Will** 39
Resist 30 cold
Saving Throws +5
Speed 10, fly 10 (hover), overland flight 15
Action Points 2

⊕ **Bite** (standard; at-will)
Reach 3; +32 vs. AC; 3d12 + 11 damage.

⊕ **Claw** (standard; at-will)
Reach 2; +32 vs. AC; 2d12 + 11 damage.

↚ **Tail Slam** (standard; at-will)
Close blast 5; +30 vs. AC; 4d8 + 11 damage, and the target is
dazed (save ends) and knocked prone.

⸎ **Furious Dragon Onslaught** (standard; at-will)
The ancient silver dragon makes a claw attack against each
enemy within reach. It also attacks one creature with a bite.

⸎ **Wing Slice** (immediate reaction, when an enemy attacks the
ancient silver dragon while flanking it; at-will)
Reach 2; targets the triggering enemy and an enemy flanking
with the triggering enemy; +32 vs. AC; 2d12 + 11 damage.

↚ **Breath Weapon** (standard; recharge ⚁ ⚂ ⚃) ✦ **Cold**
Close blast 5; +28 vs. Reflex; 4d8 + 9 cold damage, and the
target gains vulnerable 15 to all damage (save ends). *Miss:* Half
damage.

↚ **Bloodied Breath** (free, when first bloodied; encounter)
Breath weapon recharges, and the ancient silver dragon uses it.

↚ **Frightful Presence** (standard; encounter) ✦ **Fear**
Close burst 10; targets enemies; +28 vs. Will; the target is stunned
until the end of the ancient silver dragon's next turn. *Aftereffect:*
The target takes a -2 penalty to attack rolls (save ends).

Threatening Reach
An ancient silver dragon can make opportunity attacks against
all enemies in its reach (2 squares for its claw or wing, 3 squares
for its bite).

Unstoppable
An ancient silver dragon makes saving throws against ongoing
damage at the start of its turn as well as at the end of its turn.

Alignment Unaligned **Languages** Common, Draconic
Skills Athletics +30, Insight +21
Str 32 (+25) **Dex** 26 (+22) **Wis** 14 (+16)
Con 28 (+23) **Int** 16 (+17) **Cha** 24 (+21)

Aggressive and wild reptiles, drakes hunt in all reaches of the world. Enterprising individuals capture and domesticate drakes, especially those that aren't able to fly. Captured drakes can be trained, but they always possess a wild side.

BLOODSEEKER DRAKE

A bloodseeker drake is an aggressive hunter that enters a frenzy when it smells blood.

Bloodseeker Drake		Level 4 Soldier
Medium natural beast (reptile)		XP 175

Initiative +8   **Senses** Perception +7 (+12 when tracking bloodied creatures)
HP 53; **Bloodied** 26
AC 20; **Fortitude** 15, **Reflex** 17, **Will** 15
Immune fear (while within 2 squares of an ally)
Speed 6
⊕ **Bite** (standard; at-will)
   +11 vs. AC; 1d10 + 4 damage.
Blood Frenzy
   A bloodseeker drake can make an opportunity attack against any adjacent bloodied creature that shifts.
Bloodthirsty
   A bloodseeker drake gains a +3 bonus to damage rolls against bloodied targets.
Alignment Unaligned   **Languages** –
Skills Athletics +8

Str 13 (+3)	**Dex** 19 (+6)	**Wis** 10 (+2)
Con 13 (+3)	**Int** 2 (-2)	**Cha** 13 (+3)

BLOODSEEKER DRAKE LORE

Nature DC 12: Bloodseeker drakes are prized by hunters and patrols for their tracking abilities. They are hard to control, however, especially in conditions thick with the stench of blood.

HORNED DRAKE

In the wild, a pack of horned drakes can bring down much larger prey. A trained horned drake retains the instinct to fight as a team.

Horned Drake		Level 5 Skirmisher
Medium natural beast (reptile)		XP 200

Initiative +6   **Senses** Perception +3; low-light vision
HP 63; **Bloodied** 31
AC 19; **Fortitude** 19, Reflex 17, **Will** 16
Speed 6
⊕ **Bite** (standard; at-will)
   +10 vs. AC; 2d8 + 2 damage, and the horned drake shifts 2 squares.
☦ **Goring Horns** (standard; at-will)
   +11 vs. AC; 3d8 + 2 damage, and the target is knocked prone.
Pack Movement (immediate reaction, when an enemy adjacent to the horned drake is hit by a melee attack; at-will)
   The drake shifts 2 squares.

Alignment Unaligned		**Languages** –
Str 18 (+6)	**Dex** 14 (+4)	**Wis** 12 (+3)
Con 15 (+4)	**Int** 2 (-2)	**Cha** 8 (+1)

HORNED DRAKE LORE

Nature DC 12: Horned drakes spend the day sleeping in the sun, preferring to hunt at night or in the early hours of morning.

SCYTHECLAW DRAKE

Predatory cunning makes this drake dangerous. Roving through forests and grasslands in small familial units, a scytheclaw drake is a study in devious pack hunting.

Scytheclaw Drake		Level 10 Skirmisher
Medium natural beast (reptile)		XP 500

Initiative +12   **Senses** Perception +12
HP 105; **Bloodied** 52
AC 24; **Fortitude** 21, **Reflex** 23, **Will** 20
Speed 10
⊕ **Scytheclaw** (standard; at-will)
   +15 vs. AC; 1d8 + 5 damage, and the target is knocked prone. If the scytheclaw drake hits a prone target, it instead deals 2d8 + 5 damage, and ongoing 5 damage (save ends); see also *springing step*.
Overwhelming Attacker (opportunity, when an enemy adjacent to the scytheclaw drake stands up; at-will)
   The drake makes an opportunity attack against the triggering enemy. On a hit, the attack deals no damage, and the enemy remains prone.
Springing Step (free, when the scytheclaw drake hits with *scytheclaw* attack; recharge ⚃ ⚄ ⚅)
   The drake jumps 8 squares and uses *scytheclaw*. The jump does not provoke an opportunity attack from the target of the triggering attack.
Alignment Unaligned   **Languages** –
Skills Athletics +13, Stealth +15

Str 16 (+8)	**Dex** 21 (+10)	**Wis** 15 (+7)
Con 17 (+8)	**Int** 3 (+1)	**Cha** 6 (+3)

SCYTHECLAW DRAKE LORE

Nature DC 16: Scytheclaw drakes are more intelligent than other drakes, and they reveal it by using tactics of distraction. If you can see one scytheclaw, chances are good that another two or three hide nearby.

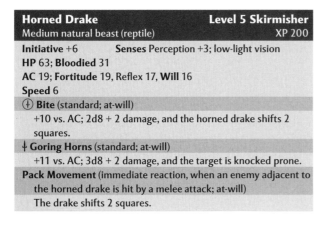

(Left to right) scytheclaw drake, fang titan drake, horned drake, and bloodseeker drake

Fang Titan Drake

The most feared of all drakes, a fang titan stalks wild places uncontested. Few predatory creatures other than dragons pose any threat to a fang titan.

Fang Titan Drake	Level 18 Elite Controller
Huge natural beast (reptile)	XP 4,000

Initiative +12   **Senses** Perception +12
HP 348; **Bloodied** 174
AC 32; **Fortitude** 31, **Reflex** 28, **Will** 28
Saving Throws +2
Speed 8
Action Points 1

⊕ **Bite** (standard; at-will)
Reach 2; targets one or two adjacent creatures; +23 vs. AC; 3d8 + 7 damage, and the target is dazed (save ends). The fang titan drake also grabs one target.

↤ **Furious Roar** (standard; encounter) ✦ **Fear**
Close burst 10; targets enemies; +22 vs. Will; the target is stunned until the end of the fang titan drake's next turn. *Aftereffect*: The target takes a -2 penalty to attack rolls (save ends).

↤ **Tail Sweep** (standard; recharge ▣▣ ▣ ▦)
Close burst 2; +22 vs. Reflex; 4d12 + 7 damage, and the target is knocked prone.

Bloodied Roar (free, when first bloodied; encounter)
Furious roar recharges, and the fang titan drake uses it.

Alignment Unaligned	**Languages** –	
Str 27 (+17)	**Dex** 16 (+12)	**Wis** 17 (+12)
Con 22 (+15)	**Int** 2 (+5)	**Cha** 7 (+7)

Fang Titan Drake Lore

Nature DC 20: Although they are rare, fang titans hunt in huge territories, killing or chasing out other large predators. Creatures that can escape the drakes' notice benefit from their unwitting protection.

Encounter Groups

Because they are wild hunters, it is rare to find these creatures working with creatures outside their own species. Although domesticated drakes are common, only the most powerful creatures can domesticate a fang titan.

Level 3 Encounter (XP 750)
✦ 2 bloodseeker drakes (level 4 brute)
✦ 2 poisonscale magi lizardfolk (level 2 artillery)
✦ 1 poisonscale collector lizardfolk (level 3 lurker)

Level 19 Encounter (XP 12,000)
✦ 1 fang titan drake (level 18 elite controller)
✦ 2 fire giants (level 18 soldier, *MM* 123)
✦ 2 fire giant forgecallers (level 18 artillery, *MM* 123)

DRAKKOTH

Stalking the jungles and forests of the world, drakkoths are draconic creatures that share the intelligence and cunning of their distant dragon kin. Drakkoths have adopted a culture and weaponry similar to those of humanoid races. Fiercely devoted to their own kind, drakkoths form warrior tribes that aggressively defend their territories.

Drakkoth Ambusher

The drakkoth ambusher fights in concert with soldier and brute allies, making surprise attacks whenever possible.

Drakkoth Ambusher Tactics

At the beginning of combat, an ambusher attempts to hit three or more enemies with *sudden rush*. Throughout combat, the ambusher prefers to attack with combat advantage and is constantly on the move, attacking with reach against prone targets while avoiding spaces adjacent to enemies.

Drakkoth Ambusher	Level 13 Skirmisher
Medium natural humanoid (reptile)	XP 800

Initiative +13   **Senses** Perception +15; low-light vision
HP 131; **Bloodied** 65; see also *drakkoth rage*
AC 27; **Fortitude** 24, **Reflex** 25, **Will** 24
Speed 7

⊕ **Glaive** (standard; at-will) ✦ **Poison, Weapon**
    Reach 2; +18 vs. AC; 4d4 damage plus 5 poison damage.

↧ **Sudden Rush** (move; recharge ⚄ ⚅)
    The drakkoth ambusher shifts its speed and makes an attack against each enemy it moves adjacent to during the move: +16 vs. Reflex; the target is knocked prone.

⬱ **Venomous Hiss** (minor; recharges when first bloodied) ✦ **Poison**
    Close blast 2; +16 vs. Reflex; 3d6 + 5 poison damage, and the target takes ongoing 5 poison damage (save ends).

Combat Advantage
    A drakkoth ambusher deals 2d6 extra damage against any target granting combat advantage to it.

Drakkoth Rage (while bloodied)
    Once per round when the drakkoth ambusher hits with an attack, it gains 10 temporary hit points.

Alignment Unaligned	**Languages** Common, Draconic	
Str 18 (+10)	**Dex** 20 (+11)	**Wis** 18 (+10)
Con 19 (+10)	**Int** 12 (+7)	**Cha** 14 (+8)

Equipment hide armor, glaive

(Left to right) drakkoth ambusher, rager, and venomshot

Drakkoth Rager

A DRAKKOTH RAGER CHARGES INTO BATTLE, oblivious to attacks against it in its single-minded fury.

Drakkoth Rager Tactics

The drakkoth rager charges haphazardly into combat, provoking opportunity attacks if necessary in order to hit three targets with *raging cleave*. The rager uses *venom hiss* as soon as it can target two or more creatures. If its foes are not clustered together, the rager focuses its attacks on the biggest threat.

Drakkoth Rager	Level 15 Elite Brute
Medium natural humanoid (reptile)	XP 2,400

Initiative +12   **Senses** Perception +12; low-light vision
HP 366; **Bloodied** 183; see also *drakkoth rage*
AC 27; **Fortitude** 30, **Reflex** 29, **Will** 29
Saving Throws +2
Speed 7
Action Points 1
⊕ **Battleaxe** (standard; at-will) ✦ **Weapon**
+18 vs. AC; 2d10 + 8 damage.
↞ **Raging Cleave** (standard; at-will) ✦ **Poison, Weapon**
Close burst 1; +18 vs. AC; 2d10 + 8 damage plus 5 poison damage.
↞ **Venomous Hiss** (minor; recharges when first bloodied) ✦ **Poison**
Close blast 2; +16 vs. Reflex; 3d6 + 5 poison damage, and the target takes ongoing 5 poison damage (save ends).
Drakkoth Rage (while bloodied)
The drakkoth rager gains a +2 bonus to attack rolls and a +5 bonus to damage rolls. In addition, once per round when the rager hits with an attack, it gains 10 temporary hit points.
Alignment Unaligned   **Languages** Common, Draconic
Str 18 (+11)   **Dex** 20 (+12)   **Wis** 20 (+12)
Con 23 (+13)   **Int** 12 (+8)   **Cha** 14 (+9)
Equipment hide armor, battleaxe

Drakkoth Venomshot

THE DRAKKOTH VENOMSHOT SUPPORTS ITS ALLIES from the edge of the fray with longbow attacks.

Drakkoth Venomshot Tactics

If a venomshot has a clear shot at a target engaged in melee, it will use its longbow attack to enhance its allies' poison attacks. Once bloodied, a venomshot will shift away from foes, try to hit a nearby enemy with its longbow, then follow up with a *venomshot hiss* in order to gain temporary hit points from *drakkoth rage*.

Drakkoth Venomshot	Level 16 Artillery
Medium natural humanoid (reptile)	XP 1,400

Initiative +13   **Senses** Perception +13; low-light vision
HP 125; **Bloodied** 63; see also *drakkoth rage*
AC 28; **Fortitude** 29, **Reflex** 28, **Will** 28
Speed 7
⊕ **Longsword** (standard; at-will) ✦ **Weapon**
+23 vs. AC; 2d8 + 4 damage.
↗ **Longbow** (standard; at-will) ✦ **Weapon**
Ranged 20/40; +23 vs. AC; 2d10 + 5 damage, and the target gains vulnerable 10 poison (save ends).
↞ **Venomshot Hiss** (minor; recharges at the start of its turn while the drakkoth venomshot is bloodied) ✦ **Poison**
Close blast 3; +21 vs. Reflex; 1d10 poison damage, and the target takes ongoing 5 poison damage (save ends).
Drakkoth Rage (while bloodied)
Once per round when the drakkoth venomshot hits with an attack, it gains 10 temporary hit points.
Alignment Unaligned   **Languages** Common, Draconic
Str 20 (+13)   **Dex** 21 (+13)   **Wis** 21 (+13)
Con 23 (+14)   **Int** 15 (+10)   **Cha** 14 (+10)
Equipment leather armor, longsword, longbow, 30 arrows

Drakkoth Lore

Nature DC 18: Drakkoths are a race of draconic creatures sometimes called dracotaurs because of their similarity in form to centaurs. Unlike dragons and dragonspawn, but similar to dragonborn, drakkoths have developed an advanced tribal culture. Drakkoths are nomadic, and the shifting boundaries of their lands can encompass vast swaths of forest or jungle.

Nature DC 23: Some drakkoth tribes are devoted to Tiamat and serve her with a bloodthirsty devotion. Others care little for the god of greed, choosing instead to honor a dragon patron (most often an elder or ancient green). A dragon that knows of this practice might seek drakkoth worshipers, inspiring (or tricking) a tribe into its service.

Encounter Groups

Drakkoths keep to themselves, although they sometimes make short-term alliances to challenge powerful targets. Additionally, they train creatures to serve them as guards and hunters.

Level 14 Encounter (XP 5,900)
✦ 1 drakkoth rager (level 15 elite brute)
✦ 2 drakkoth venomshots (level 16 artillery)
✦ 1 viscera devourer (level 12 controller, *MM* 68)

Level 16 Encounter (XP 7,200)
✦ 3 drakkoth ambushers (level 13 skirmisher)
✦ 2 drakkoth venomshots (level 16 artillery)
✦ 1 roc (level 14 elite skirmisher, *MM* 220)

DUERGAR

DISTANT KIN TO DWARVES, duergar carry the taint of a long association with infernal forces. Although they share a love of mining and metalwork with their steadfast dwarf cousins, duergar are uniformly treacherous and cruel.

DUERGAR GUARD

WIELDING A FIERY WARHAMMER, a duergar guard flings poisoned quills at its enemies.

Duergar Guard	Level 4 Soldier
Medium natural humanoid, dwarf (devil)	XP 175

Initiative +6   **Senses** Perception +4; darkvision
HP 58; **Bloodied** 29
AC 20; **Fortitude** 17, **Reflex** 15, **Will** 15
Resist 5 fire, 5 poison
Speed 5
⊕ **Warhammer** (standard; at-will) ✦ **Weapon**
  +11 vs. AC; 1d10 + 3 damage.
↗ **Infernal Quills** (minor; encounter) ✦ **Poison**
  Ranged 3; +11 vs. AC; 1d8 + 3 damage, and the target takes ongoing 2 poison damage and a –2 penalty to attack rolls (save ends both).

Infernal Anger (minor; recharge ⚃ ⚄) ✦ **Fire**
  Until the start of the duergar guard's next turn, its melee attacks deal 4 extra fire damage, and if an enemy adjacent to the guard moves, the guard shifts 1 square as an immediate reaction.
Alignment Evil   **Languages** Common, Deep Speech, Dwarven
Skills Dungeoneering +9
Str 14 (+4)   **Dex** 15 (+4)   **Wis** 15 (+4)
Con 18 (+6)   **Int** 10 (+2)   **Cha** 8 (+1)
Equipment chainmail, warhammer

DUERGAR SCOUT

A DUERGAR SCOUT ATTACKS FROM AMBUSH, sniping with its crossbow as it moves unseen among its foes.

Duergar Scout	Level 4 Lurker
Medium natural humanoid, dwarf (devil)	XP 175

Initiative +8   **Senses** Perception +9; darkvision
HP 48; **Bloodied** 24
AC 18; **Fortitude** 18, **Reflex** 16, **Will** 16
Resist 5 fire, 5 poison
Speed 5
⊕ **Warhammer** (standard; at-will) ✦ **Weapon**
  +8 vs. AC; 1d10 + 2 damage.
↗ **Crossbow** (standard; at-will) ✦ **Weapon**
  Ranged 15/30; +9 vs. AC; 1d8 + 4 damage.

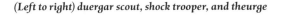

(Left to right) duergar scout, shock trooper, and theurge

➷ Infernal Quills (minor; encounter) ✦ Poison

Ranged 3; +9 vs. AC; 1d8 + 3 damage, and the target takes ongoing 2 poison damage and a -2 penalty to attack rolls (save ends both).

Shadow Attack

A duergar scout's attacks deal 2d6 extra damage while the scout is invisible.

Underdark Sneak (minor; while in dim light or darkness and adjacent to an object or a wall that occupies at least 1 square; at-will)

The duergar scout becomes invisible until the end of its next turn or until after it hits or misses with an attack.

Alignment Evil	**Languages** Common, Deep Speech, Dwarven

Skills Dungeoneering +9, Stealth +9

Str 13 (+3)	**Dex** 15 (+4)	**Wis** 14 (+4)
Con 18 (+6)	**Int** 10 (+2)	**Cha** 8 (+1)

Equipment chainmail, warhammer, crossbow, case with 10 bolts

DUERGAR THEURGE

A DUERGAR THEURGE LAUNCHES A FIERY RAIN against its foes. The approach of a theurge can drain creatures of the will to fight.

Duergar Theurge	**Level 5 Controller**
Medium natural humanoid, dwarf (devil)	XP 200

Initiative +3 **Senses** Perception +6; darkvision
HP 63; **Bloodied** 31
AC 19; **Fortitude** 16, **Reflex** 16, **Will** 18
Resist 5 fire, 5 poison
Speed 5

⊕ Warhammer (standard; at-will) ✦ Weapon
+10 vs. AC; 1d10 + 1 damage.

➷ Hellbolt (standard; at-will) ✦ Fire
Ranged 10; +9 vs. Reflex; 1d10 + 4 fire damage.

➷ Infernal Quills (minor; encounter) ✦ Poison
Ranged 3; +10 vs. AC; 1d8 + 3 damage, and the target takes ongoing 2 poison damage and a -2 penalty to attack rolls (save ends both).

↩ Wave of Despair (standard; daily) ✦ Psychic
Close blast 5; +9 vs. Will; 3d6 + 4 psychic damage, and the target is slowed and dazed (save ends both).

✴ Brimstone Hail (standard; recharge ⚄ ⚅) ✦ Fire
Area burst 2 within 15; +9 vs. Reflex; 3d6 + 4 fire damage, and the target is knocked prone.

✴ Vile Fumes (standard; recharges when first bloodied) ✦ Poison
Area burst 2 within 15; +9 vs. Fortitude; 3d6 + 4 poison damage, and the target is blinded until the end of the duergar theurge's next turn.

Alignment Evil	**Languages** Common, Deep Speech, Dwarven

Skills Arcana +9, Dungeoneering +11, Religion +9

Str 13 (+3)	**Dex** 12 (+3)	**Wis** 18 (+6)
Con 15 (+4)	**Int** 15 (+4)	**Cha** 11 (+2)

Equipment robes, warhammer

DUERGAR SHOCK TROOPER

ALREADY A FORMIDABLE OPPONENT, a shock trooper grows more imposing when bloodied—literally.

Duergar Shock Trooper	**Level 6 Brute**
Medium natural humanoid, dwarf (devil)	XP 250

Initiative +6 **Senses** Perception +6; darkvision
HP 84; **Bloodied** 42; see also *expand*
AC 18; **Fortitude** 19, **Reflex** 18, **Will** 18
Resist 5 fire, 5 poison
Speed 5

⊕ Maul (standard; at-will) ✦ Weapon
+9 vs. AC; 2d6 + 6 damage.

➷ Infernal Quills (minor; encounter) ✦ Poison
Ranged 3; +9 vs. AC; 1d8 + 4 damage, and the target takes ongoing 2 poison damage and a -2 penalty to attack rolls (save ends both).

Expand (when first bloodied; encounter) ✦ Polymorph
The duergar shock trooper becomes Large, occupying 4 squares instead of 1. Creatures and objects in the squares that the shock trooper comes to occupy are pushed 1 square. The shock trooper's reach becomes 2 and it gains a +5 bonus to damage rolls. This effect lasts until the end of the encounter.

Alignment Evil	**Languages** Common, Deep Speech, Dwarven

Skills Dungeoneering +11

Str 19 (+7)	**Dex** 16 (+6)	**Wis** 16 (+6)
Con 14 (+5)	**Int** 10 (+3)	**Cha** 8 (+2)

Equipment chainmail, maul

DUERGAR FLESHTEARER

A DUERGAR FLESHTEARER USES ITS SMOKING CLAWS to rip the life from its enemies.

Duergar Fleshtearer	**Level 11 Lurker**
Medium natural humanoid, dwarf (devil)	XP 600

Initiative +13 **Senses** Perception +9; darkvision
HP 89; **Bloodied** 44
AC 26; **Fortitude** 25, **Reflex** 24, **Will** 24
Resist 10 fire, 10 poison
Speed 5

⊕ Claw (standard; at-will)
+16 vs. AC; 1d8 + 3 damage, and ongoing 5 damage (save ends).

↓ Quill Stab (standard; requires combat advantage against the target; recharges when the duergar fleshtearer hits with its claw attack) ✦ Poison
+16 vs. AC; 1d8 damage, and the target takes ongoing 5 poison damage and a -2 penalty to attack rolls (save ends both).

➷ Infernal Quills (minor; encounter) ✦ Poison
Ranged 3; +16 vs. AC; 1d8 damage, and the target takes ongoing 5 poison damage and a -2 penalty to attack rolls (save ends both).

Shadow Scourge

While the duergar fleshtearer is invisible, its attacks deal twice the normal amount of ongoing damage.

Underdark Sneak (minor; while in dim light or darkness and adjacent to an object or a wall that occupies at least 1 square; at-will)

The duergar fleshtearer becomes invisible until the end of its next turn or until after it hits or misses with an attack.

Alignment Evil	**Languages** Common, Deep Speech, Dwarven

Skills Bluff +10, Dungeoneering +14, Stealth +14

Str 21 (+10)	**Dex** 19 (+9)	**Wis** 18 (+9)
Con 17 (+8)	**Int** 12 (+6)	**Cha** 10 (+5)

Equipment leather armor

Duergar Hellcaller

Bristling with lethal quills, the hellcaller can also summon a lesser devil to battle its foes.

Duergar Hellcaller	Level 12 Artillery
Medium natural humanoid, dwarf (devil)	XP 700

Initiative +10 **Senses** Perception +13; darkvision
HP 96; **Bloodied** 48
AC 24; **Fortitude** 23, **Reflex** 23, **Will** 25
Resist 10 fire, 10 poison
Speed 5

⊕ **Mace** (standard; at-will) ✦ **Weapon**
+19 vs. AC; 1d8 + 5 damage.

↗ **Infernal Quills** (standard; at-will) ✦ **Fire, Poison**
Ranged 10; +19 vs. AC; 1d8 + 3 fire and poison damage, and the target takes ongoing 5 fire and poison damage and a -2 penalty to attack rolls (save ends both).

↗ **Quick Quill Strike** (minor; encounter)
The duergar hellcaller makes an *infernal quills* attack.

↞ **Asmodeus's Ruby Curse** (standard; encounter) ✦ **Fear, Psychic**
Close blast 5; targets enemies; +16 vs. Will; 3d8 + 5 psychic damage, and the duergar hellcaller slides the target to the nearest space outside the blast. This forced movement provokes opportunity attacks.

❊ **Quill Storm** (standard; encounter) ✦ **Fire, Poison**
Area burst 2 within 10; +17 vs. Reflex; 1d8 fire and poison damage, and the target takes ongoing 10 fire and poison damage and a -2 penalty to attack rolls (save ends both).

Devilish Sacrifice (immediate interrupt, when an enemy makes a melee attack roll against the duergar hellcaller; encounter)
The hellcaller shifts to the nearest space beyond the triggering enemy's reach. A legion devil hellguard (MM 64) appears in the hellcaller's former space and becomes the target of the enemy's attack. The devil acts immediately after the hellcaller's initiative count.

Alignment Evil **Languages** Common, Deep Speech, Dwarven
Skills Arcana +11, Dungeoneering +13, Religion +11
Str 14 (+8) **Dex** 19 (+10) **Wis** 14 (+8)
Con 18 (+10) **Int** 11 (+6) **Cha** 22 (+12)
Equipment leather armor, mace

Duergar Blackguard

The heavily armored blackguard relentlessly pursues one enemy across the field of battle, pounding it with repeated waraxe attacks.

Duergar Blackguard	Level 13 Elite Soldier
Medium natural humanoid, dwarf (devil)	XP 1,600

Initiative +8 **Senses** Perception +8; darkvision
HP 260; **Bloodied** 130
AC 29; **Fortitude** 27, **Reflex** 25, **Will** 25
Resist 10 fire, 10 poison
Saving Throws +2
Speed 5
Action Points 1

⊕ **Blighted Warhammer** (standard; at-will) ✦ **Poison, Weapon**
+20 vs. AC; 2d10 + 3 damage, and the duergar blackguard makes a secondary attack against the target. *Secondary Attack:* +16 vs. Fortitude; the target takes ongoing 5 poison damage and a -2 penalty to attack rolls (save ends both).

↞ **Darkfire Mark** (minor 1/round; at-will) ✦ **Fire, Necrotic**
Close burst 10; targets one enemy; until the end of the duergar blackguard's next turn, the target is marked and gains no benefit from any concealment. In addition, if the target ends its next turn farther from the blackguard than it began the turn, or if it does not make an attack roll against the blackguard during its next turn, the target takes 10 fire and necrotic damage.

↞ **Quill Burst** (minor; recharge ⚃ ⚄ ⚅) ✦ **Poison**
Close burst 3; targets one enemy; +18 vs. AC; 1d8 + 4 damage, and the target takes ongoing 5 poison damage and a -2 penalty to attack rolls (save ends both).

Infernal Footwork (immediate reaction, when an enemy adjacent to the duergar blackguard moves or shifts away from it; at-will)
The blackguard shifts 2 squares and must end the shift in a space adjacent to the triggering enemy. If the triggering enemy is marked by the duergar blackguard, the blackguard then uses *blighted warhammer* against the target as a free action.

Alignment Evil **Languages** Common, Deep Speech, Dwarven
Skills Dungeoneering +15, Intimidate +15, Religion +13
Str 22 (+12) **Dex** 11 (+6) **Wis** 14 (+8)
Con 18 (+10) **Int** 19 (+10) **Cha** 18 (+10)
Equipment plate armor, heavy shield, warhammer

Duergar Blasphemer

Infernal priests of Asmodeus, duergar blasphemers punish unbelievers with poison and fire.

Duergar Blasphemer	Level 14 Controller (Leader)
Medium natural humanoid, dwarf (devil)	XP 1,000

Initiative +9 **Senses** Perception +13; darkvision
Crush Nonbelievers (Fire, Poison) aura sight; the duergar blasphemer and each ally within the aura can score critical hits on rolls of 19-20 against prone targets and deal 10 extra fire and poison damage on critical hits against prone targets.
HP 140; **Bloodied** 70
AC 28; **Fortitude** 25, **Reflex** 25, **Will** 26
Resist 10 fire, 10 poison
Speed 5

⊕ **Greatclub** (standard; at-will) ✦ **Fire, Necrotic, Weapon**
+19 vs. AC; 2d4 + 3 damage, and ongoing 5 fire and necrotic damage (save ends).

⥮ **Sinner's Slip** (immediate interrupt, when an enemy marked by the duergar blasphemer makes an attack roll against it; encounter) ✦ **Psychic**
Targets the triggering enemy; +18 vs. Will; the enemy's attack instead targets the ally of the attacker nearest to it. If no target is available, the attacker is knocked prone and takes 3d6 + 6 psychic damage.

↗ **Eyes of Asmodeus** (standard; at-will)
Ranged 10; +18 vs. Fortitude; the target is weakened and marked until the end of the duergar blasphemer's next turn. *Aftereffect:* The target is slowed (save ends). *Miss:* The target is slowed (save ends).

↗ **Infernal Quills** (standard; at-will) ✦ **Fire, Poison**
Ranged 10; +19 vs. AC; 1d8 + 4 fire and poison damage, and the target takes ongoing 5 fire and poison damage and a -2 penalty to attack rolls (save ends both).

↗ **Quick Quill Strike** (minor; encounter)
The duergar blasphemer makes an *infernal quills* attack.

↞ **Preach Submission** (minor 1/round; at-will)
Close burst 10; targets one creature; +19 vs. Will; the target is marked (save ends). If the target is already marked by the duergar blasphemer, it is knocked prone.

(Left to right) duergar fleshtearer, blackguard, and hellcaller

Alignment Evil	Languages Common, Deep Speech,	
	Dwarven	
Skills Bluff +15, Dungeoneering +18, Religion +17		
Str 14 (+9)	Dex 15 (+9)	Wis 23 (+13)
Con 20 (+12)	Int 20 (+12)	Cha 16 (+10)
Equipment greatclub, robes		

DUERGAR LORE

Nature DC 10: Duergar are kin to dwarves, but their long association with infernal powers has given them strange abilities and a thirst for blood. Their devilish nature leads duergar to prefer volcanic areas of the Underdark.

Nature DC 16: Long ago, duergar were members of a great clan of dwarves that delved deep into the Underdark and fell to a mind flayer assault. They endured uncounted years as slaves before fighting their way to freedom. Those duergar that escaped gained a perverse education from their captivity, becoming as corrupt as their former masters.

Nature DC 21: Believing that Moradin abandoned them during their enslavement, the duergar turned instead to the worship of devils. Most now take Asmodeus as their patron deity, and devilish power flows in their veins. Within their settlements, blood rites to infernal beings are common. Woe to the slave that has outlived its usefulness or angered a capricious duergar master.

ENCOUNTER GROUPS

Duergar raid, pillage, and take prisoners when it suits them, using captives as slave labor and sacrifices for their infernal altars. For their raiding parties, they summon devils and employ troglodytes, orcs, ogres, and other wicked races.

Level 4 Encounter (XP 901)
- ✦ 2 duergar guards (level 4 soldier)
- ✦ 1 duergar scout (level 4 lurker)
- ✦ 1 duergar theurge (level 5 controller)
- ✦ 4 orc drudges (level 4 minion, *MM* 203)

ELADRIN

SELF-STYLED PRINCES AND NOBLES of the Feywild, eladrin live charmed lives full of art and music. However, they are quick to anger when their wrath is provoked; an eladrin bears down upon its foes like a hurricane.

ELADRIN ARCANE ARCHER

ARCANE ARCHERS INFUSE THEIR WEAPONS with magical force, the better to destroy their enemies.

Eladrin Arcane Archer	Level 5 Artillery
Medium fey humanoid	XP 200

Initiative +6   **Senses** Perception +7; low-light vision
HP 51; **Bloodied** 25
AC 17; **Fortitude** 16, **Reflex** 18, **Will** 16
Saving Throws +5 against charm effects
Speed 6
⊕ **Short Sword** (standard; at-will) ✦ **Weapon**
   +12 vs. AC; 1d6 + 4 damage.

⊛ **Scorching Arrows** (standard; at-will) ✦ **Fire, Weapon**
   Ranged 20/40; +10 vs. AC or Reflex (whichever is lower); 1d10 damage plus 1d6 fire damage. *Effect:* The eladrin arcane archer makes the attack against the same target or a different one.
✳ **Eldritch Burst** (standard; recharge ⚁ ⚄ ⚅) ✦ **Force**
   Area burst 1 within 20; +10 vs. Fortitude; 1d10 + 5 force damage, and the target is knocked prone.
Fey Step (move; encounter) ✦ **Teleportation**
   The eladrin arcane archer teleports 5 squares.

Alignment Unaligned	**Languages** Common, Elven
Str 12 (+3)	**Dex** 18 (+6)	**Wis** 11 (+2)
Con 15 (+4)	**Int** 17 (+5)	**Cha** 15 (+4)

Equipment chainmail, longbow, 2 short swords

ELADRIN ARCANE ARCHER LORE

Arcana DC 12: Eladrin arcane archers are highly skilled warriors that employ missiles of magical fire against their enemies.

Arcana DC 17: Arcane archery is more than just a combination of magic and skill at arms. It is a complete fusion of two arts, its secrets known only to the eladrin.

(Left to right) eladrin arcane archer, coure of mischief and strife, and bladesinger

EVA WIDERMANN

ELADRIN BLADESINGER

A WHIRLING BLUR IN BATTLE, an eladrin bladesinger forms a bond with allies and enemies alike, making each fight personal.

Eladrin Bladesinger	Level 11 Skirmisher
Medium fey humanoid	XP 600

Initiative +12   **Senses** Perception +6; low-light vision
HP 114; **Bloodied** 57
AC 25; **Fortitude** 23, **Reflex** 24, **Will** 23
Saving Throws +5 against charm effects
Speed 8; see also *wyvern strike*

ⓘ **Brilliant Blade** (standard; at-will) ✦ **Radiant, Weapon**
   +16 vs. AC; 2d8 + 3 radiant damage, and the target takes a -3 penalty to attack rolls against the eladrin bladesinger until the end of the bladesinger's next turn.

✦ **Crippling Strike** (standard; encounter) ✦ **Weapon**
   The eladrin bladesinger shifts 3 squares before and after making the attack. +14 vs. Fortitude; the target is weakened and slowed (save ends both). *Miss:* The target is slowed (save ends).

✦ **Dance of Brilliance** (standard; at-will) ✦ **Radiant, Weapon**
   +16 vs. AC; 1d8 + 4 radiant damage, and the eladrin bladesinger shifts 3 squares and uses *brilliant blade* against a different target.

✦ **Wyvern Strike** (standard; encounter) ✦ **Poison, Weapon**
   The eladrin bladesinger flies 8 squares and does not provoke opportunity attacks. At any point during the move, the bladesinger makes an attack: +14 vs. Fortitude; 1d8 + 4 damage, and ongoing 10 poison damage (save ends).

Combat Shift (minor; requires combat advantage against a target adjacent to the eladrin bladesinger; at-will)
   The bladesinger shifts 1 square to a space adjacent to the target.

Fey Step (move; encounter) ✦ **Teleportation**
   The eladrin bladesinger teleports 5 squares.

Alignment Unaligned	**Languages** Common, Elven	
Str 13 (+6)	**Dex** 21 (+10)	**Wis** 13 (+6)
Con 18 (+9)	**Int** 15 (+7)	**Cha** 18 (+9)

Equipment chainmail, longsword

ELADRIN BLADESINGER LORE

Arcana DC 21: Eladrin bladesingers are highly skilled warriors equally versed in the arts of magic and combat. Bladesingers epitomize grace on the battlefield, but they are equally dedicated to honor. They treat foes with respect, and they despise those that would slaughter the helpless.

ENCOUNTER GROUPS

Eladrin warriors such as the arcane archer and the bladesinger most often seek the company of other eladrin. Coures of mischief and strife can ally themselves with any creature, although rarely for long.

Level 10 Encounter (XP 2,650)
✦ 3 eladrin bladesingers (level 11 skirmisher)
✦ 1 eladrin twilight incanter (level 8 controller, MM 102)
✦ 1 will-o'-wisp (level 10 lurker)

COURE OF MISCHIEF AND STRIFE

THIS WINSOME ELADRIN keeps to the shadows, lips curled in a wicked smile.

Coure of Mischief and Strife	Level 17 Lurker
Medium fey humanoid, eladrin	XP 1,600

Initiative +19   **Senses** Perception +11; low-light vision
HP 129; **Bloodied** 64
AC 31; **Fortitude** 28, **Reflex** 30, **Will** 28
Resist 20 radiant; **Vulnerable** necrotic (a coure of mischief and strife that takes necrotic damage is slowed until the end of its next turn)
Saving Throws +5 against charm effects
Speed 6, teleport 6

ⓘ **Rapier** (standard; at-will) ✦ **Weapon**
   +22 vs. AC; 2d8 + 6 damage.

➹ **Spark of Strife** (standard; usable only while invisible; at-will) ✦ **Charm, Psychic**
   Ranged 10; +20 vs. Will; 2d10 + 5 psychic damage, and the target is dazed until the end of its next turn. At the start of the target's next turn, it charges its nearest ally or makes a basic attack against its nearest ally as a free action. If the target's attack hits, the coure of mischief and strife uses *spark of strife* against the attacked creature as a free action.

⤾ **Winds of Luck's Mischief** (standard; encounter)
   Close burst 3; +20 vs. Will; the target misses with an attack that has an odd number on the attack roll (save ends).

Invisibility (standard; at-will) ✦ **Illusion**
   The coure of mischief and strife becomes invisible until it misses with an attack or takes damage.

Fey Step (move; encounter) ✦ **Teleportation**
   The coure of mischief and strife teleports 5 squares.

Alignment Unaligned	**Languages** Common, Elven	
Skills Bluff +18, Insight +16, Stealth +20		
Str 14 (+10)	**Dex** 24 (+15)	**Wis** 16 (+11)
Con 21 (+13)	**Int** 12 (+9)	**Cha** 21 (+13)

Equipment leather armor, rapier

COURE OF MISCHIEF AND STRIFE LORE

Arcana DC 20: Like "bralani" and "ghaele," the term "coure" is a title of nobility. Any rank associated with such a title varies among different eladrin lands and clans. However, all eladrin that attain such ranks adopt spheres of influence and are invested with powers pertaining to those spheres.

Arcana DC 25: Noble rank in eladrin society is rarely a matter of inheritance. Eladrin politics is a complex mix of popularity and mysticism beyond the comprehension of nonfey. Eladrin that attain the title of coure of mischief and strife are experts in their chosen art of discord.

ELEMENTAL

ELEMENTALS ROIL ACROSS the Elemental Chaos in infinite variety. Some occupy roles in that plane's varied environments similar to those of beasts in the world. Others pursue alien interests in their own societies.

CHILLFIRE DESTROYER

A CHILLFIRE DESTROYER IS A MASS OF RAGING FIRE held in check by a shell of elemental ice. As the creature fights, the shell slowly weakens, exposing the inferno within.

Chillfire Destroyer	Level 14 Brute
Large elemental magical beast (cold, fire)	XP 1,000

Initiative +12   **Senses** Perception +12
Leaking Firecore (Fire) aura 2; while the chillfire destroyer is bloodied, each creature that starts its turn within the aura takes 10 fire damage.
HP 173; **Bloodied** 86; see also *firecore breach*
AC 26; **Fortitude** 26, **Reflex** 25, **Will** 25
Immune disease, poison; **Resist** 10 cold, 10 fire
Speed 5

⊕ **Freezing Slam** (standard; at-will) ✦ **Cold**
Reach 2; +17 vs. AC; 1d12 + 6 damage plus 1d12 cold damage.
↓ **Trample** (standard; at-will) ✦ **Cold**
The chillfire destroyer moves its speed and can move through enemies' spaces. The destroyer makes an attack: +15 vs. Reflex; 1d10 + 6 damage plus 1d10 cold damage, and the target is knocked prone.
⟻ **Firecore Breach** (when the chillfire destroyer drops to 0 hit points) ✦ **Fire**
The destroyer does not die until the start of its next turn. Until then, the destroyer can take no actions. At the start of the destroyer's next turn, it makes an attack: close burst 3; +15 vs. Reflex; 4d10 + 6 fire damage.

Alignment Unaligned		**Languages** Primordial
Str 16 (+10)	**Dex** 20 (+12)	**Wis** 20 (+12)
Con 23 (+13)	**Int** 5 (+4)	**Cha** 12 (+8)

CHILLFIRE DESTROYER LORE

Arcana DC 18: A chillfire destroyer combines the power of fire with the strength of elemental ice. This dangerous mix results in a deadly explosion when the creature is slain. Both fire archons and ice archons seek to recruit chillfire destroyers for their forces, sometimes coming into conflict as a result.

(Left to right) windstriker, chillfire destroyer, and flamespiker

Dust Devil

A LIVING MOTE OF ELEMENTAL AIR, a dust devil is a destructive creature that sends its enemies flying.

Dust Devil	Level 3 Skirmisher
Small elemental magical beast (air, earth)	XP 150

Initiative +7 **Senses** Perception +0
HP 47; **Bloodied** 23
AC 18; **Fortitude** 14, **Reflex** 16, **Will** 14 (-2 to all defenses while slowed or immobilized)
Immune disease, poison
Speed 8

⊕ **Grasping Winds** (standard; at-will)
+8 vs. Reflex; 1d10 + 3 damage, and the dust devil slides the target 2 squares.

↯ **Gale Blast** (move; recharge ⚄ ⚅)
The dust devil shifts 5 squares and attacks each enemy it moves adjacent to (one attack per creature): +8 vs. Fortitude; the target is knocked prone.

↩ **Stinging Sands** (standard; encounter)
Close burst 3; +8 vs. Fortitude; 3d6 + 3 damage, and the target is blinded until the end of the dust devil's next turn.

Alignment Unaligned **Languages** Primordial
Skills Stealth +10
Str 8 (+0)   **Dex** 18 (+5)   **Wis** 8 (+0)
Con 15 (+3) **Int** 5 (-2)   **Cha** 15 (+3)

Dust Devil Lore

Arcana DC 15: A dust devil is a creature of wind and earth, flighty and impulsive. Because of its dependence on movement, any attack that slows a dust devil weakens it significantly.

Flamespiker

FORMED OF AIR, EARTH, AND FIRE, flamespikers are front-line warriors under the command of more powerful beings of the Elemental Chaos.

Flamespiker	Level 5 Soldier
Medium elemental magical beast (air, earth, fire)	XP 200

Initiative +6 **Senses** Perception +4
HP 66; **Bloodied** 33
AC 21; **Fortitude** 18, **Reflex** 16, **Will** 16
Immune disease, petrification, poison; **Resist** 10 fire
Speed 7

⊕ **Stonespike** (standard; at-will) ✦ Fire
Reach 2; +12 vs. AC; 1d8 damage plus 1d6 fire damage, and the target gains vulnerable 5 fire and is marked until the end of the flamespiker's next turn.

⊙ **Spikebolt** (standard; at-will)
Ranged 5/10; +12 vs. AC; 1d10 + 5 damage.

↯ **Thunderfire Thrust** (immediate reaction, when an enemy within 2 squares of the flamespiker shifts; recharge ⚄ ⚅) ✦ Fire, Thunder
The flamespiker uses *stonespike* against the triggering enemy. On a hit, the flamespiker makes a secondary attack against the same target. *Secondary Attack:* +10 vs. Fortitude; 5 thunder damage, and the target is stunned (save ends).

Alignment Unaligned **Languages** Primordial
Str 13 (+3)   **Dex** 15 (+4)   **Wis** 15 (+4)
Con 18 (+6) **Int** 6 (+0)   **Cha** 8 (+1)

Flamespiker Lore

Arcana DC 12: A flamespiker is a living shell of stone with a hollow core of roiling flame. It blasts foes with burning shards of stone, rendering targets more susceptible to subsequent fire-based attacks.

Geonid

AN ELEMENTAL OF ROCK AND EARTH, the geonid lurks in the Underdark waiting for creatures to stumble across it. When dormant, it looks like a large boulder. Only when prey draws near does it reveal its true form.

Geonid	Level 6 Lurker
Large elemental magical beast (earth)	XP 250

Initiative +10 **Senses** Perception +11; darkvision
HP 56; **Bloodied** 28
AC 20; **Fortitude** 18, **Reflex** 17, **Will** 17
Immune disease, petrification, poison
Speed 4

⊕ **Tentacle** (standard; at-will)
Reach 2; +11 vs. AC; 2d6 + 4 damage.

↯ **Capturing Grab** (standard; at-will)
Reach 2; +11 vs. AC; 1d6 + 4 damage. *Effect:* The geonid makes one more attack against the same target. If both attacks hit, the target is grabbed.

↩ **Shell Slam** (standard; at-will)
Close burst 2; +9 vs. Fortitude; the target is knocked prone. *Effect:* The geonid closes its shell. While the geonid's shell is closed, its speed is 0, it gains a +5 bonus to all defenses, and it does not have line of effect to any creature other than a creature it has grabbed. The geonid slides a creature it has grabbed into its space. The grabbed creature has line of sight and line of effect only to the geonid. The geonid does not gain its bonus to defenses against the grabbed creature. If the grabbed creature escapes, it appears in a space adjacent to the geonid. The geonid can open its shell as a minor action.

Shell Form
A geonid with its shell closed resembles a boulder. A creature can recognize the geonid as a beast by succeeding on a DC 28 Perception check.

Alignment Unaligned **Languages** Primordial
Skills Stealth +11
Str 19 (+7)   **Dex** 16 (+6)   **Wis** 17 (+6)
Con 14 (+5) **Int** 6 (+1)   **Cha** 9 (+2)

Geonid Lore

Arcana DC 17: During the war between the gods and the primordials, geonids served as guardians and watchers along the hidden pathways that honeycombed the world. Secret caches of weapons, treasure, and sleeping primordial war beasts still lurk in such places, forgotten by all but the geonids that still guard them.

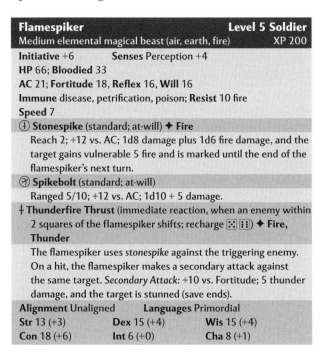

(Left to right) mud lasher, dust devil, tempest wisp, and stormstone fury

Mud Lasher

A CREATURE OF ELEMENTAL EARTH AND WATER, the mud lasher is a vicious brute that delights in drowning its foes.

Mud Lasher	Level 4 Brute
Medium elemental magical beast (earth, water)	XP 175

Initiative +4   **Senses** Perception +9; low-light vision
HP 63; **Bloodied** 31
AC 16; **Fortitude** 17, **Reflex** 15, **Will** 15
Immune disease, poison
Speed 5
⊕ **Slam** (standard; at-will)
   +7 vs. AC; 2d8 + 4 damage.
↯ **Drowning Slam** (standard; encounter)
   +5 vs. Fortitude; 2d8 + 4 damage, and ongoing 5 damage (save ends). *Miss:* Half damage.
↗ **Mud Ball** (standard; at-will)
   Ranged 10; +5 vs. Reflex; the target is slowed (save ends). If the target is already slowed, it is instead immobilized (save ends).
Amorphous Body (immediate reaction, when hit by a melee attack; encounter)
   The mud lasher shifts 3 squares.
Relentless Assault
   A mud lasher gains a +2 bonus to attack rolls against slowed or immobilized creatures.
Alignment Unaligned   **Languages** Primordial
Skills Stealth +9
Str 18 (+6)   **Dex** 15 (+4)   **Wis** 15 (+4)
Con 13 (+3)   **Int** 8 (+1)   **Cha** 11 (+2)

Mud Lasher Lore

Arcana DC 12: A mud lasher buries a victim in shallow mud, then rests atop this crude grave to feast on the slowly rotting corpse. These creatures have no interest in gold, gems, and other riches, but treasure is sometimes interred with their victims.

Rockfist Smasher

ROCKFIST SMASHERS TAKE GREAT PLEASURE in knocking foes to their knees.

Rockfist Smasher	Level 10 Brute
Large elemental magical beast (earth)	XP 500

Initiative +7   **Senses** Perception +11
HP 125; **Bloodied** 62; see also *internal avalanche*
AC 22; **Fortitude** 24, **Reflex** 21, **Will** 21
Immune disease, petrification, poison
Speed 5
⊕ **Granite Punch** (standard; at-will)
   Reach 2; +13 vs. AC; 2d10 + 6 damage, and if the target is bloodied, it is knocked prone.
Internal Avalanche (when first bloodied; encounter)
   The rockfist smasher gains 20 temporary hit points. If it has temporary hit points at the start of its next turn, it loses them and gains 1 action point that it must use during that turn.
Alignment Unaligned   **Languages** Primordial
Str 21 (+10)   **Dex** 15 (+7)   **Wis** 12 (+6)
Con 15 (+7)   **Int** 4 (+2)   **Cha** 15 (+7)

ZOLTAN BOROS & GÁBOR SZIKSZAI

ROCKFIST SMASHER LORE

Arcana DC 16: Capricious and stupid, a rockfist smasher fights its way across a battlefield at random, focusing on a specific target only after it bloodies that foe.

Arcana DC 21: More intelligent creatures of the Elemental Chaos often gather a number of rockfist smashers and keep them in chambers as traps.

SHARDSTORM VORTEX

SHARDSTORMS ARISE IN THE ELEMENTAL CHAOS like blizzards, hurling cutting slices of stone instead of snow. Among these storms lurk shardstorm vortices.

The shardstorm vortex is a scavenger, feeding on the destruction left behind by the battles of its more powerful elemental kin.

Shardstorm Vortex	Level 7 Skirmisher
Medium elemental magical beast (air, earth)	XP 300

Initiative +9   **Senses** Perception +6
Sandblast aura 1; each enemy within the aura takes a -2 penalty to all defenses.
HP 80; **Bloodied** 40
AC 21; **Fortitude** 19, **Reflex** 20, **Will** 19
Immune disease, poison
Speed 0, fly 8 (hover)
⊕ **Abrasive Slam** (standard; at-will)
   +10 vs. Fortitude; 2d8 + 2 damage.
↢ **Whirling Blast** (standard; recharge ⚄ ⚅)
   The shardstorm vortex shifts 4 squares and makes an attack: close burst 1; +10 vs. Reflex; 3d8 + 3 damage, and the vortex pushes the target 1 square. *Miss:* Half damage.

Alignment Unaligned	**Languages** Primordial	
Str 10 (+3)	**Dex** 19 (+7)	**Wis** 16 (+6)
Con 16 (+6)	**Int** 5 (+0)	**Cha** 6 (+1)

Shardstorm Vortex Funnelcloud	Level 13 Minion Skirmisher
Medium elemental magical beast (air, earth)	XP 200

Initiative +14   **Senses** Perception +10
Sandblast aura 1; each enemy within the aura takes a -2 penalty to all defenses.
HP 1; a missed attack never damages a minion.
AC 27; **Fortitude** 24, **Reflex** 26, **Will** 24
Immune disease, poison
Speed 0, fly 8 (hover)
⊕ **Abrasive Slam** (standard; at-will)
   +16 vs. Fortitude; 12 damage.
Vortex Step (move; at-will)
   The shardstorm vortex funnelcloud shifts 4 squares.

Alignment Unaligned	**Languages** Primordial	
Str 11 (+6)	**Dex** 22 (+12)	**Wis** 19 (+10)
Con 19 (+10)	**Int** 5 (+3)	**Cha** 6 (+4)

Shardstorm Vortex Whirlwind	Level 23 Minion Skirmisher
Medium elemental magical beast (air, earth)	XP 1,275

Initiative +21   **Senses** Perception +17
Sandblast aura 1; each enemy within the aura takes a -2 penalty to all defenses.
HP 1; a missed attack never damages a minion.
AC 37; **Fortitude** 35, **Reflex** 36, **Will** 34
Immune disease, poison
Speed 0, fly 8 (hover)
⊕ **Abrasive Slam** (standard; at-will)
   +26 vs. Fortitude; 15 damage.
Vortex Step (move; at-will)
   The shardstorm vortex whirlwind shifts 4 squares.

Alignment Unaligned	**Languages** Primordial	
Str 12 (+12)	**Dex** 27 (+19)	**Wis** 22 (+17)
Con 24 (+18)	**Int** 5 (+8)	**Cha** 6 (+9)

SHARDSTORM VORTEX LORE

Arcana DC 14: The shardstorm vortex is a scavenger from the Elemental Chaos. Though it is rarely the first creature to enter a fight, its potent slam attack makes it a dangerous foe.

STORMSTONE FURY

A STORMSTONE FURY IS A HULKING CREATURE of stone and thunder, both of which it unleashes at the slightest threat.

Stormstone Fury	Level 14 Artillery
Medium elemental magical beast (air, earth)	XP 1,000

Initiative +12   **Senses** Perception +9
HP 113; **Bloodied** 56
AC 26; **Fortitude** 26, **Reflex** 25, **Will** 25
Immune disease, petrification, poison; **Resist** 10 thunder
Speed 6
⊕ **Grinding Stones** (standard; at-will)
   +21 vs. AC; 1d10 + 3 damage.
↗ **Hurtling Thunderstone** (standard; at-will) ✦ **Thunder**
   Ranged 20; +21 vs. AC; 2d8 + 6 damage. *Miss:* Half damage. *Effect:* One square the target currently occupies becomes the origin square of a burst 2 attack that occurs at the start of the stormstone fury's next turn: +19 vs. Fortitude; 1d10 + 6 thunder damage.
↢ **Shrapnel Burst** (minor; recharge ⚃ ⚄ ⚅) ✦ **Thunder**
   Close burst 2; +21 vs. AC; 1d6 + 6 damage plus 1d6 thunder damage, and the stormstone fury pushes the target 2 squares.
Meld to Ground (when first bloodied; requires the stormstone fury to be on the ground; encounter) ✦ **Teleportation**
   The fury disappears, and no creatures have line of sight or line of effect to it. At the start of its next turn, the fury appears within 10 squares of its previous space.

Alignment Unaligned	**Languages** Primordial	
Str 16 (+10)	**Dex** 20 (+12)	**Wis** 15 (+9)
Con 23 (+13)	**Int** 6 (+5)	**Cha** 20 (+12)

STORMSTONE FURY LORE

Arcana DC 18: Stormstone furies are creatures of stone and living thunder. A stormstone fury has no compunction about catching allies with its attacks, so these creatures fight best alongside those resistant to thunder. Dwarves covet thundering weapons crafted from the stone of a stormstone fury's body.

TEMPEST WISP

A TEMPEST WISP SEEKS OUT other creatures it can coerce to its side of a fight, using them as shields as it targets weaker foes.

Tempest Wisp	Level 13 Controller
Medium elemental magical beast (air)	XP 800

Initiative +10   **Senses** Perception +10
HP 134; **Bloodied** 67
AC 27; **Fortitude** 26, **Reflex** 24, **Will** 24
Immune disease, poison; **Resist** insubstantial while not bloodied
Speed 0, fly 7 (hover)
ⓐ **Air Slash** (standard; at-will)
    +16 vs. Reflex; 2d8 + 5 damage.
ⓡ **Whistling Wind** (standard; at-will)
    Ranged 10; +16 vs. Reflex; 2d10 + 3 damage, and the tempest wisp slides the target 1 square.
↗ **Tumbling Updraft** (standard; recharge ⚄ ⚅)
    Ranged 10; +20 vs. Fortitude; the target is lifted up 20 feet (4 squares) and restrained (save ends). *Failed Saving Throw:* The target is lifted up another 20 feet. *Successful Saving Throw:* The target falls and takes falling damage, if applicable.
Alignment Unaligned   **Languages** Primordial
Str 15 (+8)   **Dex** 19 (+10)   **Wis** 19 (+10)
Con 22 (+12)   **Int** 9 (+5)   **Cha** 14 (+8)

TEMPEST WISP LORE

Arcana DC 18: A tempest wisp becomes solid when bloodied. Unlike many elementals, tempest wisps actively ally themselves with other creatures, hoping to stay behind them in battle.

WINDFIEND FURY

A CYCLONE OF MIST AND LIGHTNING, the windfiend fury arcs through the air like a predator.

Windfiend Fury	Level 12 Controller
Large elemental magical beast (air, water)	XP 700

Initiative +11   **Senses** Perception +10
Forceful Zephyr aura 3; the windfiend fury slides each creature that starts its turn within the aura 1 square.
HP 123; **Bloodied** 61
AC 26; **Fortitude** 24, **Reflex** 25, **Will** 24
Immune disease, poison; **Resist** 15 lightning, 15 thunder
Speed 0, fly 8 (hover)
ⓐ **Flying Debris** (standard; at-will)
    Reach 2; +17 vs. AC; 2d8 + 5 damage.
↗ **Lightning Strike** (standard; recharge ⚄ ⚅) ✦ **Lightning**
    Ranged 10; +16 vs. Fortitude; 3d8 + 5 lightning damage, and the target is dazed until the end of the windfiend fury's next turn.
↞ **Storm Burst** (standard; at-will) ✦ **Teleportation, Thunder**
    Close burst 2; +16 vs. Reflex; 1d10 + 5 thunder damage. *Effect:* The windfiend fury teleports to any space adjacent to the burst's area of effect.

(Left to right) geonid, rockfist smasher, shardstorm vortex, and windfiend fury

Alignment Unaligned	**Languages** Primordial	
Str 17 (+9)	**Dex** 21 (+11)	**Wis** 19 (+10)
Con 19 (+10)	**Int** 6 (+4)	**Cha** 16 (+9)

WINDFIEND FURY LORE

Arcana DC 16: As an opponent, the windfiend fury is difficult to pin down. If surrounded in melee, it explodes in a thunderous burst, then re-forms in another place farther away from its foes.

Arcana DC 21: Windfiend furies often accidentally cross the boundaries between planes. Swept up into a great storm on one plane, a windfiend fury can be pulled into a dangerous tempest that rages in another plane. Some archons know a way to imprison windfiend furies within magic vessels, which they then pilot to other planes using the elementals' power.

WINDSTRIKER

WINDSTRIKERS WHIRL OUT OF NOWHERE to hammer foes with potent blasts of thunderous cold.

Their lethal fury comes in fits and starts as their winds seek to enwrap targets before the windstrikers blast them.

Windstriker	Level 9 Lurker
Medium elemental magical beast (air)	XP 400

Initiative +11   **Senses** Perception +9
HP 56; **Bloodied** 28
AC 21; **Fortitude** 22, **Reflex** 20, **Will** 20
Immune disease, poison; **Resist** insubstantial
Speed 0, fly 8 (hover)

ⓘ **Windstrike** (standard; at-will) ✦ **Cold, Thunder**
    Reach 2; +14 vs. AC; 1d8 + 2 cold and thunder damage.

⽮ **Lethal Windstrike** (standard; at-will) ✦ **Cold, Thunder**
    Reach 2; targets the windstriker's quarry (see *searching wind*); +14 vs. AC; 2d12 + 5 cold and thunder damage, and the target is no longer designated as the windstriker's quarry.

➶ **Searching Wind** (standard; recharges when the windstriker hits with *lethal windstrike*) ✦ **Cold, Thunder**
    Ranged 10; +12 vs. Will; 2d6 + 5 cold and thunder damage, and the target is knocked prone. *Effect:* The target is designated as the windstriker's quarry.

Shifting Wind (immediate reaction, when the windstriker takes damage; at-will)
    Until the end of its next turn, the windstriker does not provoke opportunity attacks and can move through enemies' spaces.

Alignment Unaligned	**Languages** Primordial	
Str 14 (+6)	**Dex** 17 (+7)	**Wis** 10 (+4)
Con 20 (+9)	**Int** 5 (+1)	**Cha** 17 (+7)

WINDSTRIKER LORE

Arcana DC 14: A windstriker targets a specific foe with its attacks, trusting its defenses to protect it from opportunity attacks as it whirls across the battlefield.

ENCOUNTER GROUPS

Elementals fight most commonly alongside their own kind, or with other creatures of the Elemental Chaos. Outside that plane, elementals are found as guardians of tombs and treasure-houses, or at locations where they have been summoned by powerful magic.

Level 4 Encounter (XP 875)
✦ 2 clay scouts (level 2 lurker, *MM* 156)
✦ 3 dust devils (level 3 skirmisher)
✦ 1 human mage (level 4 artillery, *MM* 163)

Level 6 Encounter (XP 1,275)
✦ 3 dust devils (level 3 skirmisher)
✦ 2 flamespikers (level 5 soldier)
✦ 1 geonid (level 6 lurker)
✦ 1 mud lasher (level 4 brute)

Level 7 Encounter (XP 1,500)
✦ 4 flamespikers (level 5 soldier)
✦ 1 imp (level 3 lurker, *MM* 63)
✦ 2 magma hurlers (level 4 artillery, *MM* 182)
✦ 1 tiefling heretic (level 5 artillery, *MM* 250)

Level 9 Encounter (XP 2,100)
✦ 3 shardstorm vortices (level 7 skirmisher)
✦ 4 shardstorm vortex funnelclouds (level 13 minion skirmisher)
✦ 1 windstriker (level 9 lurker)

Level 12 Encounter (XP 3,700)
✦ 2 rockfist smashers (level 10 brute)
✦ 2 stormstone furies (level 14 artillery)
✦ 1 windfiend fury (level 12 controller)

Level 15 Encounter (XP 6,400)
✦ 2 chillfire destroyers (level 14 brute)
✦ 1 tempest wisp (level 13 controller)
✦ 1 beholder eye of flame (level 13 elite artillery, *MM* 32)
✦ 4 salamander firetails (level 14 skirmisher, *MM* 226)

FELL TAINT

INSUBSTANTIAL ALIEN PREDATORS from a twisted realm of madness, fell taints kill by generating insanity and despair in their victims. These unnatural horrors slip between worlds where and when the boundaries thin. Their presence alone opens any gap a bit wider, allowing more dreadful entities to pass through.

FELL TAINT LASHER

A TWISTING KNOT OF PREDATORY TENTACLES, a fell taint lasher seizes its prey to feed on the madness it inspires.

Fell Taint Lasher		Level 1 Soldier
Small aberrant magical beast		XP 100

Initiative +3　　　　**Senses** Perception +8
HP 20; **Bloodied** 10
AC 15; **Fortitude** 12, **Reflex** 12, **Will** 14
Resist insubstantial; **Vulnerable** 5 psychic
Speed 1, fly 6 (hover)

ⓐ **Tendril Caress** (standard; at-will) ✦ **Psychic**
　+5 vs. Reflex; 1d6 + 4 psychic damage.

✦ **Tendrils of Stasis** (standard; at-will) ✦ **Psychic**
　+5 vs. Will; 1d4 + 4 psychic damage, and the target is immobilized until the end of the fell taint lasher's next turn.

Fell Taint Feeding (standard; at-will) ✦ **Healing**
　Targets a helpless or unconscious creature; the fell taint lasher loses insubstantial and its fly speed until the end of its next turn, and it makes a coup de grace against the target. If the lasher kills the target, it regains all of its hit points.

Flowing Tendrils (free, when the fell taint lasher makes an opportunity attack; at-will)
　The lasher shifts 1 square.

Alignment Unaligned	**Languages** –	
Str 11 (+0)	**Dex** 12 (+1)	**Wis** 16 (+3)
Con 13 (+1)	**Int** 4 (-3)	**Cha** 10 (+0)

FELL TAINT LASHER TACTICS

A fell taint lasher quickly closes and focuses on one victim. It begins with *tendrils of stasis,* hoping to use its mind-ravaging tendrils on a target that has been immobilized. It uses *flowing tendrils* to gain and maintain flanking.

FELL TAINT PULSAR

A FELL TAINT PULSAR IS AN AMBUSH HUNTER that attempts to disable its prey with a quick attack.

Fell Taint Pulsar		Level 1 Artillery
Small aberrant magical beast		XP 100

Initiative +2　　　　**Senses** Perception +8
HP 18; **Bloodied** 9
AC 12; **Fortitude** 12, **Reflex** 13, **Will** 14
Resist insubstantial; **Vulnerable** 5 psychic
Speed 1, fly 6 (hover)

ⓐ **Tendril Caress** (standard; at-will) ✦ **Psychic**
　+4 vs. Reflex; 1d4 + 3 psychic damage.

ⓡ **Tendril Pulse** (standard; at-will) ✦ **Psychic**
　Ranged 20; +6 vs. Reflex; 2d4 + 3 psychic damage.

⤳ **Tendril Flurry** (standard; recharge ⚄ ⚅) ✦ **Psychic**
　Ranged 10; targets one, two, or three creatures; +4 vs. Reflex; 2d4 + 1 psychic damage.

Fell Taint Feeding (standard; at-will) ✦ **Healing**
　Targets a helpless or unconscious creature; the fell taint pulsar loses insubstantial and its fly speed until the end of its next turn, and it makes a coup de grace against the target. If the pulsar kills the target, it regains all of its hit points.

Alignment Unaligned	**Languages** –	
Skills Stealth +7		
Str 11 (+0)	**Dex** 14 (+2)	**Wis** 16 (+3)
Con 13 (+1)	**Int** 4 (-3)	**Cha** 10 (+0)

FELL TAINT PULSAR TACTICS

Fell taint pulsars start combat with *tendril flurry,* from hiding if possible. Afterward, they prefer to use *tendril pulse* until *tendril flurry* recharges.

FELL TAINT THOUGHT EATER

THE FELL TAINT THOUGHT EATER DOESN'T HESITATE TO take on a group of foes, using its ability to disorient its opponents to target its next meal.

Fell Taint Thought Eater		Level 2 Controller
Small aberrant magical beast		XP 125

Initiative +2　　　　**Senses** Perception +6
HP 26; **Bloodied** 13
AC 14; **Fortitude** 13, **Reflex** 13, **Will** 15
Resist insubstantial; **Vulnerable** 5 psychic
Speed 1, fly 6 (hover)

ⓐ **Tendril Caress** (standard; at-will) ✦ **Psychic**
　+6 vs. Reflex; 1d6 + 5 psychic damage.

⤳ **Spirit Haze** (standard; at-will) ✦ **Psychic**
　Ranged 10; +6 vs. Will; 1d4 + 5 psychic damage, and the target is dazed until the end of the fell taint thought eater's next turn.

↩ **Thought Fog** (standard; recharge ⚄ ⚅) ✦ **Psychic, Charm**
　Close blast 5; targets enemies; +5 vs. Will; the target is slowed (save ends). *First Failed Saving Throw:* The target is immobilized instead of slowed (save ends).

Fell Taint Feeding (standard; at-will) ✦ **Healing**
　Targets a helpless or unconscious creature; the fell taint thought eater loses insubstantial and its fly speed until the end of its next turn, and it makes a coup de grace against the target. If the thought eater kills the target, it regains all of its hit points.

Alignment Unaligned	**Languages** –	
Str 11 (+1)	**Dex** 12 (+2)	**Wis** 10 (+1)
Con 13 (+2)	**Int** 5 (-1)	**Cha** 16 (+4)

FELL TAINT THOUGHT EATER TACTICS

A fell taint thought eater closes and uses *thought fog* on as many enemies as possible. Then it moves back and uses *spirit haze* until *thought fog* recharges.

FELL TAINT WARP WENDER

THE FELL TAINT WARP WENDER SHIFTS about the battlefield, making it difficult for foes to pin it down.

Fell Taint Warp Wender		Level 4 Controller
Medium aberrant magical beast		XP 175
Initiative +5	**Senses** Perception +10	
HP 38; **Bloodied** 19		
AC 18; **Fortitude** 16, **Reflex** 16, **Will** 17		
Resist insubstantial; **Vulnerable** 5 psychic		
Speed 1, fly 6 (hover)		
⊕ **Tendril Caress** (standard; at-will) ✦ **Psychic**		
+8 vs. Reflex; 1d6 + 4 psychic damage.		
⟶ **Psychic Transposition** (standard; at-will) ✦ **Psychic,** **Teleportation**		
Ranged 10; +8 vs. Will; 1d4 + 4 psychic damage, and the target is dazed (save ends). *First Failed Saving Throw:* The fell taint warp wender swaps positions with the target.		
Fell Taint Feeding (standard; at-will) ✦ **Healing**		
Targets a helpless or unconscious creature; the fell taint warp wender loses insubstantial and its fly speed until the end of its next turn, and it makes a coup de grace against the target. If the warp wender kills the target, it regains all of its hit points.		
Alignment Unaligned	**Languages** —	
Str 11 (+2)	**Dex** 16 (+5)	**Wis** 17 (+5)
Con 15 (+4)	**Int** 6 (+0)	**Cha** 12 (+3)

FELL TAINT WARP WENDER TACTICS

A fell taint warp wender attacks foes with *psychic transposition*, keeping as many dazed as possible. If sorely pressed, the warp wender uses a move action to fly up after dazing a foe, making for a bruising fall for an enemy that fails its saving throw.

FELL TAINT LORE

Dungeoneering DC 10: Fell taints are strange, aberrant predators that kill by inflicting madness, feeding on the thoughts and emotions they steal from their foes.

Dungeoneering DC 15: The alien fell taints are only partially real. Although some aspect of them exists in the world, the rest is formed by the minds of those who view them.

Fell taints can live indefinitely without eating. They simply go dormant until a prospective meal comes near.

Fell taints come in a variety of types. Lashers must close to attack. Pulsars lurk in the shadows of high places, unleashing a flurry of mind-wrecking light rays from their eyes when prey is near. Thought eaters freeze their victims, consuming them at their leisure.

Dungeoneering DC 17: Fell taints originate in the alien Far Realm. There they are relatively weak predators, comparable to foxes in the world. They slip through weak points in the planar boundaries, seemingly finding them through instinct. When they come to the world or to other planes, they act as beacons for more deadly beings from their dread home. Their presence alone thins the barriers between planes.

ENCOUNTER GROUPS

Fell taints usually work only with their kind and other aberrant creatures of the Far Realm. Occasionally they are found with nonintelligent beings or undead. These alliances of convenience feature little cooperation and no communication.

Level 1 Encounter (XP 525)
✦ 1 fell taint thought eater (level 2 controller)
✦ 1 fell taint pulsar (level 1 artillery)
✦ 3 fell taint lashers (level 1 soldier)

Level 3 Encounter (XP 750)
✦ 1 fell taint pulsar (level 1 artillery)
✦ 1 fell taint thought eater (level 2 controller)
✦ 3 phantom warriors (level 4 soldier, *MM* 116)

Level 4 Encounter (XP 925)
✦ 2 fell taint pulsars (level 1 artillery)
✦ 1 fell taint thought eater (level 2 controller)
✦ 2 ochre jellies (level 3 elite brute, *MM* 202)

The passions and obsessions of some strong-willed eladrin can drive them even after death. When their physical forms are ruined, their spirits lash out at their slayers.

LINGERER KNIGHT

A LINGERER KNIGHT FIGHTS with dangerous desperation, seeking to accomplish a task undone in life.

Lingerer Knight	Level 16 Elite Soldier
Medium fey humanoid (undead)	XP 2,800

Initiative +17 **Senses** Perception +11; darkvision
Spiraling Despair aura 3; each enemy within the aura takes a -2 penalty to damage rolls and saving throws.
HP 152; **Bloodied** 76; see also *spiritual despondence* and *vestige transformation*
AC 32; **Fortitude** 30, **Reflex** 32, **Will** 29
Resist 10 necrotic; **Vulnerable** 5 radiant
Saving Throws +2 (+5 against charm effects)
Speed 6
Action Points 1
⊕ **Longsword** (standard; at-will) ✦ **Necrotic**
   +23 vs. AC; 1d8 + 5 necrotic damage, and ongoing 5 necrotic damage (save ends).
↓ **Double Attack** (standard; at-will)
   The lingerer knight makes two longsword attacks.
⇐ **Desperate Challenge** (standard; encounter) ✦ **Necrotic**
   Ranged 10; the target is marked until the end of the encounter or until the lingerer knight transforms into a fey-knight vestige. While marked, the target takes 8 necrotic damage whenever it makes an attack that does not include the knight.
⇐ **Spirit-Sword Circle** (standard; recharge ⚄ ⚅) ✦ **Necrotic**
   Close burst 1; +21 vs. Reflex; 2d8 + 7 necrotic damage, and ongoing 5 necrotic damage (save ends).
⇐ **Spiritual Despondence** (when first bloodied) ✦ **Necrotic**
   Close burst 3; targets enemies; no attack roll; 2d6 + 4 necrotic damage.
Fey Step (move; encounter) ✦ **Teleportation**
   The lingerer knight teleports 5 squares.
Vestige Transformation (when the lingerer knight drops to 0 hit points)
   The knight becomes a fey-knight vestige. All effects and conditions on the knight end. The vestige acts on the knight's initiative count.

Alignment Evil	**Languages** Common, Elven
Str 21 (+13)	**Dex** 25 (+15)	**Wis** 17 (+11)
Con 16 (+11)	**Int** 17 (+11)	**Cha** 19 (+12)

Equipment scale armor, longsword

FEY-KNIGHT VESTIGE

A FEY-KNIGHT VESTIGE ENTERS A FRENZY OF RAGE, stabbing with its ghostly sword to inflict terrible wounds.

Fey-Knight Vestige	Level 16 Lurker
Medium fey humanoid (undead)	XP 1,400 or 0 if encountered after lingerer knight

Initiative +19 **Senses** Perception +11; darkvision
Spiraling Despair aura 3; each enemy within the aura takes a -2 penalty to damage rolls and saving throws.
HP 75; **Bloodied** 37
AC 30; **Fortitude** 30, **Reflex** 32, **Will** 29
Resist 15 necrotic, insubstantial; **Vulnerable** 10 radiant
Speed 6, fly 6 (hover), phasing
⊕ **Ghostsword** (standard; at-will) ✦ **Necrotic**
   +19 vs. Fortitude; 1d8 + 5 necrotic damage, and the target grants combat advantage to the fey-knight vestige (save ends).
Combat Advantage ✦ **Necrotic**
   The fey-knight vestige deals 2d8 extra necrotic damage to any target granting combat advantage to it.
Desperate Dash (move; recharge ⚄ ⚅)
   The fey-knight vestige shifts 6 squares.
Fey Step (move; encounter) ✦ **Teleportation**
   The fey-knight vestige teleports 5 squares.

Alignment Evil	**Languages** Common, Elven
Skills Stealth +20	
Str 21 (+13)	**Dex** 25 (+15)	**Wis** 17 (+11)
Con 16 (+11)	**Int** 17 (+11)	**Cha** 19 (+12)

LINGERER FELL INCANTER

SURROUNDED BY A MIASMA OF DESPAIR, a lingerer fell incanter channels its hatred through its magic.

Lingerer Fell Incanter	Level 18 Elite Artillery
Medium fey humanoid (undead)	XP 4,000

Initiative +14 **Senses** Perception +15; darkvision
Spiraling Despair aura 3; each enemy within the aura takes a -2 penalty to damage rolls and saving throws.
HP 130; **Bloodied** 65; see also *vestige transformation*
AC 30; **Fortitude** 30, **Reflex** 31, **Will** 31
Resist 10 necrotic; **Vulnerable** 5 radiant
Saving Throws +2 (+5 against charm effects)
Speed 6
Action Points 1
⊕ **Quarterstaff** (standard; at-will) ✦ **Necrotic**
   +25 vs. AC; 1d8 + 5 necrotic damage, and ongoing 5 necrotic damage (save ends). The lingerer fell incanter also pushes the target 1 square.
↗ **Soul Bolt** (standard; at-will) ✦ **Necrotic**
   Ranged 10; +23 vs. Fortitude; 2d8 + 6 necrotic damage, and the target is immobilized (save ends).
↗ **Double Attack** (standard; at-will)
   The lingerer fell incanter makes two *soul bolt* attacks.
⇐ **Soul Blast** (standard; usable only while bloodied; recharge ⚄ ⚅) ✦ **Necrotic**
   Close blast 3; +21 vs. Fortitude; 2d8 + 8 necrotic damage, and the target is weakened until the end of the lingerer fell incanter's next turn.
Fey Step (move; encounter) ✦ **Teleportation**
   The lingerer fell incanter teleports 5 squares.
Vestige Transformation (when the lingerer fell incanter drops to 0 hit points)
   The fell incanter becomes a fey-incanter vestige. All effects and conditions on the fell incanter end. The vestige acts on the fell incanter's initiative count.

Alignment Evil	**Languages** Common, Elven
Str 13 (+10)	**Dex** 21 (+14)	**Wis** 22 (+15)
Con 16 (+12)	**Int** 23 (+15)	**Cha** 20 (+14)

Equipment quarterstaff

Fey-Incanter Vestige

The fey-incanter vestige thinks nothing of its own survival, wishing only to torment those who destroyed its physical form.

Fey-Incanter Vestige	Level 18 Lurker
Medium fey humanoid (undead)	XP 2,000 or 0 if encountered after lingerer fell incanter

Initiative +17   **Senses** Perception +11; darkvision
Spiraling Despair aura 3; each enemy within the aura takes a -2 penalty to attack rolls and saving throws.
HP 91; **Bloodied** 45
AC 30; **Fortitude** 28, **Reflex** 32, **Will** 30
Resist 15 necrotic, insubstantial; **Vulnerable** 10 radiant
Speed 6, fly 6 (hover), phasing

⊙ **Ray of Humility** (standard; at-will) ✦ **Necrotic**
  Ranged 5; +21 vs. Will; 1d8 + 5 necrotic damage, ongoing 5 necrotic damage, and the target must roll saving throws twice, taking the lower of the two results (save ends both).

⊀ **Ray of Spring's Rejection** (standard; recharge ⚄ ⚅) ✦ **Necrotic**
  Ranged 5; +21 vs. Will; 2d8 + 6 necrotic damage, and the target grants combat advantage to the fey-incanter vestige (save ends).

Combat Advantage ✦ **Necrotic**
  The fey-incanter vestige deals 2d8 extra necrotic damage to any target granting combat advantage to it.

Fey Step (move; encounter) ✦ **Teleportation**
  The fey-incanter vestige teleports 5 squares.

Maniacal Dash (move; recharge ⚄ ⚅)
  The fey-incanter vestige shifts 6 squares.

Alignment Evil		**Languages** Common, Elven
Skills Stealth +20		
Str 13 (+10)	**Dex** 22 (+15)	**Wis** 22 (+15)
Con 16 (+12)	**Int** 26 (+17)	**Cha** 20 (+14)

Fey Lingerer Lore

Arcana or Religion DC 20: Fey lingerers are eladrin knights and wizards who refuse to die. They are not the gracious and mannered eladrin of the fey court, but are twisted and depraved, withdrawn from elven grace. When younger, more vibrant foes challenge the lingerers' strength, they retaliate furiously.

Arcana or Religion DC 25: Fey lingerer knights pine to relive past glories; incanters seek to rediscover lost rituals and spells. When they are destroyed, fey lingerers transform into vengeful incorporeal spirits.

Encounter Groups

Fey lingerers are encountered with other undead, and even with living eladrin loyal to them.

Level 18 Encounter (XP 11,600)
✦ 2 lingerer knights (level 16 elite soldier)
✦ 1 lingerer fell incanter (level 18 elite artillery)
✦ 1 bralani of autumn winds (level 19 controller, MM 102)

Lingerer knight and fell incanter

Large, fierce humanoids of the Feywild, firbolgs live for the hunt. They value independence, courage, and the middle ground between good and evil. They are agents of destiny, death, and the unforgiving wild.

FIRBOLG HOUNDER

A FIRBOLG HOUNDER OPENLY ATTACKS PREY to distract it from the threat posed by the rest of its hunting band.

Firbolg Hounder	Level 11 Soldier
Large fey humanoid	XP 600

Initiative +11   **Senses** Perception +9; low-light vision
HP 113; **Bloodied** 56
Regeneration 5
AC 28; **Fortitude** 24, **Reflex** 23, **Will** 23
Vulnerable necrotic (if the firbolg hounder takes necrotic damage, its regeneration does not function on its next turn)
Saving Throws +2 against charm effects, immobilized, restrained, and slowed
Speed 8

ⓐ **Battleaxe** (standard; at-will) ✦ **Weapon**
Reach 2; +18 vs. AC; 1d12 + 7 damage.

✦ **Drive Prey** (standard; recharges when first bloodied) ✦ **Fear, Weapon**
Reach 2; +17 vs. Fortitude; 2d8 + 7 damage, and the firbolg hounder slides the target 2 squares. The hounder makes a secondary attack. *Secondary Attack:* +15 vs. Will; the target must move or shift away from the hounder with its first action on its next turn or be dazed until the end of that turn.

✦ **Hounding Strike** (standard; at-will) ✦ **Weapon**
Reach 2; +18 vs. AC; 1d12 + 7 damage, and the firbolg hounder slides the target 2 squares.

ⓨ **Handaxe** (standard; at-will) ✦ **Weapon**
Ranged 5/10; +17 vs. AC; 1d8 + 5 damage, and the target is knocked prone.

ⓨ **Moonfire** (minor 1/round; recharge ⚁ ⚂ ⚃)
Ranged 10; +16 vs. Will; until the end of the firbolg hounder's next turn, the target is marked and cannot benefit from invisibility or concealment.

Hunter's Leap
A firbolg hounder doesn't provoke opportunity attacks while jumping.

Alignment Unaligned   **Languages** Common, Elven
Skills Athletics +15, Intimidate +11, Nature +14, Stealth +14
Str 21 (+10)	**Dex** 18 (+9)	**Wis** 18 (+9)
Con 17 (+8)	**Int** 11 (+5)	**Cha** 12 (+6)

Equipment scale armor, light shield, battleaxe, 3 handaxes

FIRBOLG HOUNDER TACTICS

Opening with *moonfire*, the firbolg uses *drive prey* to maneuver a foe into danger. It pursues the enemy, using *hunter's leap* if necessary. The hounder then keeps the battle moving and its allies in advantageous position using *hounding strike*. It throws a handaxe only to bring down elusive prey. If severely wounded, the firbolg hounder might use *drive prey* to disengage and flee.

FIRBOLG HUNTER

THE FIRBOLG HUNTER SPECIALIZES in stalking prey, leaping from hiding to attack after sturdier allies have engaged the enemy.

Firbolg Hunter	Level 12 Skirmisher
Large fey humanoid	XP 700

Initiative +14   **Senses** Perception +16; low-light vision
HP 123; **Bloodied** 61
Regeneration 5
AC 26; **Fortitude** 22, **Reflex** 25, **Will** 24
Vulnerable necrotic (if the firbolg hunter takes necrotic damage, its regeneration does not function on its next turn)
Saving Throws +2 against charm effects, immobilized, restrained, and slowed
Speed 8

ⓐ **Spear** (standard; at-will) ✦ **Weapon**
Reach 2; +17 vs. AC; 1d10 + 6 damage.

ⓨ **Javelin** (standard; at-will) ✦ **Weapon**
Ranged 10/20; +18 vs. AC; 1d8 + 7 damage.

ⓐ/ⓨ **Crippling Strike** (standard; recharges when first bloodied)
The firbolg hunter makes a spear attack or a javelin attack. On a hit, the attack deals 2d6 extra damage, and the target is immobilized (save ends). *Aftereffect:* The target is slowed (save ends).

ⓐ/ⓨ **Mobile Attack** (standard; at-will)
The firbolg hunter moves 8 squares and makes a spear attack or a javelin attack at any point during the move. The hunter doesn't provoke opportunity attacks when moving away from its target or when making the ranged attack.

ⓨ **Moonfire** (minor 1/round; recharge ⚁ ⚂ ⚃)
Ranged 10; +16 vs. Will; until the end of the firbolg hunter's next turn, the hunter's attacks against the target deal 1d6 extra damage, and the target cannot benefit from invisibility or concealment.

Hunter's Leap
A firbolg hunter doesn't provoke opportunity attacks while jumping.

Alignment Unaligned   **Languages** Common, Elven
Skills Athletics +15, Intimidate +12, Nature +16, Stealth +17
Str 18 (+10)	**Dex** 22 (+12)	**Wis** 20 (+11)
Con 19 (+10)	**Int** 12 (+7)	**Cha** 13 (+7)

Equipment leather armor, spear, 3 javelins

FIRBOLG HUNTER TACTICS

The firbolg hunter uses *moonfire* to enhance the effectiveness of its *crippling strike* attack. It uses *hunter's leap* to escape its enemies and maneuver for combat advantage.

FIRBOLG MOON SEER

WHEN BATTLE IS JOINED, the firbolg moon seer calls down darkest fate on the enemy.

Firbolg Moon Seer	Level 14 Controller
Large fey humanoid	XP 1,000

Initiative +11 **Senses** Perception +18; low-light vision
HP 141; **Bloodied** 70
Regeneration 5
AC 28; **Fortitude** 26, **Reflex** 24, **Will** 27
Vulnerable necrotic (if the firbolg moon seer takes necrotic damage, its regeneration does not function on its next turn)
Saving Throws +2 against charm effects, immobilized, restrained, and slowed
Speed 8
⊕ **Moon Mace** (standard; at-will) ✦ **Radiant, Weapon**
  Reach 2; +18 vs. Reflex; 1d10 + 7 radiant damage, and the target is blinded until the start of its next turn.
↗ **Ban of the Raven** (standard; encounter) ✦ **Necrotic, Radiant**
  Ranged 10; +18 vs. Fortitude; 3d8 + 6 necrotic damage, attack rolls against the target can score critical hits on rolls of 18–20, and the target takes 10 extra necrotic damage from a critical hit (save ends both). *Aftereffect:* Attack rolls against the target can score critical hits on rolls of 19–20 (save ends).
↗ **Moonfire** (minor 1/round; recharge ⚄ ⚅)
  Ranged 10; +18 vs. Will; until the end of the firbolg moon seer's next turn, the target grants combat advantage to the moon seer and cannot benefit from invisibility or concealment.
⬟ **Moonstrike** (standard; recharge ⚄ ⚅) ✦ **Charm, Psychic**
  Close burst 5; targets one enemy affected by *moonfire*; +18 vs. Will; 2d8 + 6 psychic damage, and the target is dominated until the end of the firbolg moon seer's next turn.
⬟ **Spirit Hounds** (standard; recharges when first bloodied)
  Close blast 5; targets enemies; +17 vs. Reflex; 2d6 + 6 damage, and the target is slowed and cannot teleport (save ends both).
Alignment Unaligned **Languages** Common, Elven
Skills Arcana +14, Athletics +15, Nature +18, Religion +14
| **Str** 17 (+10) | **Dex** 18 (+11) | **Wis** 23 (+13) |
| **Con** 21 (+12) | **Int** 14 (+9) | **Cha** 15 (+9) |
Equipment leather armor, mace, moon mask

FIRBOLG MOON SEER TACTICS

When battle is joined, the firbolg moon seer targets one foe with *moonfire*, then makes that enemy more vulnerable with *ban of the raven*. The members of the firbolg hunt focus melee attacks on opponents affected by *ban of the raven*. The moon seer targets the largest number of enemies possible with a *spirit hounds* attack. It uses *moonstrike* late in battle—often to force the target to provide cover for the moon seer's escape.

FIRBOLG BLOODBEAR

WITH THE ABILITY TO TRANSFORM into the shape of a fearsome beast, the firbolg bloodbear is a reckless and savage opponent.

Firbolg Bloodbear	Level 15 Elite Brute
Large fey humanoid	XP 2,400

Initiative +12 **Senses** Perception +18; low-light vision
HP 240; **Bloodied** 120; see also *bloodbear form*
Regeneration 5 (10 while in bloodbear form)
AC 27; **Fortitude** 28, **Reflex** 25, **Will** 28
Vulnerable necrotic (if the firbolg bloodbear takes necrotic damage, its regeneration does not function on its next turn)
Saving Throws +2 (+4 against charm effects, immobilized, restrained, and slowed)
Speed 8
Action Points 1
⊕ **Slam** (standard; at-will)
  Reach 2; +18 vs. AC; 2d8 + 9 damage.
⊕ **Claw** (standard; usable only while in bloodbear form; at-will)
  Reach 2; +18 vs. AC; 2d12 + 9 damage.
↓ **Double Attack** (standard; at-will)
  The firbolg bloodbear makes two melee basic attacks. If the bloodbear hits with both attacks, it makes a secondary attack against the target. *Secondary Attack:* +17 vs. Fortitude; the target is grabbed.
↓ **Bloodbear Maul** (standard; recharges when bloodied)
  Reach 2; targets a creature grabbed by the firbolg bloodbear; no attack roll; 4d10 + 9 damage, and if the bloodbear is in bloodbear form, it makes a bite attack against the target as a free action.
↓ **Bite** (standard; usable only while in bloodbear form; at-will)
  +18 vs. AC; 3d12 + 9 damage, and if the target is granting combat advantage to the firbolg bloodbear, the target takes ongoing 10 damage (save ends).
↗ **Moonfire** (minor; recharge ⚄ ⚅)
  Ranged 10; +15 vs. Will; until the end of the firbolg bloodbear's next turn, the target cannot benefit from invisibility or concealment.
Bloodbear Form (when first bloodied; encounter) ✦ **Healing, Polymorph**
  The firbolg bloodbear takes the form of a humanoid-bear hybrid. It regains all of its hit points, gains regeneration 10, and gains bite and claw attacks. When the bloodbear is bloodied a second time, it reverts to its normal form until the end of the encounter.
Alignment Unaligned **Languages** Common, Elven
Skills Athletics +19, Intimidate +13, Nature +18
| **Str** 24 (+14) | **Dex** 20 (+12) | **Wis** 22 (+13) |
| **Con** 20 (+12) | **Int** 12 (+8) | **Cha** 13 (+8) |
Equipment hide armor, bear helmet

FIRBOLG BLOODBEAR TACTICS

Diving into the middle of combat, the firbolg bloodbear concentrates on one foe, attempting to grab that enemy for a *bloodbear maul* in the next round. The firbolg is reckless until it can transform into its bloodbear form. Then it acts like a berserk dire bear—only stronger and tougher—doing its best to use *bloodbear maul* again before it is forced out of bloodbear form.

Firbolg Ghostraven

From on high, this firbolg shapechanger glides into battle in its terrifying spectral form.

Firbolg Ghostraven	Level 16 Elite Lurker
Large fey humanoid	XP 2,800

Initiative +18 **Senses** Perception +18; low-light vision
HP 238; **Bloodied** 119
Regeneration 5
AC 30; **Fortitude** 28, **Reflex** 29, **Will** 28
Vulnerable necrotic (if the firbolg ghostraven takes necrotic damage, its regeneration does not function on its next turn)
Saving Throws +2 (+4 against charm effects, immobilized, restrained, and slowed)
Speed 8
Action Points 1

⊕ **Heavy War Pick** (standard; at-will) ✦ **Weapon**
   Reach 2; +21 vs. AC; 1d12 + 7 damage (crit 2d12 + 19).

‡ **Double Attack** (standard; at-will)
   The firbolg ghostraven makes two heavy war pick attacks. If the ghostraven hits two targets with the attacks, one of the targets of the ghostraven's choice is blinded (save ends).

⟑ **Moonfire** (minor 1/round; recharge ⚄ ⚅ ⚅)
   Ranged 10; +19 vs. Will; until the end of the firbolg ghostraven's next turn, the target cannot benefit from invisibility or concealment.

Ghostraven Form (minor; at-will) ✦ **Polymorph**
   Until the firbolg ghostraven attacks, it gains insubstantial and phasing and gains a fly (clumsy) speed equal to its walk speed. While in dim light or darkness, it has concealment while in this form.

Ghostraven Strike
   When the firbolg ghostraven hits a target that couldn't see the ghostraven at the start of the ghostraven's turn, the attack deals 2d8 extra damage.

Hunter's Flight
   A firbolg ghostraven doesn't provoke opportunity attacks while jumping or when moving at half speed while flying.

Alignment Unaligned **Languages** Common, Elven
Skills Athletics +18, Nature +18, Stealth +19
Str 20 (+13) **Dex** 23 (+14) **Wis** 21 (+13)
Con 17 (+11) **Int** 13 (+9) **Cha** 15 (+10)
Equipment leather armor, raven helmet, heavy war pick

Firbolg Ghostraven Tactics

The ghostraven employs *double attack* against two foes, hoping to blind one. It aims at least one attack per round at a blinded target in order to take advantage of *ghostraven strike*. Failing that, it uses *ghostraven form* to retreat into hiding to prepare another stealthy attack.

Firbolg Master of the Wild Hunt

The firbolg master of the Wild Hunt pursues one foe relentlessly across the field of battle.

Firbolg Master of the Wild Hunt	Level 22 Elite Skirmisher
Large fey humanoid	XP 8,300

Initiative +22 **Senses** Perception +24; low-light vision
HP 404; **Bloodied** 202
Regeneration 10
AC 36; **Fortitude** 33, **Reflex** 35, **Will** 34
Vulnerable necrotic (if the firbolg master of the Wild Hunt takes necrotic damage, its regeneration does not function on its next turn)
Saving Throws +2 (+4 against charm effects, immobilized, restrained, and slowed)
Speed 8, fly 8 (clumsy)
Action Points 1

⊕ **Spear of the Hunt** (standard; at-will) ✦ **Weapon**
   Reach 2; +27 vs. AC; 2d10 + 7 damage.

⟑ **Spear the Prey** (standard; at-will) ✦ **Weapon**
   Ranged 10/20; +27 vs. AC; 2d10 + 7 damage. *Effect:* The firbolg master of the Wild Hunt's spear returns after the master makes the attack.

‡ **Double Attack** (standard; at-will)
   The firbolg master of the Wild Hunt makes two *spear of the hunt* attacks.

‡/⟑ **Mortal Strike** (standard; recharges when first bloodied)
   The firbolg master of the Wild Hunt makes a *spear of the hunt* attack or a *spear the prey* attack against a bloodied enemy. On a hit, the attack becomes a critical hit and deals 6d6 extra damage. If the attack reduces the target to 0 hit points or fewer, the master gains 1 action point.

⟻ **Moonfire** (minor 1/round; at-will)
   Ranged 10; +25 vs. Will; until the end of the firbolg master of the Wild Hunt's next turn, the target is marked, grants combat advantage to the master, and cannot benefit from invisibility or concealment.

Moonhunter
   A firbolg master of the Wild Hunt's attacks deal 2d6 extra damage to a creature affected by *moonfire*.

Alignment Unaligned **Languages** Common, Elven
Skills Acrobatics +25, Athletics +23, Nature +24, Stealth +25
Str 24 (+18) **Dex** 28 (+20) **Wis** 26 (+19)
Con 18 (+15) **Int** 15 (+13) **Cha** 18 (+15)
Equipment light shield, stag helmet, longspear

Firbolg Master of the Wild Hunt Tactics

A firbolg master of the Wild Hunt places *moonfire* upon a foe quickly so that it loses no chance to take advantage of *moonhunter*. It then directs all efforts toward bloodying that foe in order to create the opportunity for a *mortal strike*. A firbolg master of the Wild Hunt can fly, and it does so mostly to avoid dangerous terrain and hazards.

(Left to right) firbolg bloodbear, master of the Wild Hunt, and ghostraven

FIRBOLG LORE

Arcana DC 20: Firbolgs are hunters of the Feywild, the creators and keepers of the Wild Hunt. Small settlements dot firbolg territory in the deep wilderness of the Feywild, perched on precarious heights, dangerous terrain, or floating motes of rock for greater defensibility.

Firbolg society is made up of clans led by the mightiest warriors, usually masters of the Wild Hunt. Clan and family ties are strong among firbolgs.

Arcana DC 25: The firbolgs' religion is centered on three deities: the Maiden (Sehanine), the Mother (Melora), and the Crone (the Raven Queen). As a people, they follow the Maiden's demands that they walk a middle road between good and evil.

Firbolg priests, who are usually female, are called moon seers and are treated with great respect. Seers and elite warriors dedicated to the deities wear masks or helmets that cover their features.

Arcana DC 30: Firbolgs love trophies and treasure, but they value other creatures' promises more than wealth. Firbolgs call a hunt to pursue oath breakers. It is said that a dark ritual can be used to call firbolgs to the world to hunt one who has broken a vow made to the ritual's performer or those the performer represents.

ENCOUNTER GROUPS

Firbolgs respect strength and forthrightness, endurance and skill. Numerous firbolgs serve other fey and mighty nonfey. They also allow others to join in Wild Hunts, which often include firbolg hounders, hunters, and moon seers. The most frightful Wild Hunts are composed of all sorts of fey led by a master of the Wild Hunt and his hounds.

Level 13 Encounter (XP 4,300)
✦ 2 centaur hunters (level 12 artillery)
✦ 2 firbolg hounders (level 11 soldier)
✦ 1 firbolg hunter (level 12 skirmisher)
✦ 1 firbolg moon seer (level 14 controller)

Level 22 Encounter (XP 22,700)
✦ 1 firbolg bloodbear (level 15 elite brute)
✦ 2 firbolg ghostravens (level 16 elite lurker)
✦ 1 firbolg master of the Wild Hunt (level 22 elite skirmisher)
✦ 2 Wild Hunt hounds (level 21 skirmisher, MM 161)

FOMORIAN

When the Feywild was young, it mirrored many aspects of the world, both foul and benign. Fomorians arose as dark reflections of the massive titans. To this day, these twisted giants continue to inhabit the Underdark of the Feywild. Their beautiful caverns house numerous eladrin slaves, cyclops followers, and other fey that have been turned to evil ways.

FOMORIAN GHOST SHAMAN

Generating a mist of darkness, the fomorian ghost shaman manipulates its foes like puppets.

Fomorian Ghost Shaman	Level 16 Elite Controller
Huge fey humanoid (giant)	XP 2,800

Initiative +11 **Senses** Perception +10; darkvision, truesight 6

Aura of Eyes aura 3; each enemy within the aura takes a -3 penalty to attack rolls against the fomorian ghost shaman and cannot shift or charge.

HP 312; **Bloodied** 156

AC 30; **Fortitude** 28, **Reflex** 26, **Will** 30

Saving Throws +2

Speed 8

Action Points 1

⊕ **Death's Touch** (standard; at-will)
Reach 3; +20 vs. Fortitude; 4d4 + 5 necrotic damage, and the target is slowed (save ends).

↗ **Evil Eye** (minor 1/round; at-will)
Ranged 5; +20 vs. Reflex; the target gains ongoing 10 necrotic damage (save ends).

↞ **Spirits of Possession** (standard; at-will) ✦ **Charm**
Close blast 3; targets creatures that have ongoing necrotic damage; +20 vs. Will; the target is dominated (save ends).

✷ **Darksoul Mist** (standard; recharge ⚄ ⚅ ⚃) ✦ **Zone**
Area burst 2 within 10; +20 vs. Fortitude; 2d8 + 7 necrotic damage, and the target is slowed (save ends). *Effect:* The burst creates a zone of darkness that lasts until the end of the encounter. The zone blocks line of sight for any creature without darkvision.

Alignment Evil		**Languages** Elven
Str 13 (+9)	**Dex** 17 (+11)	**Wis** 15 (+10)
Con 20 (+13)	**Int** 16 (+11)	**Cha** 24 (+15)

FOMORIAN GHOST SHAMAN TACTICS

A fomorian ghost shaman lurks just behind the front-line warriors, using its *evil eye* on its foes and then dominating them with *spirits of possession*.

FOMORIAN CACKLER

A fomorian cackler is a sly assassin that finds evil glee in sinking its daggers into an enemy's heart.

Fomorian Cackler	Level 17 Elite Lurker
Huge fey humanoid (giant)	XP 3,200

Initiative +17 **Senses** Perception +17; truesight 6

Cackling Depravity aura 1; each enemy within the aura takes a -2 penalty to Will.

HP 262; **Bloodied** 131

AC 31; **Fortitude** 30, **Reflex** 28, **Will** 27

Saving Throws +2

Speed 8

Action Points 1

⊕ **Disembowel** (standard; at-will) ✦ **Weapon**
Reach 3; +22 vs. AC; 2d8 + 7 damage.

↗ **Evil Eye** (minor; at-will)
Ranged 5; +20 vs. Will; the target treats the fomorian cackler as invisible (save ends).

Fomorian ghost shaman

Heartseeking Daggers (standard; at-will) ✦ **Weapon**
Ranged 10; targets one or two creatures; +22 vs. AC; 2d8 + 7 damage. *Effect:* The daggers return to the fomorian cackler after it makes the attack.

Invisible Mania
A fomorian cackler's attacks deal 4d6 extra damage against a creature that cannot see the cackler.

Size Alteration (minor; at-will)
The fomorian cackler changes its size to Medium and the cackler's reach for *disembowel* becomes 1. The cackler can use a minor action to return to its normal size and regain its normal reach.

Alignment Evil	**Languages** Elven	
Skills Bluff +14, Stealth +18		
Str 24 (+15)	**Dex** 21 (+13)	**Wis** 19 (+12)
Con 23 (+14)	**Int** 15 (+10)	**Cha** 13 (+9)
Equipment 2 daggers		

FOMORIAN CACKLER TACTICS

A fomorian cackler prefers to ambush enemies from places where a fomorian could not normally fit. It uses *evil eye* to render itself invisible to one or two targets, then concentrates its attacks on those foes to take advantage of *invisible mania*.

FOMORIAN TOTEMIST

FESTOONED WITH A CHAIN OF SEVERED HEADS, a fomorian totemist wields evil magic on the battlefield.

Fomorian Totemist	**Level 18 Elite Skirmisher**
Huge fey humanoid (giant, undead)	XP 4,000

Initiative +17 — **Senses** Perception +14; truesight 6
HP 352; **Bloodied** 176
AC 32; **Fortitude** 31, **Reflex** 29, **Will** 29
Saving Throws +2
Speed 8
Action Points 1

⊕ **Chain of Skulls** (standard; at-will) ✦ **Weapon**
Reach 4; +23 vs. AC; 2d8 + 3 damage, and ongoing 5 necrotic damage (save ends).

✦ **Voodoo** (minor 1/round; at-will)
Reach 4; +21 vs. Will; 2d6 psychic damage, and the fomorian totemist chooses one of the following three effects.
Glorious Head: The target is blinded (save ends).
Wasting Head: The target is weakened (save ends).
Bewildering Head: The target must make a melee basic attack against an ally adjacent to it.
Effect: The totemist shifts 1 square after the attack.

⊀ **Evil Eye** (minor; at-will)
Ranged 5; +21 vs. Will; 10 necrotic damage, and the target takes a –2 penalty to saving throws until the end of the fomorian totemist's next turn.

Fresh Rage
A fomorian totemist's first successful attack during its turn deals 5 extra damage.

Alignment Evil	**Languages** Elven	
Str 27 (+17)	**Dex** 22 (+15)	**Wis** 21 (+14)
Con 24 (+16)	**Int** 15 (+11)	**Cha** 23 (+15)
Equipment chain strung with skulls		

(Left to right) fomorian butcher and cackler

113

FOMORIAN TOTEMIST TACTICS

A fomorian totemist never stays still. It uses *evil eye* on the most capable foes, to prevent them from saving against its *voodoo* attacks. If any fey are among its opponents, it focuses its attacks on them.

FOMORIAN BLINDER

THE FOMORIAN BLINDER USES THE POWER of its evil eye to debilitate its foes.

Fomorian Blinder	Level 20 Elite Artillery
Huge fey humanoid (giant)	XP 5,600

Initiative +11   **Senses** Perception +18; truesight 6
HP 296; **Bloodied** 148
AC 32; **Fortitude** 31, **Reflex** 33, **Will** 31
Saving Throws +2
Speed 8
Action Points 1

⊕ **Quarterstaff** (standard; at-will) ✦ **Weapon**
     Reach 3; +27 vs. AC; 1d12 + 10 damage.

⌁ **Evil Eye** (minor; at-will)
     Ranged 10; +25 vs. Fortitude; the target is affected by the fomorian's *evil eye* (save ends). While the target is affected by *evil eye*, whenever the fomorian blinder's attack damages a creature other than the target, the target takes an equal amount of damage. The effect ends if the blinder uses *evil eye* against a different target.

⌁ **Acid Eye** (standard; at-will) ✦ **Acid, Necrotic**
     Ranged 10; targets one or two creatures; +25 vs. Reflex; 2d8 + 9 acid and necrotic damage, and the target cannot use encounter or daily attack powers until the end of the target's next turn.

✳ **Shower of Ichor** (minor; encounter) ✦ **Acid, Necrotic**
     Area burst 2 within 10; +23 vs. Reflex; 2d8 + 9 acid and necrotic damage, and ongoing 10 acid and necrotic damage (save ends).

Alignment Evil	**Languages** Elven	
Str 23 (+16)	**Dex** 12 (+11)	**Wis** 16 (+13)
Con 22 (+16)	**Int** 26 (+18)	**Cha** 23 (+16)

Equipment quarterstaff

FOMORIAN BLINDER TACTICS

A fomorian blinder uses *evil eye* against foes it thinks are most likely to attack it, especially spellcasters. It uses *acid eye* every round, spending an action point to catch bloodied foes within *shower of ichor*.

FOMORIAN BUTCHER

BRUTAL AND RELENTLESS, a fomorian butcher fixates on one opponent, trying to hack the creature to death with its falchion.

(Top to bottom) fomorian blinder and totemist

Fomorian Butcher		Level 22 Elite Brute
Huge fey humanoid (giant)		XP 8,300

Initiative +15   **Senses** Perception +16; truesight 6
HP 514; **Bloodied** 257
AC 34; **Fortitude** 36, **Reflex** 32, **Will** 33
Saving Throws +2
Speed 8
Action Points 1

⊕ **Falchion** (standard; at-will) ✦ **Weapon**
    Reach 3; +25 vs. AC; 4d4 + 14 (crit 12d4 + 24) damage.

⟡ **Evil Eye** (minor; at-will)
    Ranged 5; +23 vs. Will; the target is restrained (save ends).
    The effect ends if the fomorian butcher uses *evil eye* against a
    different target.

Fomorian Brutality
    When the fomorian butcher scores a critical hit against a target
    affected by its *evil eye*, it makes a falchion attack against the
    same target as a free action.

Fomorian Butchery
    A fomorian butcher's falchion attack deals 2d12 + 11 extra
    damage against a creature that the butcher has hit since the
    start of the butcher's last turn.

Alignment Evil	**Languages** Elven	
Str 27 (+20)	**Dex** 19 (+15)	**Wis** 10 (+11)
Con 27 (+20)	**Int** 11 (+11)	**Cha** 20 (+16)

Equipment hide armor, falchion

Fomorian Butcher Tactics

A fomorian butcher charges the most physically
dangerous-looking foe, hewing wildly with its massive
falchion. It then uses its *evil eye* to prevent the enemy
from escaping. It spends an action point to make
another falchion attack when that opponent becomes
bloodied. It concentrates on one foe, trying to do as
much damage as possible with *fomorian butchery*.

Fomorian Lore

Arcana DC 14: Fomorians have a peculiar obsession with the other denizens of the Feywild. They
loathe them passionately, but desire their subjugation,
not their destruction. In their minds, the ideal Feywild is one in which each fomorian lives as royalty,
ruling over all other creatures. For this reason, they
wage an eternal war with the eladrin and other fey,
forever seeking to achieve this impossible goal.

Arcana DC 22: Ghost shamans enslave the spirits
of those they kill. They use these spirits in combat,
but also keep them as sources of amusement, forcing them to dance or play out haunting shadow
plays. These evil giants make frequent forays into the
Shadowfell to discover its secrets.

The totemist takes heads from those it slays and
adds them to its chain of heads. Once it imbues the
heads with necromantic power, its attacks with the
chain of heads can have a different result depending
on which head strikes the foe. Fomorian totemists
often prefer a certain type of head and can become
obsessive about their collections. One might favor
eladrin heads, while another might prefer dwarves
for their long beards. Some totemists select future

victims years before coming to claim their heads,
patiently waiting for their chosen targets to "mature"
and adopt the appearance they can see with their
prescient evil eyes.

Cacklers laugh like mad fools almost constantly,
but a cackler's manic air belies its fiendish mind.
Cacklers are silent only when they seek to be hidden,
and they have extraordinary stealth for their massive height and weight. Due to their ability to change
size, cacklers sometimes adopt magic disguises to
travel among lesser creatures. When they adopt the
disguise of another creature, they easily take on its
mannerisms. Their madness allows them to assume
these other personalities with ease. However, such
personalities remain with the cackler and sometimes
emerge unbidden at later times.

Foul fomorian blinders take the eyes of other
creatures and use them to attack foes. They delight in
carrying these tiny trophies of their victims. Blinders
know the most about fomorians and their culture,
acting as the sages and scholars of their race. It's said
that if any possess the secret to a defense against the
evil eye, a blinder surely knows it.

Arcana DC 27: Fomorian butchers are the most
sadistic among fomorians and have been known to
cut slaves in half simply for the joy of it. Their simple-
minded pleasure in slaughter makes them frequent
targets for recruitment and manipulation by other
creatures. Fomorian butchers often work with devils,
greedily trading their souls and some mysterious
afterlife for the power they desire in the Feywild and
beyond.

Encounter Groups

The fomorians work with other sinister forces of the
Feywild, and with the drow.

Level 15 Encounter (XP 6,600)
✦ 1 drow arachnomancer (level 13 artillery, *MM* 94)
✦ 1 drow blademaster (level 13 elite skirmisher,
   MM 94)
✦ 1 fomorian ghost shaman (level 16 elite controller)
✦ 8 Lolthbound goblin slaves (level 12 minion
   skirmisher)

Level 21 Encounter (XP 16,300)
✦ 1 fomorian butcher (level 22 elite brute)
✦ 1 fomorian cackler (level 17 elite lurker)
✦ 1 fomorian painbringer (level 19 elite controller,
   MM 110)

Level 22 Encounter (XP 23,200)
✦ 1 fomorian blinder (level 20 elite artillery)
✦ 2 fomorian totemists (level 18 elite skirmisher)
✦ 3 fomorian warriors (level 17 elite soldier,
   MM 110)

A PROUD RACE OF HUMANOIDS infused with the energy of the Elemental Chaos, genasi vary in appearance and personality. At home strolling through the corridors of churning energy of the Elemental Chaos, they also delight in the verdant forests of the Feywild and the quaint cities of the world. Among the genasi are hot-blooded fireblades, adventuring skyspies, taciturn stoneshields, and elemental dervishes, which tap the energy of their elemental heritage.

GENASI ELEMENTAL DERVISH

A GRACEFUL MASTER OF THE DOUBLE SWORD, a genasi elemental dervish is equally capable of reaching a foe on land, through water, or in the air.

Genasi Elemental Dervish	Level 18 Elite Skirmisher	
Medium elemental humanoid (air, earth, fire, water)		XP 4,000

Initiative +17   Senses Perception +13
HP 344; Bloodied 172
AC 32; Fortitude 30, Reflex 32, Will 30
Resist 10 cold, 10 fire, 10 lightning
Saving Throws +3
Speed 6, fly 6 (hover), swim 6
Action Points 1

⊕ **Double Sword** (standard; at-will) ✦ Weapon; Varies
  +23 vs. AC; 1d8 + 7 damage, and ongoing 5 damage (save ends) of the type determined by *elemental manifestation*.

✦ **Double Attack** (standard; at-will)
  The genasi elemental dervish makes two double sword attacks.

✦ **Fiery Riposte** (immediate reaction, when the genasi elemental dervish is hit by an enemy adjacent to it; at-will) ✦ Fire
  Targets the triggering enemy; +21 vs. Reflex; the target takes ongoing 10 fire damage (save ends). If the target is already taking ongoing fire damage, that damage increases by 10.

✦ **Primordial Storm** (standard; recharge ⚄ ⚅) ✦ Weapon
  The genasi elemental dervish shifts 6 squares and can move through enemies' spaces. During its movement, the dervish makes the following three attacks in order, each against a different target.
  Promise of Storm (Thunder): +21 vs. Fortitude; 1d8 + 5 thunder damage, and the target gains vulnerable 5 thunder (save ends).
  Earth Shock: +21 vs. Fortitude; 1d8 + 5 damage, and the target is dazed until the end of its next turn.
  Lightning Cut (Lightning): +21 vs. Reflex; 1d8 + 5 lightning damage, and the target gains ongoing 10 lightning damage (save ends).

Elemental Manifestation
  At the start of a genasi elemental dervish's turn, it chooses fire, lightning, or thunder damage. The dervish's double sword attack deals that type of damage until the start of its next turn, when it can choose a different damage type.

Alignment Unaligned   Languages Common, Primordial
Skills Acrobatics +20, Athletics +21, Endurance +21, Intimidate +16, Nature +20

Str 19 (+13)	Dex 24 (+16)	Wis 18 (+13)
Con 20 (+14)	Int 16 (+12)	Cha 15 (+11)

Equipment hide armor, double sword

GENASI ELEMENTAL DERVISH TACTICS

The genasi elemental dervish adapts to its enemies' vulnerabilities. It uses *promise of storm* and *lightning cut* against defenders, and it employs *earth shock* against strikers or mobile foes.

GENASI FIREBLADE

THE GENASI FIREBLADE RUSHES INTO COMBAT, swinging its flaming blade at the nearest enemies.

Genasi Fireblade	Level 11 Brute
Medium elemental humanoid (fire)	XP 600

Initiative +6   Senses Perception +7
HP 139; Bloodied 69
AC 23; Fortitude 25, Reflex 22, Will 21
Resist 10 fire
Speed 6

⊕ **Falchion** (standard; at-will) ✦ Fire, Weapon
  +14 vs. AC; 2d4 + 6 damage (crit 4d4 + 14), and ongoing 5 fire damage (save ends).

✦ **Fiery Riposte** (immediate reaction, when the genasi fireblade is hit by an enemy adjacent to it; at-will) ✦ Fire
  Targets the attacker; +13 vs. Reflex; the target takes ongoing 5 fire damage (save ends). If the target is already taking ongoing fire damage, that damage increases by 5.

⬳ **Fan the Flames** (standard; recharge ⚄ ⚅) ✦ Fire
  Close burst 1; +12 vs. Reflex; the target takes ongoing 5 fire damage (save ends), and the target takes a -2 penalty to saving throws against ongoing fire damage until the end of the encounter.

Alignment Unaligned   Languages Common, Primordial
Skills Endurance +18, Intimidate +10

Str 22 (+11)	Dex 13 (+6)	Wis 15 (+7)
Con 19 (+9)	Int 17 (+8)	Cha 11 (+5)

Equipment hide armor, falchion

GENASI FIREBLADE TACTICS

The genasi fireblade positions itself among several enemies and uses *fan the flames* to give enemies penalties to saving throws against fire. It uses *fiery riposte* at each opportunity. If an enemy has resistance to fire, the genasi fireblade seeks other, more susceptible targets.

GENASI HYDROMANCER

THE GENASI SHARE A BOND with the essence of elemental matter. The hydromancer learns to manipulate that bond, using magic to transform itself into a being of pure water and then back to solid form.

Genasi Hydromancer — Level 8 Controller
Medium elemental humanoid (water) — XP 350

Initiative +7 **Senses** Perception +5
HP 91; **Bloodied** 45
AC 22; **Fortitude** 21, **Reflex** 20, **Will** 20
Speed 6, swim 8
Saving Throws +2 against ongoing damage

⊕ **Scimitar** (standard; at-will) ✦ **Weapon**
+13 vs. AC; 2d8 + 4 damage (crit 1d8 + 20).

⊗ **Wave Bolt** (standard; at-will)
Ranged 5; +13 vs. AC; 2d6 + 4 damage, and the genasi hydromancer slides the target 3 squares.

┼ **Drowning Touch** (standard; recharges when the target saves against this attack's ongoing damage or when it drops to 0 hit points or fewer)
+12 vs. Fortitude; the target is dazed and takes ongoing 10 damage (save ends both).

⬳ **Whirling Vortex** (standard; recharge ⚄ ⚅)
Close burst 2; targets enemies; +12 vs. Reflex; 2d8 + 6 damage, and the genasi hydromancer slides the target 3 squares.

Liquid Body (immediate interrupt, when hit by an enemy's attack; recharges when first bloodied)
The genasi hydromancer takes half damage from the triggering attack.

Swift Current (move; encounter)
The genasi hydromancer shifts 6 squares. During its movement, the hydromancer can move through enemy-occupied spaces, move across liquid, and ignore difficult terrain and hazardous terrain effects.

Alignment Unaligned **Languages** Common, Primordial
Skills Acrobatics +12, Arcana +10, Stealth +12
Str 14 (+6) **Dex** 16 (+7) **Wis** 13 (+5)
Con 19 (+8) **Int** 13 (+5) **Cha** 17 (+7)
Equipment robes, scimitar

Genasi Hydromancer Tactics

Genasi hydromancers rely on *swift current* and *liquid body* to allow them to dart into the middle of a group of enemies before unleashing *whirling vortex* to scatter foes. The hydromancer saves *drowning touch* for its deadliest foe, channeling water into the target's lungs to slay him or her.

Genasi Skyspy

A genasi skyspy uses its ability to fly for short distances to engage in hit-and-run attacks, doing as much damage as possible with its short swords before retreating to attack again elsewhere.

Genasi Skyspy — Level 7 Skirmisher
Medium elemental humanoid (air) — XP 300

Initiative +9 **Senses** Perception +9
HP 78; **Bloodied** 39
AC 20; **Fortitude** 19, **Reflex** 20, **Will** 17
Resist 5 cold
Speed 6; see also *sky jaunt*

⊕ **Short Sword** (standard; at-will) ✦ **Weapon**
+12 vs. AC; 1d6 + 4 damage, and the genasi skyspy shifts 1 square.

┼ **Swiftwind Strike** (standard; requires combat advantage against the target; at-will)
The genasi skyspy makes two short sword attacks against one target.

⬳ **Manifest Whirlwind** (standard; encounter)
Close burst 2; +10 vs. Reflex; 2d6 + 3 damage, and the target is pushed 1 square and knocked prone.

Feather-Footed
A genasi skyspy has a +2 bonus to AC against opportunity attacks.

Sky Jaunt (minor; recharge ⚄ ⚅ ⚅)
Until the end of its turn, the genasi skyspy gains a fly speed equal to its speed and can hover.

Alignment Unaligned **Languages** Common, Primordial
Skills Acrobatics +12, Endurance +7, Nature +6, Stealth +12
Str 17 (+6) **Dex** 18 (+7) **Wis** 12 (+4)
Con 14 (+5) **Int** 13 (+4) **Cha** 11 (+3)
Equipment leather armor, 2 short swords

Genasi Skyspy Tactics

The genasi skyspy engages targets and then retreats before becoming mired in combat. It capitalizes on combat advantage by moving in and striking twice with its short swords before shifting away. A skyspy that becomes locked in combat uses *manifest whirlwind* to knock enemies back, creating opportunities for escape.

Genasi Stoneshield

Immovable defender of its allies, the genasi stoneshield strides among its enemies, dealing blows with its heavy war pick.

Genasi Stoneshield — Level 10 Soldier
Medium elemental humanoid (earth) — XP 500

Initiative +8 **Senses** Perception +6
HP 106; **Bloodied** 53
AC 26; **Fortitude** 24, **Reflex** 21, **Will** 20
Saving Throws +1
Speed 5

⊕ **Heavy War Pick** (standard; at-will) ✦ **Weapon**
+17 vs. AC; 1d12 + 5 damage (crit 1d12 + 17), and the target is marked (save ends). While marked by the genasi stoneshield, the target takes a –5 penalty to damage rolls against the stoneshield's allies.

┼ **Mighty Bull Rush** (standard; at-will)
+14 vs. Fortitude; 2d6 + 5 damage, the genasi stoneshield pushes the target 1 square and shifts into the space the target left.

⬳ **Earth Shock** (minor; encounter)
Close burst 2; targets enemies; +12 vs. Fortitude; the target is knocked prone.

Stone Roots
When an effect pulls, pushes, or slides a genasi stoneshield, the stoneshield moves 1 square less than the effect specifies. Also, a stoneshield cannot be knocked prone.

Alignment Unaligned **Languages** Common, Primordial
Skills Athletics +15, Endurance +16, Intimidate +11, Nature +6
Str 20 (+10) **Dex** 12 (+6) **Wis** 12 (+6)
Con 18 (+9) **Int** 14 (+7) **Cha** 13 (+6)
Equipment plate armor, heavy war pick

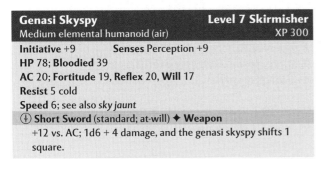

(Left to right) genasi stoneshield, skyspy, elemental dervish, and fireblade

GENASI STONESHIELD TACTICS

The genasi stoneshield enters combat with *mighty bull rush* and then marks its enemies on subsequent turns with its heavy war pick attacks. The stoneshield pursues fleeing enemies, or knocks enemies down with *earth shock*.

GENASI LORE

Arcana DC 10: Genasi have five types of manifestation: airsoul, earthsoul, firesoul, thundersoul, and watersoul. A genasi can usually manifest only one type. Each manifestation bestows different powers and resistances.

Genasi share personality traits based on their manifestations. Typically, airsouls are fickle and capricious, earthsouls are stoic and cautious, firesouls are temperamental and impulsive, thundersouls are bold and proud, and watersouls are amenable and friendly.

Arcana DC 16: Some genasi can change their elemental manifestations or manifest multiple elements. Genasi can channel their elemental manifestations through their weapons, creating blades of fire, ice, or lightning.

Arcana DC 21: Genasi were originally servants of djinns, efreets, and other primordials. In the Elemental Chaos, many genasi still serve primordials. During the war between the deities and the primordials, genasi rebelled and gained freedom. The primordials created archons to replace them.

ENCOUNTER GROUPS

Genasi sometimes accompany other natives of the Elemental Chaos: archons, djinns, efreets, and elementals. Otherwise, they roam far and wide.

Level 8 Encounter (XP 1,800)
- ✦ 3 genasi skyspies (level 7 skirmisher)
- ✦ 3 hippogriff dreadmounts (level 5 soldier, *MM* 146)
- ✦ 1 shardstorm vortex (level 7 skirmisher)

Level 10 Encounter (XP 2,700)
- ✦ 2 genasi fireblades (level 11 brute)
- ✦ 2 genasi stoneshields (level 10 soldier)
- ✦ 1 magma strider (level 10 skirmisher, *MM* 182)

Level 19 Encounter (XP 12,800)
- ✦ 2 genasi elemental dervishes (level 18 elite skirmisher)
- ✦ 1 storm archon squallshield (level 17 soldier)
- ✦ 1 storm archon tempest weaver (level 21 artillery)

GHOST LEGIONNAIRE

SLAIN IN LONG-AGO BATTLES, these soldiers fight for forgotten causes, distant memories, or a fierce loyalty to each other. Although they appear as separate soldiers, their spirits have fused into a single entity that lives and dies as a single soul. Enemies that know of the battles ghost legionnaires once fought can use that knowledge to their own advantage.

GHOST LEGIONNAIRE LORE

Religion DC 18: The ghost legionnaire has the power to possess others and force them to relive the ghost's last few moments on the battlefield. While possessed, the target can see, hear, and feel everything the ghost legionnaire experienced. The possessed creature even appears to have the same wounds that the ghost legionnaire suffered.

Religion DC 23: When wounded, legionnaires display wounds and battle damage from the fight that killed them originally, no matter what type of damage they currently take.

ENCOUNTER GROUPS

Ghost legionnaires are occasionally recruited by other undead, particularly if they fell in the same battle.

Level 15 Encounter (XP 6,000)
- ✦ 5 ghost legionnaires (level 13 soldier)
- ✦ 1 human lich wizard (level 14 elite controller, *MM* 176)

Ghost Legionnaire	Level 13 Soldier
Medium natural humanoid (undead)	XP 800

Initiative +13   **Senses** Perception +6
HP 100; **Bloodied** 50; see also *soul link*
AC 30; **Fortitude** 28, **Reflex** 26, **Will** 27
Resist 10 necrotic
Speed 6

⊕ **Devastating Cut** (standard; at-will)
  +19 vs. AC; 2d8 + 6 damage.

⊛ **Ghost Arrow** (standard; at-will) ✦ **Necrotic**
  Ranged 10/20; +17 vs. AC; 1d10 + 6 necrotic damage.

⤳ **Battle Visions** (standard; encounter) ✦ **Psychic, Reliable**
  Ranged 10/20; +16 vs. Will; 2d8 + 6 psychic damage, and the target is deafened and dominated (save ends both). While the target is dominated, the ghost legionnaire merges with the target, disappearing from sight. The legionnaire cannot attack or be attacked during this time. When the target saves, the legionnaire appears in a square adjacent to the target. Until the end of the encounter, the target gains a +5 bonus to History checks for *call of history*.

Soul Link
  At the start of the encounter, ghost legionnaires' hit points combine into one sum. Damage to a legionnaire deducts from that total. When that total is reduced to 0, all legionnaires are destroyed simultaneously.

Call of History
  Any character can make a DC 25 History check as a minor action to attempt to learn more about the ghost legionnaire. If the check succeeds, the legionnaire gains vulnerable 10 to that character's next attack.

Alignment Unaligned		**Languages** Common
Skills Acrobatics +16, Athletics +18		
Str 25 (+13)	**Dex** 21 (+11)	**Wis** 11 (+6)
Con 18 (+10)	**Int** 11 (+6)	**Cha** 26 (+14)

RALPH HORSLEY

Giants inhabit the various climates of the world and elsewhere. From the tallest peak to the frozen tundra, from the Feywild to the Shadowfell, these hulking creatures thrive.

Eldritch Giant

Eldritch giants come from a different time—an earlier age when the primordials made the world. Although fashioned from fire, stone, and storm, the primordials' wondrous creation was heavily invested with magic, and the eldritch giants aided their primordial lords in the world's formation. Although their powers have ebbed since those days, eldritch giants remember their ancient mastery of magic and forever seek to regain it.

Eldritch Giant	Level 18 Skirmisher
Large fey humanoid (giant)	XP 2,000

Initiative +12 **Senses** Perception +20; low-light vision
HP 171; **Bloodied** 85
AC 32; **Fortitude** 29, **Reflex** 31, **Will** 33
Resist 10 force
Saving Throws +5 against charm effects
Speed 8, teleport 6

⊕ **Eldritch Blade** (standard; at-will) ✦ **Force, Weapon**
Reach 2; +21 vs. Reflex; 3d6 + 7 force damage.

⊙ **Force Missile** (standard; at-will) ✦ **Force**
Ranged 20; +21 vs. Reflex; 2d6 + 7 force damage.

↙ **Sweeping Sword** (standard; encounter) ✦ **Force, Weapon**
Close blast 2; +21 vs. AC; 3d6 + 7 force damage, and the target is knocked prone. *Special*: When charging, the eldritch giant can use this power in place of a melee basic attack.

Consume Magic (minor 1/round; at-will)
Targets an adjacent conjuration or zone created by an enemy; +21 vs. the Will of the creator of the conjuration or zone; the conjuration or zone is destroyed, and its effects end. The eldritch giant's attacks deal 3d6 extra force damage until the end of its next turn.

Eldritch Field (minor; recharge ⚄ ⚅) ✦ **Zone**
Close blast 5; the blast creates a zone of rippling magic that lasts until the end of the encounter or until the eldritch giant uses this power again. The zone is difficult terrain, and the giant's attacks deal 1d6 extra force damage against creatures within the zone.

Alignment Evil **Languages** Elven, Giant
Skills Arcana +21, Insight +20
Str 21 (+14)	Dex 12 (+10)	Wis 22 (+15)
Con 19 (+13)	Int 24 (+16)	Cha 13 (+10)

Eldritch Giant Tactics

When combat begins, the eldritch giant creates its eldritch blade—a sword of pure force—as a free action. The giant charges in with *sweeping sword*, thereafter teleporting about the battlefield. It tries to make every attack with combat advantage, resorting to *force missile* only against those who evade it in melee.

Eldritch Titan	Level 21 Elite Skirmisher
Huge fey humanoid (giant)	XP 6,400

Initiative +12 **Senses** Perception +22; low-light vision
HP 394; **Bloodied** 197
AC 35; **Fortitude** 32, **Reflex** 34, **Will** 36
Resist 10 force
Saving Throws +2 (+7 against charm effects)
Speed 8, teleport 6
Action Points 1

⊕ **Eldritch Hammer** (standard; at-will) ✦ **Force, Weapon**
Reach 3; +26 vs. AC; 3d8 + 7 force damage.

⊙ **Force Ram** (standard; at-will) ✦ **Force**
Ranged 20; +24 vs. Reflex; 2d8 + 8 force damage, and the eldritch titan pushes the target 5 squares.

‡ **Eldritch Fury** (standard; at-will)
The eldritch titan makes two *eldritch hammer* attacks. *Special*: When charging, the titan can use this power in place of a melee basic attack.

↙ **Force Hammer** (standard; encounter) ✦ **Force, Weapon**
Close blast 3; +24 vs. Fortitude; 3d8 + 8 force damage, and the target is pushed 3 squares and knocked prone. *Miss*: Half damage, and eldritch titan pushes the target 3 squares.

Consume Magic (minor 1/round; at-will)
Targets an adjacent conjuration or zone created by an enemy; +21 vs. the Will of the creator of the conjuration or zone; the conjuration or zone is destroyed, and its effects end. The eldritch titan's attacks deal 3d8 extra force damage until the end of its next turn.

Eldritch Field (minor; recharge ⚄ ⚅) ✦ **Zone**
Close blast 5; the blast creates a zone of rippling magic that lasts until the end of the encounter or until the eldritch titan uses this power again. The zone is difficult terrain, and the giant's attacks deal 1d8 extra force damage against creatures within the zone.

Alignment Evil **Languages** Elven, Giant
Skills Arcana +23, Insight +22
Str 23 (+16)	Dex 10 (+10)	Wis 24 (+17)
Con 21 (+15)	Int 26 (+18)	Cha 16 (+13)
Equipment warhammer

Eldritch Titan Tactics

An eldritch titan bathes an area in *eldritch field* at the start of a fight, then makes a *force hammer* attack to knock as many of its foes prone as it can. It uses its *eldritch fury* attacks as often as possible.

ELDRITCH GIANT LORE

Arcana DC 20: Eldritch giants dwell near fonts of magical power. They guard such places jealously, leaving them only to seek out more magical power, such as an artifact or a piece of lost knowledge. Eldritch titans lord over their lesser kin, jealously guarding the greatest items and secrets of magic for themselves.

Arcana DC 25: An eldritch giant's skin is tattooed with magical patterns that protect it and allow it to absorb conjurations and zones to bolster its attacks. These patterns also grant the giant the ability to teleport on flows of arcane energy. A particular eldritch giant or titan might have access to other magical powers, as well as rituals and magic items.

ENCOUNTER GROUPS

Eldritch giants can occasionally be found with other magic users, but they are unreliable allies. They prefer magical servants and delight in enslaving weaker creatures.

Level 18 Encounter (XP 10,600)
- ✦ 3 eldritch giants (level 18 skirmisher)
- ✦ 1 prismatic chaos shard (level 16 artillery)
- ✦ 2 blue slaads (level 17 brute, *MM* 238)

Level 23 Encounter (XP 25,900)
- ✦ 2 eldritch titans (level 21 elite skirmisher)
- ✦ 2 nothic eyes of Vecna (level 22 lurker)
- ✦ 1 phoenix (level 19 elite brute, *MM* 220)

FROST GIANT

FROST GIANTS LIVE IN BITTER NORTHERN LANDS and among frigid mountains where they subsist by hunting and raiding. They are brutal, superstitious, and murderous creatures among whom only might makes right.

Frost Giant	Level 17 Brute
Large elemental humanoid (cold, giant)	XP 1,600

Initiative +11 **Senses** Perception +13
HP 201; **Bloodied** 100; see also *dying swipe*
AC 29; **Fortitude** 32, **Reflex** 27, **Will** 28
Resist 15 cold
Speed 8 (ice walk)
⊕ **Icy Greataxe** (standard; at-will) ✦ **Cold, Weapon**
　　Reach 2; +20 vs. AC; 4d6 + 7 (crit 8d6 + 31) cold damage.
ⴕ **Dying Swipe** (when the frost giant drops to 0 hit points)
　　The frost giant makes an *icy greataxe* attack.
ⴕ **Chilling Strike** (standard; recharge ⚄ ⚅) ✦ **Cold, Weapon**
　　Reach 2; +20 vs. AC; 2d6 + 7 cold damage, and the target gains vulnerable 10 cold (save ends).
⤳ **Icy Handaxe** (standard; at-will) ✦ **Cold, Weapon**
　　Ranged 5/10; +20 vs. AC; 2d8 + 7 cold damage.
Icebound Footing
　　When an effect pulls, pushes, or slides a frost giant, the giant moves 2 squares less than the effect specifies. Also, a frost giant can make a saving throw to avoid being knocked prone.

Alignment Evil	**Languages** Giant

Skills Athletics +19
Str 23 (+14)　　**Dex** 16 (+11)　　**Wis** 20 (+13)
Con 21 (+13)　　**Int** 10 (+8)　　**Cha** 12 (+9)
Equipment hide armor, greataxe, 3 handaxes

FROST GIANT TACTICS

A frost giant prefers to charge into melee with an *icy greataxe* attack. It follows up with *chilling strike*. It throws an *icy handaxe* only when it has no other options.

(Left to right) frost giant ice shaper, frost titan, and frost giant

Frost Giant Ice Shaper — Level 19 Controller (Leader)

Large elemental humanoid (cold, giant) — XP 2,400

Initiative +12   **Senses** Perception +16
HP 182; **Bloodied** 91
AC 32; **Fortitude** 32, **Reflex** 29, **Will** 33
Resist 15 cold
Speed 8 (ice walk)

ⓘ **Freezing Flail** (standard; at-will) ✦ **Cold, Weapon**
Reach 2; +24 vs. AC; 2d12 + 4 cold damage.

➵ **Freezing Bolt** (standard; at-will) ✦ **Cold**
Ranged 20; +22 vs. Reflex; 2d12 + 4 cold damage, and the target is immobilized (save ends).

➵ **Ice Slide** (minor 1/round; at-will)
Ranged 10; +22 vs. Fortitude; the frost giant ice shaper slides the target 3 squares.

❄ **Wall of Frost** (standard; recharge ▣) ✦ **Cold, Conjuration**
Area wall 12 within 10; the frost giant ice shaper conjures a wall of swirling snow that lasts until the end of the ice shaper's next turn. The wall is 6 squares high and blocks line of sight. The wall's space is lightly obscured and is difficult terrain. A creature that starts its turn adjacent to the wall takes 5 cold damage, and a creature that enters a square of the wall or starts its turn there takes 15 cold damage. *Sustain Minor:* The wall persists.

Ice Armor (standard; recharge ⚅ ▣)
One ally within 10 squares of the frost giant ice shaper gains resist 10 to all damage until the end of the ice shaper's next turn.

Icebound Footing
When an effect pulls, pushes, or slides a frost giant ice shaper, the ice shaper moves 2 squares less than the effect specifies. Also, an ice shaper can make a saving throw to avoid being knocked prone.

Alignment Evil   **Languages** Giant, Primordial
Skills Arcana +14, Heal +21, Intimidate +20
Str 21 (+14)   **Dex** 16 (+12)   **Wis** 25 (+16)
Con 22 (+15)   **Int** 10 (+9)   **Cha** 22 (+15)
Equipment chainmail, flail

Frost Giant Ice Shaper Tactics

A frost giant ice shaper uses *wall of frost* to divide the battlefield favorably. It then uses *ice slide* and *freezing bolt* attacks to move its enemies into advantageous positions and keep them there. The ice shaper uses *ice armor* on whichever ally provides the most protection.

Frost Titan — Level 20 Elite Brute

Huge elemental humanoid (cold, giant) — XP 5,600

Initiative +14   **Senses** Perception +16
Fimbulwinter Breath (Cold) aura 2; enemies treat the aura's area as difficult terrain. Each enemy that starts its turn within the aura takes 5 cold damage.
HP 466; **Bloodied** 233; see also *furious swipe*
AC 32; **Fortitude** 34, **Reflex** 29, **Will** 33
Resist 15 cold
Saving Throws +2
Speed 8 (ice walk)
Action Points 1

ⓘ **Icy Greataxe** (standard; at-will) ✦ **Cold, Weapon**
Reach 3; +23 vs. AC; 2d8 + 9 (crit 4d8 + 25) cold damage, and ongoing 10 cold damage (save ends).

✦ **Furious Swipe** (free, when first bloodied and again when the frost titan drops to 0 hit points)
The titan makes an *icy greataxe* attack.

✦ **Cold-Blooded Kick** (minor 1/round; at-will)
Reach 3; +21 vs. Reflex; 1d8 + 9 damage, and the target is pushed 2 squares and knocked prone.

➵ **Ice Bolts** (standard; recharge ⚄ ▣)
Ranged 20; targets one or two creatures; +21 vs. Fortitude; 1d8 + 9 cold damage, and the target is slowed (save ends).

↢ **Blast of Winter** (standard; encounter)
Close blast 5; +21 vs. Reflex; 3d8 + 6 cold damage, ongoing 10 cold damage (save ends), and the target is immobilized until the end of the frost titan's next turn. *Miss:* Half damage.

Glacial Footing
When an effect pulls, pushes, or slides a frost titan, the titan moves 4 squares less than the effect specifies. Also, a frost titan can make a saving throw to avoid being knocked prone.

Alignment Evil   **Languages** Giant, Primordial
Skills Athletics +24
Str 28 (+19)   **Dex** 19 (+14)   **Wis** 23 (+16)
Con 23 (+16)   **Int** 12 (+11)   **Cha** 16 (+13)
Equipment greataxe

Frost Titan Tactics

Initially, a frost titan unleashes *blast of winter*. It then uses *cold-blooded kick* and *icy greataxe* attacks to drive foes before it. A frost titan prefers melee, and it uses *ice bolts* and its *Fimbulwinter breath* aura to prevent foes from escaping.

Frost Giant Lore

Arcana DC 22: In their arctic lands, frost giants dwell in glacial caves or crude fortresses carved of stone and ice. From these holds, frost giants hunt game and raid for slaves and plunder. The mightiest frost giant in a clan, called a jarl, leads weaker giants though intimidation and violence.

Ice shapers, the frost giants' seers, gain respect from their kind for their auguries and wisdom. They engender fear with their cruelty and ferocity.

Arcana DC 27: A few frost giants have magical powers and can use runes, sorcery, and foul rituals. Such powers give a giant influence in its clan, if not outright leadership.

Encounter Groups

Frost giants enslave or ally with other creatures that prefer the cold. When they raid more temperate climes, they come by other sorts of slaves. Mammoths, remorhazes, white dragons, and similar creatures are found with frost giants.

Level 19 Encounter (XP 12,000)
✦ 2 frost giants (level 17 brute)
✦ 1 frost giant ice shaper (level 19 controller)
✦ 1 remorhaz (level 21 elite brute)

Level 21 Encounter (XP 19,200)
✦ 2 frost titans (level 20 elite brute)
✦ 2 ice archon frostshapers (level 20 controller, MM 21)
✦ 1 ice archon rimehammer (level 19 soldier, MM 20)

(Left to right) stone giant, stone titan, and stone giant runecarver

STONE GIANT

ATOP FORBIDDING PEAKS and in the deep reaches of mountain ranges dwell stone giants. These rockbound beings show little concern for smaller creatures, and they distrust strangers. A stone giant aroused to violence can be as startling and pitiless as an avalanche.

STONE GIANT LORE

Arcana DC 25: Stone giants move slowly and quietly among the mountains and within their rocky cave homes, blending with the terrain so well that they can easily waylay foes or go unnoticed. Brooding and contemplative, stone giants can rest in thought for years, sitting like statues. With weapons and thrown stones, they are expert hunters. When roused to anger, a stone giant is able to move its bulk with precision and quickness.

Particularly at night and during thunderstorms, stone giants play by throwing rocks at each other—the losing side is the one hit more often. During such contests, the giants seldom watch out for unexpected passersby. Such heedless "games" give stone giants a rougher reputation than they might deserve.

Arcana DC 30: Stone giants are artistic and craft-oriented, especially with stone. Runecarvers use arcane lore to craft runes of ancient magic upon surfaces. With these spells set in stone, they smite foes. The art of rune magic might have originated with ancient stone giants, although dwarf artificers surely disagree.

STONE GIANT TACTICS

A stone giant hides among the cliffs and ambushes approaching enemies with hurled rocks. It then rushes in with *staggering sweep* to drive foes back. It stays in melee until opponents retreat, then goes back to hurling rocks until any threat is out of range.

Stone Giant	Level 14 Soldier
Large elemental humanoid (earth, giant)	XP 1,000

Initiative +12   **Senses** Perception +12; low-light vision
HP 140; **Bloodied** 70
AC 30; **Fortitude** 27, **Reflex** 24, **Will** 26
Immune petrification
Speed 8 (earth walk)
⊕ **Stone Greatclub** (standard; at-will) ✦ **Weapon**
    Reach 2; +21 vs. AC; 2d10 + 4 damage, and the target is marked until the end of the stone giant's next turn.
† **Hardened Threat** (opportunity, when a creature marked by the stone giant and within its reach moves or shifts; at-will)
    The giant makes a *stone greatclub* attack against the triggering creature.
⤢ **Hurl Rock** (standard; at-will)
    Ranged 20; +21 vs. AC; 2d8 + 6 damage.

↩ **Staggering Sweep** (standard; recharges when first bloodied) ✦
Weapon

Close blast 2; +19 vs. AC; 2d10 + 4 damage, and the target is
pushed 2 squares and marked until the end of the stone giant's
next turn. *Effect:* The giant shifts 2 squares but must remain
within 2 squares of any creatures marked by it.

Stone Bones (immediate interrupt, when the stone giant is hit by
an attack; not usable while bloodied; at-will)

The giant gains resist 5 to all damage against the triggering
attack.

Alignment Unaligned	**Languages** Giant	
Skills Athletics +18, Stealth +15		
Str 22 (+13)	**Dex** 16 (+10)	**Wis** 20 (+12)
Con 20 (+12)	**Int** 10 (+7)	**Cha** 11 (+7)
Equipment greatclub		

Stone Giant Runecarver Tactics

The stone giant runecarver attacks from range, using
rocks with specially inscribed runes. It starts with
rune of stony sleep and follows with *rune of thundering
echo*. It focuses its melee attacks on slowed opponents
to take advantage of its *grasping stone* power.

Stone Giant Runecarver	**Level 16 Controller (Leader)**
Large elemental humanoid (earth, giant)	XP 1,400

Initiative +9 　　　　**Senses** Perception +14; low-light vision

Hardened Focus aura 5; each petrified enemy within the aura
loses all resistances and gains vulnerable 5 to all damage.

HP 155; **Bloodied** 77

AC 30; **Fortitude** 28, **Reflex** 27, **Will** 29

Immune petrification

Speed 8 (earth walk)

⊕ **Enruned War Pick** (standard; at-will) ✦ **Weapon**

Reach 2; +21 vs. AC; 2d8 + 9 (crit 4d8 + 25) damage, and the
target is slowed (save ends).

❇ **Rune of Stony Sleep** (standard; recharge ⚅) ✦ **Zone**

Area burst 1 within 10; +21 vs. Fortitude; 2d8 + 6 damage, and
the target is slowed (save ends). *First Failed Saving Throw:* The
target is petrified instead of slowed (save ends). *Effect:* The burst
creates a zone of magical runes that lasts until the end of the
encounter. Each enemy that starts its turn within the zone takes
a –2 penalty to saving throws against slowed and immobilized.

❇ **Rune of Thundering Echo** (standard; recharge ⚄ ⚅)

Area burst 1 within 10; +21 vs. Fortitude; 2d8 + 6 thunder
damage. If the target is slowed or immobilized, it takes ongoing
10 thunder damage (save ends).

Grasping Stone

When a stone giant runecarver hits a slowed creature with an
attack that would cause the creature to become slowed, that
creature is immobilized until the end of the runecarver's next turn.

Stone Bones (immediate interrupt, when the stone giant
runecarver is hit by an attack; not usable while bloodied; at-will)

The runecarver gains resist 5 to all damage against the
triggering attack.

Alignment Unaligned	**Languages** Giant, Primordial	
Skills Arcana +17, Athletics +18, Stealth +17		
Str 21 (+13)	**Dex** 12 (+9)	**Wis** 23 (+14)
Con 19 (+12)	**Int** 18 (+12)	**Cha** 15 (+10)
Equipment warhammer		

Stone Titan Tactics

Displaying speed, agility, and stealth, a stone titan
uses *launch quakestone* from hiding, continuing to

toss boulders until enemies come close enough for
a quick rush into melee. Next, the titan moves to
catch numerous foes with an *avalanche stomp* attack.
It then lays about with its massive fists until it has a
chance to use *launch quakestone* again. The stone titan
continues to launch ranged attacks against retreating
adversaries until those foes are out of range.

Stone Titan	**Level 18 Elite Soldier**
Huge elemental humanoid (earth, giant)	XP 4,000

Initiative +15 　　　**Senses** Perception +15; low-light vision

Slipstone Distortion aura 1; each enemy that starts its turn within
the aura is marked until the end of the stone titan's next turn.

HP 348; **Bloodied** 174

AC 34; **Fortitude** 33, **Reflex** 28, **Will** 30

Immune petrification

Saving Throws +2

Speed 8 (earth walk)

Action Points 1

⊕ **Slam** (standard; at-will)

Reach 3; +25 vs. AC; 3d6 + 7 damage, and marked targets take
an extra 2d6 damage.

ϯ **Hardened Threat** (opportunity, when a creature marked by the
stone titan and within its reach moves or shifts; at-will)

The titan makes a slam attack against the triggering creature.

⊛ **Launch Boulder** (standard; at-will)

Ranged 20; +23 vs. AC; 2d10 + 7 damage.

↩ **Avalanche Stomp** (standard; encounter)

Close burst 3; +21 vs. Fortitude; 3d10 + 7 damage, and the
target is grabbed by earth and stone. The stone titan does not
need to use an action to sustain the grab. The earth and stone
has a Fortitude and Reflex of 28 against escape attempts. *Miss:*
Half damage.

❇ **Launch Quakestone** (standard; recharge ⚄ ⚅)

Area burst 1 within 20; +23 vs. AC; 1d10 + 7 damage, and
the target is knocked prone and dazed (save ends). *Miss:* Half
damage, and the target is knocked prone.

Stone Bones (immediate interrupt, when the stone titan is hit by
an attack; not usable while bloodied; at-will)

The titan gains resist 5 to all damage against the triggering attack.

Alignment Unaligned	**Languages** Giant, Primordial	
Skills Arcana +16, Athletics +21, Stealth +18		
Str 26 (+17)	**Dex** 18 (+13)	**Wis** 22 (+15)
Con 22 (+15)	**Int** 14 (+11)	**Cha** 16 (+12)

Encounter Groups

Stone giants keep pets and, rare among their kin,
have ties other than those of master and slave with
galeb duhrs and azers. Sometimes giants with non-
evil ways can be found among stone giants. Evil stone
giants might ally with other evil giants.

Level 15 Encounter (XP 6,400)

✦ 3 stone giants (level 14 soldier)
✦ 1 stone giant runecarver (level 16 controller)
✦ 1 nabassu gargoyle (level 18 lurker, *MM* 115)

Level 18 Encounter (XP 11,200)

✦ 2 stone titans (level 18 elite soldier)
✦ 1 azer taskmaster (level 17 controller, *MM* 23)
✦ 4 azer warriors (level 17 minion, *MM* 22)

Gnolls honor chaos and carnage above all else. Their devotion to the demon lord Yeenoghu drives them to commit acts of butchery.

DEATHPLEDGED GNOLL

A DEATHPLEDGED GNOLL VOWS TO DIE destroying the enemies of Yeenoghu. Its dark oath and a thirst for blood make this creature a frightful foe.

Deathpledged Gnoll		Level 5 Brute
Medium natural humanoid		XP 200

Initiative +4   Senses Perception +4; low-light vision
HP 74; Bloodied 37; see also *claws of Yeenoghu*
AC 18; Fortitude 18, Reflex 16, Will 16
Resist see *claws of Yeenoghu*
Speed 7
Action Points see *claws of Yeenoghu*
⊕ **Bone Claw** (standard; at-will) ✦ **Weapon**
    +8 vs. AC; 2d6 + 9 damage (2d6 + 11 damage while bloodied).
Claws of Yeenoghu (when the deathpledged gnoll first drops to 0 hit points) ✦ **Healing**
    The deathpledged regains 5 hit points, gains 1 action point, and gains resist 15 to all damage. At the end of its next turn, the deathpledged drops to 0 hit points.
Pack Attack
    A deathpledged gnoll's melee attacks deal 5 extra damage against an enemy that has two or more gnoll allies adjacent to it.

Alignment Chaotic evil	Languages Abyssal, Common

Skills Intimidate +5

Str 18 (+6)	Dex 15 (+4)	Wis 15 (+4)
Con 14 (+4)	Int 9 (+1)	Cha 7 (+0)

Equipment leather armor, bone claws (spiked gauntlets)

DEATHPLEDGED GNOLL LORE

Nature DC 12: In return for its vow to its demon lord Yeenoghu, a deathpledged gnoll can temporarily shrug off death with potent demonic powers.

FANG OF YEENOGHU

Gnolls are known for their rituals honoring the demon lord Yeenoghu. The fangs of Yeenoghu are the shamans that lead these rites.

Fang of Yeenoghu	Level 7 Skirmisher (Leader)
Medium natural humanoid	XP 300

Initiative +9   Senses Perception +3; low-light vision
HP 77; Bloodied 38
AC 21; Fortitude 18, Reflex 19, Will 18
Speed 8
⊕ **Cudgel of Bloody Teeth** (standard; at-will) ✦ **Disease, Weapon**
    +12 vs. AC; 1d10 + 6 damage (1d10 + 8 while bloodied), and the fang of Yeenoghu makes a secondary attack against the same target. *Secondary Attack:* +10 vs. Fortitude; the target is exposed to level 6 slavering canker (see below).
↯ **Relentless Push** (standard; at-will) ✦ **Weapon**
    The fang of Yeenoghu shifts 2 squares before the attack: +12 vs. AC; 1d10 + 6 damage (1d10 + 8 while bloodied), and the fang of Yeenoghu pushes the target 1 square. *Effect:* One ally within 5 squares of the fang of Yeenoghu shifts 1 square as a free action.
↢ **Howl of the Demon** (standard; recharge ⚁⚁)
    Close burst 5; targets each ally of level 10 or lower in the burst; the target makes a melee basic attack as a free action.
Pack Attack
    A fang of Yeenoghu's melee attacks deal 5 extra damage against an enemy that has two or more gnoll allies adjacent to it.

Alignment Chaotic evil	Languages Abyssal, Common

Skills Insight +8, Intimidate +11, Religion +8

Str 16 (+6)	Dex 19 (+7)	Wis 11 (+3)
Con 13 (+4)	Int 10 (+3)	Cha 16 (+6)

Equipment hide armor, cudgel of bloody teeth (greatclub)

FANG OF YEENOGHU LORE

Nature DC 14: Fangs of Yeenoghu earn their place in the demon lord's ranks by capturing slaves and sending them to serve Yeenoghu in the Abyss.

Nature DC 19: A cudgel of bloody teeth is a gruesome greatclub studded with teeth and crusted with blood. While a fang of Yeenoghu fights, its cudgel of bloody teeth continually oozes fresh blood and spittle. Once its wielder is killed, the cudgel quickly rots away.

Nature DC 21: Those gnolls that serve as fodder for the gnoll gorger are rewarded for their sacrifice by the fang of Yeenoghu. A gnoll slain by a gorger has its teeth added to the cudgel of bloody teeth, allowing it to taste the blood of its enemies even in death.

Slavering Canker	Level 6 Disease	Endurance improve DC 23, maintain DC 19, worsen DC 18 or lower

| The target is cured. | ◀ **Initial Effect:** The target takes a -1 penalty to attack rolls and damage rolls. | ◀▶ The target takes a -2 penalty to attack rolls and damage rolls, and regains 5 fewer than the normal number of hit points from healing effects. | ▶ **Final State:** The target is weakened, and must rest for twice as long as normal to gain the benefit of a short rest or an extended rest. |

GNOLL GORGER

ALL GNOLLS DEVOUR THE FLESH OF SENTIENTS, but gorgers gain strength in battle by feasting on their own kind.

Gnoll Gorger	Level 7 Brute
Medium natural humanoid	XP 300

Initiative +6   **Senses** Perception +3; low-light vision
HP 96; **Bloodied** 48
AC 19; **Fortitude** 20, **Reflex** 18, **Will** 18
Speed 7
⊕ **Bite** (standard; at-will)
  +10 vs. AC; 2d6 + 8 damage (2d6 + 10 while bloodied).
Gorge (minor 1/round; at-will) ✦ **Healing**
  The gnoll gorger feeds upon an ally adjacent to it. The ally takes 5 damage, and the gorger regains 10 hit points.
Pack Attack
  A gnoll gorger's melee attacks deal 5 extra damage against an enemy that has two or more gnoll allies adjacent to it.
Alignment Chaotic evil   **Languages** Abyssal, Common
Skills Intimidate +11, Stealth +11
Str 20 (+8)	**Dex** 17 (+6)	**Wis** 11 (+3)
Con 16 (+6)	**Int** 9 (+2)	**Cha** 17 (+6)
Equipment leather armor

GNOLL GORGER TACTICS

A gnoll gorger recklessly charges into combat, laying into foes with its bite attack. It uses its *gorge* power each round, focusing on the most robust allies available.

GNOLL GORGER LORE

Nature DC 14: Gnoll gorgers draw strength from the blood of their kin. They feast on the flesh of allies in combat to restore vigor, inspiring themselves to greater savagery.

ENCOUNTER GROUPS

Gnoll packs often include demons, slave troops, and beasts trained for war. Gnolls are sometimes encountered in the service of others, acting as shock troops for giants and other powerful monsters.

Level 4 Encounter (XP 925)
✦ 2 deathpledged gnolls (level 5 brute)
✦ 1 corruption corpse (level 4 artillery, *MM* 274)
✦ 1 gnoll demonic scourge (level 8 brute, *MM* 132)

Level 7 Encounter (XP 1,600)
✦ 1 fang of Yeenoghu (level 7 skirmisher)
✦ 3 gnoll gorgers (level 7 brute)
✦ 1 beholder gauth (level 5 elite artillery)

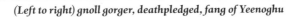

(Left to right) gnoll gorger, deathpledged, fang of Yeenoghu

GNOME

ALL GNOMES SHARE A CONNECTION TO THE FEYWILD, but that connection can manifest itself in starkly different ways. Some gnomes are naturally adept at channeling arcane currents, while others use the power of the beast within them.

GNOME MISTWALKER

GNOMES ARE MASTERS OF ILLUSION MAGIC. A mistwalker combines this expertise with melee prowess to ambush or harass enemies.

Gnome Mistwalker		Level 5 Lurker
Small fey humanoid		XP 200

Initiative +9   **Senses** Perception +3; low-light vision
HP 51; **Bloodied** 25
AC 20; **Fortitude** 16, **Reflex** 17, **Will** 16
Speed 5

⊕ **War Pick** (standard; at-will) ✦ **Weapon**
+10 vs. AC; 1d8 + 4 damage (crit 1d8 + 12).

† **Mistwalker's Strike** (standard; recharge ⚁ ⚂ ⚃) ✦ **Illusion**
The gnome mistwalker becomes invisible until the end of its next turn. In addition, it shifts 2 squares and makes a war pick attack.

Combat Advantage
A gnome mistwalker deals 1d6 extra damage against any creature granting combat advantage to it.

Fade Away (immediate reaction, when the gnome mistwalker takes damage; encounter) ✦ **Illusion**
The gnome mistwalker becomes invisible until after it hits or misses with an attack or until the end of its next turn.

Reactive Stealth
If the gnome mistwalker has cover or concealment when it rolls initiative at the start of an encounter, it can make a Stealth check to become hidden.

Blur of Movement (immediate reaction, when the gnome mistwalker is hit by an enemy; at-will) ✦ **Teleportation**
The mistwalker teleports 1 square.

Alignment Unaligned		**Languages** Common, Elven
Skills Stealth +10		
Str 10 (+2)	Dex 16 (+5)	Wis 13 (+3)
Con 15 (+4)	Int 11 (+2)	Cha 14 (+4)
Equipment hide armor, war pick		

GNOME MISTWALKER TACTICS

Mistwalkers flash across the battlefield to impale foes upon their picks. They rely on *blur of movement* to escape their enemies and to use *mistwalker's strike*.

GNOME MISTWALKER LORE

Nature DC 12: Mistwalkers are gnome warriormages and brigands. These robbers build warrens of tunnels around forest roads, cloak them with illusions, and use them to ambush caravans laden with goods useful to spellcasters.

GNOME ENTROPIST

GNOME ENTROPISTS SEE THE POTENTIAL for change in all things, and they use the power of chaos to hinder and debilitate their foes.

Gnome Entropist	Level 8 Artillery
Small fey humanoid	XP 350

Initiative +7   **Senses** Perception +3; low-light vision
HP 71; **Bloodied** 35
AC 20; **Fortitude** 19, **Reflex** 19, **Will** 21 (+2 to all defenses against ranged attacks)
Speed 5

⊕ **Acid Dagger** (standard; at-will) ✦ **Acid, Weapon**
+15 vs. AC; 1d4 damage plus 1d6 + 4 acid damage.

↗ **Entropic Arc** (standard; at-will)
Ranged 10; +13 vs. Reflex; 2d8 + 4 damage (crit 2d8 + 20).

↞ **Primordial Yell** (standard; recharges when first bloodied) ✦ **Thunder**
Close blast 3; +13 vs. Fortitude; 2d10 + 4 thunder damage, and the target is deafened and cannot take immediate actions or opportunity actions until the end of the gnome entropist's next turn.

✳ **Chaos Flare** (standard; encounter)
Area burst 1 within 15; +13 vs. Will; 3d8 + 5 damage, and the target is blinded (save ends).

Fade Away (immediate reaction, when the gnome entropist takes damage; encounter) ✦ **Illusion**
The entropist becomes invisible until after it hits or misses with an attack or until the end of its next turn.

Reactive Stealth
If the gnome entropist has cover or concealment when it rolls initiative at the start of an encounter, it can make a Stealth check to become hidden.

Alignment Unaligned	**Languages** Common, Elven
Skills Arcana +10, Bluff +14, Stealth +12	

Str 10 (+4)	Dex 17 (+7)	Wis 8 (+3)
Con 17 (+7)	Int 12 (+5)	Cha 20 (+9)

Equipment dagger, robes

GNOME ENTROPIST TACTICS

A gnome entropist announces its presence to enemies with a *chaos flare*, then stays on the fringe of combat making *entropic arc* attacks. It uses *primordial yell* to elude foes trying to force it into close combat, falling back on *acid dagger* attacks only if cornered.

GNOME ENTROPIST LORE

Nature DC 14: Gnome entropists target their foes with power channeled from the Elemental Chaos. Their innate ties to the magic of the Feywild interfere with this extraplanar power, driving some mad.

GNOME WOLVERINE

THOUGH SMALL IN STATURE, a gnome wolverine is as fierce in combat as its namesake.

Gnome Wolverine	Level 9 Skirmisher
Small fey humanoid	XP 400

Initiative +9 **Senses** Perception +10; low-light vision
HP 95; **Bloodied** 47
AC 23 (26 against opportunity attacks); **Fortitude** 22, **Reflex** 20, **Will** 20
Speed 5 (7 when charging)

⊕ **Waraxe** (standard; at-will) ✦ **Weapon**
   +14 vs. AC; 1d12 + 6 damage.

↯ **Shrieking Strike** (standard; recharges when first bloodied) ✦ **Weapon**
   +14 vs. AC; 2d12 + 5 damage, and one enemy adjacent to the target takes 1d12 damage. *Effect*: The gnome wolverine gains a +3 bonus to all defenses until the start of its next turn. *Special*: When charging, the wolverine can use this power in place of a melee basic attack.

↯ **Unbalancing Swipe** (standard; at-will) ✦ **Weapon**
   +12 vs. Reflex; 1d12 + 6 damage, and the gnome wolverine slides the target 2 squares. On a critical hit, the target is also knocked prone.

Fade Away (immediate reaction, when the gnome wolverine takes damage; encounter) ✦ **Illusion**
   The wolverine becomes invisible until after it hits or misses with an attack or until the end of its next turn.

Reactive Stealth
   If a gnome wolverine has cover or concealment when it rolls initiative at the start of an encounter, it can make a Stealth check to become hidden.

Vicious Fury (when the gnome wolverine bloodies an enemy or reduces an enemy to 0 hit points or fewer; at-will)
   The wolverine shifts 5 squares and gains a +3 bonus to damage rolls until the end of its next turn.

Alignment Unaligned	**Languages** Common, Elven	
Skills Athletics +14, Intimidate +12, Stealth +12		
Str 20 (+9)	**Dex** 17 (+7)	**Wis** 12 (+5)
Con 15 (+6)	**Int** 10 (+4)	**Cha** 17 (+7)

Equipment hide armor, waraxe

GNOME WOLVERINE TACTICS

The gnome wolverine throws itself into battle with *shrieking strike*, then wades through foes with *unbalancing swipe* attacks. It reserves *fade away* to reposition itself if cornered, or to set up another *shrieking strike* attack once it is bloodied.

GNOME WOLVERINE LORE

Nature DC 14: A gnome wolverine has a fierceness that belies the stature and reputation of its race. A berserker fury drives a wolverine in battle, and its power increases with each foe it drops.

(Top to bottom) gnome entropist and wolverine

ENCOUNTER GROUPS

Gnomes most often work with their own kind and with other creatures of the Feywild. However, a gnome's capricious nature means that such alliances are typically brief.

Level 8 Encounter (XP 1,850)
   ✦ 1 gnome entropist (level 8 artillery)
   ✦ 2 gnome wolverines (level 9 skirmisher)
   ✦ 2 spriggan giantsouls (level 8 brute)

Level 10 Encounter (XP 2,600)
   ✦ 3 gnome entropists (level 8 artillery)
   ✦ 2 phase spiders (level 8 skirmisher)
   ✦ 1 satyr piper (level 8 controller, *MM* 228)
   ✦ 1 will-o'-wisp (level 10 lurker)

Goblins are often subservient to the devotees of dark gods and other powerful masters. Such leaders appeal to the goblins' hostile and barbarous natures.

Bugbear Wardancer

Like all bugbears, the wardancer is full of bluster and purpose. These warriors are a force to be reckoned with as they sow destruction across the battlefield.

Bugbear Wardancer Tactics

A bugbear wardancer relishes punishing as many enemies as possible, and so prefers to choose a different target each round. It will attack a foe within reach first, and if it hits it uses its move action to get into position to attack a new foe, setting up a flanking position with an ally that can then attack and similarly move.

Bugbear Wardancer Lore

Nature DC 12: A bugbear wardancer leaps and howls as it arcs its vicious flail through the ranks of its foes. Its wide-reaching attacks and single-minded fury make it a dangerous foe.

Nature DC 17: Wardancers dedicate themselves to particular exarchs of Bane, forming small sects whose members create their own rival forms of battle dance.

Nature DC 19: More intelligent goblins who lead bugbear wardancers train them thoroughly, teaching them how to avoid harming their allies in combat. Through strict conditioning, hobgoblins sometimes plant command words in wardancers' minds to control them when they get out of hand.

Bugbear Wardancer	Level 6 Skirmisher
Medium natural humanoid	XP 250

Initiative +9   **Senses** Perception +5; low-light vision
HP 70; **Bloodied** 35
AC 20; **Fortitude** 18, **Reflex** 19, **Will** 18
Speed 7

⊕ **Flail Dance** (standard; at-will) ✦ **Weapon**
+9 vs. Fortitude; 2d6 + 4 damage, the target is pushed 2 squares and knocked prone, and the bugbear wardancer shifts 1 square.

↤ **Flail Barrier** (standard; recharge ⚄ ⚅) ✦ **Weapon**
Close burst 2; targets enemies; no attack roll; 5 damage, and the bugbear wardancer takes half damage from weapon attacks until the end of its next turn.

↤ **Flail Assault** (standard; encounter) ✦ **Weapon**
Close burst 2; +9 vs. Reflex; 2d6 damage, and the target is pushed 2 squares and knocked prone.

Combat Advantage
A bugbear wardancer deals 1d6 extra damage against any creature granting combat advantage to it.

Alignment Evil	**Languages** Common, Goblin	
Str 16 (+6)	**Dex** 19 (+7)	**Wis** 14 (+5)
Con 14 (+5)	**Int** 11 (+3)	**Cha** 16 (+6)

Equipment hide armor, heavy flail

(Left to right) goblin acolyte of Maglubiyet, bugbear wardancer, and Lolthbound goblin

GOBLIN ACOLYTE OF MAGLUBIYET

Maglubiyet, goblin exarch of Bane, inspires the radical devotion of a sect of combatants seeking to mold themselves in his image.

Goblin Acolyte of Maglubiyet		Level 1 Controller
Small natural humanoid		XP 100

Initiative +0   **Senses** Perception +3; low-light vision
Life Scourge aura 2; each creature within the aura cannot regain hit points.
HP 29; **Bloodied** 14
AC 15; **Fortitude** 12, **Reflex** 12, **Will** 14
Speed 6
ⓘ **Slashing Shroud** (standard; at-will) ✦ **Illusion, Weapon**
     +6 vs. AC; 1d10 + 3 damage, and the goblin acolyte of Maglubiyet becomes invisible to the target until the end of the acolyte's next turn.
↗ **Hand of Maglubiyet** (standard; at-will) ✦ **Force**
     Ranged 10; +5 vs. Fortitude; 1d6 + 5 force damage, and the goblin acolyte of Maglubiyet chooses either to slide the target 3 squares or to immobilize the target until the end of the acolyte's next turn.
↗ **Maglubiyet's Fists** (standard; recharge ⚄ ⚅)
     The goblin acolyte of Maglubiyet makes two *hand of Maglubiyet* attacks, each against a different target.
Goblin Tactics (immediate reaction, when the goblin acolyte of Maglubiyet is missed by a melee attack; at-will)
     The acolyte shifts 1 square.
Alignment Evil	**Languages** Common, Goblin	
Skills Diplomacy +6, Intimidate +6		
Str 11 (+0)	**Dex** 10 (+0)	**Wis** 16 (+3)
Con 13 (+1)	**Int** 13 (+1)	**Cha** 13 (+1)
Equipment battleaxe		

GOBLIN ACOLYTE OF MAGLUBIYET TACTICS

A goblin acolyte moves freely across the battlefield, using *hand of Maglubiyet* to keep foes away from its allies or to hold more powerful combatants in place. It makes *slashing shroud* attacks with abandon, sticking close to badly wounded foes so that its *life scourge* aura prevents them from healing.

GOBLIN ACOLYTE OF MAGLUBIYET LORE

Nature DC 5: Acolytes of Maglubiyet devote their lives to the goblin exarch of Bane, modeling themselves in his image and drawing power from their faith.

Nature DC 10: An acolyte of Maglubiyet seeks signs of its patron's favor in all it does, such as thunder rolling at an auspicious moment or a bird of prey landing on a nearby tree. Such symbols can drive superstitious acolytes to fight against impossible odds, and an unfavorable sign can just as easily make them flee a fight before it even begins.

LOLTHBOUND GOBLIN

Centuries spent as slaves to the drow have driven some goblins to a mad devotion to the dark elves and their demon queen.

Lolthbound Goblin		Level 3 Soldier
Small natural humanoid		XP 150

Initiative +6   **Senses** Perception +3; darkvision
HP 45; **Bloodied** 22
AC 19; **Fortitude** 15, **Reflex** 16, **Will** 15; see also *drow inspiration*
Speed 6
ⓘ **War Pick** (standard; at-will) ✦ **Weapon**
     +10 vs. AC; 1d8 + 5 damage (crit 1d8 + 13), and the target is marked until the end of the Lolthbound goblin's next turn.
⸸ **Stinging Blow** (standard; encounter) ✦ **Poison, Weapon**
     +10 vs. AC; 1d8 + 5 poison damage (crit 1d8 + 13), and if the target is taking ongoing poison damage, that ongoing damage increases by 5.
↞ **Lolthbound Shriek** (standard; encounter) ✦ **Thunder**
     Close blast 5; targets creatures that are not drow, spiders, or goblins; +8 vs. Fortitude; 2d10 thunder damage.
Drow Inspiration (while within 5 squares of a drow ally)
     The Lolthbound goblin gains a +2 bonus to attack rolls and all defenses.
Drow Protector (immediate interrupt, when a drow ally adjacent to the Lolthbound goblin is targeted by an attack; at-will)
     The triggering attack targets the goblin instead.
Goblin Tactics (immediate reaction, when the Lolthbound goblin is missed by a melee attack; at-will)
     The goblin shifts 1 square.
Alignment Evil	**Languages** Common, Elven, Goblin	
Str 14 (+3)	**Dex** 17 (+4)	**Wis** 14 (+3)
Con 13 (+2)	**Int** 8 (+0)	**Cha** 9 (+0)
Equipment leather armor, war pick		

Lolthbound Goblin Slave	Level 12 Minion Skirmisher
Small natural humanoid (goblin)	XP 175

Initiative +13   **Senses** Perception +10; darkvision
HP 1; a missed attack never damages a minion.
AC 26; **Fortitude** 24, **Reflex** 25, **Will** 24; see also *drow inspiration*
Speed 6
ⓘ **Stinging Pick** (standard; at-will) ✦ **Poison, Weapon**
     +17 vs. AC; 7 poison damage, and if the target is affected by ongoing poison damage, that ongoing damage increases by 5.
↗ **Hand Crossbow** (standard; at-will) ✦ **Weapon**
     Ranged 10/20; +17 vs. AC; 5 damage (7 if the Lolthbound goblin slave moved 3 or more squares during its turn).
Drow Inspiration (while within 5 squares of a drow ally)
     The Lolthbound goblin slave gains a +2 bonus to attack rolls and all defenses.
Goblin Tactics (immediate reaction, when missed by a melee attack; at-will)
     The Lolthbound goblin slave shifts 1 square.
Alignment Evil	**Languages** Common, Elven, Goblin	
Str 19 (+10)	**Dex** 21 (+11)	**Wis** 19 (+10)
Con 14 (+8)	**Int** 8 (+5)	**Cha** 9 (+5)
Equipment leather armor, war pick, hand crossbow, case with 10 bolts		

Lolthbound Goblin Tactics

Lolthbound goblins are dedicated to protecting their drow masters, fighting close to them to take advantage of *drow inspiration* and *drow protector* powers. A Lolthbound goblin uses *stinging blow* to maximize ongoing poison damage dealt by allies, reserving its *Lolthbound shriek* until surrounded.

Lolthbound Goblin Slave Lore

Nature DC 16: Lolthbound goblin slaves are goblins brutalized by the drow. They are granted the power to fight in the name of the Spider Queen, but they have no will of their own.

Hobgoblin Fleshcarver

DEFINED BY ITS SPECIALIZED WEAPONS, the hobgoblin fleshcarver is dedicated to perfecting the art of battle.

Hobgoblin Fleshcarver	Level 6 Elite Controller
Medium natural humanoid	XP 500

Initiative +7   **Senses** Perception +4; low-light vision
Fleshcarver's Trap aura 2; each enemy that starts its turn within the aura takes 5 damage the first time it moves during that turn.
HP 146; **Bloodied** 73
AC 20 (22 with *phalanx soldier*); **Fortitude** 18, **Reflex** 19, **Will** 18
Saving Throws +2
Speed 6
Action Points 1
⊕ **Glaive** (standard; at-will) ✦ **Weapon**
     Reach 2; +11 vs. AC; 2d4 + 4 damage.
⊗ **Toxic Dart** (standard; at-will) ✦ **Poison, Weapon**
     Ranged 6/12; +11 vs. AC; 1d6 + 4 poison damage, and the target is slowed (save ends). If the target was already slowed, it is instead immobilized (save ends).
⊗ **Defensive Dart** (immediate reaction, when the hobgoblin fleshcarver is hit by an enemy's melee attack; recharge ⚄ ⚅)
     The fleshcarver shifts 2 squares and uses *toxic dart* against the triggering enemy.
↞ **Glaive Flurry** (standard; at-will) ✦ **Weapon**
     Close burst 2; targets enemies; +11 vs. AC; 3d4 + 4 damage, and the hobgoblin fleshcarver slides the target 2 squares. The target must end the slide within 3 squares of the fleshcarver.
Hobgoblin Resilience (immediate reaction, when the hobgoblin fleshcarver becomes subject to an effect; encounter)
     The fleshcarver rolls a saving throw against the triggering effect.
Phalanx Soldier
     A hobgoblin fleshcarver gains a +2 bonus to AC while at least one hobgoblin ally is adjacent to it.

Alignment Evil	**Languages** Common, Goblin	
Str 14 (+5)	**Dex** 19 (+7)	**Wis** 12 (+4)
Con 17 (+6)	**Int** 12 (+4)	**Cha** 16 (+6)

Equipment chain armor, glaive, 10 poisoned darts

Hobgoblin Fleshcarver Tactics

A fleshcarver uses its *glaive flurry* for multiple purposes: to knock enemies back toward groups of allies, to drive foes into positions where they are flanked, or pull foes back if they try to get away. Until it becomes bloodied, a fleshcarver is aggressive and keeps enemies near it if possible. It becomes more defensive once bloodied and uses its dart powers more frequently.

Hobgoblin fleshcarvers aren't afraid to call a retreat when a battle appears unwinnable. They coordinate their movement so that they stay adjacent to allies as they retreat, to benefit from *phalanx soldier*. By using *toxic dart*, they try to keep enemies from pursuing them at full speed.

Hobgoblin Fleshcarver Lore

Nature DC 12: A hobgoblin fleshcarver carries a jagged glaive and poisoned darts. Each glaive is crafted by a fleshcarver and perfectly shaped and weighted to match that hobgoblin's fighting style. The poison used on the fleshcarver's darts is harvested from serpents the fleshcarver hunts as a part of its training.

Nature DC 17: Fleshcarvers pride themselves on their martial ability, and welcome challenges from other weapon users. Still, pride won't draw a fleshcarver away from the thick of combat.

Goblin Encounter Groups

Goblins can be encountered in almost any context: as an invading horde, mercenaries in the pay of other villains, or slaves beholden to dangerous masters.

Level 1 Encounter (XP 550)
✦ 1 goblin acolyte of Maglubiyet (level 1 controller)
✦ 3 goblin warriors (level 1 skirmisher, *MM* 137)
✦ 1 Lolthbound goblin (level 3 soldier)

Level 6 Encounter (XP 1,200)
✦ 2 bugbear wardancers (level 6 skirmisher)
✦ 2 bugbear warriors (level 5 brute, *MM* 135)
✦ 1 barghest battle lord (level 7 controller)

Level 6 Encounter (XP 1,350)
✦ 1 hobgoblin fleshcarver (level 6 elite controller)
✦ 3 hobgoblin soldiers (level 3 soldier, *MM* 139)
✦ 2 dire wolves (level 5 skirmisher, *MM* 264)

Level 13 Encounter (XP 4,100)
✦ 4 Lolthbound goblin slaves (level 12 minion skirmisher)
✦ 1 drow priest (level 15 controller, *MM* 95)
✦ 2 blade spiders (level 10 brute, *MM* 246)
✦ 2 drow warriors (level 11 lurker, *MM* 94)

GOLEM

CREATED TO GUARD THEIR MASTERS and their masters' secrets, golems have no sense of self and follow orders without question.

BONE GOLEM

BUILT FROM THE BONES OF MANY CREATURES, these massive conglomerations stab their foes with sharpened bone. They serve well those who seek to disorient their enemies through pain, or those who are partial to macabre trappings.

Bone Golem		Level 12 Elite Brute
Large natural animate (construct)		XP 1,400

Initiative +11 **Senses** Perception +9; darkvision
Bone Spikes aura 1; each enemy that enters the aura takes 5 damage.
HP 302; **Bloodied** 151; see also *bone death*
AC 24; **Fortitude** 25, **Reflex** 24, **Will** 22
Immune disease, poison, sleep
Saving Throws +2
Speed 6 (cannot shift)
Action Points 1
⊕ **Bone Spur** (standard; at-will)
　　Reach 2; +15 vs. AC; 2d8 + 9 damage.
↯ **Double Spurs** (standard; at-will)
　　The bone golem makes two *bone spur* attacks, each against a different target. If both attacks hit, the targets are dazed until the end of the golem's next turn.
↢ **Bone Volley** (standard; recharge ⚅⚅)
　　Close burst 3; +13 vs. Reflex; 4d8 + 6 damage, and the target is dazed (save ends).
↯↢ **Bone Death** (free, when first bloodied and again when the bone golem drops to 0 hit points)
　　The golem uses *bone volley* if the power is not expended; otherwise, it makes a *bone spur* attack.
Osseous Retaliation
　　A creature that makes an opportunity attack against a bone golem takes 2d6 damage.
Alignment Evil **Languages** –
Str 22 (+12) **Dex** 20 (+11) **Wis** 17 (+9)
Con 21 (+11) **Int** 3 (+2) **Cha** 3 (+2)

BONE GOLEM LORE

　　Arcana or Nature DC 21: Bone golems are constructs created by dark-hearted mages and priests to serve as guardians. Although they look like undead, they are merely animated matter.

ENCOUNTER GROUPS

Like many golems, bone golems are constructed by arcane magic wielders for protection or enforcement.

Level 13 Encounter (XP 4,200)
✦ 1 bone golem (level 12 elite brute)
✦ 4 horde ghouls (level 13 minion)
✦ 1 human lich wizard (level 14 elite controller, *MM 176)

CHAIN GOLEM

IMBUED WITH MAGIC, these humanoid conglomerations of metal links enwrap foes in crushing chains. They specialize in pounding enemies, pulling them close, and immobilizing them.

Chain Golem		Level 22 Elite Soldier
Huge natural animate (construct)		XP 8,300

Initiative +19 **Senses** Perception +19; darkvision
Entangling Chains aura 3; each enemy that starts its turn within the aura is slowed until the end of its turn.
HP 418; **Bloodied** 209
AC 38; **Fortitude** 35, **Reflex** 32, **Will** 34
Immune disease, poison, sleep
Saving Throws +2
Speed 8 (cannot shift)
Action Points 1
⊕ **Chain** (standard; at-will)
　　Reach 3; +29 vs. AC; 2d8 + 9 damage, and the chain golem pulls the target 2 squares.
↯ **Berserk Attack** (immediate reaction, when the chain golem is damaged by an attack while bloodied; at-will)
　　The golem makes a chain attack against a target adjacent to it.
↯ **Chain Smash** (standard; at-will)
　　The chain golem makes two chain attacks, each against a different target.
↢ **Chain Grab** (standard; at-will)
　　Close burst 2; +27 vs. Reflex; 2d8 + 9 damage, and the target is pulled 1 square and grabbed. While the target is grabbed by the chain golem, the golem can move away from the target without ending the grab. When the golem ends its move, it must slide the target into a space adjacent to it or the grab ends.
Stable Footing
　　A chain golem ignores difficult terrain.
Alignment Unaligned **Languages** –
Str 28 (+20) **Dex** 22 (+17) **Wis** 26 (+19)
Con 25 (+18) **Int** 3 (+7) **Cha** 3 (+7)

CHAIN GOLEM TACTICS

The job of the chain golem is to keep melee combatants and skirmishing characters occupied at the center of the battlefield. It accomplishes this goal with its chain and *chain grab* attacks, then lays about with *chain smash*.

CHAIN GOLEM LORE

　　Arcana or Nature DC 21: Modeled after chain devils, chain golems often act as guardians over prisoners. Chain golems draw their foes in by wrapping them in chains, then pummel them mercilessly.

Clay Golem

THE PONDEROUS-LOOKING CLAY GOLEM has surprising speed. These brutes are favored by those who seek to inflict significant, sometimes unmendable, damage.

Clay Golem	Level 15 Elite Brute
Large natural animate (construct)	XP 2,400

Initiative +15; see also *hasty reaction*   **Senses** Perception +11; darkvision

Aura of Misjudgment aura 3; each enemy within the aura cannot shift.

HP 368; **Bloodied** 184

AC 27; **Fortitude** 31, **Reflex** 25, **Will** 27

Immune disease, poison, sleep

Saving Throws +2

Speed 6 (cannot shift)

Action Points 1

ⓘ **Slam** (standard; at-will)

   Reach 2; +19 vs. AC; 3d8 + 7 damage, and the target cannot regain hit points (save ends).

✦ **Clay Smash** (standard; at-will)

   The clay golem makes two slam attacks, each against a different target.

✦ **Berserk Attack** (immediate reaction, when the clay golem is damaged by an attack while bloodied; at-will)

   The golem makes a slam attack against a creature adjacent to it.

Hasty Reaction

   A clay golem rolls initiative twice, taking the higher of the two results.

Unstoppable (move; encounter)

   The clay golem moves 8 squares and can move through enemies' spaces. Opportunity attacks against the golem triggered by this movement take a -10 penalty to damage rolls.

Alignment Unaligned	**Languages** –	
Str 26 (+15)	**Dex** 14 (+9)	**Wis** 18 (+11)
Con 24 (+14)	**Int** 3 (+3)	**Cha** 3 (+3)

Clay Golem Lore

Arcana or Nature DC 23: A clay golem's partially melted form looks slow, but that appearance is deceptive. Clay golems bear a curse from their creation that sometimes prevents foes' wounds from healing.

Encounter Groups

Like all golems, clay golems serve their masters regardless of intent or motivation.

Level 15 Encounter (XP 6,200)
✦ 1 clay golem (level 15 elite brute)
✦ 1 shadar-kai gloom lord (level 14 artillery)
✦ 2 shadow snakes (level 16 skirmisher, MM 240)

Iron Golem

INFUSED WITH POTENT TOXINS, iron golems thunder toward foes and bash them into mush.

Iron Golem	Level 20 Elite Soldier
Large natural animate (construct)	XP 5,600

Initiative +14   **Senses** Perception +10; darkvision

Noxious Fumes (Poison) aura 2; while the iron golem is bloodied, each creature that enters the aura or starts its turn there takes 5 poison damage.

HP 386; **Bloodied** 193; see also *toxic death*

AC 36; **Fortitude** 36, **Reflex** 30, **Will** 28

Immune disease, poison, sleep

Saving Throws +2

Speed 6 (cannot shift)

Action Points 1

ⓘ **Iron Blade** (standard; at-will)

   Reach 2; +27 vs. AC; 2d10 + 3 damage, and the target is marked (save ends).

✦ **Cleave** (standard; at-will)

   The iron golem makes two *iron blade* attacks, each against a different target.

✦ **Dazing Fist** (immediate interrupt, when a creature marked by the iron golem and within its reach moves or shifts; at-will)

   Reach 2; targets the triggering creature; +25 vs. Fortitude; the target is dazed (save ends).

◁ **Breath Weapon** (standard; recharge ⚄ ⚅) ✦ **Poison**

   Close blast 3; +25 vs. Fortitude; 3d8 + 9 poison damage, and ongoing 5 poison damage (save ends).

◁ **Toxic Death** (when first bloodied and again when the iron golem drops to 0 hit points) ✦ **Poison**

   Close burst 3; +25 vs. Fortitude; 2d8 + 6 poison damage, and ongoing 10 poison damage (save ends).

Alignment Unaligned	**Languages** –	
Str 27 (+18)	**Dex** 15 (+12)	**Wis** 11 (+10)
Con 25 (+17)	**Int** 3 (+6)	**Cha** 3 (+6)

Equipment longsword

Iron Golem Juggernaut — Level 26 Elite Soldier

Huge natural animate (construct) — XP 18,000

Initiative +19   **Senses** Perception +15; darkvision

Noxious Fumes aura 3; while the iron golem juggernaut is
bloodied, any creature that enters the aura or starts its turn
there takes 10 poison damage.

HP 488; **Bloodied** 244; see also *toxic death*

AC 42; **Fortitude** 43, **Reflex** 38, **Will** 36

Immune disease, poison, sleep

Saving Throws +2

Speed 6 (cannot shift)

Action Points 1

⊕ **Iron Blade** (standard; at-will)

  Reach 3; +33 vs. AC; 3d10 + 5 damage, and the target is marked
(save ends).

⊥ **Cleave** (standard; at-will)

  The iron golem juggernaut makes two *iron blade* attacks, each
against a different target.

⊥ **Dazing Fist** (immediate interrupt, when a creature marked by
the iron golem juggernaut and within its reach moves or shifts;
at-will)

  Reach 3; targets the triggering creature; +31 vs. Fortitude; the
target is dazed (save ends).

↩ **Breath Weapon** (standard; recharge ⚅ ⚅) ✦ **Poison**

  Close blast 5; +31 vs. Fortitude; 4d8 + 9 poison damage, and
ongoing 5 poison damage (save ends).

↩ **Toxic Death** (when first bloodied and again when the iron
golem juggernaut drops to 0 hit points) ✦ **Poison**

  Close burst 5; +31 vs. Fortitude; 3d10 + 6 poison damage, and
ongoing 10 poison damage (save ends).

Alignment Unaligned   **Languages** —

Str 30 (+23)   **Dex** 18 (+17)   **Wis** 14 (+15)

Con 28 (+22)   **Int** 3 (+9)   **Cha** 3 (+9)

Equipment longsword

IRON GOLEM LORE

Arcana or Nature DC 27: Iron golems are art-
fully crafted giant metal warriors. Potent toxins leak
from holes in their exteriors.

ENCOUNTER GROUPS

Although most golems begin their semblance of life at
the hands of a spellcaster, they can pass through the
hands of several owners during their life spans.

Level 24 Encounter (XP 34,000)
- ✦ 1 iron golem juggernaut (level 26 elite soldier)
- ✦ 1 storm gorgon (level 26 skirmisher, *MM* 143)
- ✦ 1 djinn skylord (level 25 controller)

ENCOUNTER GROUPS

Some golems remain undisturbed for centuries. Adventurers would be hard-pressed to guess their orders,
much less who gave those orders in the first place.

Level 21 Encounter (XP 20,300)
- ✦ 1 chain golem (level 22 elite soldier)
- ✦ 1 dark naga (level 21 elite controller, *MM* 194)
- ✦ 1 iron golem (level 20 elite soldier)

A RECLUSIVE AND NOMADIC RACE, towering goliaths prefer high mountains to civilized lowlands. Daring competitors, goliaths enjoy testing themselves.

Goliath Sunspeaker	Level 7 Artillery
Medium natural humanoid	XP 300

Initiative +5   **Senses** Perception +9
HP 64; **Bloodied** 32
AC 19; **Fortitude** 19, **Reflex** 18, **Will** 20
Speed 6

ⓐ **Sunspeaker's Hand** (standard; at-will) ✦ **Radiant**
  +12 vs. Reflex; 1d8 + 3 radiant damage.

➢ **Solar Sphere** (standard; at-will) ✦ **Implement, Radiant**
  Ranged 20; +12 vs. Reflex; 2d8 + 3 radiant damage.

➢ **Sun Rays** (standard; recharge ⚄ ⚅) ✦ **Fire or Radiant, Implement**
  Ranged 10; targets one or two creatures; +12 vs. Reflex; 1d8 + 3 fire or radiant damage, and ongoing 5 damage of the type dealt to the target (save ends).

↢ **Flaring Leap** (move; encounter) ✦ **Fire**
  The goliath sunspeaker jumps 3 squares and then moves its remaining speed. During this movement, the sunspeaker gains a +4 bonus to all defenses. The square in which the sunspeaker began its move erupts with fire 2 squares high. A creature that starts its turn adjacent to the fire takes 1d6 + 3 fire damage. A creature that enters the square or starts its turn there takes 2d6 + 3 fire damage. The fire blocks line of sight and lasts until the end of the sunspeaker's next turn. *Sustain Minor:* The fire persists.

⁙ **Call Down the Sun** (standard; encounter) ✦ **Implement, Radiant**
  Area burst 3 within 20; +11 vs. Reflex; 2d6 + 3 radiant damage. *Miss:* Half damage.

Stone's Endurance (minor; encounter)
  The goliath sunspeaker gains resist 5 to all damage until the end of its next turn.

Alignment Unaligned   **Languages** Common
Skills Arcana +8, Athletics +10, Insight +9, Nature +9
Str 14 (+5)	**Dex** 15 (+5)	**Wis** 12 (+4)
Con 16 (+6)	**Int** 10 (+3)	**Cha** 17 (+6)

Equipment leather armor, orb

Goliath Guardian	Level 9 Soldier
Medium natural humanoid	XP 400

Initiative +8   **Senses** Perception +7
HP 96; **Bloodied** 48
AC 25; **Fortitude** 22, **Reflex** 20, **Will** 22
Speed 6

ⓐ **Bastard Sword** (standard; at-will) ✦ **Weapon**
  +16 vs. AC; 1d10 + 7 damage, and the target is marked until the end of the goliath guardian's next turn. If the target is prone, it cannot stand up until the end of the guardian's next turn.

† **Ram's Charge** (standard; recharge ⚄ ⚅) ✦ **Weapon**
  +14 vs. Fortitude; 1d6 + 3 damage, the target is pushed 2 squares and knocked prone, and the goliath guardian shifts 2 squares and makes a bastard sword attack against the target. *Special:* When charging, the guardian can use this power in place of a melee basic attack.

Stone's Endurance (minor; encounter)
  The goliath guardian gains resist 5 to all damage until the end of its next turn.

Warrior's Leap
  A goliath guardian can jump without provoking opportunity attacks.

Alignment Unaligned   **Languages** Common
Skills Athletics +13, Insight +12, Nature +12
Str 19 (+8)	**Dex** 14 (+6)	**Wis** 16 (+7)
Con 16 (+7)	**Int** 10 (+4)	**Cha** 10 (+4)

Equipment scale armor, light shield, bastard sword

ENCOUNTER GROUPS

Goliaths keep sturdy pets and the company of brave creatures. However, a goliath might also choose to work with dwarves, galeb duhrs, or goblins.

Level 9 Encounter (XP 2,100)
✦ 1 galeb duhr rockcaller (level 11 controller, *MM* 114)
✦ 3 goliath guardians (level 9 soldier)
✦ 1 goliath sunspeaker (level 7 artillery)

CHIPPY

GRAY RENDER

Widely feared throughout the world, a gray render kills everything in its path. This creature feeds upon flesh and terror alike, working itself into a mindless rampage.

Gray Render	Level 19 Elite Brute
Large natural humanoid	XP 4,800

Initiative +10   **Senses** Perception +15; blindsight 10
HP 452; **Bloodied** 226; see also *rampage*
AC 31; **Fortitude** 34, **Reflex** 27, **Will** 28
Saving Throws +2
Speed 8
Action Points 1

⊕ **Claw** (standard; at-will)
Reach 2; +22 vs. AC; 1d12 + 8 damage, and the target is grabbed.

↓ **Double Attack** (standard; at-will)
The gray render makes two claw attacks. If both attacks hit the same target, the target takes ongoing 10 damage (save ends).

↓ **Body Sweep** (immediate reaction, when the gray render is hit by an enemy's melee attack while the gray render has a creature grabbed; requires a grabbed creature; at-will) ✦ **Weapon**
The gray render uses the grabbed creature as a weapon; +22 vs. Reflex; targets the triggering enemy; 2d12 + 8 damage, and the grey render pushes the target 4 squares. The grabbed creature takes half the damage dealt by this attack.

↓ **Dismembering Bite** (standard; encounter)
Targets a creature grabbed by the gray render; +20 vs. Fortitude; 3d12 + 8 damage, and the target is dazed (save ends).

Rampage (while bloodied)
The gray render's claw attack also knocks a target prone.

Alignment Chaotic evil   **Languages** —
Skills Athletics +23
Str 27 (+17)   **Dex** 13 (+10)   **Wis** 15 (+11)
Con 26 (+17)   **Int** 2 (+5)   **Cha** 10 (+9)

GRAY RENDER TACTICS

A gray render approaches battle mindlessly and fearlessly. It moves toward the nearest opponent, attacking in a fury and attempting to grab it. Once the render has a creature grabbed, it uses *dismembering bite* and *body sweep* at the first opportunity. The gray render flies into a destructive rage when bloodied, mindlessly clawing and knocking opponents about until it is killed or until it destroys its enemies.

GRAY RENDER LORE

Nature DC 22: Although gray renders are natural creatures that mostly inhabit the world, many scholars have come to believe that their roots can be traced back to the Elemental Chaos, where they gained their chaotic, destructive impulses.

Nature DC 27: Entropy is bound within the existence of gray renders, causing them to leave a path of wanton devastation in their wake. Renders are drawn toward footholds of civilization, such as homesteads and outlying settlements, where they unleash their destructive urges.

ENCOUNTER GROUPS

Gray renders are too instinctively chaotic and vicious to band with other creatures for long, but predators and scavengers follow in the wake of gray renders to exploit the destruction they cause.

Level 18 Encounter (XP 11,800)
✦ 1 bodak skulk (level 16 lurker)
✦ 1 gray render (level 19 elite brute)
✦ 2 guulvorg worgs (level 16 elite brute, *MM* 265)

Level 20 Encounter (XP 14,800)
✦ 1 dire bulette (level 18 elite skirmisher, *MM* 38)
✦ 1 gray render (level 19 elite brute)
✦ 3 nabassu gargoyles (level 18 lurker, *MM* 115)

Combining the best of two proud lineages, half-elves are adaptable and diplomatic. They often travel widely and seek out new experiences. Naturally gifted leaders, they frequently become quite powerful.

HALF-ELF LORE

Nature DC 12: Half-elves combine the grace of elves with the drive of humans, adding their own stunning charisma to the mix. Keen-witted and free-spirited, half-elves follow their hearts wherever they lead—along bright paths or down dark roads.

HALF-ELF BANDIT CAPTAIN

With a flair for the dramatic to accompany a mastery of blades, the half-elf bandit captain is flamboyant in everything it does. Bold and self-reliant, a half-elf bandit captain leads through charisma and remains vigilant against treachery. The bandit captain takes enough risks in pursuit of gold; trust is one gamble too many.

Half-Elf Bandit Captain	Level 6 Skirmisher (Leader)	
Medium natural humanoid		XP 250

Initiative +9   **Senses** Perception +8; low-light vision
HP 69; **Bloodied** 34
AC 20; **Fortitude** 18, **Reflex** 19, **Will** 18
Speed 6

⊕ **Longsword** (standard; at-will) ✦ **Weapon**
+11 vs. AC; 1d8 + 4 damage, and the half-elf bandit captain shifts 1 square.

⊙ **Dagger** (standard; at-will) ✦ **Weapon**
Ranged 5/10; +11 vs. AC; 1d4 + 4 damage.

↯/⊙ **Slash and Dash** (standard; recharge ⚄ ⚅ ▦)
The half-elf bandit captain makes a longsword attack, shifts 2 squares, and makes a dagger attack.

↯ **Triggering Slash** (standard; recharge ⚄ ▦) ✦ **Weapon**
+11 vs. AC; 1d8 + 4 damage, and one ally shifts 1 square and makes a melee basic attack as a free action.

Alignment Unaligned   **Languages** Common, Elven
Skills Athletics +11, Diplomacy +11, Insight +8, Stealth +12
| **Str** 16 (+6) | **Dex** 19 (+7) | **Wis** 11 (+3) |
| **Con** 13 (+4) | **Int** 10 (+3) | **Cha** 16 (+6) |
Equipment leather armor, longsword, 6 daggers

HALF-ELF BANDIT CAPTAIN TACTICS

The half-elf bandit captain leads with *slash and dash,* then uses *triggering slash* to enable an ally to move into flanking position.

HALF-ELF BANDIT CAPTAIN LORE

Nature DC 12: Half-elf leaders tend to rely on charisma to keep followers in line, and half-elf bandit captains are no different. That charm can be a liability, though, if followers believe it's been used to lie to them.

HALF-ELF CON ARTIST

Many half-elves are diplomats and peacemakers, capable of finding the common ground between any two groups. Others use their talents for their own interests. They can find the common ground between their hands and your money pouch with disconcerting ease.

The half-elf con artist mixes audacity with personal magnetism to achieve astounding results. A few honeyed words or a smile and a shrug can set foes to fighting one another or give an enemy reason to hesitate. Yet the con artist wounds with more than words. The con artist's sleight of hand has put a blade in the back of many an erstwhile ally.

Half-Elf Con Artist	Level 7 Controller	
Medium natural humanoid		XP 300

Initiative +6   **Senses** Perception +2; low-light vision
HP 77; **Bloodied** 38
AC 20; **Fortitude** 17, **Reflex** 20, **Will** 20
Speed 6

⊕ **Dagger** (standard; at-will) ✦ **Weapon**
+12 vs. AC; 1d4 + 4 damage.

↯ **Deceptive Maneuver** (standard; at-will) ✦ **Charm**
+10 vs. Will; the target makes a basic attack against one of its allies of the half-elf con artist's choice.

⊙ **Silver Deception** (standard; recharge ⚄ ▦) ✦ **Charm**
Ranged 10; +10 vs. Will; the target is dominated until the end of the half-elf con artist's next turn.

⬅ **Pathetic Appeal** (standard; encounter) ✦ **Charm**
Close burst 5; +10 vs. Will; targets enemies; the target cannot attack the half-elf con artist (save ends). If the con artist makes an attack roll against the target, that target makes a saving throw against this effect.

Combat Advantage
A half-elf con artist deals 2d6 extra damage against any creature granting combat advantage to it.

Grifter's Flight (move; encounter)
The half-elf con artist shifts 6 squares and can make a Stealth check without a penalty for moving.

Alignment Unaligned   **Languages** Common, Elven
Skills Bluff +12, Insight +7, Stealth +11, Thievery +11
| **Str** 10 (+3) | **Dex** 17 (+6) | **Wis** 9 (+2) |
| **Con** 13 (+4) | **Int** 12 (+4) | **Cha** 19 (+7) |
Equipment fine clothes, dagger

HALF-ELF CON ARTIST TACTICS

A half-elf con artist usually prefers to avoid a fight, although sometimes its schemes put it at the wrong end of a sword. If a con artist does stand and fight, it uses *deceptive maneuver* to force enemies into attacking each other. The con artist relies on *pathetic appeal* and *grifter's flight* to save itself when cornered.

HALF-ELF CON ARTIST LORE

Nature DC 14: Their natural charm grants half-elves an advantage in con games and elaborate swindles, drawing many to use their charisma for selfish reasons. Half-elves with long practice at such sleight of tongue develop an almost magical ability to fool foes and use friends.

HALF-ELF BALEFUL THAUMATURGE

THE WIELDER OF DREADFUL MAGIC, a half-elf baleful thaumaturge can make a battlefield a place of horror for enemies. Intelligent and wary, the half-elf thaumaturge has labored long to gain power and has gained much as a result. Of course, even with such vast powers, there are always more to be gained.

Half-Elf Baleful Thaumaturge	Level 24 Artillery
Medium natural humanoid	XP 6,050

Initiative +15   **Senses** Perception +14; low-light vision
HP 169; **Bloodied** 84
AC 36; **Fortitude** 32, **Reflex** 35, **Will** 38
Speed 6

⊕ **Infernal Slam** (standard; at-will) ✦ **Teleportation**
  +29 vs. Will; 2d6 + 10 damage, and the half-elf baleful thaumaturge slides the target 3 squares and then teleports 3 squares.

⊗ **Soul Bite** (standard; at-will) ✦ **Implement**
  Ranged 10; + 29 vs. Reflex; 2d8 + 10 damage, and the half-elf baleful thaumaturge gains 10 temporary hit points.

↞ **Mouths of Hell** (standard; encounter) ✦ **Implement, Psychic, Zone**
  Close blast 5; +27 vs. Will; 3d12 + 9 psychic damage, and the half-elf baleful thaumaturge gains 10 temporary hit points. *Effect:* The blast creates a zone filled with ghostly maws that lasts until the end of the encounter. Each creature that starts its turn within the zone takes 15 psychic damage. The thaumaturge gains 5 temporary hit points whenever the zone damages a creature.

⁛ **Wall of Shadow Teeth** (standard; recharge ⚄ ⚅) ✦ **Conjuration, Implement, Necrotic**
  Area wall 8 within 10; the half-elf baleful thaumaturge conjures a wall of shadow teeth that lasts until the end of the thaumaturge's next turn. The wall is 2 squares high and attacks each creature that starts its turn within the wall or adjacent to it: +27 vs. Fortitude; 3d8 + 9 necrotic damage, and the target is immobilized (save ends). *Sustain Minor:* The wall persists.

Bloody Step (minor; usable only when the half-elf baleful thaumaturge has 5 or more temporary hit points; at-will) ✦ **Teleportation**
  The thaumaturge loses 5 temporary hit points and teleports 8 squares.

Alignment Unaligned   **Languages** Common, Elven
Skills Arcana +24, Bluff +27, Streetwise +27

Str 14 (+14)	**Dex** 16 (+15)	**Wis** 15 (+14)
Con 19 (+16)	**Int** 25 (+19)	**Cha** 30 (+22)

Equipment wand

HALF-ELF BALEFUL THAUMATURGE TACTICS

The baleful thaumaturge opens with *wall of shadow teeth*, hoping to keep a few enemies immobilized, and then uses *mouths of hell*. If engaged in melee, the half-elf uses *infernal slam* to move enemies into the area of *mouths of hell*. Otherwise the half-elf uses *soul bite* and attempts to stay out of melee.

HALF-ELF BALEFUL THAUMATURGE LORE

Nature or Arcana DC 24: The path to the power that a baleful thaumaturge follows presents no end of difficulties and sacrifice, but thaumaturges who persevere achieve power unthinkable to most mortals. Blood sacrifices, both their own and that of others, give baleful thaumaturges access to dark forces with which the thaumaturge must cajole and bargain (something at which half-elves excel).

ENCOUNTER GROUPS

Half-elves travel throughout the world and are commonly found beyond its borders as well. They associate with a vast array of peoples and creatures.

Level 7 Encounter (XP 1,500)
✦ 1 half-elf bandit captain (level 6 skirmisher)
✦ 2 halfling prowlers (level 6 lurker, *MM* 153)
✦ 6 human bandits (level 2 skirmisher, *MM* 162)

Level 25 Encounter (XP 38,200)
✦ 1 eladrin lich wizard (level 24 elite controller, *MM* 176)
✦ 2 half-elf baleful thaumaturges (level 24 artillery)
✦ 2 slaughterstone hammerers (level 25 soldier)

(Left to right) half-elf bandit captain and baleful thaumaturge

HALF-ORC

Bold and brash, half-orcs combine the physical strength of orcs with the resourcefulness of humans. These cunning warriors are at home both in the city and in the wild.

HALF-ORC HUNTER

THE HALF-ORC HUNTER IS A SKILLED TRACKER and a brash fighter, rushing into battle with little regard for its own safety.

Half-Orc Hunter	Level 5 Skirmisher
Medium natural humanoid	XP 200

Initiative +7   **Senses** Perception +8; low-light vision
HP 62; **Bloodied** 31
AC 19; **Fortitude** 18, **Reflex** 18, **Will** 16
Speed 6 (8 when charging)

⊕ **Battleaxe** (standard; at-will) ✦ **Weapon**
+10 vs. AC; 1d10 + 5 damage.

⊗ **Longbow** (standard; at-will) ✦ **Weapon**
Ranged 20/40; +10 vs. AC; 1d10 + 5 damage.

↟ **Evasive Chop** (standard; at-will) ✦ **Weapon**
The half-orc hunter shifts 1 square before and after the attack; +10 vs. AC; 1d10 + 5 damage.

Draw First Blood
A half-orc hunter's melee attacks deal 1d10 extra damage against any creature that has not yet taken damage during the encounter.

Furious Assault (free, when the half-orc hunter damages an enemy; encounter)
The hunter's attack deals 1d10 extra damage.

Alignment Unaligned	**Languages** Common, Giant

Skills Endurance +9, Nature +8

Str 16 (+5)	**Dex** 17 (+5)	**Wis** 13 (+3)
Con 14 (+4)	**Int** 10 (+2)	**Cha** 8 (+1)

Equipment leather armor, battleaxe, longbow, 20 arrows

HALF-ORC HUNTER TACTICS

The half-orc hunter tears into unwounded foes to benefit from *draw first blood*, often also using *furious assault* on its first successful strike. The hunter then moves onto the next unhurt target, trusting its allies to finish off the wounded. When no enemies are unwounded, a hunter backs off to concentrate bow fire on the softest targets.

HALF-ORC DEATH MAGE

SOME HALF-ORCS ARE DRAWN to the service of Yurtrus, an exarch of Gruumsh who is a master of disease, misery, and death. These half-orcs master secret rites of Yurtrus. In battle, they wear white robes and carry staffs of black wood.

Half-Orc Death Mage	Level 6 Controller
Medium natural humanoid	XP 250

Initiative +7   **Senses** Perception +6; low-light vision
HP 66; **Bloodied** 33
AC 19; **Fortitude** 17, **Reflex** 19, **Will** 18
Speed 6

⊕ **Quarterstaff** (standard; at-will) ✦ **Weapon**
+11 vs. AC; 1d8 + 5 damage.

↟ **Rotting Touch** (standard; at-will) ✦ **Necrotic**
+10 vs. Fortitude; 1d6 + 4 necrotic damage, and the target loses necrotic resistance or immunity and takes ongoing 5 necrotic damage (save ends both).

⤳ **Bolt of Putrescence** (standard; recharge ⚃ ⚅) ✦ **Implement**
Ranged 10; +10 vs. Reflex; 2d8 + 5 damage, and the target takes a –5 penalty to all defenses until the end of the half-orc death mage's next turn.

✳ **Swarm of Flies** (standard; encounter) ✦ **Implement, Zone**
Area burst 1 within 10; +10 vs. Fortitude; 2d6 + 5 damage, and the burst creates a zone of swarming flies that lasts until the end of the encounter. Each creature that starts its turn within the zone takes 5 damage and does not have line of sight to squares more than 3 squares away from it. As a minor action, the half-orc death mage can move the zone 2 squares.

Furious Assault (free, when the half-orc death mage damages an enemy; encounter)
The death mage's attack deals 1d10 extra damage.

Death Mark (when an enemy reduces the half-orc death mage to 0 hit points) ✦ **Necrotic**
The triggering enemy takes 2d10 + 5 necrotic damage.

Alignment Evil	**Languages** Common, Giant

Skills Arcana +9, Intimidate +8, Religion +9

Str 15 (+5)	**Dex** 18 (+7)	**Wis** 17 (+6)
Con 10 (+3)	**Int** 13 (+4)	**Cha** 10 (+3)

Equipment robes, quarterstaff

HALF-ORC DEATH MAGE TACTICS

A death mage remains at the rear of battle. From there, it can rain its spells upon its foes without fear of reprisal. It uses *swarm of flies* to force its enemies to break up, leaving them isolated and vulnerable to its orc allies. *Bolt of putrescence* is useful against heavily armored targets. Unlike many evil creatures, the death mage has no fear of dying for its master. If the battle goes poorly, it strides into melee to use *rotting touch* and eventually *death mark*.

HALF-ORC SCARTHANE

As its ritual scars testify, a half-orc scarthane is a terrifying fury on the battlefield.

Half-Orc Scarthane	Level 7 Brute
Medium natural humanoid	XP 300

Initiative +6   **Senses** Perception +3; low-light vision
HP 96; **Bloodied** 48; see also *wounded retaliation*
AC 20; **Fortitude** 22, **Reflex** 20, **Will** 17
Speed 6 (8 when charging)
⊕ **Greataxe** (standard; at-will) ✦ **Weapon**
+10 vs. AC; 1d12 + 8 (crit 1d12 + 20) damage.
⊠ **Wounded Retaliation** (immediate reaction, when first bloodied; encounter)
The half-orc scarthane makes a greataxe attack.
⊠ **Bloodfury Attack** (standard; usable only while bloodied; encounter) ✦ **Healing, Weapon**
+10 vs. AC; 2d12 + 2 damage, and the half-orc scarthane regains 10 hit points.
Blood for Blood ✦ **Healing**
When the half-orc scarthane hits a bloodied target, the attack deals 1d6 extra damage, and the scarthane regains 5 hit points.
Furious Assault (free, when the half-orc scarthane damages an enemy; encounter)
The scarthane's attack deals 1d10 extra damage.
Alignment Unaligned   **Languages** Common, Giant
Skills Athletics +13, Endurance +11, Intimidate +7
Str 21 (+8)   **Dex** 17 (+6)   **Wis** 11 (+3)
Con 16 (+6)   **Int** 10 (+3)   **Cha** 8 (+2)
Equipment greataxe

HALF-ORC SCARTHANE TACTICS

The half-orc scarthane focuses attacks on one creature if possible to get the foe to a bloodied state as quickly as possible, taking advantage of *blood for blood*. The scarthane uses *bloodfury attack* at the first possible chance.

HALF-ORC LORE

Nature DC 12: Half-orcs combine the daring of humans and the ferocity of orcs. Proud of their strength and decisiveness, half-orcs are often impolitic in social situations.

The origins of half-orcs are mysterious. Some say they are the product of crossbreeding between savage tribes. Others point to an ancient program to create the ultimate warrior. Still others say their origins are divine. All or none of these explanations might be true.

Half-orc hunters are found among many communities. Half-orc scarthanes are most often found living savage lives alongside full-blooded orcs, bearing ritual scars that prove their ferocity and worthiness.

ENCOUNTER GROUPS

Half-orcs exist between two cultures, and they often walk the line between wilderness and settled lands. Thus, they're adaptable to a wide range of associates.

Level 6 Encounter (XP 1,400)
✦ 2 half-orc hunters (level 5 skirmisher)
✦ 1 human hexer (level 7 controller)
✦ 4 human berserkers (level 4 brute, *MM* 163)

Level 9 Encounter (XP 2,100)
✦ 4 half-orc scarthanes (level 7 brute)
✦ 1 orc chieftain (level 8 elite brute, *MM* 204)
✦ 1 orc eye of Gruumsh (level 5 controller, *MM* 204)

When these feathered predators are on the hunt, the silent skies become a dangerous battleground.

Blood Hawk

Blood hawks are aggressive hunters that use their razor-sharp claws to deal grievous wounds.

Blood Hawk		Level 1 Skirmisher
Small natural beast		XP 100

Initiative +5   **Senses** Perception +1
HP 27; **Bloodied** 13
AC 15; **Fortitude** 12, **Reflex** 14, **Will** 12
Speed 2 (clumsy), fly 6

ⓐ **Claw Rake** (standard; at-will)
+6 vs. AC; 1d6 + 5 damage, and the target takes ongoing 2 damage, or ongoing 5 damage if the blood hawk is bloodied (save ends).

ⴕ **Flyby Attack** (standard; at-will)
The blood hawk flies 6 squares and makes a *claw rake* attack at any point during that movement. The blood hawk doesn't provoke opportunity attacks when moving away from the target.

Alignment Unaligned   **Languages** –
Str 13 (+1)	**Dex** 16 (+3)	**Wis** 13 (+1)
Con 11 (+0)	**Int** 2 (–4)	**Cha** 7 (–2)

Frost Hawk

Native to the Elemental Chaos, the frost hawk is a fearsome aerial hunter often found in the world in search of prey.

Frost Hawk		Level 7 Skirmisher
Small elemental beast (cold)		XP 300

Initiative +9   **Senses** Perception +6
HP 80; **Bloodied** 40
AC 21; **Fortitude** 19, **Reflex** 20, **Will** 19
Immune disease, poison; **Resist** 10 cold
Speed 2 (clumsy), fly 8

ⓐ **Ice Talons** (standard; at-will) ✦ **Cold**
+12 vs. AC; 1d6 + 5 damage plus 1d6 cold damage.

ⴕ **Flyby Attack** (standard; at-will)
The frost hawk flies 8 squares and makes an *ice talons* attack at any point during that movement. The frost hawk doesn't provoke opportunity attacks when moving away from the target.

↞ **Freezing Screech** (standard; at-will) ✦ **Cold**
Close blast 3; +10 vs. Fortitude; 1d8 + 5 cold damage, and the target is slowed (save ends).

Shattering Strike
A frost hawk's melee attacks deal 2d6 extra cold damage against a slowed creature.

Alignment Unaligned   **Languages** –
Str 14 (+5)	**Dex** 19 (+7)	**Wis** 16 (+6)
Con 16 (+6)	**Int** 2 (–1)	**Cha** 8 (+2)

Hawk Lore

Arcana DC 19: Although they originate in the Elemental Chaos, frost hawks can be found in the high places and cold regions of the world. A frost hawk's screech can hinder the movement of opponents, making them more vulnerable to its attacks.

Nature DC 10: Blood hawks are deadly raptors trained as hunters by many races. Their lethal claws deal wounds that continue to bleed, and their flying attacks make them difficult to engage.

Encounter Groups

Like most raptors, blood hawks and frost hawks can be encountered among their own kind or as hunting birds trained by other creatures.

Level 2 Encounter (XP 725)
✦ 3 blood hawks (level 1 skirmisher)
✦ 1 bloodseeker drake (level 4 soldier)
✦ 2 elf archers (level 2 artillery, *MM* 106)

Level 6 Encounter (XP 1,400)
✦ 2 frost hawks (level 7 skirmisher)
✦ 1 orc bloodrager (level 7 elite brute, *MM* 204)
✦ 1 orc eye of Gruumsh (level 5 controller, *MM* 204)

HOMUNCULUS

HOMUNCULI ACT AS TIRELESS GUARDIANS for specific locations, relics, or creatures. Their creators imbue these constructs with a singular purpose, but many homunculi have outlived their original masters.

STONEFIST DEFENDER

A DRIVEN AND DEADLY FOE, a stonefist defender serves a designated creature as a bodyguard and combat partner.

Stonefist Defender		Level 2 Skirmisher
Small natural animate (construct, homunculus)		XP 125

Initiative +6   **Senses** Perception +4; darkvision
HP 38; **Bloodied** 19
AC 16; **Fortitude** 13, **Reflex** 14, **Will** 14
Immune disease, poison
Speed 8
⊕ **Spiked Fist** (standard; at-will)
    +7 vs. AC; 1d8 + 5 damage.
Guard Creature
    A stonefist defender gains a +2 bonus to attack rolls against any enemy adjacent to its guarded creature (see the "Guard" sidebar).
Synchronized Flank
    While a stonefist defender is flanking an enemy with its guarded creature, its attacks deal 1d6 extra damage against the flanked enemy.
Tumble (move; at-will)
    The stonefist defender shifts 3 squares.

Alignment Unaligned		**Languages** –
Skills Acrobatics +9		
Str 12 (+2)	**Dex** 17 (+4)	**Wis** 17 (+4)
Con 14 (+3)	**Int** 11 (+1)	**Cha** 7 (-1)

WAYNE ENGLAND

ARBALESTER

AN ARBALESTER IS A DEADLY RANGED ATTACKER, lobbing volleys of bolts at intruders in the area it guards.

Arbalester		Level 4 Artillery
Medium natural animate (construct, homunculus)		XP 175

Initiative +6   **Senses** Perception +9; darkvision
HP 43; **Bloodied** 21
AC 16; **Fortitude** 15, **Reflex** 17, **Will** 15
Immune disease, poison
Speed 6
⊕ **Slam** (standard; at-will)
    +11 vs. AC; 1d6 + 4 damage.
↗ **Bolt** (standard; at-will)
    Ranged 20/40; +11 vs. AC; 1d10 + 4 damage.
↗ **Double Shot** (standard; recharge ⚁ ⚂ ⚃)
    The arbalester makes two bolt attacks, each against a different target. The targets must be within 5 squares of each other.
Guard Area
    If an enemy is within an arbalester's guarded area (see the "Guard" sidebar) at the start of the arbalester's turn, the arbalester recharges *double shot*.

Alignment Unaligned	**Languages** –	
Str 15 (+4)	**Dex** 18 (+6)	**Wis** 15 (+4)
Con 13 (+3)	**Int** 5 (-1)	**Cha** 8 (+1)

ENCOUNTER GROUPS

Homunculi can be found as servants and companions to spellcasters, or as tireless guards in ancient tombs and treasure vaults.

Level 3 Encounter (XP 750)
✦ 3 stonefist defenders (level 2 skirmisher)
✦ 1 arbalester (level 4 artillery)
✦ 1 dwarf hammerer (level 5 soldier, *MM* 97)

> ### GUARD
>
> A homunculus can be attuned to a specific area or creature. Attuning the homunculus takes 1 minute and can be done only by the homunculus's creator or its new owner (as designated by its creator). The homunculus gains certain powers and benefits in this guard role.
>   **Guarded Area:** An area up to 5 squares on a side.
>   **Guarded Creature:** A creature, typically the homunculus's creator.

DIVERSE AND MULTIFACETED, humans possess the potential for both greatness and villainy.

HUMAN CAVALIER

MOUNTED ON A WARHORSE, a human cavalier wears its enemies down with lance and broadsword.

Human Cavalier	Level 7 Soldier (Leader)
Medium natural humanoid	XP 300

Initiative +8 **Senses** Perception +9
Battle Acumen aura sight; each ally within the aura gains a +2 bonus to initiative.
HP 78; **Bloodied** 39
AC 23; **Fortitude** 20, **Reflex** 18, **Will** 19
Speed 5

⊕ **Broadsword** (standard; at-will) ✦ **Weapon**
+14 vs. AC; 1d10 + 5 damage, and the target is marked until the end of the human cavalier's next turn.

↟ **Champion's Retort** (immediate interrupt, when an enemy marked by the human cavalier makes a melee attack against an ally adjacent to it; at-will) ✦ **Weapon**
Targets the triggering enemy; +13 vs. AC; 1d6 + 5 damage.

↟ **Lancer** (standard; usable only while mounted; at-will) ✦ **Weapon**
+14 vs. AC; 1d10 + 5 damage, and the target is knocked prone.

Hasty Parry (immediate interrupt, when an enemy marked by the human cavalier makes a melee attack against an ally adjacent to it; encounter)
The triggering enemy's attack targets the cavalier instead of the ally, and the cavalier gains a +3 bonus to AC against that attack.

Alignment Unaligned **Languages** Common
Skills Athletics +12, Diplomacy +11
Str 19 (+7)	**Dex** 13 (+4)	**Wis** 12 (+4)
Con 14 (+5)	**Int** 10 (+3)	**Cha** 16 (+6)
Equipment heavy shield, plate armor, broadsword, longspear

HUMAN DIABOLIST

THE HUMAN DIABOLIST IS A PRACTITIONER of evil magic. A diabolist wields fire as its favored weapon.

Human Diabolist	Level 20 Artillery
Medium natural humanoid	XP 2,800

Initiative +14 **Senses** Perception +10
HP 147; **Bloodied** 73
AC 32; **Fortitude** 32, **Reflex** 31, **Will** 33
Speed 6

⊕ **Kukri** (standard; at-will) ✦ **Fire, Weapon**
+25 vs. AC; 1d6 + 4 damage plus 2d6 fire damage. The human diabolist rerolls any damage die result of 1 until the result is greater than 1.

⊕ **Dark Fire** (standard; at-will) ✦ **Fire, Implement, Necrotic**
Ranged 15; +27 vs. Reflex; 2d10 + 7 fire and necrotic damage.

↣ **Hell Blight** (minor; at-will) ✦ **Implement**
Ranged sight; no attack roll; the target is hell-blighted (save ends). A hell-blighted target that takes fire damage from the human diabolist cannot spend a healing surge until the end of the diabolist's next turn. If the diabolist uses this power on a new target, the previous target is no longer hell-blighted.

↣ **Sulfurous Flash** (standard; at-will) ✦ **Fire, Implement**
Ranged 5; +27 vs. Fortitude; 2d4 + 6 fire damage, and the human diabolist has concealment against the target until the end of the diabolist's next turn.

❋ **Darkfire Storm** (standard; encounter) ✦ **Fire, Implement, Necrotic**
Area burst 2 within 20; +25 vs. Reflex; 2d6 + 7 fire and necrotic damage, and ongoing 10 fire and necrotic damage (save ends).

Infernal Deflection (immediate interrupt, when the human diabolist is hit by a melee or ranged attack; recharge ⚄ ⚅) ✦ **Fire**
The diabolist takes half damage from the triggering attack, and the attacker takes 15 fire damage.

Life from Fire
Whenever a human diabolist takes fire damage, it gains 10 temporary hit points.

Alignment Evil **Languages** Common
Skills Arcana +19, Bluff +21, Stealth +19
Str 10 (+10)	**Dex** 18 (+14)	**Wis** 11 (+10)
Con 21 (+15)	**Int** 11 (+10)	**Cha** 23 (+16)
Equipment leather armor, kukri, rod

HUMAN DIRE BEAST HUNTER

THE HUMAN DIRE BEAST HUNTER WAITS IN AMBUSH for prey, armed with spear, net, and poison.

Human Dire Beast Hunter	Level 9 Artillery
Medium natural humanoid	XP 400

Initiative +8   **Senses** Perception +12
HP 76; **Bloodied** 38
AC 22; **Fortitude** 21, **Reflex** 22, **Will** 21
Speed 6
⊕ **Spear** (standard; at-will) ✦ **Weapon**
  +16 vs. AC; 2d8 + 5 damage.
⊗ **Poisoned Crossbow** (standard; at-will) ✦ **Poison, Weapon**
  Ranged 15/30; +16 vs. AC; 2d8 + 3 damage, and ongoing 5
  poison damage (save ends).
➹ **Trapping Net** (standard; requires a net; encounter)
  Ranged 3; +16 vs. Reflex; the target is restrained (save ends).
Alignment Unaligned   **Languages** Common
Skills Acrobatics +13, Athletics +11, Endurance +12
Str 14 (+6)   **Dex** 19 (+8)   **Wis** 17 (+7)
Con 16 (+7)   **Int** 16 (+7)   **Cha** 11 (+4)
Equipment crossbow with 40 poisoned bolts, spear, net

HUMAN DREAD ASSASSIN

A HUMAN DREAD ASSASSIN HAS ONE MARK. The assassin's goal is to kill that mark, no matter the cost.

Human Dread Assassin	Level 22 Lurker
Medium natural humanoid	XP 4,150

Initiative +23   **Senses** Perception +22
HP 161; **Bloodied** 80; see also *assassin's determination*
AC 36; **Fortitude** 32, **Reflex** 34, **Will** 32
Speed 7
⊕ **Zealot's Scimitar** (standard; at-will) ✦ **Necrotic, Poison, Weapon**
  +26 vs. AC; 1d8 + 5 damage (crit 2d8 + 13), and ongoing 10
  poison and necrotic damage (save ends).
Cloak of Zeal (move 1/round; at-will)
  The human dread assassin gains concealment until the end of
  its next turn and shifts 3 squares.
Deadly Blade (minor; usable while the human dread assassin has
  cover or concealment; recharge ⚄ ⚅)
  The target of the assassin's next attack grants combat
  advantage to it, and the assassin's attack deals 5d6 extra
  damage on a hit.
Assassin's Determination (when first bloodied; encounter)
  The human dread assassin recharges *deadly blade*. If it is already
  recharged, the assassin regains 20 hit points.
Alignment Unaligned   **Languages** Common
Skills Intimidate +22, Stealth +24
Str 17 (+14)   **Dex** 26 (+19)   **Wis** 13 (+12)
Con 23 (+17)   **Int** 18 (+15)   **Cha** 22 (+17)
Equipment scimitar

HUMAN GLADIATOR

A CONSUMMATE ATHLETE, the human gladiator knows all the tricks of close combat.

Human Gladiator	Level 14 Elite Soldier
Medium natural humanoid	XP 2,000

Initiative +12   **Senses** Perception +9
Fighting Focus aura 1; each enemy that starts its turn within the
  aura is marked until the start of its next turn.
HP 276; **Bloodied** 138
AC 30; **Fortitude** 26, **Reflex** 26, **Will** 24
Saving Throws +2
Speed 6
Action Points 1
⊕ **Gladius** (standard; at-will) ✦ **Weapon**
  +21 vs. AC; 2d8 + 6 damage.
↯ **Knock to the Dirt** (minor; encounter)
  +19 vs. Fortitude; the target is knocked prone.
↯ **Well-Placed Kick** (minor; recharge ⚄ ⚅)
  +19 vs. Reflex; the target is dazed and slowed (save ends both).
↯ **Sand in the Eyes** (minor; encounter)
  +19 vs. Fortitude; the target is blinded (save ends).
⟳ **Gladius Display** (standard; at-will) ✦ **Weapon**
  Close burst 1; targets enemies; +19 vs. Reflex; 2d8 + 6 damage.
Alignment Unaligned   **Languages** Common
Skills Acrobatics +15, Athletics +18
Str 22 (+13)   **Dex** 16 (+10)   **Wis** 14 (+9)
Con 18 (+11)   **Int** 12 (+8)   **Cha** 17 (+10)
Equipment light shield, scale armor, gladius (short sword)

HUMAN INSANE NOBLE

A HUMAN INSANE NOBLE RUSHES around the battlefield, making attacks at a maddening pace. Insane nobles are reckless, with no regard for their own safety.

Human Insane Noble		Level 23 Elite Skirmisher
Medium natural humanoid		XP 10,200

Initiative +19   **Senses** Perception +11
HP 428; **Bloodied** 214; see also *ignoble fury*
AC 37; **Fortitude** 35, **Reflex** 35, **Will** 36
Saving Throws +2
Speed 6
Action Points 1

⊕ **Scepter** (standard; at-will) ✦ **Weapon**
+28 vs. AC; 3d8 + 6 damage.

↯ **Flurry of Madness** (standard; at-will)
The insane noble shifts 6 squares and makes one scepter attack against each enemy it moves adjacent to.

↯ **Ignoble Fury** (immediate reaction, when first bloodied) ✦ **Weapon**
Close burst 1; targets enemies; +26 vs. AC; 3d8 + 6 damage, and the target is knocked prone.

Sheer Madness
An insane noble does not provoke opportunity attacks.

Alignment Chaotic evil   **Languages** Common
Skills Endurance +23

Str 16 (+14)	Dex 22 (+17)	Wis 11(+11)
Con 22 (+17)	Int 15 (+13)	Cha 24 (+18)

Equipment scepter (mace)

HUMAN HEXER

CEREMONIAL STAFF IN HAND, the human hexer has an array of spells to change the course of a battle.

Human Hexer		Level 7 Controller
Medium natural humanoid		XP 300

Initiative +3   **Senses** Perception +16
HP 77; **Bloodied** 38
AC 20; **Fortitude** 17, **Reflex** 18, **Will** 19
Speed 6

⊕ **Staff** (standard; at-will) ✦ **Weapon**
+12 vs. AC; 1d6 + 1 damage.

↗ **Beast Curse** (standard; recharge ⚄ ⚅) ✦ **Polymorph**
Ranged 10; targets a hexed enemy; +11 vs. Fortitude; until the end of the human hexer's next turn, the target becomes a Tiny animal. While in this form, the target cannot use powers.

⬅ **Hex** (minor; at-will) ✦ **Charm, Implement**
Close burst 10; targets enemies; +11 vs. Will; the target is hexed (save ends). While the target is hexed, it takes a -2 penalty to attack rolls and damage rolls against the human hexer.

❈ **Capricious Earth** (standard; encounter) ✦ **Charm, Implement**
Area burst 3 within 10; targets hexed creatures; +11 vs. Will; 1d10 + 3 damage, and the human hexer slides the target 3 squares and the target is knocked prone.

Hex Jump (move; encounter) ✦ **Teleportation**
The human hexer either teleports 5 squares or swaps positions with one hexed creature within 5 squares of it.

Alignment Unaligned   **Languages** Common
Skills Arcana +10, Nature +11

Str 10 (+3)	Dex 11 (+3)	Wis 17 (+6)
Con 13 (+4)	Int 15 (+5)	Cha 14 (+5)

Equipment robes, staff

Human Javelin Dancer

RANGING OVER THE BATTLEFIELD, the human javelin dancer is a study in deadly grace.

Human Javelin Dancer	Level 6 Skirmisher
Medium natural humanoid	XP 250

Initiative +8 **Senses** Perception +4
HP 70; **Bloodied** 35
AC 20; **Fortitude** 18, **Reflex** 19, **Will** 17
Speed 6

⊕ **Spear** (standard; at-will) ✦ **Weapon**
+11 vs. AC; 1d8 + 3 damage.

⊬ **Mobile Attack** (standard; at-will)
The human javelin dancer shifts 3 squares and makes one spear attack during the move.

⌁ **Javelin** (standard; at-will) ✦ **Weapon**
Ranged 10/20; +12 vs. AC; 1d6 + 3 damage.

Adept Retreat
A human javelin dancer does not grant combat advantage from running.

Skirmish
If a human javelin dancer ends its move at least 4 squares from the square where it started the move, its attacks deal 1d6 extra damage until the start of its next turn.

Alignment Unaligned	**Languages** Common

Skills Athletics +10

Str 15 (+5)	**Dex** 16 (+6)	**Wis** 13 (+4)
Con 14 (+5)	**Int** 10 (+3)	**Cha** 10 (+3)

Equipment leather armor, light shield, 4 javelins, spear

Human Knife Fighter

THE HUMAN KNIFE FIGHTER MAKES A BLOODY MESS of enemies' ranks, popping up, knife in hand, where least expected.

Human Knife Fighter	Level 7 Elite Skirmisher
Medium natural humanoid	XP 600

Initiative +8 **Senses** Perception +14
HP 162; **Bloodied** 81
AC 21; **Fortitude** 19, **Reflex** 19, **Will** 19
Saving Throws +2
Speed 7
Action Points 1

⊕ **Wounding Dagger** (standard; at-will) ✦ **Weapon**
+12 vs. AC (crit 19–20); 1d6 + 6 damage (crit 1d6 + 12) and ongoing 5 damage (save ends).

⊬ **Dance of the Knife** (standard; at-will) ✦ **Weapon**
+12 vs. AC (crit 19–20); 1d6 + 6 damage (crit 1d6 + 12). *Effect:* The human knife fighter shifts 2 squares after the attack and makes one more attack against the same target or a different one. The knife fighter then shifts 2 squares.

Peerless Tumbler (move; recharge ⚅ ⚅)
The human knife fighter shifts 4 squares, ignoring difficult terrain.

Combat Advantage
A human knife fighter deals 2d6 extra damage against any target granting combat advantage to it.

Alignment Unaligned	**Languages** Common

Skills Stealth +11

Str 15 (+5)	**Dex** 17 (+6)	**Wis** 16 (+6)
Con 17 (+6)	**Int** 13 (+4)	**Cha** 12 (+4)

Equipment dagger, net

Human Mystagogue

SPEAKING A SUPERNAL WORD OF POWER, the human mystagogue manipulates both its enemies' perceptions and the battle's direction.

Human Mystagogue	Level 20 Controller (Leader)
Medium natural humanoid	XP 2,800

Initiative +11 **Senses** Perception +22
Shared Clarity aura 10; each ally within the aura gains a +2 bonus to saving throws.
HP 188; **Bloodied** 94
AC 33; **Fortitude** 31, **Reflex** 32, **Will** 33
Speed 6

⊕ **Mystery's Touch** (standard; at-will) ✦ **Implement, Psychic**
+24 vs. Reflex; 2d8 + 7 psychic damage, and the target takes a –2 penalty to attack rolls against the human mystagogue until the end of the mystagogue's next turn.

⌁ **Bend Perception** (standard; at-will) ✦ **Illusion, Implement, Psychic**
Ranged 20; +22 vs. Will; 2d6 + 7 psychic damage, and until the end of the human mystagogue's next turn, the target is slowed and takes a –2 penalty to attack rolls and saving throws.

⬳ **Awestrike** (standard; recharge ⚄ ⚅) ✦ **Healing, Implement, Psychic**
Close burst 5; targets enemies; +22 vs. Will; 2d6 + 7 psychic damage, the human mystagogue slides the target 6 squares, and the target is dazed (save ends). *Effect:* The mystagogue slides one ally in the burst 6 squares, and that ally regains 10 hit points.

Veil of Inscrutability (immediate reaction, when the human mystagogue is missed by a melee or ranged attack; at-will)
The mystagogue shifts 2 squares and gains a +2 bonus to AC and Reflex until the end of its next turn.

Alignment Unaligned	**Languages** Common, Supernal

Skills Arcana +21, Insight +22, Religion +21

Str 12 (+11)	**Dex** 12 (+11)	**Wis** 24 (+17)
Con 20 (+15)	**Int** 22 (+16)	**Cha** 15 (+12)

Equipment robes, holy symbol

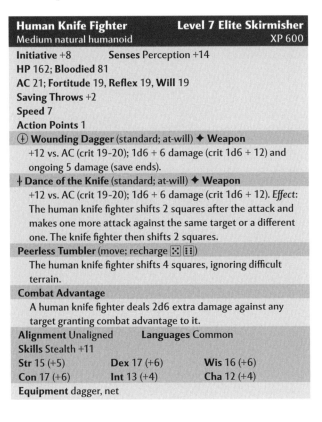

HUMAN NOBLE

WITH SILVER TONGUES, human nobles remind assailants of the lethal price of harming the gentry.

Human Noble	Level 5 Controller (Leader)
Medium natural humanoid	XP 200

Initiative +3 **Senses** Perception +3
HP 60; **Bloodied** 30
AC 19; **Fortitude** 17, **Reflex** 17, **Will** 18; see also *protected*
Speed 5

ⓐ **Longsword** (standard; at-will) ✦ **Weapon**
+10 vs. AC; 1d8 + 3 damage.

⟻ **Appoint Champion** (standard; at-will)
Close burst 10; targets one ally; the target makes a basic attack as a free action and shifts 1 square before or after the attack.

⟻ **Inspirational Authority** (standard; encounter)
Close burst 10; targets one ally; the target uses an at-will, encounter, or recharge attack power as a free action.

⟻ **Urge Hesitation** (standard; encounter) ✦ **Charm**
Close burst 5; targets enemies; +9 vs. Will; the target cannot use a standard action during its next turn.

Protected
A human noble gains a +2 bonus to all defenses while an ally is adjacent to it.

Alignment Unaligned **Languages** Common
Skills Diplomacy +10, Insight +8, Intimidate +10
| **Str** 15 (+4) | **Dex** 12 (+3) | **Wis** 12 (+3) |
| **Con** 12 (+3) | **Int** 14 (+4) | **Cha** 16 (+5) |
Equipment chainmail, light shield, longsword

HUMAN PIRATE

HUMAN PIRATES ARE BANDITS OF THE SEA, raiding ships and seaports.

Human Pirate	Level 9 Skirmisher
Medium natural humanoid	XP 400

Initiative +8 **Senses** Perception +5
HP 95; **Bloodied** 47
AC 23; **Fortitude** 21, **Reflex** 21, **Will** 20
Speed 7

ⓐ **Cutlass** (standard; at-will) ✦ **Weapon**
+14 vs. AC; 2d6 + 5 damage.

Rigging Monkey (minor; encounter)
The human pirate gains a climb speed of 7 until the end of its next turn.

Scurvy Dog's Flank
A human pirate gains a +1 bonus to attack rolls against an enemy it is flanking, and its attacks deal 2d6 extra damage to that creature.

Alignment Unaligned **Languages** Common
Skills Acrobatics +11, Athletics +11
| **Str** 14 (+6) | **Dex** 15 (+6) | **Wis** 12 (+5) |
| **Con** 15 (+6) | **Int** 9 (+3) | **Cha** 11 (+4) |
Equipment cutlass (short sword)

HUMAN PIRATE TACTICS

Human pirates climb in the rigging of ships, using *rigging monkey* to keep enemies on their toes. Pirates stay near the water. If on a boat, they stay near the edge of the boat.

HUMAN PIRATE CAPTAIN

A HUMAN PIRATE CAPTAIN WADES INTO BATTLE, swinging a cutlass and taunting its enemies.

Human Pirate Captain	Level 10 Soldier (Leader)
Medium natural humanoid	XP 500

Initiative +10 **Senses** Perception +12
HP 104; **Bloodied** 52
AC 26; **Fortitude** 22, **Reflex** 22, **Will** 22
Speed 7

ⓐ **Cutlass** (standard; at-will) ✦ **Weapon**
+16 vs. AC; 2d6 + 6 damage, and the target is slowed (save ends).

⟻ **Call to Arms** (when first bloodied; encounter)
Close burst 10; targets allies; the target makes a melee basic attack or shifts 3 squares as a free action.

⟻ **Vicious Mockery** (minor; recharge ⚅⚅)
Close burst 5; targets one enemy; the target provokes an opportunity attack from each enemy that is adjacent to it.

Rigging Monkey (minor; encounter)
The human pirate captain gains a climb speed of 7 until the end of its next turn.

Scurvy Dog's Flank
A human pirate captain gains a +1 bonus to attack rolls against an enemy it is flanking, and its attacks deal 2d6 extra damage to that creature.

Alignment Unaligned **Languages** Common
Skills Acrobatics +13, Athletics +13
| **Str** 16 (+8) | **Dex** 16 (+8) | **Wis** 14 (+7) |
| **Con** 16 (+8) | **Int** 13 (+6) | **Cha** 16 (+8) |
Equipment cutlass (short sword)

Human Slaver

A HUMAN SLAVER RELIES ON MACE AND SCOURGE to subdue and capture its victims.

Human Slaver	Level 8 Brute
Medium natural humanoid	XP 350

Initiative +7   **Senses** Perception +4
HP 102; **Bloodied** 51
AC 20; **Fortitude** 20, **Reflex** 20, **Will** 19
Speed 6
⊕ **Thump and Lash** (standard; at-will) ✦ **Weapon**
     +11 vs. AC; 2d8 + 6 damage, and the target takes a –2 penalty to melee attack rolls until the end of its next turn.
↓ **Slaver's Tangle** (standard; requires a scourge; recharge ⚄ ⚅ ⚅)
     ✦ **Weapon**
     +11 vs. AC; 2d8 + 6 damage, and the target is immobilized and takes a –2 penalty to melee attack rolls until the end of its next turn.
Alignment Evil   **Languages** Common
Skills Intimidate +11
Str 17 (+7)   **Dex** 16 (+7)   **Wis** 10 (+4)
Con 12 (+5)   **Int** 10 (+4)   **Cha** 14 (+6)
Equipment leather armor, mace, scourge (whip)

Human Slaver Tactics

The human slaver focuses on a single target with *slaver's tangle*. The slaver then either moves on to other enemies or delivers punishing mace-and-scourge combos to immobilized victims with *thump and lash*.

Human Lore

Nature DC 10: Human cavaliers ride horses or griffons. Cavaliers are prized as battle leaders, and they are often hired to lead nonhuman troops.

Human gladiators are accustomed to fighting a wide array of combatants. Although some gladiators are kept as slaves, others become wealthy by defeating foes in arena matches.

Human nobles claim that their families' status grants them leadership skills. However, once in combat some nobles find that they are unable to cope with bloodshed, and freeze up or run away.

Pirate captains keep their rowdy crews in line with a mixture of threats and bribes. Humans who have run afoul of the law become pirates to avoid capture and to satisfy the human need for new experiences and adventures.

Human slavers are themselves slaves to greed and power. They have great influence over their slaves, but the promise of freedom sometimes causes those slaves to revolt and remove the slaver from the picture—by any means necessary.

Nature DC 15: Human diabolists trade their souls for power. Both humans and devils share a lust for power, and many of a diabolist's other traits might be considered infernal.

Human javelin dancers dance around foes, hurling javelins like thunderbolts with uncanny accuracy.

Human knife fighters, trained for battle in alley fights and tavern brawls, tumble around the battlefield to slip blades into just the right places.

Human mystagogues are often found at the centers of cults.

Nature DC 20: Human dire beast hunters can be bounty hunters seeking to capture exotic creatures and sell them to the highest bidder, or they can be pompous nobles seeking to one-up other members of the nobility by mounting bigger and more exotic heads in their great rooms.

Human hexers practice a mixture of arcane and primal magic. While some work in harmony with nature, others pervert primal magic to command the spirits of the earth against their will.

Encounter Groups

Humans are versatile and familiar. They have a knack for turning up nearly everywhere.

Level 6 Encounter (XP 1,350)
✦ 2 half-orc hunters (level 5 skirmisher)
✦ 8 human lackeys (level 7 minion, *MM* 162)
✦ 1 human slaver (level 8 brute)

Level 7 Encounter (XP 1,500)
✦ 1 cacklefiend hyena (level 7 brute, *MM* 166)
✦ 1 human hexer (level 7 controller)
✦ 1 human knife fighter (level 7 elite skirmisher)
✦ 4 human lackeys (level 7 minion, *MM* 162)

Level 7 Encounter (XP 1,700)
✦ 3 human cavaliers (level 7 soldier)
✦ 1 human noble (level 5 controller)
✦ 4 warhorses (level 3 brute, *MM* 159)

Level 9 Encounter (XP 2,050)
✦ 1 human pirate captain (level 10 soldier)
✦ 3 human pirates (level 9 skirmisher)
✦ 1 human slaver (level 8 brute)

Level 19 Encounter (XP 13,200)
✦ 1 goristro (level 19 elite brute, *MM* 55)
✦ 2 human diabolists (level 20 artillery)
✦ 1 human mystagogue (level 20 controller)

Level 21 Encounter (XP 16,650)
✦ 1 half-elf baleful thaumaturge (level 24 artillery)
✦ 1 human dread assassin (level 22 lurker)
✦ 1 human insane noble (level 23 elite skirmisher)

LEGENDARY FOR THEIR DEADLY HEADS and strange powers, hydras give any group of heroes pause. Driven by hunger, hydras lurk at the edges of civilization, plaguing border communities.

RAZOR HYDRA

THE RAZOR HYDRA GLITTERS with metal growing from its scales.

Razor Hydra	Level 16 Solo Brute
Large natural beast (reptile)	XP 7,000

Initiative +13   **Senses** Perception +17; all-around vision
HP 640; **Bloodied** 320; see also *regenerating heads* and *ferocity*
AC 28; **Fortitude** 29, **Reflex** 27, **Will** 26
Saving Throws +5
Speed 7
Action Points 2

⊕ **Bite** (standard; at-will)
Reach 2; +19 vs. AC; 1d8 + 4 damage, and the target takes ongoing 5 damage (save ends). If the razor hydra hits a target that is already taking untyped ongoing damage, that target's ongoing damage increases by 5.

⨎ **Hydra Fury** (standard; at-will)
The razor hydra makes four bite attacks, plus an additional attack for each head it has grown (see *regenerating heads*).

⨎ **Ferocity** (when the razor hydra drops to 0 hit points)
The hydra makes a *hydra fury* attack.

Blood-Hungry
A razor hydra gains a +2 bonus to attack rolls against bloodied creatures and creatures taking untyped ongoing damage.

Many-Headed
Each time a razor hydra would become dazed or stunned, it instead loses one attack while using *hydra fury* during its next turn. The hydra can be dazed or stunned multiple times.

Regenerating Heads
When a razor hydra first reaches 480, 320, and 160 hit points, a head is destroyed. At the start of the hydra's next turn after a head is destroyed, two heads grow in the lost head's place, and the hydra gains an additional bite attack with *hydra fury*.

Threatening Reach
A razor hydra can make opportunity attacks against all enemies within its reach (2 squares).

Alignment Unaligned		**Languages** —
Str 21 (+13)	**Dex** 20 (+13)	**Wis** 18 (+12)
Con 24 (+15)	**Int** 2 (+4)	**Cha** 8 (+7)

HEROSLAYER HYDRA

A CREATURE OUT OF LEGEND, the heroslayer hydra earned its name from the heroes who fell to its fangs.

(Back to front) heroslayer hydra and razor hydra

JIM NELSON

Heroslayer Hydra — Level 20 Solo Brute

Heroslayer Hydra	Level 20 Solo Brute
Huge natural beast (reptile)	XP 14,000

Initiative +14   **Senses** Perception +19; all-around vision
HP 776; **Bloodied** 388; see also *regenerating heads*
AC 32; **Fortitude** 34, **Reflex** 30, **Will** 30
Saving Throws +5
Speed 6
Action Points 2

⊕ **Bite** (standard; at-will)
   Reach 3; +25 vs. AC; 1d10 + 8 damage.

‡ **Hydra Fury** (standard; at-will)
   The heroslayer hydra makes five bite attacks, plus an additional attack for each head it has grown (see *regenerating heads*). A target hit by more than one bite attack in a round takes 10 extra damage.

‡ **Rampage** (standard; recharges when a critical hit is scored against the heroslayer hydra)
   The hydra makes one bite attack against each enemy within reach. On a hit, the target takes ongoing 10 damage (save ends).

Heroslayer
   While a heroslayer hydra is marked, it gains a +2 bonus to attack rolls and a +5 bonus to damage rolls against the creature that marked it.

Many-Headed
   Each time a heroslayer hydra would become dazed or stunned, it instead loses one attack while using *hydra fury* during its next turn. The hydra can be dazed or stunned multiple times.

Regenerating Heads
   When a heroslayer hydra first reaches 582, 388, and 194 hit points, a head is destroyed. At the start of the hydra's next turn after a head is destroyed, two heads grow in the lost head's place, and the hydra gains an additional bite attack with *hydra fury*.

Threatening Reach
   A heroslayer hydra can make opportunity attacks against all enemies within its reach (3 squares).

Alignment Chaotic evil   **Languages** —
Str 23 (+16)   **Dex** 19 (+14)   **Wis** 18 (+14)
Con 26 (+18)   **Int** 2 (+6)   **Cha** 9 (+9)

CHAOS HYDRA

HAILING FROM THE ELEMENTAL CHAOS, the chaos hydra draws upon elemental energy. As the chaos hydra generates more heads, it becomes more cunning.

Chaos Hydra — Level 22 Solo Brute

Chaos Hydra	Level 22 Solo Brute
Huge elemental beast (reptile)	XP 20,750

Initiative +16   **Senses** Perception +20; all-around vision
HP 848; **Bloodied** 424; see also *chaosborn*
AC 34; **Fortitude** 36, **Reflex** 32, **Will** 31
Resist 20 variable (2/encounter)
Saving Throws +5
Speed 7
Action Points 2

⊕ **Frostfire Bite** (standard; at-will) ✦ **Cold, Fire**
   Reach 3; +25 vs. AC; 3d8 + 5 cold and fire damage.

⊕ **Storm Bite** (standard; at-will) ✦ **Lightning, Thunder**
   Reach 3; +25 vs. AC; 3d8 + 5 lightning and thunder damage.

‡ **Hydra Fury** (standard; at-will)
   The chaos hydra makes a *storm bite* attack, a *frostfire bite* attack, and each additional attack it has gained through the growth of a head (see *chaosborn*).

‡ **Crushing Maw** (standard; at-will)
   Reach 3; +25 vs. AC; 1d8 + 5 damage, and the target is slowed and takes ongoing 10 damage (save ends both).

‡ **Mind Bite** (standard; at-will)
   Reach 3; +25 vs. AC; 1d8 + 5 damage, and the target is dazed (save ends).

‡ **Paralyzing Fang** (standard; at-will)
   Reach 3; +25 vs. AC; 1d8 + 5 damage, and the target is immobilized and takes a -2 penalty to all defenses (save ends both).

‡ **Venom Tooth** (standard; at-will) ✦ **Poison**
   Reach 3; +25 vs. AC; 1d8 +5 damage, and ongoing 10 poison damage (save ends).

Chaosborn
   A chaos hydra starts with two heads. When the hydra first reaches 636, 424, and 212 hit points, it grows an additional head. Roll a d4 at each increment to determine which attack the new head makes:
   1—*Crushing Maw*, 2—*Mind Bite*, 3—*Paralyzing Fang*, or 4—*Venom Tooth*. A hydra can gain the same attack multiple times through this effect.

Many-Headed
   Each time a chaos hydra would become dazed or stunned, it instead loses one attack, determined randomly, while using *hydra fury* during its next turn. The hydra can be dazed or stunned multiple times.

Threatening Reach
   A chaos hydra can make opportunity attacks against all enemies within its reach (3 squares).

Alignment Chaotic evil   **Languages** —
Str 26 (+19)   **Dex** 20 (+16)   **Wis** 19 (+15)
Con 28 (+20)   **Int** 2 (+7)   **Cha** 10 (+11)

HYDRA LORE

Arcana DC 22: Originally a native of the Elemental Chaos, the chaos hydra has filtered into the other planes. A chaos hydra's two heads contain elemental energy, which its bite unleashes on enemies.

Arcana DC 27: As a chaos hydra is hurt, its body generates more heads. The bite attack of a generated head can vary randomly.

Nature DC 22: When one head of a razor hydra sinks its fangs into an enemy, the other heads become obsessed with the taste of that enemy's blood. Razor hydras are also known as blood hydras for their ability to detect the scent of blood.

Nature DC 27: Heroslayer hydras dwell in mountain caves. In early times, humanoids stalked razor hydras to collect the hydras' serrated teeth, which were valued as weapons because they cause victims to bleed long after receiving wounds.

ENCOUNTER GROUPS

Opportunistic scavengers, such as carrion crawlers and shardstorm vortex whirlwinds, follow rampaging hydras. A powerful creature such as a minotaur cabalist occasionally captures a hydra to guard its lair.

Level 16 Encounter (XP 7,800)
✦ 1 minotaur cabalist (level 13 controller, *MM* 190)
✦ 1 razor hydra (level 16 solo brute)

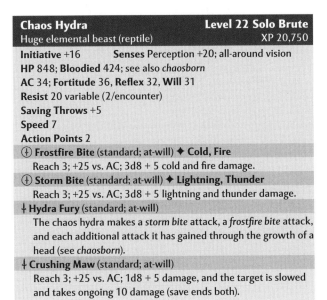

SLY AND SECRETIVE, KENKUS thrive in the underbelly of the civilized world. Like the ravens they resemble, these avian humanoids are opportunistic. They do not allow laws or morality to stand in their way.

KENKU RUFFIAN

KENKU RUFFIANS RELY ON NUMBERS. They flock around their foes to take them down.

Kenku Ruffian	Level 3 Minion Skirmisher
Medium natural humanoid	XP 38

Initiative +4   **Senses** Perception +3; low-light vision
HP 1; a missed attack never damages a minion.
AC 17; **Fortitude** 15, **Reflex** 16, **Will** 15
Speed 6
⊕ **Club** (standard; at-will) ✦ **Weapon**
    +8 vs. AC; 5 damage.
Flock Effect
    A kenku ruffian gains a +3 bonus instead of +2 while flanking, and it grants a +3 bonus instead of +2 while aiding another.
Mimicry
    A kenku ruffian can mimic sounds and voices. A successful Insight check opposed by the ruffian's Bluff check allows a listener to determine that the effect is faked.
Alignment Unaligned   **Languages** Common
Skills Stealth +9

Str 12 (+2)	**Dex** 17 (+4)	**Wis** 14 (+3)
Con 14 (+3)	**Int** 9 (+0)	**Cha** 11 (+1)

Equipment leather armor, club

KENKU RUFFIAN TACTICS

Before combat begins, one or two kenku ruffians go to get help. Once the fighting starts, ruffians use *flock effect* to boost their leaders' attacks and to make accurate attacks together.

KENKU WARRIOR

THE KENKU WARRIOR PRACTICES a flitting martial art, dodging seemingly at random toward and away from foes.

Kenku Warrior	Level 3 Skirmisher
Medium natural humanoid	XP 150

Initiative +6   **Senses** Perception +3; low-light vision
HP 44; **Bloodied** 22
AC 17; **Fortitude** 14, **Reflex** 15, **Will** 14
Speed 6
⊕ **Dagger** (standard; at-will) ✦ **Weapon**
    +8 vs. AC; 1d4 + 6 damage.
⊙ **Dagger** (standard; at-will) ✦ **Weapon**
    Ranged 5/10; +8 vs. AC; 1d4 + 6 damage.
† **Fluttering Attack** (standard; at-will)
    The kenku warrior shifts 4 squares and makes a basic attack during that movement.
Combat Advantage
    A kenku warrior deals 1d6 extra damage on melee attacks against any target granting combat advantage to it.
Flock Effect
    A kenku warrior gains a +3 bonus instead of +2 while flanking, and it grants a +3 bonus instead of +2 while aiding another.
Mimicry
    A kenku warrior can mimic sounds and voices. A successful Insight check opposed by the warrior's Bluff check allows a listener to determine that the effect is faked.
Alignment Unaligned   **Languages** Common

Str 14 (+3)	**Dex** 17 (+4)	**Wis** 14 (+3)
Con 12 (+2)	**Int** 9 (+0)	**Cha** 11 (+1)

Equipment leather armor, 6 daggers

KENKU WARRIOR TACTICS

The kenku warrior uses its mobility and *fluttering attack* to keep itself and its flockmates in flanking positions. The combination of combat advantage and *flock effect* then metes out the damage.

KENKU RINGLEADER

KENKU RINGLEADERS LEAD SMALL KENKU BANDS on raids or heists, acting as muscle when stealth and trickery fail. If the city watch or a rival gang shows up, the ringleader signals the crew's retreat.

Kenku Ringleader	Level 4 Soldier (Leader)
Medium natural humanoid	XP 175

Initiative +8   **Senses** Perception +3; low-light vision
HP 54; **Bloodied** 27
AC 20; **Fortitude** 16, **Reflex** 16, **Will** 15
Speed 6
⊕ **Spiked Chain** (standard; at-will) ✦ **Weapon**
    Reach 2; +11 vs. AC; 2d4 + 5 damage, and the target is marked until the end of the kenku ringleader's next turn.
⊙ **Sling** (standard; at-will) ✦ **Weapon**
    Ranged 10/20; +11 vs. AC; 1d6 + 5 damage.
† **Press the Attack** (standard; at-will) ✦ **Weapon**
    Reach 2; targets an enemy marked by the kenku; +11 vs. AC; 2d4 + 5 damage, and the target is knocked prone.
⬅ **Flock Reaction** (minor; recharge ⚄ ⚅ ⚅)
    Close burst 3; targets kenkus; the target shifts 1 square as a free action.
Flock Effect
    A kenku ringleader gains a +3 bonus instead of +2 while flanking, and it grants a +3 bonus instead of +2 while aiding another.
Mimicry
    A kenku ringleader can mimic sounds and voices. A successful Insight check opposed by the ringleader's Bluff check allows a listener to determine that the effect is faked.
Alignment Unaligned   **Languages** Common
Skills Bluff +10, Intimidate +10

Str 13 (+3)	**Dex** 18 (+6)	**Wis** 12 (+3)
Con 14 (+4)	**Int** 10 (+2)	**Cha** 16 (+5)

Equipment leather armor, sling, spiked chain

KENKU RINGLEADER TACTICS

A kenku ringleader first advances upon and attacks the most dangerous-looking enemies. It then directs allies into flanking positions using the shifting ability granted by *flock reaction*. It uses *press the attack* at every chance.

Aware of the details of any situation, a ringleader withdraws if a battle goes badly for its crew. It does not surrender unless it must do so to survive.

KENKU SNEAK

THE KENKU SNEAK LURKS IN HIDING and strikes from the shadows.

Kenku Sneak	Level 4 Lurker
Medium natural humanoid	XP 175

Initiative +10   **Senses** Perception +4; low-light vision
HP 42; **Bloodied** 21
AC 18; **Fortitude** 15, **Reflex** 17, **Will** 15
Speed 7 (4 while invisible)
ⴲ **Dagger** (standard; at-will) ✦ **Weapon**
    +9 vs. AC; 1d4 + 6 damage.
⤤ **Dagger** (standard; at-will) ✦ **Weapon**
    Ranged 5/10; +9 vs. AC; 1d4 + 6 damage.
Disappear into the Flock
    While it has cover from other kenkus, a kenku sneak can make a Stealth check to become hidden.
Flock Effect
    A kenku sneak gains a +3 bonus instead of +2 while flanking, and it grants a +3 bonus instead of +2 while aiding another.
Hidden Strike
    A kenku sneak deals 2d4 + 4 extra damage against any target from which it is hidden.
Mimicry
    A kenku sneak can mimic sounds and voices. A successful Insight check opposed by the sneak's Bluff check allows a listener to determine that the effect is faked.
Sniper
    A hidden kenku sneak that misses with a ranged attack remains hidden.
Alignment Unaligned   **Languages** Common
Skills Bluff +8, Stealth +11, Thievery +11
Str 15 (+4)   **Dex** 18 (+6)   **Wis** 14 (+4)
Con 12 (+3)   **Int** 13 (+3)   **Cha** 13 (+3)
Equipment leather armor, 6 daggers

KENKU SNEAK TACTICS

The kenku sneak uses *disappear into the flock* and focuses on enemies not in the main melee group that are close enough for the sneak to reach while hidden.

KENKU WING MAGE

THE KENKU WING MAGE USES AIR MAGIC and glowing feathers of force to harm and hamper foes.

Kenku Wing Mage	Level 5 Artillery
Medium natural humanoid	XP 200

Initiative +3   **Senses** Perception +3; low-light vision
HP 50; **Bloodied** 25
AC 17; **Fortitude** 15, **Reflex** 17, **Will** 18
Speed 6; see *wings of the flock*
ⴲ **Dagger** (standard; at-will) ✦ **Weapon**
    +9 vs. AC; 1d4 + 3 damage.
⤤ **Murder of Crows** (standard; at-will) ✦ **Force, Implement**
    Ranged 20; +10 vs. Reflex; 1d6 + 4 force damage, and the target grants combat advantage to the kenku wing mage (save ends).
↞ **Hurricane Blast** (standard; recharge ⚄ ⚅) ✦ **Force, Implement**
    Close blast 3; +8 vs. Fortitude; 1d6 + 6 force damage, and the kenku wing mage slides the target 3 squares.
✻ **Death Flock** (standard; encounter) ✦ **Force, Implement**
    Area burst 1 within 20; +8 vs. Reflex; 1d6 + 6 force damage, and the target is dazed (save ends).
Flock Effect
    A kenku wing mage gains a +3 bonus instead of +2 while flanking, and it grants a +3 bonus instead of +2 while aiding another.
Mimicry
    A kenku wing mage can mimic sounds and voices. A successful Insight check opposed by the wing mage's Bluff check allows a listener to determine that the effect is faked.
Wings of the Flock (minor; encounter) ✦ **Force**
    The kenku wing mage gains fly 6 (hover; altitude limit 4) until the end of the encounter.
Alignment Unaligned   **Languages** Common
Skills Stealth +8
Str 9 (+1)   **Dex** 13 (+3)   **Wis** 13 (+3)
Con 14 (+4)   **Int** 18 (+6)   **Cha** 15 (+4)
Equipment robes, dagger, orb

KENKU WING MAGE TACTICS

The kenku wing mage uses *wings of the flock* to move to a place with cover from where it can rain destruction upon its enemies with *murder of crows*, *hurricane blast*, and *death flock*. Rooftops and tree branches are ideal locations.

Kenku Assassin

Sly and deceitful, a kenku assassin favors poison. Unlike other kenkus, assassins rarely surrender.

Kenku Assassin	Level 5 Elite Skirmisher
Medium natural humanoid	XP 400

Initiative +8   **Senses** Perception +6; low-light vision
HP 126; **Bloodied** 63
AC 19; **Fortitude** 16, **Reflex** 17, **Will** 16
Saving Throws +2
Speed 6
Action Points 1

ⓣ **Venomous Stab** (standard; at-will) ✦ **Poison, Weapon**
   +10 vs. AC; 1d6 + 5 damage, and the target is slowed (save ends).

ⓡ **Venomous Shot** (standard; at-will) ✦ **Poison, Weapon**
   Ranged 15/30; +10 vs. AC; 1d8 + 4 poison damage, and the target is slowed (save ends).

↯ **Fluttering Attack** (standard; at-will)
   The kenku assassin shifts 4 squares and uses *venomous stab* during that move.

↯ **Gouging Talons** (immediate reaction, when an enemy attacks the kenku assassin; at-will)
   Targets the triggering enemy; +10 vs. AC; 1d6 + 2 damage.

⬚ **Feather Burst** (minor; encounter)
   Close burst 2; targets enemies; no attack roll; the target is blinded until the end of the kenku assassin's turn.

Flock Effect
   A kenku assassin gains a +3 bonus instead of +2 while flanking, and it grants a +3 bonus instead of +2 while aiding another.

Mimicry
   A kenku assassin can mimic sounds and voices. A successful Insight check opposed by the assassin's Bluff check allows a listener to determine that the effect is faked.

Alignment Unaligned   **Languages** Common
Skills Bluff +9, Stealth +11, Thievery +11
Str 13 (+3)   **Dex** 18 (+6)   **Wis** 9 (+1)
Con 15 (+4)   **Int** 13 (+3)   **Cha** 15 (+4)
Equipment leather armor, shortbow, short sword, 20 arrows

Kenku Assassin Tactics

The kenku assassin avoids melee until it hits at least one enemy with a *venomous shot*. Then it uses *fluttering attack* to poison more enemies. When necessary, the assassin uses *feather burst* to extricate itself, and possibly its allies, from melee. Kenku assassins fight to the death if escape is not possible.

Kenku Lore

Nature DC 12: These opportunistic avians live in tightly knit clans called flocks. Flocks are suspicious of outsiders, even other kenkus. They move in groups and are exceptionally good at working together.

Nature DC 17: Kenkus live predominantly in civilized regions but can be found throughout the world. Flocks live in or near major cities, often secretly. Flocks run a wide variety of criminal enterprises, favoring schemes and cons. They frequently use their ability to mimic sounds and voices. Violence is not their first choice, but kenkus can be formidable adversaries once steel is drawn.

Encounter Groups

Kenku flocks keep a wide variety of monsters as short-term company. Only those who overcome the kenkus' naturally suspicious nature remain part of a flock for long.

Level 2 Encounter (XP 700)
✦ 2 bloodseeker drakes (level 4 soldier)
✦ 2 kenku warriors (level 3 skirmisher)
✦ 1 pseudodragon (level 3 lurker, MM 91)

Level 3 Encounter (XP 779)
✦ 1 kenku ringleader (level 4 soldier)
✦ 8 kenku ruffians (level 3 minion)
✦ 2 kenku warriors (level 3 skirmisher)

Level 3 Encounter (XP 824)
✦ 2 blood hawks (level 1 skirmisher)
✦ 4 kenku ruffians (level 3 minion skirmisher)
✦ 1 kenku sneak (level 4 lurker)
✦ 3 spiretop drakes (level 1 skirmisher)

Level 4 Encounter (XP 922)
✦ 1 human berserker (level 4 brute, MM 163)
✦ 1 kenku ringleader (level 4 soldier)
✦ 6 kenku ruffians (level 3 minion skirmisher)
✦ 2 kenku sneaks (level 4 lurker)

Level 5 Encounter (XP 1,200)
✦ 1 half-elf bandit captain (level 6 skirmisher)
✦ 2 human berserkers (level 4 brute, MM 163)
✦ 1 kenku assassin (level 5 elite skirmisher)
✦ 1 kenku wing mage (level 5 artillery)

KRENSHAR

KRENSHARS ARE POWERFUL, CATLIKE CREATURES with faces that peel back to expose the bones and muscles of their skulls. This hideous sight, combined with a krenshar's savage roars, freezes its foes in terror.

Krenshar		Level 4 Controller
Medium natural beast		XP 175

Initiative +5 **Senses** Perception +7; low-light vision
Fearsome Visage aura 5; each enemy within the aura takes a -2 penalty to saving throws against fear effects.
HP 55; **Bloodied** 27
AC 18; **Fortitude** 16, **Reflex** 16, **Will** 14
Speed 8
⊕ **Hooking Swipe** (standard; at-will)
+8 vs. AC; 1d6 + 4 damage, and the target is knocked prone.
↩ **Roaring Skull** (standard; recharge ⚄ ⚅) ✦ **Fear, Thunder**
Close blast 5; +7 vs. Will; 1d8 + 4 thunder damage, and the target is dazed (save ends). If the target was already dazed, it is also weakened as long as it remains dazed.
↩ **Unnerving Skull** (minor 1/round; at-will) ✦ **Fear, Gaze**
Close burst 5; targets one creature; +8 vs. Will; the target takes a -2 penalty to attack rolls (save ends).
Alignment Unaligned **Languages** —
Skills Intimidate +5, Stealth +9
| **Str** 17 (+5) | **Dex** 17 (+5) | **Wis** 10 (+2) |
| **Con** 15 (+4) | **Int** 2 (-2) | **Cha** 12 (+3) |

KRENSHAR BLOOD SLAYER

KRENSHAR BLOOD SLAYERS ARE SLIGHTLY LARGER than their more common cousins. They lead krenshar prides, tracking prey with their uncanny ability to smell blood.

Krenshar Blood Slayer		Level 5 Brute
Medium natural beast		XP 200

Initiative +5 **Senses** Perception +7; low-light vision
Fearsome Visage aura 5; each enemy within the aura takes a -2 penalty to saving throws against fear effects.
HP 75; **Bloodied** 37
AC 17; **Fortitude** 18, **Reflex** 17, **Will** 15
Speed 8
⊕ **Claw** (standard; at-will)
+8 vs. AC; 1d6 + 4 damage.
↯ **Grabbing Claws** (standard; at-will)
The krenshar blood slayer makes two claw attacks. If both attacks hit the same target, that target is grabbed.
↯ **Bite** (standard; at-will)
Targets a creature grabbed by the krenshar blood slayer; no attack roll; 2d6 + 8 damage.
↩ **Unnerving Skull** (minor 1/round; at-will) ✦ **Fear, Gaze**
Close burst 5; targets one creature; +8 vs. Will; the target takes a -2 penalty to attack rolls (save ends).
Alignment Unaligned **Languages** —
Skills Intimidate +5
| **Str** 18 (+6) | **Dex** 16 (+5) | **Wis** 10 (+2) |
| **Con** 15 (+4) | **Int** 2 (-2) | **Cha** 13 (+3) |

KRENSHAR LORE

Nature DC 12: Krenshars roam hills, plains, and forests in small prides. Krenshars born with blood red spots on their hides become guardians of the pride. Other krenshars act as hunters and caregivers to young.

Nature DC 17: Gnolls, hobgoblins, and humans trap and domesticate krenshars. Trainers are often injured or killed while taming them, because repressing a stressed krenshar's instinct to reveal its skull is difficult.

KRENSHAR ENCOUNTER GROUPS

Krenshars are usually encountered with members of their pride or with humanoids that have tamed them.

Level 5 Encounter (XP 1,125)
✦ 2 deathpledged gnolls (level 5 brute)
✦ 3 krenshars (level 4 controller)
✦ 1 krenshar blood slayer (level 5 brute)

Level 6 Encounter (XP 1,450)
✦ 2 human javelin dancers (level 6 skirmisher)
✦ 1 human slaver (level 8 brute)
✦ 3 krenshar blood slayers (level 5 brute)

Poisonscale lizardfolk favor cruel toxins and relentless hit-and-run tactics. Swamps and jungles are the favored homes of the varied tribes of these scaled humanoids.

Poisonscale Magus

The poisonscale magus uses toxic magic to hurl death from a distance.

Poisonscale Magus	Level 2 Artillery
Medium natural humanoid (reptile)	XP 125

Initiative +2   Senses Perception +8
HP 32; Bloodied 16
AC 14; Fortitude 14, Reflex 16, Will 16
Speed 6 (swamp walk)
⊕ **Dagger** (standard; at-will) ✦ **Weapon**
  +6 vs. AC; 1d6 + 3 damage.
↗ **Poison Blood** (standard; at-will) ✦ **Poison**
  Ranged 10/20; +7 vs. Fortitude; 1d6 + 3 poison damage, and ongoing 5 poison damage (save ends).
↗ **Corrupt Poison** (minor; at-will) ✦ **Poison**
  Ranged 10/20; targets a creature taking ongoing poison damage; +7 vs. Fortitude; the poisonscale magus slides the target 3 squares, and the target is slowed (save ends).
❖ **Poison Barrage** (standard; encounter) ✦ **Poison**
  Area burst 3 within 10; +5 vs. Fortitude; 1d6 + 3 poison damage, and the target gains vulnerable 5 poison (save ends). *Miss:* Half damage, and the target gains vulnerable 5 poison until the end of its next turn.
Alignment Unaligned   Languages Draconic
Skills Athletics +7, Arcana +9
Str 12 (+2)   Dex 12 (+2)   Wis 14 (+3)
Con 14 (+3)   Int 15 (+3)   Cha 8 (+0)
Equipment dagger

Poisonscale Slitherer

Among the weakest of lizardfolk, the cowardly poisonscale slitherers prefer to fight alongside their stronger kin.

Poisonscale Slitherer	Level 2 Soldier
Medium natural humanoid (reptile)	XP 125

Initiative +6   Senses Perception +7
HP 36; Bloodied 18
AC 17; Fortitude 14, Reflex 15, Will 13
Speed 5 (swamp walk)
⊕ **Spear** (standard; at-will) ✦ **Weapon**
  +8 vs. AC; 1d10 + 3 damage.
↗ **Javelin** (standard; encounter) ✦ **Poison, Weapon**
  Ranged 10/20; +6 vs. AC; 1d6 + 3 damage, and the poisonscale slitherer makes a secondary attack against the same target. *Secondary Attack:* +4 vs. Fortitude; 2d6 + 3 poison damage.
Slitherer Bravery
  A poisonscale slitherer gains a +2 bonus to attack rolls while it is adjacent to at least one ally.
Slitherer Stability
  A poisonscale slitherer cannot be knocked prone and ignores forced movement.

Alignment Unaligned   Languages Draconic
Skills Athletics +8, Stealth +9
Str 14 (+3)   Dex 17 (+4)   Wis 12 (+2)
Con 12 (+2)   Int 8 (+0)   Cha 8 (+0)
Equipment spear, 2 javelins

Poisonscale Savage

The poisonscale savage wades confidently into combat with a huge club, its tail dripping toxic sweat.

Poisonscale Savage	Level 2 Brute
Medium natural humanoid (reptile)	XP 125

Initiative +3   Senses Perception +2
Aura of Poison aura 1; each enemy within the aura takes a -2 penalty to saving throws against ongoing poison damage.
HP 45; Bloodied 22
AC 13; Fortitude 16, Reflex 15, Will 14
Speed 6 (swamp walk)
⊕ **Greatclub** (standard; at-will) ✦ **Weapon**
  +5 vs. AC; 2d6 + 3 damage.
⊕ **Poison Tail** (minor; at-will) ✦ **Poison**
  +4 vs. AC; the target takes ongoing 5 poison damage (save ends).
↗ **Javelin** (standard; encounter) ✦ **Poison, Weapon**
  Ranged 10/20; +5 vs. AC; 1d6 + 3 damage, and ongoing 5 poison damage (save ends).
Alignment Unaligned   Languages Draconic
Skills Athletics +9
Str 17 (+4)   Dex 14 (+3)   Wis 12 (+2)
Con 15 (+3)   Int 8 (+0)   Cha 8 (+0)
Equipment greatclub, javelin

Poisonscale Collector

The poisonscale collector uses blinding poison to incapacitate and kill foes.

Poisonscale Collector	Level 3 Lurker
Medium natural humanoid (reptile)	XP 150

Initiative +8   Senses Perception +8
HP 36; Bloodied 18
AC 18; Fortitude 14, Reflex 16, Will 15
Speed 6 (swamp walk)
⊕ **Dagger** (standard; at-will) ✦ **Poison, Weapon**
  +8 vs. AC; 1d6 + 2 damage, and ongoing 5 poison damage (save ends).
↓ **Blinding Poison** (standard; at-will)
  Targets a creature taking ongoing poison damage; +6 vs. Fortitude; 1d6 + 3 damage, and the target is blinded (save ends).
↓ **End Strike** (standard; at-will)
  Targets a creature that cannot see the poisonscale collector; +8 vs. AC; 2d6 + 3 damage.
Poison Strike
  A poisonscale collector gains a +2 bonus to damage rolls against any enemy taking ongoing poison damage.
Alignment Unaligned   Languages Draconic
Skills Athletics +7, Stealth +9
Str 13 (+2)   Dex 17 (+4)   Wis 14 (+3)
Con 12 (+2)   Int 10 (+1)   Cha 8 (+0)
Equipment dagger

(Left to right) poisonscale myrmidon, savage, and magus

POISONSCALE MYRMIDON

COMPARED WITH OTHER LIZARDFOLK, the poison-scale myrmidon wielding a club is a disciplined combatant.

Poisonscale Myrmidon		Level 3 Soldier
Medium natural humanoid (reptile)		XP 150

Initiative +5   **Senses** Perception +2
HP 47; **Bloodied** 23
AC 20; **Fortitude** 15, **Reflex** 14, **Will** 13
Speed 6 (swamp walk)
① **Club** (standard; at-will) ✦ **Weapon**
   +10 vs. AC; 1d10 + 3 damage, and the target is marked until the end of the poisonscale myrmidon's next turn.
Poison Strike
   A poisonscale myrmidon gains a +2 bonus to damage rolls against any enemy taking ongoing poison damage.
Alignment Unaligned   **Languages** Draconic
Skills Athletics +9
Str 17 (+4)   **Dex** 15 (+3)   **Wis** 12 (+2)
Con 15 (+3)   **Int** 10 (+1)   **Cha** 8 (+0)
Equipment club, turtle shell shield (light shield)

POISONSCALE LORE

Nature DC 10: Although poisonscale slitherers are less hale than other lizardfolk, they have powerful tails that stabilize them in battle.

Poisonscale collectors are specially trained hunters with two important duties: collecting the toxic plants and creatures that poisonscales eat to produce their poison, and taking captives for slavery or sacrifice.

Among poisonscales, magi are honored advisors. Because of their toxic magic, they live short lives.

Poisonscale myrmidons lack other poisonscales' ability to produce poison, but they make up for it with greater strength and thicker scales.

Poisonscale savages enjoy "counting coup" by touching enemies with their tails. When they defeat their enemies, they take trophies from the bodies.

ENCOUNTER GROUPS

Lizardfolk hunt in mixed groups, taking roles in hunting parties according to their diverse talents.

Level 3 Encounter (XP 850)
✦ 1 greenscale darter (level 5 lurker, *MM* 178)
✦ 2 greenscale hunters (level 4 skirmisher, *MM* 178)
✦ 2 poisonscale collectors (level 3 lurker)

LYCANTHROPE

HEREDITARY SHAPESHIFTERS, lycanthropes are feared in communities both large and small. In its natural form, a lycanthrope appears as a blend of humanoid and beast, but it can choose to wear a humanoid disguise or an animal shape.

WEREBOAR

WEREBOARS ARE BRUTISH HUMANOIDS that are easily angered and that transform into lycanthropic form when incited. A wereboar is a provocateur, and seeks out fights in taverns and on city streets, where it can use its size and strength in close quarters.

Wereboar — **Level 6 Brute**
Large natural humanoid (shapechanger) — XP 250

Initiative +3 **Senses** Perception +4
HP 61; **Bloodied** 33; see also *bloodied resilience* and *death strike*
Regeneration 5
AC 17; **Fortitude** 21, **Reflex** 16, **Will** 17
Immune moontusk fever; **Vulnerable** silver (if the wereboar takes damage from a silver weapon, its regeneration does not function on its next turn)
Speed 6 (8 in boar form)

Maul (standard; usable only while in humanoid form; at-will) ✦ **Weapon**
+9 vs. AC; 2d6 + 6 damage.

Gore (standard; usable only while in boar form; at-will) ✦ **Disease**
+9 vs. AC; 1d8 + 6 damage, ongoing 5 damage (save ends), and the target is exposed to moontusk fever (see below).

Death Strike (when the werebear drops to 0 hit points)
The wereboar makes a gore or a maul attack.

Bloodied Resilience (while bloodied)
The wereboar gains a +2 bonus to all defenses and deals ongoing 10 damage with its gore attack instead of ongoing 5 damage.

Change Shape (minor; at-will) ✦ **Polymorph**
A wereboar can alter its physical form to appear as a dire boar (*MM* 35) or a unique humanoid (see "Change Shape," page 216).

Alignment Evil **Languages** Common
Skills Athletics +13, Endurance +11, Intimidate +8

Str 20 (+8)	**Dex** 10 (+3)	**Wis** 12 (+4)
Con 16 (+6)	**Int** 10 (+3)	**Cha** 11 (+3)

Equipment hide armor, maul

WEREBOAR TACTICS

A wereboar looks for any opportunity to utilize its boar form. It engages in battle with minimal cause, charging opponents and using its gore attack.

Moontusk Fever — **Level 6 Disease** — **Endurance** improve DC 17, maintain DC 12, worsen DC 11 or lower

The target is cured.	◀ **Initial Effect:** The target takes a -2 penalty to saving throws while bloodied.	◀▶ While bloodied, the target can roll only one saving throw at the end of its turn, even if it is affected by multiple effects.	▶ **Final State:** When the subject rolls a saving throw while bloodied, it rolls two dice and takes the lower of the two results.

TOMÁS GIORELLO

Weretiger

WERETIGERS ARE CAUTIOUS COMBATANTS. A weretiger uses stealth to stalk an enemy, waiting for the opportune moment to strike.

Weretiger	Level 11 Elite Skirmisher
Large natural humanoid (shapechanger)	XP 1,200

Initiative +9   **Senses** Perception +12; low-light vision
HP 172; **Bloodied** 86
Regeneration 10
AC 25; **Fortitude** 23, **Reflex** 22, **Will** 22
Immune moon rage; **Vulnerable** silver (if the weretiger takes damage from a silver weapon, its regeneration does not function on its next turn)
Saving Throws +2
Speed 6 (8 in tiger form)
Action Points 1

ⓐ **Katar** (standard; usable only while in humanoid form; at-will)
    ✦ **Weapon**
    +16 vs. AC; 2d6 + 6 damage (crit 4d6 + 18).
ⓐ **Bite** (standard; usable only while in tiger form; at-will) ✦
    Disease
    +16 vs. AC; 1d8 + 5 damage, and the target is exposed to moon rage (see below).
↯ **Feline Fury** (standard; at-will)
    The weretiger makes two melee basic attacks. It shifts 1 square between the attacks.
↯ **Pounce** (standard; usable only when charging; recharge ⚄ ⚅)
    +16 vs. AC; 2d8 + 5 damage, and the target is pushed 1 square and knocked prone. The weretiger then shifts into the target's vacated space.
↯ **Slashing Recoil** (immediate reaction, when an attack misses the weretiger; at-will)
    The weretiger makes a melee basic attack and shifts 2 squares.
Change Shape (minor; at-will) ✦ **Polymorph**
    A weretiger can alter its physical form to appear as a dire tiger or a unique humanoid (see "Change Shape," page 216).

Alignment Evil	**Languages** Common	

Skills Acrobatics +12, Bluff +11, Insight +12, Stealth +12

Str 17 (+8)	**Dex** 14 (+7)	**Wis** 14 (+7)
Con 15 (+7)	**Int** 12 (+6)	**Cha** 13 (+6)

Equipment leather armor, 2 katars

WERETIGER TACTICS

A weretiger prefers to focus on one adversary at a time using *feline fury* and retreats if engaged by a second opponent. If this happens, the weretiger charges with *pounce* to reengage.

Moon Rage	Level 11 Disease	Endurance improve DC 21, maintain DC 16, worsen DC 15 or lower

◁ The target is cured.

◁ Initial Effect: The target takes a −2 penalty to attack rolls as its hands begin to grow fur and claws.

◁▷ The target gains a Strength-based claw attack that deals 1d6 damage. The target can no longer wield weapons or hold implements. This effect remains as long as the subject is diseased.

▷ Final State: The target's predatory instincts take over. When the target attacks a creature in combat, it can attack no other creatures until that target is dead or until the end of the encounter.

WEREWOLF LORD

At the center of many lycanthropic clans, a werewolf lord calls the shots. The most feared of its kind, the werewolf lord is larger, stronger, and smarter than a werewolf and is a vicious adversary.

Werewolf Lord	Level 13 Elite Brute (Leader)
Large natural humanoid (shapechanger)	XP 1,600

Initiative +7   **Senses** Perception +8; low-light vision
Blood Moon aura 5; the werewolf lord and any ally within the aura gain a +2 bonus to attack rolls and a +5 bonus to damage rolls against bloodied targets.
HP 264; **Bloodied** 132
Regeneration 10
AC 25; **Fortitude** 27, **Reflex** 22, **Will** 24
Immune greater moon fever; **Vulnerable** silver (if the werewolf lord takes damage from a silver weapon, its regeneration does not function on its next turn)
Saving Throws +2
Speed 6 (8 in wolf form)
Action Points 1
⊕ **Falchion** (standard; usable only while in humanoid form; at-will)
   ✦ **Weapon**
   +16 vs. AC; 4d4 + 6 damage (crit 8d4 + 22).
⊕ **Bite** (standard; usable only while in wolf form; at-will) ✦
   Disease
   +16 vs. AC; 2d12 + 3 damage, and the target is exposed to greater moon frenzy (see below).
↯ **Canine Fury** (standard; at-will)
   The werewolf lord makes two melee basic attacks.
↯ **Speed of the Wolf** (standard; usable only in wolf form; recharge ⚅ ⚄)
   The werewolf lord shifts 6 squares and makes a bite attack.
⬳ **Savage Howl** (minor; encounter)
   Close burst 10; each ally in the burst gains 15 temporary hit points. In addition, each ally that has a bite attack makes a bite attack as a free action.
Change Shape (minor; at-will) ✦ **Polymorph**
   A werewolf lord can alter its physical form to appear as a dire wolf (MM 264) or a unique humanoid (see "Change Shape," page 216).
Alignment Evil   **Languages** Common
Skills Athletics +17, Bluff +14, Endurance +14, Intimidate +14

Str 22 (+12)	**Dex** 12 (+7)	**Wis** 15 (+8)
Con 17 (+9)	**Int** 13 (+7)	**Cha** 16 (+9)

Equipment chain armor, falchion

WEREWOLF LORD TACTICS

The impressive physique of a werewolf lord often leads foes to underestimate its cunning. A werewolf lord guides the attacks of its group, inspiring its allies to greater ferocity with its *savage howl* and its *blood moon* aura.

LYCANTHROPE LORE

Nature DC 16: Lycanthropy is hereditary, and lycanthropes mate with other lycanthropes to produce lycanthropic offspring. Some lycanthropes can also mate with humanoids, producing lycanthropic children. However, the blood is diluted in this way, and such children never change forms or instead become shifters.

Nature DC 21: Legend says that Melora created lycanthropes, and they are affected by the full moon and silver because of a feud between Melora and Sehanine. Lycanthropes are most active on nights with a full moon. Silver, the moon metal, cuts them to the quick.

ENCOUNTER GROUPS

As shapechangers, lycanthropes can be found with a wide variety of creatures. But only those who can keep up with the bestial fury of lycanthropes remain connected to them for long.

Level 6 Encounter (XP 1,200)
✦ 2 half-orc hunters (level 5 skirmisher)
✦ 1 human hexer (level 7 controller)
✦ 2 wereboars (level 6 brute)

Level 12 Encounter (XP 3,500)
✦ 1 eladrin bladesinger (level 11 skirmisher)
✦ 2 weretigers (level 11 elite skirmisher)
✦ 1 will-o'-wisp (level 10 lurker)

Level 13 Encounter (XP 4,250)
✦ 1 werewolf pack lord (level 13 elite brute)
✦ 3 werewolves (level 8 brute, MM 181)
✦ 4 worgs (level 9 brute, MM 265)

Greater Moon Frenzy	Level 13 Disease	Endurance improve DC 23, maintain DC 18, worsen DC 17 or lower
◀ The target is cured.	◀▶ **Initial Effect:** The target takes a –2 penalty to Will.	◀▶ While bloodied, the target must make a saving throw at the end of each turn. If the saving throw fails, the target makes a melee attack on its next turn against a random target within 5 squares of it. If no targets are within 5 squares, the target does nothing but move in a randomly chosen direction.	▶ **Final State:** The target attacks the nearest creature in its line of sight. If it cannot see any other creatures, it does nothing but move in a randomly chosen direction.

MAMMOTH

MAMMOTHS ARE FURRY, ELEPHANTLIKE CREATURES that roam the freezing steppes. The furious Nyfellar mammoth, a creature made partially of ice, hits foes like an avalanche.

Nyfellar Mammoth	Level 17 Brute
Huge elemental beast (mount)	XP 1,600

Initiative +6 **Senses** Perception +10
HP 202; **Bloodied** 101
AC 29; **Fortitude** 33, **Reflex** 24, **Will** 28
Resist 10 cold
Speed 8 (ice walk)
⊕ **Gore** (standard; at-will)
  Reach 2; +20 vs. AC; 2d10 + 10 damage.
↯ **Stamp** (standard; at-will) ✦ **Cold**
  +18 vs. Fortitude; 2d6 + 10 damage plus 1d6 cold damage, and the target is knocked prone.
↯ **Blizzard Trample** (standard; recharges when the Nyfellar mammoth is first bloodied or when it takes cold damage)
  The Nyfellar mammoth moves 8 squares and can move through enemy-occupied spaces, making one stamp attack against each of those enemies.
↯ **Tusk Toss** (standard; recharge ⚁ ⚂ ⚃)
  Reach 2; +18 vs. Fortitude; 1d10 + 5 damage, and the mammoth slides the target 5 squares. The target falls from a height of up to 30 feet (6 squares) into the space where it ends the slide and takes falling damage, if applicable.
Bitterwind Charge (while mounted by a friendly rider of 17th level or higher; at-will) ✦ **Mount**
  When charging, the Nyfellar mammoth can use *blizzard trample* or *tusk toss* instead of a melee basic attack. After the mammoth's attack, its rider makes a melee basic attack as a free action.
Icebound Footing
  When an effect pulls, pushes, or slides the Nyfellar mammoth, the mammoth moves 2 squares less than the effect specifies. The mammoth can make a saving throw to avoid being knocked prone.
Alignment Unaligned **Languages** —
Str 30 (+18) **Dex** 10 (+8) **Wis** 18 (+12)
Con 22 (+14) **Int** 2 (+4) **Cha** 9 (+7)

NYFELLAR MAMMOTH TACTICS
The Nyfellar mammoth charges enemies with a stamp and then uses *tusk toss.* It fights until those threatening it flee or until it dies.

MAMMOTH LORE
Arcana DC 20: The massive Nyfellar mammoths have their origins in Nyfell, the frozen land in the Elemental Chaos from which frost giants hail. Frost giants brought these beasts to the world. Because Nyfellar mammoths can subsist on a variety of food and ice, they can live in inhospitable frozen regions.

ENCOUNTER GROUPS
Frost giants use Nyfellar mammoths for warfare and raids. A favorite frost giant tactic is to ready an attack against the victim of a *tusk toss.*

Level 17 Encounter (XP 9,200)
✦ 2 frost giants (level 17 brute)
✦ 2 Nyfellar mammoths (level 17 brute)
✦ 1 rimefire griffon (level 20 skirmisher, *MM* 147)

TOMÁS GIORELLO

Valuing order and oaths of service, a marut hones its skills for a particular purpose. Maruts serve other entities as mercenaries or serve their own mysterious ends.

Marut Castigator

Marut castigators identify those who violate the law, subduing them for judgment.

Marut Castigator	Level 21 Skirmisher
Medium immortal humanoid	XP 3,200

Initiative +19 **Senses** Perception +21; truesight 10
HP 146; **Bloodied** 73
Regeneration 10
AC 35; **Fortitude** 33, **Reflex** 34, **Will** 33
Immune sleep; **Resist** 10 thunder
Speed 8, fly 4 (hover), teleport 4
⊕ **Double Sword** (standard; at-will) ✦ **Lightning, Weapon**
   +26 vs. AC; 3d8 + 5 damage. The marut castigator can choose to have the attack deal lightning damage.
↯ **Double Attack** (standard; recharge ⚄ ⚅ ⚃)
   The marut castigator makes two double sword attacks.
↯ **Punisher's Lash** (standard; at-will) ✦ **Lightning**
   Reach 2; +23 vs. Reflex; 2d6 + 7 lightning damage, and the target is slowed and cannot teleport until the end of the marut castigator's next turn.
↯ **Thunderbolt Strike** (standard; recharges when both attacks of *double attack* hit) ✦ **Teleportation, Thunder**
   The marut castigator teleports 4 squares and makes a double sword attack that deals 2d6 extra thunder damage.
Alignment Unaligned   **Languages** Supernal
Skills Acrobatics +22
Str 22 (+16)   **Dex** 25 (+17)   **Wis** 22 (+16)
Con 20 (+15)   **Int** 14 (+12)   **Cha** 15 (+12)
Equipment double sword

Marut Prosecutor

A marut prosecutor's word is marut law. Woe to any who fail to obey that law when a marut is near.

Marut Prosecutor	Level 21 Controller (Leader)
Medium immortal humanoid	XP 3,200

Initiative +13   **Senses** Perception +21; truesight 10
HP 147; **Bloodied** 73
Regeneration 10
AC 35; **Fortitude** 32, **Reflex** 33, **Will** 33
Immune sleep; **Resist** 10 thunder
Speed 8, fly 4 (hover), teleport 4
⊕ **Slam** (standard; at-will) ✦ **Thunder**
   +26 vs. AC; 1d10 + 4 damage plus 1d6 thunder damage, and the target is slowed (save ends).
↗ **Dictum** (minor; at-will)
   Ranged 10; +22 vs. Fortitude; the target is immobilized (save ends).
⬰ **Biting Testimony** (standard; at-will) ✦ **Psychic**
   Close burst 10; targets one enemy; +25 vs. Will; 3d6 + 7 psychic damage, and the target takes a -2 penalty to attack rolls, skill checks, and ability checks (save ends).

⬰ **Sigil of Indictment** (minor; usable only when no creature is affected by this power; at-will) ✦ **Psychic**
   Close burst 10; targets one enemy; +25 vs. Will; until the end of the marut prosecutor's next turn, the target grants combat advantage to the prosecutor, and the prosecutor and its allies deal 5 extra psychic damage against the creature. *Sustain Minor:* The effect persists.
Justice Restrained
   A slowed, immobilized, or restrained creature takes a -2 penalty to attack rolls against a marut prosecutor.
Alignment Unaligned   **Languages** Supernal
Skills Insight +21, Intimidate +22
Str 18 (+14)   **Dex** 16 (+13)   **Wis** 23 (+16)
Con 21 (+15)   **Int** 23 (+16)   **Cha** 24 (+17)

Marut Prosecutor Tactics

The prosecutor singles out one enemy—preferably one who has violated the marut's creed—and places a *sigil of indictment* on it. The prosecutor then uses *dictum* to prevent escape and *biting testimony* to break the enemy's spirit by shouting out the enemy's crimes, failures, or flaws.

Marut Executioner

The marut executioner slays those who oppose marut actions or who do not repay maruts for aid.

Marut Executioner	Level 22 Brute
Medium immortal humanoid	XP 4,150

Initiative +17   **Senses** Perception +13; truesight 10
HP 205; **Bloodied** 102
Regeneration 10
AC 34; **Fortitude** 34, **Reflex** 33, **Will** 34
Immune sleep; **Resist** 10 thunder
Speed 8, fly 4 (hover), teleport 4
⊕ **Double Axe** (standard; at-will) ✦ **Thunder, Weapon**
   +25 vs. AC; 2d10 + 4 damage plus 2d8 thunder damage. On a critical hit, the target is also knocked prone.
↯ **Warranted Stroke** (standard; recharges when first bloodied) ✦ **Thunder**
   Targets a bloodied creature; +27 vs. AC; 4d6 + 8 damage plus 2d8 thunder damage, and the target is knocked prone. If this attack reduces the target to 0 hit points or fewer, the marut executioner gains 1 action point.
⬰ **Execution's Call** (standard; encounter) ✦ **Thunder**
   Close blast 5; targets enemies; +23 vs. Fortitude; 2d6 + 7 thunder damage, and the marut executioner pulls the target into a space adjacent to it. *Miss:* Half damage.
⬰ **Slayer's Fury** (standard; encounter) ✦ **Thunder, Weapon**
   Close burst 1; targets enemies; +23 vs. AC; 2d10 + 4 damage plus 2d8 thunder damage. On a critical hit, the target is also knocked prone.
Alignment Unaligned   **Languages** Supernal
Skills Endurance +23, Intimidate +23
Str 26 (+19)   **Dex** 23 (+17)   **Wis** 15 (+13)
Con 25 (+18)   **Int** 14 (+13)   **Cha** 24 (+18)
Equipment double axe

(Left to right) marut castigator, executioner, and prosecutor

MARUT LORE

Religion DC 22: Maruts require no sustenance. Maruts take no slaves, but they sometimes have mortal servitors in their astral fortresses. They do accept or request services as payment for completed tasks—so maruts might accept indentured servitude or other compulsory services. Although maruts rarely mistreat their servants, they are strict and uncompassionate taskmasters.

Religion DC 27: Although maruts are thought of as a unified race, they divide themselves along ethical and militaristic lines into units they call cadres. Marut cadres dedicated to philosophies other than the upholding of oaths and the fair dispensing of justice also exist. A few cadres serve the Raven Queen.

BARGAINING WITH MARUTS

A marut is an inscrutable being of cosmic balance. It is insightful and careful, but it is fallible. While under contract, a marut acts in its employer's interests. Only a reasoned appeal to a marut's beliefs, proof that a contract contains falsehood, or a mission of greater importance can cause a marut to abandon its task. Maruts might undertake tasks that support their beliefs without requesting payment.

Religion DC 29: Maruts favor strict interpretation of laws and contracts and the upholding of oaths. The love of order and battle they share with angels is more than coincidental. Maruts consider themselves to be astral spirits of the air, despite the fact that they appear to be made of solid stone and to be clad in metal. The designation makes sense. Maruts fly without wings, and they live and roam about in mobile fortresses floating on the Astral Sea.

ENCOUNTER GROUPS

Maruts of various cadres work together and with other races when a task furthers their overarching beliefs. They do so under contract.

Level 21 Encounter (XP 17,500)
+ 1 djinn vizier (level 20 artillery)
+ 2 marut castigators (level 21 skirmisher)
+ 2 marut executioners (level 22 brute)

Level 23 Encounter (XP 27,750)
+ 2 marut castigators (level 21 skirmisher)
+ 1 marut prosecutor (level 21 controller)
+ 3 rakshasa dread knights (level 24 soldier, *MM* 218)

MYCONID

INSIDIOUS FUNGAL MENACES from Feywild caverns polluted by the fomorians, myconids strive only to spread across their territories, contaminating those places with their presence.

MYCONID ROTPRIEST

THE MYCONID ROTPRIEST IS THE COLONY'S HEALER and scapegoat, taking the damage of others so that the colony as a whole can survive.

Myconid Rotpriest		Level 3 Brute (Leader)
Medium fey humanoid (plant)		XP 150

Initiative +2   **Senses** Perception +3; tremorsense 10
HP 48; **Bloodied** 24; see also *life burst*
Regeneration 5
AC 15; **Fortitude** 16, **Reflex** 13, **Will** 16
Vulnerable radiant (if the myconid rotpriest takes radiant damage, its regeneration does not function until the end of the rotpriest's next turn)
Speed 5
(⊕) **Stipe Staff** (standard; at-will) ✦ **Weapon**
    +6 vs. AC; 2d10 + 3 damage.
(↙) **Decomposing Spray** (standard; at-will) ✦ **Necrotic**
    Close burst 3; +6 vs. Fortitude; 1d10 + 3 necrotic damage.
(↙) **Life Burst** (when reduced to 0 hit points) ✦ **Healing**
    Close burst 1; targets living creatures; the target regains 10 hit points.
Roots of the Colony (free, when the myconid rotpriest is hit by an attack while a myconid ally is within 5 squares of it; at-will)
    The rotpriest takes half damage from the attack, and the myconid ally takes the same amount of damage.
Sacrifice for the Colony (free, when a myconid ally uses *roots of the colony* to deal damage to the myconid rotpriest; at-will)
    The rotpriest takes the damage dealt to the ally, and the ally takes none.
Alignment Unaligned   **Languages** –
Str 10 (+1)   **Dex** 12 (+2)   **Wis** 15 (+3)
Con 18 (+5)   **Int** 10 (+1)   **Cha** 18 (+5)
Equipment quarterstaff

MYCONID ROTPRIEST TACTICS

A rotpriest positions itself among allies in combat, absorbing their damage with *roots of the colony* and *sacrifice for the colony* and then regenerating. It uses *decomposing spray* when it can hit multiple targets. Otherwise, it uses its *stipe staff* to bludgeon enemies into submission.

MYCONID SOVEREIGN

THE MYCONID SOVEREIGN COMMANDS the allegiance of its colony. This towering fungal leader holds silent court over its underlings.

Myconid Sovereign		Level 4 Controller (Leader)
Large fey humanoid (plant)		XP 175

Initiative +2   **Senses** Perception +0; tremorsense 10
HP 58; **Bloodied** 29
AC 18; **Fortitude** 18, **Reflex** 14, **Will** 15
Speed 6
(⊕) **Slam** (standard; at-will)
    +9 vs. AC; 2d6 + 3 damage.
(↙) **Spore Burst** (standard; recharge ⚄ ⚅ ⚅) ✦ **Poison**
    Close blast 3; targets nonplants; +8 vs. Will; 1d8 + 3 poison damage, and the target is dazed until the end of the myconid sovereign's next turn.
(↙) **Commanding Spores** (standard; at-will)
    Close burst 5; targets one plant ally in burst; the target shifts 1 square.
Roots of the Colony (free, when the myconid sovereign is hit by an attack while a myconid ally is within 5 squares of it; at-will)
    The myconid sovereign takes half of the damage from the attack, and the myconid ally takes the same amount of damage.
Alignment Unaligned   **Languages** telepathy 5
Str 7 (+0)   **Dex** 11 (+2)   **Wis** 8 (+1)
Con 18 (+6)   **Int** 7 (+0)   **Cha** 12 (+3)

MYCONID SOVEREIGN TACTICS

A myconid sovereign fights behind other myconids, relying on them for protection. It uses *commanding spores* to create a defensive wall of myconids. Because other myconids are immune to *spore burst*, the sovereign uses that attack against enemies that are engaged in melee with its allies.

MYCONID GUARD

MYCONID GUARDS ARE A COLONY'S PROTECTORS and shock troops.

Myconid Guard		Level 4 Soldier
Medium fey humanoid (plant)		XP 175

Initiative +5   **Senses** Perception +3; tremorsense 10
HP 56; **Bloodied** 28
AC 18; **Fortitude** 17, **Reflex** 16, **Will** 14
Speed 6
(⊕) **Spiny Strike** (standard; at-will)
    +11 vs. AC; 2d6 + 3 damage.
(↙) **Pacification Spores** (standard; encounter) ✦ **Poison**
    Close burst 1; +9 vs. Will; 1d6 + 3 poison damage, and the target cannot take a standard action until the end of the myconid guard's next turn.
Roots of the Colony (free, when the myconid guard is hit by an attack while a myconid ally is within 5 squares of it; at-will)
    The myconid guard takes half damage from the attack, and the myconid ally takes the same amount of damage.
Alignment Unaligned   **Languages** –
Str 18 (+6)   **Dex** 16 (+5)   **Wis** 12 (+3)
Con 16 (+5)   **Int** 8 (+1)   **Cha** 10 (+2)

(Left to right) myconid guard, rotpriest, sovereign, and guard

Myconid Guard Tactics

When a colony comes under attack, myconid guards charge into combat. They use *pacification spores* to incapacitate enemies, and they attempt to subdue other enemies with *spiny strike* attacks.

Myconid Lore

Arcana DC 12: Myconids are plant creatures touched by the madness of the fomorians. Although not necessarily evil, myconids strive to expand their territory and numbers, which pits them against other creatures competing for the same resources. Myconids like dark places and often prefer the Underdark and the Shadowdark to their home plane.

Because of the inherent resilience of a colony of myconids, other races cultivate them for cheap labor or enslave them. Drow, fomorians, and shadar-kai command myconids in great numbers.

Arcana DC 17: Vast mushroom forests sprawl over tracts of the Feywild and areas of the Underdark and the Shadowdark, providing myconids with ideal conditions under which to thrive and to multiply. Other fungal creatures represent a full range of predators of and prey for myconids.

Arcana DC 19: Myconids communicate with each other by releasing spores. These spores convey raw emotions such as fear, satisfaction, and desire. A colony's sovereign is the only myconid that can communicate with other types of creatures, which it does by using its telepathy.

Encounter Groups

Shadowfell- and Underdark-dwelling civilizations co-opt myconid colonies. Myconids can thrive in a wide range of places, including forest glades, deep dungeons, and the strange landscapes of the Feywild.

Level 3 Encounter (XP 850)
+ 1 deathjump spider (level 4 skirmisher)
+ 2 myconid guards (level 4 soldier)
+ 1 myconid rotpriest (level 3 brute)
+ 1 myconid sovereign (level 4 controller)

Level 4 Encounter (XP 875)
+ 2 arbalesters (level 4 artillery)
+ 1 green slime (level 4 lurker)
+ 2 myconid guards (level 4 soldier)

Level 5 Encounter (XP 1,100)
+ 1 geonid (level 6 lurker)
+ 2 myconid rotpriests (level 4 brute)
+ 2 rust monsters (level 6 skirmisher)

NEOGI SEE THE WORLD in terms of ownership. The strong rule and possess the weak. Slavery and trade form the foundations of neogi culture, making neogi reliable merchants to devils, giants, drow, and other dark forces.

NEOGI SLAVER

THE NEOGI SLAVER SEEKS to bring foes to their knees rather than kill them. Dead slaves aren't worth much on the market.

Neogi Slaver	Level 10 Controller (Leader)
Medium aberrant magical beast	XP 500

Initiative +7 — Senses Perception +8; darkvision
HP 106; Bloodied 53
AC 24; Fortitude 21, Reflex 22, Will 23
Immune dazed
Speed 8, climb 6 (spider climb)
ⓐ Bite (standard; at-will) ✦ Poison
  +14 vs. AC; 1d6 + 3 damage, and ongoing 5 poison damage (save ends). *First Failed Saving Throw:* The target is slowed (save ends).
⤳ Charm Bolt (standard; at-will) ✦ Charm
  Ranged 12; +15 vs. Will; the target takes a -2 penalty to attack rolls on attacks that include the neogi slaver as a target (save ends). *First Failed Saving Throw:* The target treats the slaver as invisible (save ends).
⤺ Psychic Shackle (standard; recharge ⚄ ⚅) ✦ Psychic
  Close blast 3; +15 vs. Will; 3d6 + 2 psychic damage, and the target is dazed until the start of the neogi slaver's next turn.
⤺ Thrall Goad (minor; encounter)
  Close burst 6; targets allies; the target makes a saving throw with a +5 bonus.
Alignment Evil — Languages Common, Deep Speech, telepathy 12
Skills Bluff +20, Diplomacy +20, Insight +18, Intimidate +20
Str 11 (+5) — Dex 14 (+7) — Wis 17 (+8)
Con 18 (+9) — Int 19 (+9) — Cha 21 (+10)

NEOGI SLAVER TACTICS

The neogi slaver fights just behind the front line, using *charm bolt* to reduce the threat from any enemy targeting it. *Psychic shackle* softens groups of enemies for capture.

NEOGI SPAWN SWARM

A SWARM OF NEOGI SPAWN moves toward anything that is neither neogi nor marked as the slave of one, and then tries to eat it.

Neogi Spawn Swarm	Level 10 Brute
Medium aberrant magical beast (swarm)	XP 500

Initiative +9 — Senses Perception +8; darkvision
Swarm Attack aura 1; each enemy that starts its turn within the aura takes 5 poison damage.
HP 131; Bloodied 65; see also *psychic scream*
AC 23; Fortitude 22, Reflex 21, Will 22
Immune dazed; Resist half damage from melee and ranged attacks; Vulnerable 10 against close and area attacks
Speed 6, climb 6 (spider climb)
ⓐ Bite (standard; at-will) ✦ Poison
  +13 vs. AC; 2d6 + 4 damage, and ongoing 5 poison damage (save ends). *First Failed Saving Throw:* The target is also slowed (save ends).
⤺ Psychic Scream (when first bloodied and again when the neogi spawn swarm drops to 0 hit points) ✦ Psychic
  Close burst 1; targets enemies; +11 vs. Will; 2d6 + 2 psychic damage, and the target is dazed (save ends).
Alignment Evil — Languages Deep Speech
Str 18 (+9) — Dex 19 (+9) — Wis 17 (+8)
Con 21 (+10) — Int 5 (+2) — Cha 21 (+10)

NEOGI SPAWN SWARM TACTICS

These partially formed slugs have no higher goal than to sate their endless hunger and no tactical plans beyond consuming the flesh of any creature present.

NEOGI GREAT OLD MASTER

UNQUESTIONED RULERS OF THEIR TRADE CLANS, great old masters are living brood nests. Each carries within itself the fertile eggs of a whole neogi clan, as well as larval masses developing into neogi spawn.

Neogi Great Old Master	Level 16 Controller
Large aberrant magical beast	XP 1,400

Initiative +10 — Senses Perception +12; darkvision
Thrall Field aura 1; each enemy within the aura takes a -4 penalty to saving throws.
HP 157; Bloodied 78; see also *larva burst*
AC 30; Fortitude 27, Reflex 28, Will 29
Immune dazed
Speed 6, climb 4 (spider climb)
ⓐ Scythe Claw (standard; at-will)
  Reach 3; +21 vs. AC; 2d8 + 7 damage, and the target is knocked prone.
⤳ Enslaving Bolt (standard; at-will) ✦ Charm, Psychic
  Ranged 12; +20 vs. Will; 2d6 + 7 psychic damage, and the target is slowed (save ends). *First Failed Saving Throw:* The target takes a -2 penalty to attack rolls on attacks that include the neogi great old master as a target. *Second Failed Saving Throw:* The target is dominated (save ends). *Third Failed Saving Throw:* If the target is bloodied, it is dominated until it takes an extended rest.
⤺ Larva Burst (when first bloodied; encounter) ✦ Zone
  Close burst 2; targets enemies; +20 vs. Reflex; 2d10 + 5 damage, and the target is slowed (save ends). *Effect:* The burst creates a zone of squirming grubs and larvae that lasts until the end of the encounter. The zone is difficult terrain.
⤺ Psychic Shackle (standard; recharge ⚄ ⚅) ✦ Psychic
  Close blast 4; +20 vs. Will; 3d6 + 7 psychic damage, and the target is dazed until the start of the neogi great old master's next turn.
Alignment Evil — Languages Common, Deep Speech, telepathy 12
Skills Bluff +20, Diplomacy +20, Insight +18, Intimidate +20
Str 20 (+13) — Dex 14 (+10) — Wis 18 (+12)
Con 21 (+13) — Int 22 (+14) — Cha 24 (+15)

Neogi Great Old Master Tactics

When forced into battle as the leader of its clan, a neogi great old master moves to the center of conflict, uses its long, scythelike legs for *scythe claw* attacks, and uses *enslaving bolt* to dominate its enemies.

Neogi Lore

Dungeoneering DC 16: Neogi see everything in terms of ownership and lay claim to everything not already claimed by a creature more powerful than they are. Travelers of dark lands and strange realms, neogi embark on trade missions to barter with powerful evil creatures. They buy and sell slaves, exotic goods, and odd magic baubles.

Dungeoneering DC 21: Neogi originate in the Far Realm. They avoid the deadly mind flayers. Once owned by illithidlike beings in the Far Realm, neogi also avoid entanglements with illithids in the world.

Great old masters rule every neogi trade clan. Drooling horrors, they brim with vile intellect and the unborn spawn of their clans.

Neogi spawn are adolescents with small brains to match their relatively tiny bodies. They tumble about neogi colonies under the watchful eyes of their guardians.

Encounter Groups

Neogi rarely appear without slaves in tow. Some slaves fall so fully under neogi control that the slaves willingly aid their masters in combat.

Level 13 Encounter (4,800 XP)
✦ 3 neogi slavers (level 10 controller)
✦ 1 neogi spawn swarm (level 10 brute)
✦ 2 umber hulks (level 12 elite soldier, *MM* 256)

Level 15 Encounter (6,150 XP)
✦ 5 kuo-toa guards (level 16 minion, *MM* 172)
✦ 2 kuo-toa harpooners (level 14 soldier, *MM* 172)
✦ 1 neogi great old master (level 16 controller)
✦ 2 neogi slavers (level 10 controller)

(Back to front) neogi great old master and neogi slaver

NOTHIC

ABERRANT CREATURES CARRIED TO THE PLANES on drifting pieces of the Far Realm, nothics have fragmented intellects strung together by tenuous sanity. Typically controlled by a more powerful master, a nothic's propensity for random, seemingly insane actions makes it more like an amusing pet than a servitor.

NOTHIC CACKLER

THE NOTHIC CACKLER GIBBERS and capers madly about, hardly seeming to care about foes even in the midst of combat.

Nothic Cackler	Level 15 Artillery
Medium aberrant humanoid	XP 1,200

Initiative +11   **Senses** Perception +9; darkvision, truesight 10
HP 116; **Bloodied** 58
AC 27; **Fortitude** 28, **Reflex** 29, **Will** 25
Speed 6
⊕ **Claw** (standard; at-will)
   +21 vs. AC; 1d6 + 5 damage.
↗ **Mind Rot** (standard; at-will) ✦ **Charm, Psychic**
   Ranged 10; +20 vs. Will; 2d6 + 3 psychic damage, and the nothic cackler slides the target 6 squares. The target then makes a melee basic attack against a target of the cackler's choice.
↗ **Rotting Gaze** (standard; at-will) ✦ **Necrotic**
   Ranged 10; targets one, two, or three enemies; +18 vs. Fortitude; 2d6 + 5 necrotic damage, and the target takes a -2 penalty to all defenses (save ends).

↜ **Maddening Cackle** (standard; recharge ⚄ ⚅) ✦ **Fear, Psychic**
   Close burst 3; targets enemies; +18 vs. Will; 2d8 + 6 psychic damage, and the nothic cackler pushes the target 2 squares. At the start of the target's next turn, the cackler slides the target 2 squares.
Distorted Visage
   When a nothic cackler moves at least 4 squares during its turn, it gains a +2 bonus to AC and Reflex until the end of its next turn.

Alignment Unaligned   **Languages** Deep Speech
Skills Stealth +16
Str 19 (+11)   **Dex** 19 (+11)   **Wis** 14 (+9)
Con 20 (+12)   **Int** 9 (+6)   **Cha** 10 (+7)

NOTHIC MINDBLIGHT

AS MOROSE AND SEDENTARY as the nothic cackler is crazed, the nothic mindblight uses the dizzying effect of its single eye to disorient enemies and sow chaos among their ranks.

Nothic Mindblight	Level 19 Controller
Medium aberrant humanoid	XP 2,400

Initiative +14   **Senses** Perception +11; darkvision, truesight 10
Eye Lure aura 3; the nothic mindblight slides each creature that starts its turn within the aura 2 squares.
HP 180; **Bloodied** 90
AC 32; **Fortitude** 32, **Reflex** 32, **Will** 29
Speed 6
⊕ **Claw** (standard; at-will) ✦ **Necrotic**
   +24 vs. AC; 2d6 + 3 damage, and ongoing 5 necrotic damage (save ends).
↗ **Eye of Insanity** (standard; recharges when no creature is dominated by the nothic mindblight) ✦ **Fear**
   Ranged 5; +23 vs. Will; the target is dominated (save ends). *Aftereffect:* The target is dazed until the end of its next turn.
↜ **Necrotic Eye** (standard; at-will) ✦ **Necrotic**
   Close blast 5; +23 vs. Fortitude; the target takes ongoing 10 necrotic damage (save ends).
⁜ **Mesmerizing Visage** (standard; recharge ⚄ ⚅) ✦ **Charm, Psychic**
   Area burst 2 within 10; targets enemies; +23 vs. Will; 2d8 + 6 psychic damage, and the target takes a -1 penalty to saving throws (save ends). *First Failed Saving Throw:* The target takes a -3 penalty to saving throws instead of -1 (save ends).

Alignment Unaligned   **Languages** Deep Speech
Skills Stealth +19
Str 21 (+14)   **Dex** 20 (+14)   **Wis** 15 (+11)
Con 20 (+14)   **Int** 10 (+9)   **Cha** 12 (+10)

⟨ 03

DES HANLEY

NOTHIC EYE OF VECNA

EYES OF VECNA HAVE STRONG CONNECTIONS to Vecna, and their powers can inflict withering attacks upon enemies, rotting the flesh.

Nothic Eye of Vecna	Level 22 Lurker (Leader)
Medium aberrant humanoid	XP 4,150

Initiative +23 **Senses** Perception +15; darkvision, truesight 10

Soul Decay aura 3; each undead ally within the aura at the start of the nothic eye of Vecna's turn makes a melee basic attack against an enemy as a free action.

HP 162; **Bloodied** 81

AC 36; **Fortitude** 34, **Reflex** 36, **Will** 32

Speed 6

ⓘ **Claw** (standard; at-will) ✦ **Necrotic**

+27 vs. AC; 2d12 + 6 necrotic damage, and the target is immobilized and takes a -2 penalty to saving throws (save ends both).

✦ **Mobile Melee Attack** (standard; at-will)

The nothic eye of Vecna moves its speed and makes a claw attack during the move. The eye of Vecna does not provoke opportunity attacks while moving away from the target of this attack.

⟵ **Eye Rot** (minor; recharges when the nothic eye of Vecna is not invisible to any creature)

Close burst 10; targets enemies; only one attack roll against all enemies; +28 vs. Fortitude; the eye of Vecna is invisible to the target (save ends).

Invisible Advantage

When a nothic eye of Vecna hits a creature that cannot see it, one ally adjacent to the target makes an opportunity attack against the target.

Alignment Unaligned   **Languages** Deep Speech

Skills Stealth +24

Str 23 (+17)	**Dex** 26 (+19)	**Wis** 18 (+15)
Con 24 (+18)	**Int** 12 (+12)	**Cha** 14 (+13)

NOTHIC LORE

Dungeoneering DC 18: Nothics are aberrant creatures that have drifted into the world and into other planes from the Far Realm. They have a semblance of intellect, but their hold on sanity is tenuous. A nothic can be identified by its awkward gait and its single eye, which can afflict enemies with various conditions. Nothics cackle maddeningly for no apparent reason.

Dungeoneering DC 23: Nothics serve powerful creatures that enjoy their erratic and amusing behavior. Nothic are also vicious combatants; they defend their masters with devotion.

Dungeoneering DC 25: Nothics live among the undead and in cults of Vecna, serving as guardians and jesters. Nothics in Vecna cults develop terrible gifts granted by the god of secrets. Their strong psychic connections to the Maimed God allow Vecna to see through the eye of any such nothic upon which he focuses attention, allowing him to gather secrets and keep tabs on those in his service.

ENCOUNTER GROUPS

The typical nothic is a cross between a court jester and a torturer in the court of a powerful evil creature. Barely sane, nothics perform functions other creatures might not consider.

Level 14 Encounter (XP 5,400)
✦ 1 mind flayer infiltrator (level 14 lurker, *MM* 188)
✦ 2 nothic cacklers (level 15 artillery)
✦ 2 war trolls (level 14 soldier, *MM* 254)

Level 18 Encounter (XP 10,000)
✦ 2 aboleth lashers (level 17 brute, *MM* 8)
✦ 1 death hag (level 18 soldier, *MM* 151)
✦ 2 nothic mindblights (level 19 controller)

Level 21 Encounter (XP 16,550)
✦ 3 bodak reavers (level 18 soldier, *MM* 36)
✦ 1 dark naga (level 21 elite controller, *MM* 194)
✦ 1 nothic eye of Vecna (level 22 lurker)

DECEPTIVE HUMANOIDS IMBUED with supernatural powers, oni dominate their surroundings, becoming leaders to be reckoned with.

ONI DEVOURER

ONI DEVOURERS COMMONLY SERVE more powerful, evil spellcasters. By day, they disguise themselves as ascetics, beggars, and priests. At night, they become ghoulish monstrosities hunting humanoids for food.

Oni Devourer	Level 7 Soldier
Medium natural humanoid	XP 300

Initiative +8   **Senses** Perception +3; darkvision
HP 78; **Bloodied** 39
AC 23; **Fortitude** 19, **Reflex** 19, **Will** 18
Speed 6, climb 4
ⓘ **Claws** (standard; at-will)
   +14 vs. AC; 1d6 + 3 damage, and the target is slowed (save ends).
☩ **Devour** (standard; recharge ⚅ ⚅)
   +14 vs. AC; 2d6 + 3 damage, and the target takes a –5 penalty to saving throws (save ends).
↗ **Hypnotic Glare** (standard; encounter) ✦ **Charm, Gaze**
   Ranged 10; +12 vs. Will; the target is pulled 5 squares and dazed (save ends).

Deceptive Veil (minor; at-will) ✦ **Illusion**
   The oni devourer can disguise itself to appear as any Medium natural humanoid. A creature can see through the disguise with a successful Insight check versus the devourer's Bluff check.
Alignment Evil   **Languages** Common, Giant
Skills Bluff +13, Stealth +11
Str 17 (+6)   **Dex** 17 (+6)   **Wis** 11 (+3)
Con 14 (+5)   **Int** 10 (+3)   **Cha** 14 (+5)

ONI OVERLORD

BRUTAL THUGS DEVOTED to avarice and bloodshed, oni overlords command groups of violent cronies. Oni overlords aren't as subtle as their brethren, and they make ostentatious displays of wealth and power.

Oni Overlord	Level 12 Elite Brute (Leader)
Large natural humanoid	XP 1,400

Initiative +7   **Senses** Perception +8; darkvision
Threatening Leader (Psychic) aura 5; each ally within the aura gains a +5 bonus to damage rolls and takes 5 psychic damage if it misses all targets with an attack.
HP 296; **Bloodied** 148
AC 24; **Fortitude** 25, **Reflex** 24, **Will** 26
Saving Throws +2
Speed 7, fly 8 (clumsy)
Action Points 1
ⓘ **Greatclub** (standard; at-will) ✦ **Weapon**
   Reach 2; +15 vs. AC; 4d4 + 6 damage, and each creature adjacent to the target takes 5 damage.
☩ **Overlord's Smash** (standard; at-will)
   The oni overlord makes a greatclub attack, shifts 1 square, and then makes a second greatclub attack against a different target.
⟵ **Overlord's Blast** (standard; recharges when first bloodied) ✦ **Necrotic, Poison**
   Close blast 5; +16 vs. Fortitude; 5d6 + 5 necrotic and poison damage, and the target gains vulnerable 5 necrotic and vulnerable 5 poison until the end of the oni overlord's next turn.
⟵ **Crush the Will** (free, when the oni overlord damages an enemy; recharge ⚅ ⚅) ✦ **Fear**
   Close burst 5; targets enemies; +15 vs. Will; the target grants combat advantage to the overlord until the end of the overlord's next turn.
Violent Reward (immediate reaction, when an ally within 10 squares of the oni overlord damages an enemy; at-will)
   The triggering ally gains 5 temporary hit points.
Deceptive Veil (minor; at-will) ✦ **Illusion**
   The oni overlord can disguise itself to appear as any Medium or Large humanoid. A creature can see through the disguise with a successful Insight check versus the overlord's Bluff check.
Alignment Evil   **Languages** Common, Giant
Skills Arcana +15, Insight +13, Intimidate +17
Str 21 (+11)   **Dex** 12 (+7)   **Wis** 14 (+8)
Con 18 (+10)   **Int** 18 (+10)   **Cha** 22 (+12)
Equipment hide armor, greatclub

ONI THUNDERER

ONI THUNDERERS DELIGHT in the pure mayhem of battle. An oni thunderer whips itself into a frenzy as it spins, and then lashes out at its enemies.

Oni Thunderer	Level 22 Skirmisher
Large natural humanoid	XP 4,150

Initiative +21   **Senses** Perception +21; darkvision
HP 206; **Bloodied** 103
AC 36; **Fortitude** 33, **Reflex** 35, **Will** 34
Speed 8, teleport 8
⊕ **Spiked Chain** (standard; at-will) ✦ **Thunder, Weapon**
   Reach 3; +28 vs. AC; 1d12 + 5 damage plus 1d8 thunder damage, and the target is grabbed and pulled into a space adjacent to the oni.
⟵ **Thunderclap Portal** (standard; recharge ⚄ ⚅ ⚅) ✦ **Teleportation, Thunder**
   The oni thunderer teleports 8 squares before or after the attack: close burst 2; targets enemies; +25 vs. Reflex; 2d12 + 8 thunder damage, and the oni thunderer pushes the target 2 squares. If the thunderer has the target grabbed, the attack deals 2d12 extra damage to the grabbed creature, and the grab ends.
Chain Dance (immediate reaction, when the oni thunderer is hit by an attack; at-will) ✦ **Teleportation**
   The thunderer teleports 3 squares.
Deceptive Veil (minor, at-will) ✦ **Illusion**
   The oni thunderer can disguise itself to appear as any Medium or Large humanoid. A creature can see through the disguise with a successful Insight check versus the thunderer's Bluff check.
Alignment Chaotic evil   **Languages** Common, Giant
Skills Acrobatics +24, Athletics +23, Bluff +23, Stealth +24
Str 23 (+17)   **Dex** 27 (+19)   **Wis** 20 (+16)
Con 22 (+17)   **Int** 16 (+14)   **Cha** 24 (+18)
Equipment leather armor, spiked chain

ONI LORE

Nature DC 16: Oni devourers disguise themselves by day, attacking and eating victims at night.

Oni overlords are tyrants that rule over an organization of lackeys. They seek wealth, power, and control, and don't care who they step on to get it.

Nature DC 21: Oni devourers serve a variety of masters, including oni, vampires, hags, and cultists of Zehir. In isolated areas of the world, large groups of devourers infiltrate and take over monasteries, small towns, and trading outposts, using such locations' innocent appearances as a cover. In one case, a group of oni devourers occupied a mountaintop monastery for almost thirty years before adventurers linked them to cases of missing pilgrims and petitioners.

Although they love combat and bloodshed, oni overlords sometimes negotiate with potential victims if they can see an easy benefit. They take on a human appearance when they do so, but are usually identifiable by their excessive jewelry.

Nature DC 26: Oni thunderers serve powerful creatures, including dragons, demons, and even undead. They command respect from their masters, leaving employers at inopportune moments if slighted.

ENCOUNTER GROUPS

Oni keep packs of shadow hounds or trolls as pets or guardians. They fight alongside death giants and titans, and serve powerful dragons or balor demons.

Level 7 Encounter (XP 1,700)
- ✦ 2 oni devourers (level 7 soldier)
- ✦ 1 oni night haunter (level 8 elite controller, *MM* 200)
- ✦ 1 troll (level 9 brute, *MM* 254)

Level 12 Encounter (XP 3,900)
- ✦ 1 oni overlord (level 12 elite brute)
- ✦ 3 minotaur warriors (level 10 soldier, *MM* 190)
- ✦ 2 scytheclaw drakes (level 10 skirmisher)

Level 22 Encounter (XP 20,750)
- ✦ 2 death giants (level 22 brute, *MM* 120)
- ✦ 3 oni thunderers (level 22 skirmisher)

THE ONLY PURPOSE OOZES SERVE in the world is to wipe clean the dilapidated, forgotten, and ruined places and free them of vermin, refuse, and adventurers.

ABOLETHIC SKUM

SOMETIMES AN ABOLETH'S ENSLAVEMENT of a humanoid foe goes wrong and the foe becomes a barely sentient pile of aqueous sludge. Out of its remnants of fear and shame, the abolethic skum hungers to destroy anything that reminds it of what it once was.

Abolethic Skum		Level 18 Minion Brute
Medium aberrant beast (aquatic, blind, ooze)		XP 500

Initiative +13 **Senses** Perception +14; blindsight 10, tremorsense 10

Psychic Dissonance aura 1; each creature within the aura gains vulnerable 5 psychic damage.

HP 1; a missed attack never damages a minion.

AC 30; **Fortitude** 32, **Reflex** 30, **Will** 26

Immune gaze; **Resist** 20 acid

Speed 2, swim 8

⊕ **Slam** (standard; at-will)

+20 vs. Fortitude; 16 damage, and the target is pushed 1 square or slowed until the end of the abolethic skum's next turn.

Aqueous Form

An abolethic skum is invisible while in water.

Alignment Unaligned	**Languages** —	
Str 16 (+12)	**Dex** 19 (+13)	**Wis** 11 (+9)
Con 23 (+15)	**Int** 4 (+6)	**Cha** 4 (+6)

ABOLETHIC SKUM TACTICS

An abolethic skum likes to fight in its element, slamming enemies into nearby water. Without water nearby, or if accompanied by a master that has psychic attack powers, the skum keeps enemies close and slowed.

BLACK PUDDING

THIS MERCURIAL OOZE SLITHERS on the ground like a massive pool of tar, waiting to turn anything it encounters into sludge.

Black Pudding		Level 8 Elite Brute
Large natural beast (blind, ooze)		XP 700

Initiative +6 **Senses** Perception +4; blindsight 10, tremorsense 10

HP 163; **Bloodied** 86

AC 20; **Fortitude** 22, **Reflex** 20, **Will** 18

Immune gaze; **Resist** 15 acid

Saving Throws +2

Speed 4, climb 3

Action Points 1

⊕ **Slam** (standard; at-will) ✦ **Acid**

+9 vs. Fortitude; 2d6 + 4 acid damage, and ongoing 5 acid damage (save ends).

↔ **Engulf** (standard; at-will) ✦ **Acid**

Close blast 3; +9 vs. Fortitude; 2d6 + 4 acid damage, and the target is grabbed. *Sustain Standard:* The black pudding sustains the grab, and the target takes 2d6 acid damage and loses a healing surge. A target that has no healing surges instead takes damage equal to its level.

Mercurial Body

A black pudding ignores difficult terrain and does not provoke opportunity attacks by moving.

Split (when the black pudding is hit by a weapon attack; at-will)

A black pudding spawn appears in a square adjacent to the black pudding or in the nearest unoccupied square.

Alignment Unaligned	**Languages** —	
Str 15 (+6)	**Dex** 14 (+6)	**Wis** 11 (+4)
Con 19 (+8)	**Int** 1 (-1)	**Cha** 1 (-1)

Black Pudding Spawn		Level 8 Minion Brute
Medium natural beast (blind, ooze)		XP 88

Initiative +6 **Senses** Perception +4; blindsight 10, tremorsense 10

HP 1; a missed attack never damages a minion.

AC 22; **Fortitude** 24, **Reflex** 22, **Will** 20

Immune gaze; **Resist** 15 acid

Speed 4, climb 3

⊕ **Slam** (standard; at-will) ✦ **Acid**

+9 vs. Fortitude; 10 acid damage.

Mercurial Body

A black pudding spawn ignores difficult terrain and does not provoke opportunity attacks by moving.

Alignment Unaligned	**Languages** —	
Str 15 (+6)	**Dex** 14 (+6)	**Wis** 11 (+4)
Con 19 (+8)	**Int** 1 (-1)	**Cha** 1 (-1)

BLACK PUDDING TACTICS

A black pudding has no discernible tactics, seeking only to eat the closest targets. It has no sense of self-preservation.

GRAY OOZE

WRETCHED PILES OF STINKING PUS, gray oozes seek
to dissolve the bones of other creatures into slime,
which they use to increase their bulk.

Gray Ooze		Level 2 Skirmisher
Small natural beast (blind, ooze)		XP 125

Initiative +5	Senses Perception +2; blindsight 10, tremorsense 10

Stench aura 2; each creature within the aura takes a -2 penalty to
attack rolls.
HP 43; **Bloodied** 21
AC 15; **Fortitude** 13, **Reflex** 15, **Will** 13
Immune gaze; **Resist** 5 acid
Speed 5, climb 3

ⓐ **Bone Melt** (standard; at-will) ✦ **Acid**
+5 vs. Fortitude; 1d6 + 5 acid damage, and the target takes a
cumulative -2 penalty to Fortitude each time it hits (save ends).
Slimy (minor; at-will)
The gray ooze shifts 2 squares.

Alignment Unaligned	**Languages** –	
Skills Stealth +12		
Str 11 (+1)	**Dex** 15 (+3)	**Wis** 11 (+1)
Con 19 (+5)	**Int** 1 (-4)	**Cha** 1 (-4)

GRAY OOZE TACTICS

Gray oozes attack in groups, softening up enemies
with *bone melt* so their attacks are increasingly likely
to hit.

GREEN SLIME

THE GREEN SLIME SLITHERS up cavern walls and waits
to drop on sources of heat. It devours flesh, bone, and
metal with equal aplomb.

Green Slime		Level 4 Lurker
Medium natural beast (blind, ooze)		XP 175

Initiative +9	Senses Perception +2; blindsight 10, tremorsense 10

HP 47; **Bloodied** 23
AC 20; **Fortitude** 23, **Reflex** 17, **Will** 20
Immune gaze; **Resist** 5 acid; **Vulnerability** 5 fire, 5 radiant
Speed 4, climb 4

ⓐ **Engulf** (standard; at-will) ✦ **Acid**
+7 vs. Reflex; 1d6 + 3 acid damage, and the target is engulfed
(save ends). While engulfed, the target takes ongoing 5 acid
damage and is restrained. While a target is engulfed, attacks
that target the green slime deal half damage to the slime and
half damage to the engulfed creature. While it has a creature
engulfed, the slime can make attacks only against the engulfed
creature.
Rapid Dissolution
A green slime's attacks deal 1d6 extra acid damage to a
creature that is taking ongoing acid damage.

Alignment Unaligned	**Languages** –	
Skills Stealth +11		
Str 11 (+2)	**Dex** 16 (+5)	**Wis** 11 (+2)
Con 17 (+5)	**Int** 3 (-2)	**Cha** 1 (-3)

GREEN SLIME TACTICS

In battle, a green slime attacks the nearest creature
and uses *rapid dissolution* to dissolve the creature into
slime.

OOZE LORE

Nature DC 10: Gray oozes are major nuisances
in archaeological expeditions. Having fed on buried
bones, they seek fresher targets among excavators
and adventurers.

Dwarves consider green slime to be among the
greatest nuisances hindering mining. The best way to
destroy green slime is with fire or light.

Nature DC 14: Black puddings are dungeon-
scavenging oozes covered in thick coatings of tarlike
acid that eats away at everything, including rock,
bone, and metal.

Nature DC 15: Gray oozes are especially dangerous in numbers or in close proximity to monsters that
can take advantage of their bone-softening threat.

Nature DC 20: Abolethic skums are the results
of failed attempts by aboleths to turn humanoids into
servitors.

Nature DC 25: Aboleths and other psychic monsters use an abolethic skum's jarring psychic presence
to soften up enemies for psychic attacks.

ENCOUNTER GROUPS

Oozes show up everywhere, regardless of whether
other denizens of their environs want them or not.

Level 4 Encounter (XP 900)
✦ 1 ankheg (level 3 elite lurker)
✦ 2 green slimes (level 4 lurker)
✦ 2 gray oozes (level 2 skirmisher)

Level 8 Encounter (XP 1,750)
✦ 2 black puddings (level 8 elite brute)
✦ 1 darkmantle enveloper (level 8 lurker)

Level 19 Encounter (XP 12,200)
✦ 10 abolethic skums (level 18 minion brute)
✦ 2 aboleth lashers (level 17 brute, *MM* 8)
✦ 1 aboleth overseer (level 18 elite controller, *MM* 8)

PHOELARCH

The plumed humanoid phoelarch and the bird-like phoera represent two forms of one creature, half natural and half elemental. Phoelarchs are humanoid creatures with flames rippling over their skin. They seek freedom and adventure. When the phoelarch is slain, it is consumed in a burst of fire and the phoera explodes into being from the Elemental Chaos, intent on revenge.

PHOELARCH MAGE

PHOELARCH MAGES HARBOR SOULS OF FIRE that burn with the desire for freedom.

PHOELARCH MAGE TACTICS

A phoelarch mage prefers to hang back, using its potent ranged and area attacks.

Phoelarch Mage	Level 12 Artillery
Medium natural humanoid	XP 350

Initiative +10   **Senses** Perception +12
Phoenix Heat (Fire) aura 1; each creature that enters the aura or starts its turn there takes 5 fire damage.
HP 93; **Bloodied** 46; see also *rise from the ashes*
AC 24; **Fortitude** 23, **Reflex** 23, **Will** 25
Resist 10 fire; **Vulnerable** 5 cold
Speed 6
⊕ **Burning Dagger** (standard; at-will) ✦ **Fire, Weapon**
   +16 vs. AC; 1d4 + 6 fire damage.
⦾ **Phoenix Ray** (standard; at-will) ✦ **Fire**
   Ranged 20; +17 vs. Reflex; 2d8 + 5 fire damage.
⬱ **Rise from the Ashes** (when the phoelarch mage drops to 0 hit points) ✦ **Fire, Zone**
   Close burst 2; +13 vs. Reflex; 3d8 + 5 fire damage. *Effect:* The burst creates a zone of fire that lasts until the end of the encounter. Each creature that enters the zone or starts its turn there takes 5 fire damage. In addition, when the phoelarch mage's next turn would occur, a phoera appears within the zone.
❉ **Flames of the Phoenix** (standard; recharge ⚄ ⚅) ✦ **Fire**
   Area burst 2 within 20; +15 vs. Reflex; 1d8 + 5 fire damage, and ongoing 5 fire damage (save ends).
Alignment Unaligned   **Languages** Common, Primordial
Skills Insight +17, Diplomacy +15
Str 13 (+7)	**Dex** 19 (+10)	**Wis** 22 (+12)
Con 15 (+8)	**Int** 16 (+9)	**Cha** 18 (+10)
Equipment dagger

PHOELARCH MAGE LORE

Nature DC 16: Phoelarch mages harness their innate command of fire. They prefer adventuring with mentors to researching ancient knowledge. Some mages search for their phoera counterparts in the hope of improving their magic.

PHOELARCH WARRIOR

PHOELARCH WARRIORS ARE BRAVE in the face of danger, often flitting among the blades of their enemies and responding with fire.

PHOELARCH WARRIOR TACTICS

The phoelarch warrior takes risks, deliberately provoking opportunity attacks to test an enemy's willingness to be harmed by *burning step*.

Phoelarch Warrior	Level 12 Skirmisher
Medium natural humanoid (fire)	XP 350

Initiative +14   **Senses** Perception +8
Phoenix Heat (Fire) aura 1; each creature that enters the aura or starts its turn there takes 5 fire damage.
HP 114; **Bloodied** 57; see also *rise from the ashes*
AC 26; **Fortitude** 23, **Reflex** 25, **Will** 25
Resist 10 fire; **Vulnerable** 5 cold
Speed 7
⊕ **Burning Falchion** (standard; at-will) ✦ **Fire, Weapon**
   +17 vs. AC; 2d4 + 6 fire damage (crit 4d4 +14 fire damage).
⬱ **Rise from the Ashes** (when the phoelarch warrior drops to 0 hit points) ✦ **Fire, Zone**
   Close burst 2; +13 vs. Reflex; 3d8 + 5 fire damage. *Effect:* The burst creates a zone of fire that lasts until the end of the encounter. Each creature that enters the zone or starts its turn there takes 5 fire damage. In addition, when the phoelarch warrior's next turn would occur, a phoera appears within the zone.
Burning Step ✦ **Fire**
   Any creature that hits the phoelarch warrior with an opportunity attack takes 3d6 fire damage.
Alignment Unaligned   **Languages** Common, Primordial
Skills Acrobatics +17, Athletics +12
Str 13 (+7)	**Dex** 23 (+12)	**Wis** 14 (+8)
Con 10 (+6)	**Int** 10 (+6)	**Cha** 18 (+10)
Equipment falchion

PHOELARCH WARRIOR LORE

Nature DC 16: Phoelarch warriors are seldom found in armies, preferring the freedom of mercenary work. As creatures that value liberty, all but the most unscrupulous phoelarch warriors refuse to work for those that keep slaves.

PHOERA

PHOERAS SOAR THROUGH THE ELEMENTAL CHAOS with concerns alien to their phoelarch counterparts.

PHOERA TACTICS

A phoera fights in a violent rage and often harms allies as well as enemies with its close attacks. It starts combat by using *feathers of flame*, preferably on multiple enemies. Then it focuses its claw attacks on a target that seems susceptible to fire damage, using *feathers of flame* again whenever the power recharges. When pressed by multiple foes, the phoera uses *flyby attack* to reposition itself.

(Left to right) phoelarch warrior, phoera, and phoelarch mage

Phoera	Level 12 Skirmisher
Medium elemental magical beast (fire)	XP 350

Initiative +14   **Senses** Perception +8

Phoenix Heat (Fire) aura 2; each creature that enters the aura or starts its turn there takes 5 fire damage.

HP 114; **Bloodied** 57; see also *death burst*

AC 26; **Fortitude** 23, **Reflex** 25, **Will** 25

Resist 15 fire; **Vulnerable** 5 cold

Speed 6, fly 10

Action Points 1

⊕ **Claw** (standard; at-will) ✦ Fire

+17 vs. AC; 1d4 + 5 damage, and ongoing 5 fire damage (save ends).

⟻ **Feathers of Flame** (standard; recharge ⚄ ⚅ ⚅) ✦ Fire

Close blast 4; +15 vs. Reflex; 3d6 + 5 fire damage.

↯/⟻ **Flyby Attack** (standard; encounter) ✦ Fire

The phoera flies its speed without provoking opportunity attacks, and it makes a claw attack or a *feathers of flame* attack at any point during the move.

⟻ **Death Burst** (when the phoera drops to 0 hit points) ✦ Fire, Zone

Close burst 2; +13 vs. Reflex; 3d8 + 5 fire damage. *Effect:* The burst creates a zone of fire that lasts until the end of the encounter. Each creature that enters the zone or starts its turn there takes 5 fire damage.

Alignment Unaligned   **Languages** Common, Primordial

Str 13 (+7)	**Dex** 23 (+12)	**Wis** 14 (+8)
Con 10 (+6)	**Int** 10 (+6)	**Cha** 18 (+10)

PHOELARCH LORE

Arcana DC 16: Phoeras are birdlike creatures that fly through the skies of the Elemental Chaos. When angered, a phoera fights viciously.

Arcana or Nature DC 21: Each phoelarch shares a soul with a phoera. The two are inextricably linked, and the death of one summons the angry form of the other. As long as its other half survives, a slain phoelarch or phoera eventually returns to life. A phoera and phoelarch that share a soul can differ as much as any two creatures. Each half has only a vague sense of the other's personality and emotions.

ENCOUNTER GROUPS

Phoelarchs prefer to ally with free-spirited creatures. Their wanderlust leads them to travel to many distant lands; they can be found almost anywhere.

Level 12 Encounter (XP 3,700)
✦ 1 briar witch dryad (level 13 elite controller, MM 96)
✦ 1 phoelarch warrior (level 12 elite skirmisher)
✦ 4 snaketongue zealots (level 12 minion, MM 272)

REMORHAZ

REMORHAZES USE THEIR INTENSE INTERNAL HEAT to burrow through the ice and rock of their arctic homes, preying on any creatures they come across, even giants and dragons.

Remorhaz	Level 21 Elite Brute
Huge elemental beast	XP 6,400

Initiative +18 **Senses** Perception +15; low-light vision
Blistering Heat (Fire) aura 2; each creature that starts its turn within the aura takes 10 fire damage.
HP 480; **Bloodied** 240
AC 33; **Fortitude** 33, **Reflex** 34, **Will** 32
Saving Throws +2
Speed 6, burrow 4 (tunneling)
Action Points 1

⊕ **Bite** (standard; at-will)
Reach 2; +24 vs. AC; 2d12 + 10 damage, and the target is grabbed.

↓ **Swallow** (minor; at-will) ✦ **Fire**
Reach 2; targets a creature grabbed by the remorhaz; +24 vs. Fortitude; the target is swallowed and is no longer grabbed. While swallowed, the target is restrained and takes 10 damage plus 10 fire damage at the start of the remorhaz's turn. The swallowed creature has line of sight and line of effect only to the remorhaz, and no creature has line of sight or line of effect to the target. The swallowed creature can make only melee or close attacks. If the swallowed creature deals 30 damage to the remorhaz with an attack, the remorhaz regurgitates the creature into an adjacent square, and the creature is no longer swallowed. When the remorhaz dies, the target is no longer swallowed and can escape as a move action, appearing in the remorhaz's former space.

↓ **Trample** (standard; at-will)
The remorhaz moves its speed and can enter enemies' spaces. The remorhaz makes an attack against each enemy whose space it enters: +22 vs. Reflex; 2d10 + 5 damage, and the target is knocked prone.

← **Immolating Carapace** (standard; recharge ⚄⚅) ✦ **Fire**
Close burst 1; +24 vs. Reflex; 3d10 + 5 fire damage, and the target takes ongoing 10 fire damage until it ends its turn in a space that is not adjacent to the remorhaz.

Enraged Heat (immediate reaction, when a creature hits the remorhaz with a melee attack; usable only while bloodied; at-will) ✦ **Fire**
The triggering creature takes 10 fire damage.

Alignment Unaligned **Languages** —
| **Str** 23 (+16) | **Dex** 26 (+18) | **Wis** 21 (+15) |
| **Con** 20 (+15) | **Int** 5 (+7) | **Cha** 10 (+10) |

REMORHAZ TACTICS

A remorhaz burrows to reach an isolated enemy and grabs it with its bite attack, then attempts to swallow it whole.

REMORHAZ LORE

Arcana DC 22: A remorhaz generates intense heat, especially when enraged. Remorhazes are infamous for swallowing their prey whole, though they dislike trying to digest meals that are also causing them damage.

Arcana DC 27: Remorhazes are wild creatures, but they are sometimes trained by frost giants for use as guardians.

ENCOUNTER GROUPS

Frost giants are among the few creatures that have been known to risk training remorhazes.

Level 18 Encounter (XP 11,200)
✦ 1 frost giant (level 17 brute)
✦ 1 remorhaz (level 21 elite brute)
✦ 1 rime hound (level 17 elite skirmisher)

RETRIEVER

RETRIEVERS ARE ARACHNOID MONSTROSITIES created by the primordials to seek out their foes with unerring accuracy. As constructs, they are built to follow the directions of powerful creatures.

Retriever		Level 27 Soldier
Huge elemental animate		XP 11,000

Initiative +24   **Senses** Perception +20; darkvision, truesight 10

HP 248; **Bloodied** 124

AC 43; **Fortitude** 39, **Reflex** 40, **Will** 38

Immune charm, fear; **Resist** 5 to all damage

Speed 8

⊕ **Claws** (standard; at-will)
Reach 3; +34 vs. AC; 2d8 + 8 damage.

⊕ **Retrieve** (standard; usable only while the retriever does not have a creature grabbed; at-will)
Reach 3; +30 vs. Fortitude; 2d8 + 8 damage, and the target is grabbed. The retriever can move a creature it has grabbed without making a Strength attack.

↗ **Eye Rays** (standard; one ray recharges each round—roll a d4 to determine which) ✦ **Acid, Cold, Fire, Thunder**
The retriever fires all the rays as a single standard action, but each must target a different creature: ranged 10; +32 vs. Reflex.
1—Acid Ray: 2d10 + 9 acid damage, and the target is blinded (save ends).
2—Cold Ray: 2d10 + 9 cold damage, and the target is immobilized (save ends).
3—Fire Ray: 2d10 + 9 fire damage, and ongoing 15 fire damage (save ends).
4—Thunder Ray: 2d10 + 9 thunder damage, and the target is stunned (save ends).

Self-Repair (standard; recharges when first bloodied) ✦ **Healing**
The retriever regains 20 hit points and gains a +4 bonus to AC until the start of its next turn.

Unerring Accuracy (standard; daily) ✦ **Teleportation**
The retriever senses the general location of the target or nearest creature of the type it was commanded to locate. The retriever teleports to a space that is within 10 squares of the target. The target need not be on the same plane as the retriever when it uses this power.

Alignment Unaligned	**Languages** –	
Str 26 (+21)	**Dex** 29 (+22)	**Wis** 25 (+20)
Con 24 (+20)	**Int** 2 (+9)	**Cha** 10 (+13)

RETRIEVER TACTICS

A retriever uses *eye rays* whenever possible. In any round when the retriever has access to at least two rays, it fires them, even if doing this provokes opportunity attacks. If it does not, it savages foes with its claws. When directed to find a target, a retriever concentrates its attacks on that creature until it can grab the target using *retrieve*.

RETRIEVER LORE

Arcana DC 26: Retrievers are unrivaled assassins and kidnappers that have the ability to find a designated target even across interplanar distances. Their eye rays can easily destroy or neutralize targets.

Arcana DC 31: Retrievers have a single-minded intellect, and in the eons since the cosmic war they have continued tirelessly to pursue whatever tasks they were given before being separated from their primordial masters.

Demons have learned the secret of commanding retrievers, turning these constructs into another tool for their destructive impulses.

ENCOUNTER GROUPS

If they aren't acting alone on some ancient mission, retrievers are seen alongside demons that have taken control of them.

Level 26 Encounter (XP 43,100)
✦ 1 abyssal rotfiend (level 26 controller)
✦ 1 marilith (level 24 elite skirmisher, *MM* 57)
✦ 2 retrievers (level 27 soldier)

Rust monsters roam caverns and dungeons seeking metals to devour, making them a nightmare for any civilized creature dwelling underground.

RUST MONSTER

A rust monster typically attacks the nearest large source of metal, so the most heavily armored enemy is often its target.

Rust Monster	Level 6 Skirmisher
Medium natural beast	XP 250

Initiative +10   **Senses** Perception +5; low-light vision
HP 66; **Bloodied** 33
AC 20; **Fortitude** 16, **Reflex** 21, **Will** 17
Speed 8

⊕ **Bite** (standard; at-will)
> +11 vs. AC; 1d10 + 5 damage, and if the target is wearing heavy armor, the armor is rusting until the end of the encounter. While the armor is rusting, the target takes a cumulative -1 penalty to AC, to a maximum penalty of -5.

↓ **Dissolve Metal** (standard; encounter) ✦ **Reliable**
> Targets a creature wearing or wielding a rusting magic item of 10th level or lower or any non-magic rusting item; +9 vs. Reflex; the rusting item is destroyed.

Rusting Defense (when the rust monster is hit by a weapon attack; at-will)
> The weapon used in the triggering attack is rusting until the end of the encounter. While the weapon is rusting, the target takes a cumulative -1 penalty to damage rolls on attacks that use the weapon, to a maximum penalty of -5.

Residuum Recovery
> A rust monster consumes any item it destroys. The *residuum* from any magic items the monster has destroyed can be retrieved from its stomach. The *residuum* is worth the market value of the item (not one-fifth the value).

Alignment Unaligned	**Languages** —	
Str 8 (+2)	**Dex** 20 (+8)	**Wis** 15 (+5)
Con 10 (+3)	**Int** 2 (-1)	**Cha** 12 (+4)

RUST MONSTER TACTICS

A hunger for metal drives the rust monster, and it heads straight for the closest enemy wearing metal armor or brandishing a metal melee weapon. A rust monster isn't clever, and often provokes opportunity attacks as it turns to its next target. Usually, after a rust monster dissolves a suit of armor or a few weapons, it retreats, content with its belly full of rust.

YOUNG RUST MONSTER SWARM

Young rust monster swarms swirl around many foes, seeking a taste of all the metals they can see.

Young Rust Monster Swarm	Level 9 Soldier
Medium natural beast (swarm)	XP 400

Initiative +12   **Senses** Perception +5; low-light vision
Swarm Attack aura 1; each enemy that starts its turn within the aura takes 3 damage. If the enemy has a rusting item, that enemy is also slowed until the end of its turn.
HP 92; **Bloodied** 46
AC 25; **Fortitude** 19, **Reflex** 24, **Will** 19
Resist half damage from melee and ranged attacks; **Vulnerable** 10 against close and area attacks
Speed 6

⊕ **Swarm of Teeth** (standard; at-will)
> +14 vs. Reflex; 2d8 + 1 damage, and if the target is wearing heavy armor, the armor is rusting until the end of the encounter. While the armor is rusting, the target takes a cumulative -1 penalty to AC, to maximum penalty of -5.

Rusting Defense (when the rust monster swarm is hit by a weapon attack; at-will)
> The weapon used in the triggering attack is rusting until the end of the encounter. While the weapon is rusting, the target takes a cumulative -1 penalty to damage rolls on attacks that use the weapon, to a maximum penalty of -5.

Alignment Unaligned	**Languages** —	
Str 8 (+3)	**Dex** 22 (+10)	**Wis** 13 (+5)
Con 12 (+5)	**Int** 2 (+0)	**Cha** 12 (+5)

DWEOMER EATER

SOME RUST MONSTERS DEVELOP A TASTE FOR MAGIC and eat items infused with arcane energy in order to grow larger and stronger.

Dweomer Eater	Level 11 Skirmisher
Large natural beast	XP 600

Initiative +13   **Senses** Perception +9; low-light vision
HP 110; **Bloodied** 55
AC 25; **Fortitude** 20, **Reflex** 25, **Will** 23
Speed 8

⊕ **Bite** (standard; at-will)
+16 vs. AC; 2d6 + 6 damage, and if the target is wearing magic armor, the armor is decaying until the end of the encounter. While the armor is decaying, the armor's enhancement bonus takes a cumulative -1 penalty, to the maximum of the armor's enhancement bonus.

⦿ **Dissolve Item** (standard; recharge ⚅⚅) ✦ **Reliable**
Targets a creature wearing or wielding a decaying magic item of 15th level or lower; +14 vs. Reflex; the decaying magic item is destroyed.

Magic Consumption (when the dweomer eater is hit by an attack that uses a magic implement or weapon; at-will)
The implement or weapon used in the triggering attack is decaying until the end of the encounter. While the implement or weapon is decaying, the target takes a cumulative -1 penalty to that implement's or weapon's enhancement bonus, to a maximum penalty equal to the item's enhancement bonus.

Residuum Recovery
A dweomer eater consumes any item it destroys. The *residuum* from any magic items the dweomer eater has destroyed can be retrieved from its stomach. The *residuum* is worth the market value of the item (not one-fifth the value).

Alignment Unaligned	**Languages** –	
Str 12 (+6)	**Dex** 23 (+11)	**Wis** 18 (+9)
Con 14 (+7)	**Int** 2 (+1)	**Cha** 13 (+6)

RUST MONSTER LORE

Nature DC 14: Rust monsters devour metals to survive. Most spend their lives leaching minerals from stone, but purer manufactured metals draw them like blood draws sharks.

Since their food is scarce, rust monsters typically have only one or two young per brood. In places where food is plentiful, such as near a lode of metal ore, a pair of rust monsters can have dozens of offspring.

Nature DC 19: A rust monster that feeds on *residuum* retains it within its body. The *residuum* can be retrieved after its death. Those that have eaten a large amount of *residuum*, called dweomer eaters, eventually absorb it, growing in size and becoming hungry for more magic.

ENCOUNTER GROUPS

Rust monsters are creatures of opportunity, so their allies often avoid using metal tools or weapons. Lizardfolk sometimes use rust monsters to help even the odds against well-armed enemies.

Level 6 Encounter (XP 1,250)
✦ 2 blackscale bruiser lizardfolk (level 6 brute, MM 179)
✦ 1 greenscale marsh mystic lizardfolk (level 6 controller, MM 179)
✦ 2 rust monsters (level 6 skirmisher)

Level 8 Encounter (XP 1,750)
✦ 1 dweomer eater (level 11 skirmisher)
✦ 1 spriggan witherer (level 8 artillery)
✦ 2 young rust monster swarms (level 9 soldier)

A GUIDE TO USING RUST MONSTERS

For a PC, the threat of losing gear can be greater than the threat of being reduced to 0 hp. Because of this fact, rust monsters can be more terrifying for players to face than a rampaging red dragon. A character who loses his or her armor becomes extremely vulnerable, and a character who has lost a magic weapon won't be as effective in later encounters. When a rust monster consumes a PC's weapon, it effectively gives that PC a significant penalty on attack and damage rolls until he or she can find a suitable replacement weapon. A PC who loses armor to a rust monster suffers an even more dramatic reduction in AC unless replacement armor can be found.

The possibility of recovering *residuum* from a rust monster or a dweomer eater alleviates this disadvantage to some degree, but the PCs will still need to find time to rest and use the Create Magic Item ritual, and they might even need to "head back to town" to find a way to replace the item. But you don't want an encounter with a rust monster to be one that forces the PCs to stop adventuring. When you include a rust monster in an encounter, think about ways to allow the PCs to carry on, with perhaps less optimal gear. For example, the PCs might have had a previous encounter that provided armor or weapons that they wouldn't normally use, or the PCs might be able to fashion clubs or other simple weapons out of nearby materials.

Eventually, though, the PCs should have an opportunity to regain their lost equipment by using the *residuum* found in the monster. Although a PC might lose an item, it is intended that the loss be only temporary, which is why the *residuum* recovered from a rust monster is equal to the full value of the destroyed item. How the PCs deal with the loss is what makes the rust monster fun. Be wary of PCs who try to abuse a rust monster's powers to their advantage by using rust monsters to consume items the PCs would otherwise sell for one-fifth value. In such cases, you should reduce the resulting *residuum* to one-fifth value, effectively making the rust monster a free Disenchant Magic Item ritual.

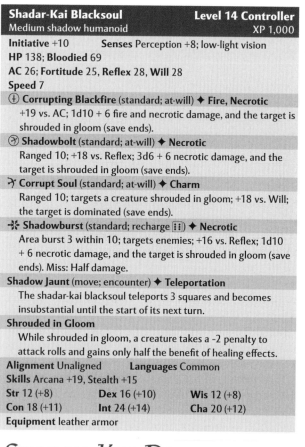

THESE SHADOWY HUMANOIDS pursue pleasure and pain, depravity and hedonistic excess—any rush of sensation to forestall the Shadowfell's gloom.

SHADAR-KAI LORE

Arcana DC 18: Shadar-kai seek new experiences and a rush of sensation. Characters who risk bargaining with the shadar-kai should offer an intense or diverting experience as their part in the deal.

Arcana DC 23: Long ago, the shadar-kai bound themselves by oath and blood to the service of the Raven Queen. However, they found their extended lives threatened by the omnipresent malaise of the Shadowfell. Realizing that sensation, even pain, was the only way to forestall their home's soul-draining gloom, the shadar-kai became a race of extremes.

SHADAR-KAI BLACKSOUL

A SHADAR-KAI BLACKSOUL KILLS FROM A DISTANCE, targeting foes with bolts of necrotic energy.

Shadar-Kai Blacksoul	Level 14 Controller
Medium shadow humanoid	XP 1,000

Initiative +10   **Senses** Perception +8; low-light vision
HP 138; **Bloodied** 69
AC 26; **Fortitude** 25, **Reflex** 28, **Will** 28
Speed 7

⊕ **Corrupting Blackfire** (standard; at-will) ✦ **Fire, Necrotic**
+19 vs. AC; 1d10 + 6 fire and necrotic damage, and the target is shrouded in gloom (save ends).

⊙ **Shadowbolt** (standard; at-will) ✦ **Necrotic**
Ranged 10; +18 vs. Reflex; 3d6 + 6 necrotic damage, and the target is shrouded in gloom (save ends).

⌁ **Corrupt Soul** (standard; at-will) ✦ **Charm**
Ranged 10; targets a creature shrouded in gloom; +18 vs. Will; the target is dominated (save ends).

✳ **Shadowburst** (standard; recharge ⚄⚅) ✦ **Necrotic**
Area burst 3 within 10; targets enemies; +16 vs. Reflex; 1d10 + 6 necrotic damage, and the target is shrouded in gloom (save ends). Miss: Half damage.

Shadow Jaunt (move; encounter) ✦ **Teleportation**
The shadar-kai blacksoul teleports 3 squares and becomes insubstantial until the start of its next turn.

Shrouded in Gloom
While shrouded in gloom, a creature takes a -2 penalty to attack rolls and gains only half the benefit of healing effects.

Alignment Unaligned   **Languages** Common
Skills Arcana +19, Stealth +15
Str 12 (+8)	**Dex** 16 (+10)	**Wis** 12 (+8)
Con 18 (+11)	**Int** 24 (+14)	**Cha** 20 (+12)

Equipment leather armor

SHADAR-KAI DAWNKILLER

A SHADAR-KAI DAWNKILLER USES STEALTH and mobility to remain unseen, slicing its enemies with lethal curved knives.

Shadar-Kai Dawnkiller	Level 14 Lurker
Medium shadow humanoid	XP 1,000

Initiative +18   **Senses** Perception +16; low-light vision
HP 106; **Bloodied** 53
AC 28; **Fortitude** 26, **Reflex** 28, **Will** 25
Speed 7

⊕ **Kukri** (standard; at-will) ✦ **Weapon**
+19 vs. AC; 2d6 + 6 damage, and the target is shrouded in gloom (save ends).

✝ **Shade Strike** (standard; at-will) ✦ **Necrotic**
+19 vs. AC; targets an enemy shrouded in gloom; 2d8 + 6 necrotic damage, and the target is blinded (save ends).

Shadow Jaunt (move; encounter) ✦ **Teleportation**
The shadar-kai dawnkiller teleports 3 squares and becomes insubstantial until the start of its next turn.

Shadows of the Raven Queen ✦ **Necrotic**
The shadar-kai dawnkiller's melee attacks deal 2d6 extra necrotic damage against a target that cannot see the dawnkiller.

Shrouded in Gloom
While shrouded in gloom, a creature takes a -2 penalty to attack rolls and gains only half the benefit of healing effects.

Alignment Unaligned   **Languages** Common
Skills Acrobatics +19, Stealth +19
Str 20 (+12)	**Dex** 24 (+14)	**Wis** 18 (+11)
Con 16 (+10)	**Int** 14 (+9)	**Cha** 11 (+7)

Equipment leather armor, 2 kukris

SHADAR-KAI GLOOM LORD

SHADAR-KAI GLOOM LORDS COMMAND THE SHADOWS and construct prisons from them.

Shadar-Kai Gloom Lord	Level 14 Artillery
Medium shadow humanoid	XP 1,000

Initiative +10   **Senses** Perception +8; low-light vision
HP 108; **Bloodied** 54
AC 26; **Fortitude** 25, **Reflex** 28, **Will** 26
Speed 7

⊕ **Corrupting Blackfire** (standard; at-will) ✦ **Fire, Necrotic**
+19 vs. AC; 2d8 + 6 fire and necrotic damage, and the target is shrouded in gloom (save ends).

⊙ **Shadowbolt** (standard; at-will) ✦ **Necrotic**
Ranged 10; +19 vs. Reflex; 2d8 + 6 necrotic damage, and the target is shrouded in gloom (save ends).

⊙ **Shadowcage** (standard; at-will) ✦ **Necrotic**
Ranged 10; targets a creature shrouded in gloom; +19 vs. Reflex; 3d6 + 6 necrotic damage, and the target is restrained and cannot see creatures more than 2 squares away from it (save ends both).

Shadow Jaunt (move; encounter) ✦ **Teleportation**
The shadar-kai gloom lord teleports 3 squares and becomes insubstantial until the start of its next turn.

Shrouded in Gloom
While shrouded in gloom, a creature takes a -2 penalty to attack rolls and gains only half the benefit of healing effects.

Alignment Unaligned   **Languages** Common
Skills Arcana +19, Stealth +15
Str 12 (+8)	**Dex** 16 (+10)	**Wis** 12 (+8)
Con 18 (+11)	**Int** 24 (+14)	**Cha** 20 (+12)

Equipment leather armor

(Left to right) shadar-kai painbearer, gloom lord, dawnkiller, and blacksoul

SHADAR-KAI PAINBEARER

GRACEFUL DANCERS OF DEATH, shadar-kai painbearers earned their name from the spiked chains they wield.

Shadar-Kai Painbearer	Level 15 Skirmisher (leader)
Medium shadow humanoid	XP 1,200

Initiative +16 — **Senses** Perception +11; low-light vision
Shadow weft aura 5; each shadar-kai ally within the aura shifts 1 square as a free action after it hits with a melee attack.
HP 144; **Bloodied** 72
AC 29; **Fortitude** 27, **Reflex** 29, **Will** 27
Speed 7

⊕ **Shadow Chain** (standard; at-will) ✦ **Weapon**
Reach 2; +20 vs. AC; 2d8 + 6 damage, and the target is shrouded in gloom (save ends).

↯ **Shadow Dance** (standard; recharge ⚅ ⚅) ✦ **Necrotic**
The shadar-kai painbearer shifts 7 squares and makes three shadow chain attacks during the move, each against a different target. The painbearer's second and third attacks deal 2d6 extra necrotic damage for each prior attack that has hit. A creature that is shrouded in gloom and is hit by an attack is blinded (save ends).

Shadow Boon (immediate reaction, when an ally within 10 squares of the shadar-kai painbearer misses with an attack; encounter)
The triggering ally rerolls the attack roll.

Shadow Jaunt (move; encounter) ✦ **Teleportation**
The shadar-kai painbearer teleports 3 squares and becomes insubstantial until the start of its next turn.

Shrouded in Gloom
While shrouded in gloom, a creature takes a –2 penalty to attack rolls and gains only half the benefit of healing effects.

Alignment Unaligned — **Languages** Common
Skills Acrobatics +19, Stealth +19
Str 20 (+12) — **Dex** 24 (+14) — **Wis** 18 (+11)
Con 16 (+10) — **Int** 14 (+9) — **Cha** 11 (+7)
Equipment leather armor, spiked chain

ENCOUNTER GROUPS

Shadar-kai frequently ally with other creatures of the Shadowfell, such as bodaks, boneclaws, and dark ones. Powerful shadar-kai favor nightmares as steeds.

Level 13 Encounter (XP 4,600)
✦ 1 bodak skulk (level 16 lurker, *MM* 36)
✦ 2 shadar-kai dawnkillers (level 14 lurker)
✦ 1 shadar-kai painbearer (level 15 skirmisher)

Level 14 Encounter (XP 5,400)
✦ 1 shadar-kai blacksoul (level 14 controller)
✦ 2 shadar-kai gloom lords (level 14 artillery)
✦ 2 shadar-kai painbearers (level 15 skirmisher)

To SAHUAGIN AND OTHER UNDERSEA PREDATORS, the shark is a totemic inspiration, a creature of blood frenzy and relentless hunger. To creatures that live above the waves, the sight of a shark's fin cutting the surface heralds doom.

FLESHTEARER SHARK

THE FLESHTEARER SHARK LOOKS like a creature from another age. For thousands of years, these sharks have hunted in oceans and lakes. Mariners greatly fear the fleshtearer, for even the sturdy hulls of ships cannot always withstand the rending teeth of this voracious beast.

Fleshtearer Shark	Level 10 Brute
Large natural beast (aquatic)	XP 500

Initiative +8 **Senses** Perception +9; low-light vision
HP 128; **Bloodied** 64
AC 22; **Fortitude** 23, **Reflex** 21, **Will** 22
Speed 1 (clumsy), swim 8
⊕ **Bite** (standard; at-will)
+13 vs. AC; 2d8 + 7 damage.
↟ **Lockjaw Charge** (standard; usable only while the fleshtearer shark is not grabbing a creature; at-will)
The shark charges and makes the following attack in place of a melee basic attack: +14 vs. AC; 2d8 + 7 damage, and the target is grabbed. When the grab ends, the target takes ongoing 5 damage (save ends).
↟ **Shredding Teeth** (standard; at-will)
Targets a creature grabbed by the fleshtearer shark; no attack roll; 3d8 + 7 damage.
Feeding Frenzy (when the fleshtearer shark starts its turn within 5 squares of a bloodied creature; at-will)
The shark must make a bite attack against a creature adjacent to it. If the shark is grabbing a creature, the grab ends.
Waterborne
While in water, a fleshtearer shark gains a +2 bonus to damage rolls against any creature without a swim speed.
Alignment Unaligned **Languages** —
Str 21 (+10) **Dex** 16 (+8) **Wis** 18 (+9)
Con 18 (+9) **Int** 2 (+1) **Cha** 15 (+7)

FLESHTEARER SHARK TACTICS
Unless spurred into combat by its master or another beast, a fleshtearer shark lurks just outside its prey's sight. The fleshtearer shark charges into battle using *lockjaw charge*, and it continues using *lockjaw charge* to attempt to grab nearby foes even if doing that means provoking opportunity attacks when moving away from adjacent enemies. Even when facing formidable prey, a fleshtearer shark does not flee, fighting fiercely to the death.

FLESHTEARER SHARK LORE
Nature DC 10: Fleshtearer sharks are not confined to the open ocean. They also prowl rivers and underground lakes in their search for prey. A fleshtearer shark feeds constantly, making it a threat to any visitor to or inhabitant of the aquatic realm. Its teeth cause bleeding wounds.

Nature DC 16: Formidable aquatic creatures such as kuo-toas and sahuagin usually give the fleshtearer shark a wide berth, although some have managed to tame the beasts. They use the creatures as weapons on raids of large ships, ensuring that any sailors who fall overboard meet a quick end.

Nature DC 21: In the deepest watery caverns of the Underdark and in the farthest reaches of the oceans, fleshtearer sharks sometimes live for hundreds of years, growing to massive size. Vast swaths of water become uninhabitable because of the presence of such a beastly predator.

ENCOUNTER GROUPS
Sharks often ally with sahuagin, kuo-toas, and other underwater denizens.

Level 10 Encounter (XP 2,700)
✦ 2 fleshtearer sharks (level 10 brute)
✦ 1 sahuagin baron (level 10 elite brute, *MM* 224)
✦ 2 sahuagin priests (level 8 artillery, *MM* 224)

JIM NELSON

SKELETON

Skeletons rarely exist without purpose. Whether crafted through necromantic ritual or raised from a tomb, they relentlessly attack when compelled to kill.

Bonecrusher Skeleton

Swift bonecrusher skeletons leap into combat fearlessly and wield greatclubs with whiplike speed.

Bonecrusher Skeleton		Level 7 Soldier
Large natural animate (undead), minotaur		XP 300

Initiative +10   **Senses** Perception +6; darkvision
HP 80; **Bloodied** 40
AC 22; **Fortitude** 21, **Reflex** 21, **Will** 19
Immune disease, poison; **Resist** 10 necrotic; **Vulnerable** 5 radiant
Speed 8

⊕ **Greatclub** (standard; at-will) ✦ **Weapon**
   Reach 2; +13 vs. AC; 1d10 + 5 damage.
↓ **Crushing Blow** (standard; recharge ⚅⚅) ✦ **Weapon**
   Reach 2; +13 vs. AC; 2d10 + 5 damage, and the target is knocked prone.
Threatening Reach
   A bonecrusher skeleton can make opportunity attacks against all enemies within its reach (2 squares).

Alignment Unaligned   **Languages** —
Str 20 (+8)   **Dex** 21 (+8)   **Wis** 16 (+6)
Con 16 (+6)   **Int** 3 (-1)   **Cha** 3 (-1)
Equipment greatclub

Skeletal Steed

A skeletal steed with a skeletal rider is the basic mounted unit of an undead army.

Skeletal Steed		Level 3 Skirmisher
Large natural animate (mount, undead)		XP 150

Initiative +6   **Senses** Perception +2; darkvision
HP 47; **Bloodied** 23
AC 17; **Fortitude** 15, **Reflex** 16, **Will** 14
Immune disease, poison
Speed 8

⊕ **Kick** (standard; at-will)
   +8 vs. AC; 1d8 + 2 damage.
↓ **Mobile Melee Attack** (standard; at-will)
   The skeletal steed moves its speed and makes a kick attack during the move. The steed does not provoke opportunity attacks while moving away from the target of this attack.
← **Death Shriek** (minor; recharge ⚄ ⚅) ✦ **Fear**
   Close burst 3; targets enemies; +6 vs. Will; the target takes a -2 penalty to attack rolls (save ends).
Mount of the Dead (while mounted by a friendly rider of 3rd level or higher) ✦ **Mount**
   When the skeletal steed uses *mobile melee attack*, the rider makes a melee basic attack during the move as a free action. The rider can choose to forego its basic attack and the steed's attack to instead use one of the rider's melee attack powers during the move.

Alignment Unaligned   **Languages** —
Str 12 (+2)   **Dex** 17 (+4)   **Wis** 13 (+2)
Con 15 (+3)   **Int** 3 (-3)   **Cha** 3 (-3)

Skeleton Lore

   Religion DC 12: Bonecrusher skeletons arise from the bones of ogres, minotaurs, oni, giants, and other large creatures.
   Skeletal steeds rarely arise alone; they awaken from death with their riders or are created by rituals as mounts. Without need of rest or sustenance, these creatures provide tireless service to any warrior.

Encounter Groups

Skeletons do little of their own volition, so bonecrusher skeletons are often found as guards and skeletal steeds as mounts.

Level 5 Encounter (XP 1,025)
✦ 1 deathlock wight (level 4 controller, *MM* 262)
✦ 3 skeletal steeds (level 3 skirmisher)
✦ 2 wights (level 5 skirmisher, *MM* 262)

Level 6 Encounter (XP 1,450)
✦ 3 bonecrusher skeletons (level 7 soldier)
✦ 1 orc eye of Gruumsh (level 5 controller, *MM* 204)
✦ 1 zombie hulk (level 8 brute, *MM* 275)

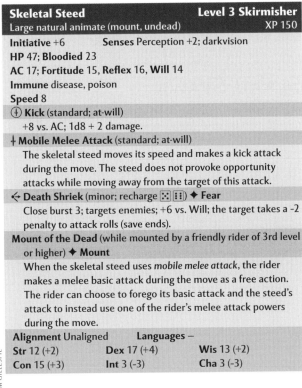

ADAM GILLESPIE

Through a haze of madness, slaads see a world with too much order and too many constraints. Their disruptive attacks create disorder, but rarely on a large scale; their chaotic nature deters them from banding into effective armies.

Flux Slaad

Mutable flux slaads alter their defenses and vulnerabilities in response to enemy attacks.

Flux Slaad Tactics

A flux slaad goes into *flux rage* early in a fight, throwing itself into the midst of its enemies and trying to slash down as many as possible. It then uses *claw slash* and shifts using *piercing reaction* to move into flanking position or out of harm's way.

Flux Slaad	Level 9 Skirmisher
Medium elemental humanoid	XP 400

Initiative +8   **Senses** Perception +10; low-light vision
HP 98; **Bloodied** 49
AC 23; **Fortitude** 23, **Reflex** 21, **Will** 21
Resist 5 variable (see also *slaad vulnerability shift*); **Vulnerable** 10 variable (see also *slaad vulnerability shift*)
Speed 7, teleport 2
⊕ **Claw Slash** (standard; at-will)
    +14 vs. AC; 2d8 + 3 damage.
↯ **Flux Rage** (standard; recharges when first bloodied)
    The flux slaad shifts 2 squares and makes one *claw slash* attack against each creature it moves adjacent to during the shift.
Piercing Reaction (immediate reaction, when the flux slaad takes damage from an attack; at-will)
    The slaad shifts 1 square.
Slaad Vulnerability Shift
    A flux slaad starts the encounter with vulnerable 10 to one of the following six damage types, randomly determined: 1—cold, 2—fire, 3—lightning, 4—necrotic, 5—psychic, or 6—thunder. It has resist 5 to the other five types. When the slaad takes damage of the type to which it's vulnerable, its vulnerability changes to one of the other five damage types, randomly determined, and it gains resistance to the type it was previously vulnerable to.
Alignment Unaligned   **Languages** Common, Primordial
Str 16 (+7)   **Dex** 15 (+6)   **Wis** 13 (+5)
Con 18 (+8)   **Int** 7 (+2)   **Cha** 14 (+6)

Flux Slaad Lore

Arcana DC 19: Flux slaads sometimes accidentally slip through weak points between the planes; this commonly occurs near gatherings of bullywugs. The flux slaads often end up ruling tribes of bullywugs, which revere them as demon lords.

Arcana DC 21: Flux slaads garner little respect from their more deadly kin. In addition to being smaller and weaker than most, they are incapable of spawning. Many flux salads thus lord over what creatures they may, often showing surprising restraint in their violent and unpredictable rages.

Slaad Spawn

Slaad spawn are not self-aware. They desire only to cause chaos and carnage, with no care for their own or their allies' safety.

Slaad Spawn Tactics

A slaad spawn prefers to use *chaotic slam* on the closest opponent, especially when the opponent is close to other enemies.

Arcana DC 25: Not all slaads reproduce through the implantation of chaos phage. Some are themselves infected with an aberrant form of chaos phage. These slaads grow embryos within their own bodies. This painful experience causes blood- and pus-filled boils on a slaad's body. Only injury releases the young slaads. This damage, and the dangerous nature of the spawn, cause many slaad spawners to avoid unleashing the spawn from their flesh.

Encounter Groups

Slaads usually fight alongside other slaads, because their motives are inscrutable to most others.

Level 8 Encounter (XP 1,950)
✦ 1 death shard (level 8 artillery)
✦ 3 flux slaads (level 9 skirmisher)
✦ 2 slaad tadpoles (level 5 lurker, *MM* 237)

Level 17 Encounter (XP 8,400)
✦ 2 blue slaads (level 17 brute, *MM* 238)
✦ 1 green slaad (level 18 controller, *MM* 238)
✦ 8 slaad spawns (level 17 minion)

SLAAD SPAWNER

Some slaads can reproduce through budding. A slaad spawner is covered in bulbous, quivering boils that rupture when the spawner is attacked, revealing small slaad spawns.

Slaad spawner is a template you can apply to any large slaad monster.
Prerequisite: Large slaad, level 15

Slaad Spawner	Elite Controller
Humanoid	XP Elite

Saving Throws +2
Action Points 1
Hit Points None additional
Powers
Spawn Slaad (immediate reaction, when the slaad spawner is hit by an attack; at-will)

A slaad spawn appears in a space adjacent to the slaad spawner. It takes its turn in the initiative order after the slaad spawner. PCs do not earn experience points for killing slaad spawns created by this power.

Slaad Spawn	Level 17 Minion Skirmisher
Small elemental humanoid	XP 400

Initiative +17 — **Senses** Perception +10; low-light vision
HP 1; a missed attack never damages a minion.
AC 31; **Fortitude** 30, **Reflex** 31, **Will** 26
Speed 5, teleport 3
⊕ **Bite** (standard; at-will)
+22 vs. AC; 13 damage.
✝ **Chaotic Slam** (standard; at-will)
The slaad spawn jumps a distance up to its speed and then attacks an adjacent enemy: +22 vs AC; 12 damage and the target is knocked prone. *Miss:* The slaad spawn explodes and is reduced to 0 hit points. The spawn then makes the following close burst 1 attack: +20 vs Reflex; 9 damage.
Alignment Chaotic evil — **Languages** —
| Str 17 (+11) | Dex 24 (+15) | Wis 14 (+10) |
| Con 22 (+14) | Int 3 (+4) | Cha 7 (+6) |

Slaad Spawn Lore

Arcana DC 20: From the moment of its gory birth from a living host, a young slaad presents a threat to all around it. Dim-witted and voracious, the slaad spawn must eat swiftly and well, or the chaotic energies contained within its body become unstable and explode. Assuming it survives those first bloody moments of life, the young slaad grows swiftly and, after just a few days, begins to display the appearance and powers that will define it in adulthood.

SLAUGHTERSTONE CONSTRUCT

THESE DEADLY AUTOMATONS were originally designed by dwarves for use as guardians of underground fortresses. The secret of their construction has since been stolen or duplicated by many others.

SLAUGHTERSTONE EVISCERATOR

THIS GREAT STONE INSECTILE CONSTRUCT is capable of tearing through hordes of enemies in very little time with its whirling serrated blades.

Slaughterstone Eviscerator		Level 18 Brute
Large natural animate (construct)		XP 2,000

Initiative +15   **Senses** Perception +9; darkvision
Whirling Blades aura 2; each creature that starts its turn within the aura takes 10 damage.
HP 212; **Bloodied** 106
AC 30; **Fortitude** 31, **Reflex** 30, **Will** 28
Immune disease, poison, sleep
Speed 6
⊕ **Eviscerating Blade** (standard; at-will)
    Reach 2; +21 vs. AC; 2d12 + 8 damage (crit 4d12 + 32).
⚔ **Whirling Bladestorm** (standard; recharge ⚄⚅)
    Close burst 2; +21 vs. AC; 1d12 + 8 damage (crit 2d12 +20).
Tunnel Fighting
    A slaughterstone eviscerator takes no penalty to attack rolls while squeezing and does not grant combat advantage while squeezing.

Alignment Unaligned	**Languages** –	
Str 25 (+16)	**Dex** 22 (+15)	**Wis** 10 (+9)
Con 22 (+15)	**Int** 1 (+4)	**Cha** 3 (+5)

SLAUGHTERSTONE EVISCERATOR TACTICS

Though it is quite capable of fighting in confined spaces, the slaughterstone eviscerator is best employed when it is allowed to wade into a mass of opponents to use its *whirling bladestorm* attack against several opponents at once.

SLAUGHTERSTONE HAMMERER

POUNDING STONE HAMMERS mount the sides of this great construct whose every step is like thunder. These automatons lay waste to all in their path with uncaring precision.

Slaughterstone Hammerer		Level 25 Soldier
Large natural animate (construct)		XP 7,000

Initiative +14   **Senses** Perception +12; darkvision
Thunder Step aura 2; each creature that starts its turn within the aura is slowed until the start of its next turn.
HP 233; **Bloodied** 116
AC 41; **Fortitude** 40, **Reflex** 35, **Will** 35
Immune disease, poison, sleep
Speed 6
⊕ **Slam** (standard; at-will)
    Reach 2; +32 vs. AC; 2d8 + 10 damage, and the target is knocked prone.
⟂ **Hammerstrike** (standard; at-will)
    Reach 2; +28 vs. Fortitude; 2d8 + 10 damage, and the target is dazed (save ends).
Tunnel Fighting
    A slaughterstone hammerer takes no penalty to attack rolls while squeezing and does not grant combat advantage while squeezing.

Alignment Unaligned	**Languages** –	
Str 28 (+21)	**Dex** 11 (+12)	**Wis** 10 (+12)
Con 25 (+19)	**Int** 1 (+7)	**Cha** 3 (+8)

SLAUGHTERSTONE HAMMERER TACTICS

The slaughterstone hammerer strides forward, striking down all who oppose it. It uses *hammerstrike* against a particularly tough opponent that survives one or more slam attacks.

SLAUGHTERSTONE SLICER

CRAFTING SUCH POWERFUL CONSTRUCTS required dwarves of epic skill. When such legendary masters could not be found, others mimicked their work with less reliable results. A slaughterstone slicer is similar to an eviscerator, but it lacks the eviscerator's supreme defenses and accuracy.

Slaughterstone Slicer	Level 11 Elite Brute
Large natural animate (construct)	XP 1,200

Initiative +11   **Senses** Perception +5; darkvision
Whirling Blades aura 2; each creature that starts its turn within the aura takes 5 damage.
HP 276; **Bloodied** 138
AC 23; **Fortitude** 24, **Reflex** 23, **Will** 19
Immune disease, poison, sleep
Saving Throws +2
Speed 6
Action Points 1

⊕ **Slicing Blade** (standard; at-will)
Reach 2; +14 vs. AC; 2d8 + 6 damage (crit 4d8 + 22).

↤ **Whirling Bladestorm** (standard; at-will)
Close burst 2; +14 vs. AC; 2d8 + 6 damage (crit 4d8 + 22).

↤ **Bloodied Bladestorm** (free, when first bloodied; encounter)
Whirling bladestorm recharges, and the slaughterstone slicer uses it.

Critical Malfunction (when the slaughterstone slicer scores a critical hit or is subject to a critical hit)
The slicer is dazed until the end of its next turn.

Tunnel Fighting
A slaughterstone slicer takes no penalty to attack rolls while squeezing and does not grant combat advantage while squeezing.

Alignment Unaligned	**Languages** –	
Str 22 (+11)	**Dex** 18 (+9)	**Wis** 10 (+5)
Con 18 (+9)	**Int** 1 (+0)	**Cha** 3 (+1)

SLAUGHTERSTONE SLICER TACTICS

A slaughterstone slicer fights like an eviscerator, but its tendency to malfunction makes it a less reliable combatant. It stays close to several enemies at once to increase the damage from *slicing blade* and *whirling bladestorm*.

SLAUGHTERSTONE CONSTRUCT LORE

Arcana or Nature DC 25: The creation of a slaughterstone construct requires the secrets of legendary dwarven craft and a solid block of stone upon which heroes have shed blood.

ENCOUNTER GROUPS

Slaughterstone constructs can be found alongside the fighting forces of nearly every intelligent race that has the will to use such monstrosities in battle.

Level 11 Encounter (XP 3,400)
✦ 1 duergar blasphemer (level 14 controller)
✦ 2 duergar fleshtearers (level 11 lurker)
✦ 1 slaughterstone slicer (level 11 elite brute)

Level 18 Encounter (XP 10,400)
✦ 2 eldritch giants (level 18 skirmisher)
✦ 1 nothic mindblight (level 19 controller)
✦ 2 slaughterstone eviscerators (level 18 brute)

Level 25 Encounter (XP 39,150)
✦ 1 beholder eye of chaos (level 25 elite artillery)
✦ 1 oni thunderer (level 22 skirmisher)
✦ 3 slaughterstone hammerers (level 25 soldier)

SOME SAY THE GODS CREATED SPHINXES to test the mettle of heroes or to protect sacred locations; others say they are primordials birthed in a time before gods.

SPHINX MYSTERY

THESE CREATURES AMUSE THEMSELVES by asking their prey for answers to riddles or for obscure bits of lore and interpretations of prophecy.

Sphinx Mystery	Level 19 Brute
Large immortal magical beast	XP 2,400

Initiative +15   **Senses** Perception +23; low-light vision
HP 224; **Bloodied** 112
AC 31; **Fortitude** 30, **Reflex** 31, **Will** 32
Speed 6, fly 6
Action Points 1

ⓐ **Ancient Claws** (standard; at-will)
    Reach 2; + 22 vs. AC; 3d10 + 5 damage.
ⓐ **Bite of Ages** (standard; at-will)
    Reach 2; + 22 vs. AC; 1d10 + 5 damage, and the target is knocked prone and immobilized (save ends).
ⓡ **Riddle Me This** (minor; at-will) ✦ **Psychic**
    Ranged 10; the sphinx mystery compels the target to contemplate a riddle. The target is dazed until the end of the encounter or until it answers the riddle. To determine the answer, a creature must spend a minor action and succeed at a DC 25 History check. A target that does not attempt to answer the riddle during its turn takes 2d8 psychic damage at the end of its turn. An ally can provide the answer and end the effect. If an ally ends the effect, the target takes 2d8 psychic damage.
ⓣ **Corrective Mauling** (standard; recharges when an enemy fails the History check for *riddle me this*)
    Reach 2; +22 vs. AC; 4d10 + 10 damage, and the target is knocked prone.
ⓒ **Great Roar** (standard; encounter) ✦ **Thunder**
    Close blast 5; +22 vs. Fortitude; 3d10 + 10 thunder damage, and the target is pushed 5 squares and knocked prone.

Alignment Unaligned	**Languages** Common, Dwarven,
	Elven, Primordial, Supernal

Skills Insight +26

Str 25 (+16)	**Dex** 23(+15)	**Wis** 28 (+18)
Con 24 (+16)	**Int** 27(+17)	**Cha** 28 (+18)

SPHINX MYSTERY TACTICS

The sphinx mystery prefers to toy with its victims by presenting riddles and enigmas before pouncing. It uses *riddle me this* repeatedly to get the question game going.

SPHINX MYSTERY LORE

Arcana DC 27: Sphinxes love toying with their prey. If the victim plays along with the riddles, a sphinx might continue to ask riddles rather than attack outright.

ENCOUNTER GROUPS

Sphinxes cooperate with other creatures that can tolerate the way they toy with their prey. Their need to pose riddles and questions often trumps tactical realities in combat, making them precarious allies.

Level 16 Encounter (XP 7,600)
✦ 2 nothic cacklers (level 15 artillery)
✦ 2 savage minotaurs (level 16 brute, *MM* 191)
✦ 1 sphinx mystery (level 19 brute)

SPIDER

GIANT ARACHNIDS CRAWL everywhere in the world and in the planes beyond. Their webs can be found strung in dark forests, ancient ruins, damp caverns, abandoned buildings, or sewers—anywhere that prey can be caught and devoured.

BRISTLE SPIDER

THIS MASSIVE SPIDER hunts within vast overgrown jungles, where the plant life is large enough to afford numerous places from which it can surprise the unwary. Bristle spiders have also been known to make lairs underground, where larger caverns and dungeon chambers offer places in which they can hide and stalk their prey.

BRISTLE SPIDER TACTICS

A bristle spider uses *bristle blast* to disorient its enemies, then *acidic poison spray* to slow them. It uses its action point to make both attacks in the first round of combat. Then it closes in to bite dazed or blinded enemies.

BRISTLE SPIDER LORE

Nature DC 18: Ettercaps and drow prize these large arachnids as companions and guardians. Other races have been known to employ and train them as well.

Nature DC 23: Bristle spiders were long ago bred by the oni to serve as mounts and servants in the vast jungles of the world.

Bristle Spider		Level 15 Elite Lurker
Huge natural beast (spider)		XP 2,400

Initiative +18   **Senses** Perception +8; tremorsense 10
HP 232; **Bloodied** 116
AC 29; **Fortitude** 27, **Reflex** 29, **Will** 23
Saving Throws +2
Speed 8, climb 6 (spider climb)
Action Points 1

⊕ **Bite** (standard; at-will) ✦ **Poison**
   Reach 2; +20 vs. AC; 1d10 + 6 damage, and the target is slowed and takes ongoing 10 poison damage (save ends both).

↞ **Acidic Poison Spray** (standard; at-will) ✦ **Acid, Poison**
   Close blast 5; +18 vs. Reflex; 2d8 + 6 acid and poison damage, and the target is slowed and takes ongoing 10 acid and poison damage (save ends both).

↞ **Bristle Blast** (minor; recharge ⚃ ⚄ ⚅)
   Close blast 5; +18 vs. Fortitude; the target is blinded and dazed until the start of the bristle spider's next turn.

Web Walker
   A bristle spider ignores the effects of spider webs and spider swarms.

Alignment Unaligned   **Languages** –
Skills Stealth +17
Str 20 (+12)   **Dex** 24 (+14)   **Wis** 13 (+8)
Con 20 (+12)   **Int** 3 (+3)   **Cha** 6 (+5)

ENCOUNTER GROUPS

These crafty predators hunt alone and in pairs. They are attracted by battle, and ally with drow or driders to prey on their enemies.

Level 14 Encounter (XP 5,200)
✦ 1 bristle spider (level 15 elite lurker)
✦ 1 drow blademaster (level 13 elite skirmisher, MM 94)
✦ 1 drow priest (level 15 controller, MM 95)

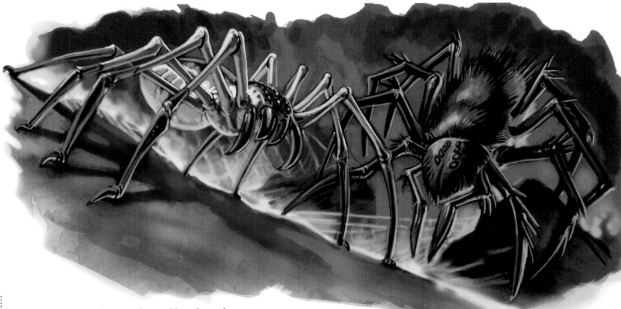

Phase spider and bristle spider

PHASE SPIDER

THESE CUNNING FEYWILD PREDATORS have been known to cross into the world in search of prey. Like their natural cousins, they can be found in nearly any environment.

Phase Spider	Level 8 Skirmisher
Large fey beast (spider)	XP 350

Initiative +11   **Senses** Perception +7; tremorsense 10
HP 87; **Bloodied** 43
AC 22; **Fortitude** 19, **Reflex** 21, **Will** 18
Speed 6, climb 6 (spider climb), teleport 6
ⓐ **Bite** (standard; at-will) ✦ **Poison, Sleep**
  +13 vs. AC; 1d8 + 5 damage, and the target is slowed (save ends). *First Failed Saving Throw:* The target is knocked unconscious instead of slowed (save ends).
↯ **Ethereal Bite** (standard; recharge ⚄ ⚅) ✦ **Teleportation**
  The phase spider teleports 10 squares and makes a bite attack.
↯ **Ethereal Repulsion** (immediate interrupt, when an enemy moves adjacent to the phase spider; at-will) ✦ **Teleportation**
  Targets the triggering enemy; +11 vs. Will; the spider teleports the target 4 squares.
Alignment Unaligned   **Languages** –
Skills Stealth +14
Str 17 (+7)   **Dex** 20 (+9)   **Wis** 17 (+7)
Con 15 (+6)   **Int** 5 (+1)   **Cha** 10 (+4)

PHASE SPIDER TACTICS

A phase spider prefers to surprise its prey, using its *ethereal bite* attack to teleport in, bite an enemy, and then teleport out of harm's way. Possessing superior mobility through their natural ability to teleport, phase spiders rarely engage a single enemy for longer than a round or two before moving on to another opponent.

Phase spiders use hit-and-run tactics in order to wear down their prey.

PHASE SPIDER LORE

Arcana DC 20: Though able to sustain them-selves on the blood of any living creature, phase spiders prefer to dine on fey victims. They have been known to divert their attention away from easier prey in order to attack such creatures.

Arcana DC 25: Phase spiders are the result of ancient magical experimentation by the eladrin, done in an effort to create a creature that can be trained to infiltrate the dark halls of the drow.

ENCOUNTER GROUPS

Phase spiders hunt both alone and in packs. They have also been known to work alongside other power-ful fey creatures, particularly eladrin.

Level 7 Encounter (XP 1,650)
✦ 2 eladrin fey knights (level 7 soldier, *MM* 102)
✦ 3 phase spiders (level 8 skirmisher)

TOMB SPIDER

THESE VORACIOUS KILLERS are true creatures of the Shadowfell insofar as they create undead as a part of their life cycle. Tomb spiders constantly look for opportunities to cross over into the world, frequently making their lairs in graveyards or cata-combs where they can find dead bodies in which to lay their eggs.

Tomb Spider	Level 11 Elite Controller
Large shadow beast (spider)	XP 1,200

Initiative +9   **Senses** Perception +12; tremorsense 10
HP 226; **Bloodied** 113
AC 25; **Fortitude** 23, **Reflex** 22, **Will** 22
Resist 10 necrotic
Saving Throws +2
Speed 6, climb 6 (spider climb)
Action Points 1
ⓐ **Bite** (standard; at-will) ✦ **Necrotic, Poison**
  +16 vs. AC; 1d8 + 5 damage, and the target is dazed and takes ongoing 10 necrotic and poison damage (save ends both). In addition, the target cannot use *second wind* until the end of the encounter.
↗ **Web Net** (minor 1/round; at-will)
  Ranged 10; +15 vs. Reflex; the target is restrained and gains vulnerable 5 necrotic (save ends both).
✷ **Webbed Terrain** (standard; recharge ⚄ ⚅) ✦ **Zone**
  Area burst 3 within 10; +15 vs. Reflex; the target is immobilized (save ends). *Effect:* The burst creates a zone of spider webs that lasts until the end of the encounter. The zone is difficult terrain.
Web Walker
  A tomb spider ignores the effects of spider webs and spider swarms.
Alignment Evil   **Languages** –
Skills Athletics +15 (+25 when jumping), Stealth +13
Str 21 (+10)   **Dex** 18 (+9)   **Wis** 15 (+7)
Con 17 (+8)   **Int** 3 (+1)   **Cha** 18 (+9)

TOMB SPIDER TACTICS

A tomb spider uses its *webbed terrain* attack to divide the field of battle. It uses *web net* to restrain as many opponents as possible, biting them as opportunity allows. If it becomes bloodied, the tomb spider uses its considerable jumping and climbing abilities to escape, allowing it to return later to renew the fight.

TOMB SPIDER LORE

Arcana DC 16: A tomb spider lays its eggs in a humanoid corpse, creating an animate mummy in which hundreds of tiny tomb spiders reside until the creature splits open. Tomb spiders are frequently employed by followers of Orcus, which delight in their natural ability to create undead as part of their reproductive cycle.

Tomb Spider Broodswarm

A TOMB SPIDER BROODSWARM ISSUES FORTH from the corpse in which it was laid.

Tomb Spider Broodswarm	Level 10 Lurker
Medium shadow beast (spider, swarm)	XP 500

Initiative +14   **Senses** Perception +5; tremorsense 10
Swarm Attack aura 1; each enemy that starts its turn within the
    aura is slowed until the start of its next turn.
HP 84; **Bloodied** 42
AC 24; **Fortitude** 21, **Reflex** 22, **Will** 20
Resist half damage from melee and ranged attacks; **Vulnerable** 5
    against close and area attacks
Speed 5, climb 5 (spider climb)
⊕ **Dread Fangs** (standard; at-will) ✦ **Necrotic, Poison**
    +13 vs. Reflex; 1d6 + 5 necrotic damage, and the target is
    immobilized and takes ongoing 5 necrotic and poison damage
    (save ends both).
Shadow Drift (standard; recharge ⚄ ⚅)
    The tomb spider broodswarm shifts 5 squares and gains a +4
    bonus to all defenses until the start of its next turn.
Web Walker
    A tomb spider broodswarm ignores the effects of spider webs
    and spider swarms.

Alignment Evil	**Languages** –	
Skills Stealth +15		
Str 15 (+7)	**Dex** 21 (+10)	**Wis** 11 (+5)
Con 18 (+9)	**Int** 1 (+0)	**Cha** 18 (+9)

Tomb Spider Broodswarm Tactics

A tomb spider broodswarm attacks the nearest living creature unless commanded to do otherwise by its parent tomb spider. These masses of infant tomb spiders use *shadow drift* to move around living obstacles.

Encounter Groups

Tomb spiders usually establish lairs near crypts or catacombs where humanoid corpses can be found. They have been known to aid powerful undead creatures as well as followers of Orcus.

Level 11 Encounter (XP 3,300)
✦ 3 crimson acolytes (level 7 skirmisher, *MM* 210)
✦ 1 deathpriest of Orcus (level 9 controller, *MM* 210)
✦ 1 tomb spider (level 11 elite controller)
✦ 2 battle wights (level 9 soldier, *MM* 262)

SPRIGGAN

Spriggans are gnomes altered by fomorian magic. These perverse fey now wander the rough country of the Feywild and the world, pillaging for food and riches and delighting in the slaying of foes.

Spriggan Giantsoul

Giantsouls build upon the evil they inherited from fomorian domination, gaining strength as well as the ability to stretch their arms to a giant's reach.

Spriggan Giantsoul		Level 8 Brute
Small fey humanoid		XP 350

Initiative +6 **Senses** Perception +7; low-light vision
HP 106; **Bloodied** 53
AC 20; **Fortitude** 21, **Reflex** 19, **Will** 20
Speed 6
ⓘ **Slam** (standard; at-will)
  +11 vs. AC; 2d6 + 5 damage, or 2d6 + 9 damage while the spriggan giantsoul is bloodied.
✦ **Giantsoul Slam** (standard; recharge ⚃ ⚄ ⚅)
  Reach 2; +13 vs. AC; 2d6 + 5 damage, and the target is knocked prone. While the spriggan giantsoul is bloodied, the damage increases to 2d6 + 9.
✦ **Surprise Slam** (immediate interrupt, when an enemy within 2 squares of the spriggan giantsoul attacks an ally; encounter)
  Giantsoul slam recharges, and the giantsoul uses it against the triggering enemy.
Redcap Zeal (when the spriggan giantsoul bloodies an enemy or reduces an enemy to 0 hit points or fewer; encounter)
  The giantsoul gains 1d10 + 3 temporary hit points.
Alignment Evil **Languages** Elven
Skills Athletics +14, Intimidate +10, Stealth +12
Str 18 (+8) **Dex** 15 (+6) **Wis** 17 (+7)
Con 16 (+7) **Int** 10 (+4) **Cha** 12 (+5)
Equipment hide armor, iron-shod boots

Spriggan Powrie

Capering in iron-shod boots, powries seek to splash their feet in the blood of foes.

Spriggan Powrie	Level 7 Skirmisher
Small fey humanoid	XP 300

Initiative +9 **Senses** Perception +9; low-light vision
HP 79; **Bloodied** 39
AC 21 (23 against opportunity attacks); **Fortitude** 19, **Reflex** 20, **Will** 18
Speed 6
ⓘ **Sickle** (standard; at-will) ✦ **Weapon**
  +12 vs. AC; 1d6 + 3 damage, and ongoing 5 damage (save ends).
✦ **Hamstring** (standard; recharges when first bloodied) ✦ **Weapon**
  +12 vs. AC; 1d6 + 3 damage, and the target is knocked prone, is slowed until the end of the spriggan powrie's next turn, and takes ongoing 5 damage (save ends).
✦ **Punt the Fallen** (minor 1/round; at-will)
  Targets a prone creature; +12 vs. Fortitude; 1d6 + 3 damage, and the spriggan powrie pushes the target 3 squares.

Blood Slide
  A spriggan powrie does not provoke opportunity attacks for moving out of a space adjacent to a bloodied creature or a creature that is taking ongoing damage.
Combat Advantage
  When a spriggan powrie hits a creature that is taking ongoing damage and is granting combat advantage to the powrie, the powrie's attack increases the ongoing damage by 5.
Redcap Zeal (when the spriggan powrie bloodies an enemy or reduces an enemy to 0 hit points or fewer; encounter)
  The powrie gains 1d8 + 2 temporary hit points.
Alignment Evil **Languages** Elven
Skills Athletics +11, Stealth +14, Thievery +12
Str 16 (+6) **Dex** 18 (+7) **Wis** 12 (+4)
Con 15 (+5) **Int** 10 (+3) **Cha** 15 (+5)
Equipment leather armor, 2 sickles, iron-shod boots

Spriggan Thorn

A spriggan thorn carries a curse of brambles, which it can lay upon an enemy with a glance.

Spriggan Thorn	Level 6 Soldier
Small fey humanoid	XP 250

Initiative +7 **Senses** Perception +9; low-light vision
HP 71; **Bloodied** 35
AC 22; **Fortitude** 18, **Reflex** 17, **Will** 19
Speed 5
ⓘ **Short Sword** (standard; at-will) ✦ **Weapon**
  +13 vs. AC; 1d6 + 3 damage, and ongoing 5 damage (save ends).
⟁ **Mark of Thorns** (standard; encounter)
  Close burst 5; targets one enemy; the target is affected by the mark of thorns until the end of the encounter. While affected by the mark of thorns, the target cannot make opportunity attacks against the spriggan thorn, and the target takes 4 damage at the end of any turn in which it did not attack the thorn. In addition, at the start of the target's turn, each of the target's allies adjacent to the target takes 4 damage.
Drowsing Puncture (minor; recharges when first bloodied)
  If the spriggan thorn hits with its next short sword attack, the target of the attack is dazed until the end of the thorn's next turn and is knocked prone.
Redcap Zeal (when the spriggan thorn bloodies an enemy or reduces an enemy to 0 hit points or fewer; encounter)
  The thorn gains 1d8 + 2 temporary hit points.
Alignment Evil **Languages** Elven
Skills Athletics +12, Stealth +11
Str 17 (+6) **Dex** 15 (+5) **Wis** 12 (+4)
Con 15 (+5) **Int** 10 (+3) **Cha** 18 (+7)
Equipment chainmail, light shield, short sword, iron-shod boots

(Left to right) spriggan powrie, spriggan giantsoul, and spriggan thorn

SPRIGGAN WITHERER

SPRIGGAN WITHERERS USE THEIR MAGIC to command the weather and to soak the earth in the blood of their foes.

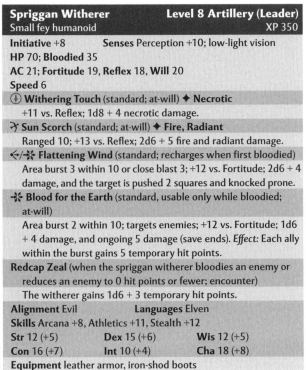

Spriggan Witherer		Level 8 Artillery (Leader)
Small fey humanoid		XP 350

Initiative +8 **Senses** Perception +10; low-light vision
HP 70; **Bloodied** 35
AC 21; **Fortitude** 19, **Reflex** 18, **Will** 20
Speed 6

ⓔ **Withering Touch** (standard; at-will) ✦ **Necrotic**
+11 vs. Reflex; 1d8 + 4 necrotic damage.

↗ **Sun Scorch** (standard; at-will) ✦ **Fire, Radiant**
Ranged 10; +13 vs. Reflex; 2d6 + 5 fire and radiant damage.

↺/✵ **Flattening Wind** (standard; recharges when first bloodied)
Area burst 3 within 10 or close blast 3; +12 vs. Fortitude; 2d6 + 4 damage, and the target is pushed 2 squares and knocked prone.

✵ **Blood for the Earth** (standard, usable only while bloodied; at-will)
Area burst 2 within 10; targets enemies; +12 vs. Fortitude; 1d6 + 4 damage, and ongoing 5 damage (save ends). *Effect:* Each ally within the burst gains 5 temporary hit points.

Redcap Zeal (when the spriggan witherer bloodies an enemy or reduces an enemy to 0 hit points or fewer; encounter)
The witherer gains 1d6 + 3 temporary hit points.

Alignment Evil **Languages** Elven
Skills Arcana +8, Athletics +11, Stealth +12
Str 12 (+5)	**Dex** 15 (+6)	**Wis** 12 (+5)
Con 16 (+7)	**Int** 10 (+4)	**Cha** 18 (+8)

Equipment leather armor, iron-shod boots

SPRIGGAN LORE

Arcana DC 14: Spriggans, also known also as red-caps for their habit of dipping their hats and clothing in blood, prefer to live in dark burrows under rugged terrain. They supplement their stores by raiding and extorting tribute from weaker creatures.

Arcana DC 19: Gnomes were once fomorian slaves, and many fled to the world to elude their oppressors. Those that did not make their way to freedom were twisted into spriggans.

ENCOUNTER GROUPS

Spriggans ally with creatures willing to tolerate their bloody ways. They keep dangerous plants and animals near their homes to dissuade intruders. Fomorians and evil eladrin use spriggans as spies and scouts.

Level 9 Encounter (XP 2,150)
✦ 1 eladrin twilight incanter (level 8 controller, *MM* 102)
✦ 1 shambling mound (level 9 brute, *MM* 232)
✦ 2 spriggan giantsouls (level 8 brute)
✦ 2 spriggan witherers (level 8 artillery)

Sprites exist in great variety in the Feywild and are as common as birds. Most present no threat beyond twittering laughter in the shadows, but some gather in dangerous swarms.

UMBRAL SPRITE SWARM

DARK FEY WITH A TASTE FOR BLOOD and a penchant for causing chaos, umbral sprites gather in the rare pockets of shadow within the Feywild and hunt any creatures that step into their domain.

Umbral Sprite Swarm	Level 4 Controller
Medium fey humanoid (swarm)	XP 175

Initiative +6   **Senses** Perception +8; blindsight 6
Swarm Attack aura 1; each enemy that starts its turn within the aura takes 3 damage.
HP 55; **Bloodied** 27
AC 18; **Fortitude** 15, **Reflex** 17, **Will** 15
Resist half damage from melee and ranged attacks; **Vulnerable** 5 against close and area attacks
Speed 4, fly 6 (hover)

ⓘ **Swarm of Fangs and Blades** (standard; at-will)
+10 vs. AC; 1d6 + 4 damage.

⟳ **Darkwave** (standard; recharge ⚄ ⚅) ✦ **Necrotic, Zone**
Close burst 3; +8 vs. Reflex; 2d8 + 4 necrotic damage. *Effect:* The burst creates a zone of darkness that lasts until the end of the umbral sprite swarm's next turn. The zone blocks line of sight.

Fade Away (immediate reaction, when the umbral sprite swarm takes damage; encounter) ✦ **Illusion**
The umbral sprite swarm is invisible until after it hits or misses with an attack or until the end of its next turn.

Alignment Unaligned	**Languages** Elven

Skills Stealth +11
| **Str** 8 (+1) | **Dex** 18 (+6) | **Wis** 13 (+3) |
| **Con** 15 (+4) | **Int** 13 (+3) | **Cha** 15 (+4) |

UMBRAL SPRITE SWARM TACTICS
The umbral sprite swarm flies into the midst of its opponents and uses its *darkwave* attack. The swarm then flits about to make the most of its *swarm of fangs and blades* until its *darkwave* attack recharges.

UMBRAL SPRITE SWARM LORE
Arcana DC 12: Although umbral sprite swarms come from the Feywild, those that make their way into the world frequently gather in areas where they might be able to cross over into the Shadowfell. Gnomes and spriggans have been known to employ umbral sprite swarms as a diversion while they pursue goals too subtle for the sprites to aid directly.

ENCOUNTER GROUPS
Sprite swarms often fight alongside other fey creatures. They are generally not found near large towns or cities, preferring more rural areas.

Level 5 Encounter (XP 1,050)
- ✦ 2 ettercap fang guards (level 4 soldier, *MM* 107)
- ✦ 2 fey panthers (level 4 skirmisher, *MM* 213)
- ✦ 2 umbral sprite swarms (level 4 controller)

STAR SPAWN

WARLOCKS AND SAGES KNOW that when one looks up at the stars, some stars glare back with hunger. When a star hangs in the correct position in the sky and its light strikes the world at precisely the right angle, the star spawn walk the world. Star spawn are utterly malevolent beings.

STAR SPAWN LORE

Dungeoneering DC 20: The star spawn are creatures sent by the baleful stars of the night sky, accursed celestial objects that gaze upon the world with a mixture of hatred, anger, and hunger. The spawn are the avatars of these stars, sent to wreak havoc. Some stars have only one spawn, but others manifest a multitude of creatures. The spawn of a particular star appear only once a year at most, but sometimes a spawn becomes trapped in the world and continues its depredations until slain.

Dungeoneering DC 25: Sometimes cults form around a star spawn. Some star spawn simply devour their worshipers, but others tolerate their presence and use them as allies. Warlocks who have the star pact flock to star spawn. Whether they serve, study, or slay them depends on a particular warlock's goals and attitudes.

Dungeoneering DC 27: Star spawn are known to appear before great tribulations and at the convergence of unparalleled levels of power. During great wars, battles between divine beings, and the preparation of mighty rituals, the spawn appear across the land. The star called Allabar, a wandering object known as the Opener of the Way, courses across the sky, causing the spawn of any stars it nears to manifest upon the world. Some believe that Allabar is a trickster star that merely spreads havoc between the world and its kin. Others claim that Allabar itself is the greatest of the stars, a strange being from beyond the world, manipulating the other stars to its own end. What that end could be, and the role played by the star spawn, none as yet can guess. Before his disappearance, the warlock Thulzar claimed that he had successfully charted the incursions of all star spawn since the fall of Bael Turath. His research showed an emerging pattern, but he, his tower, and all his works simply vanished one starless night, leaving behind only a smooth, glass-coated crater.

HERALD OF HADAR

HADAR'S DULL RED GLOW is barely visible in the night sky, as the star slowly burns down into a lifeless, dead cinder. According to the Revelations of Melech, Hadar was once the brightest star in the sky, but during the calamities that led to the fall of Bael Turath, it surged into a searing brand of light and then faded into a blood-red ember. Hadar now hangs on the edge of annihilation. A herald of Hadar is an avatar of Hadar's dying gasps, a fiendish monster that grows stronger in the presence of living creatures.

Herald of Hadar	Level 15 Brute
Medium aberrant humanoid	XP 1,200

Initiative +9 **Senses** Perception +11; darkvision
HP 180; **Bloodied** 90
AC 27; **Fortitude** 27, **Reflex** 26, **Will** 27
Speed 6
ⓐ **Hungry Claws** (standard; at-will)
  +18 vs. AC; 1d10 + 5 damage. *Effect:* The herald of Hadar makes one more *hungry claws* attack against the same target or a different one.
⸸ **Feeding Frenzy** (standard; encounter)
  +18 vs. AC; 1d10 + 5 damage. *Effect:* The herald of Hadar makes three more *hungry claws* attacks against the same target or different ones. No more than two of the attacks can target the same creature.
↞ **Breath of a Dying Star** (standard; encounter)
  Close blast 5; +18 vs. Reflex; 2d10 + 5 damage, and the target cannot spend healing surges or regain hit points (save ends).
Hadar's Hunger (immediate reaction, when a creature within 5 squares of the herald of Hadar spends a healing surge; at-will)
  The herald chooses one of the following options:
  The herald shifts 3 squares and must end the move closer to the triggering creature.
  The herald uses a *hungry claws* attack.
  The herald regains the use of one of its encounter powers.
  The herald gains a +2 bonus to attack rolls until the end of its next turn.
Alignment Chaotic evil   **Languages** telepathy 10
Str 17 (+10)   **Dex** 15 (+9)   **Wis** 18 (+11)
Con 20 (+12)   **Int** 10 (+7)   **Cha** 15 (+9)

Maw of Acamar	Level 15 Controller
Large aberrant humanoid	XP 1,200

Initiative +9 **Senses** Perception +11; darkvision
Hungry Star aura 5; each creature within the aura must spend 3 extra squares of movement for each square it moves farther away from the maw of Acamar.
HP 145; **Bloodied** 77
AC 29; **Fortitude** 27, **Reflex** 26, **Will** 27
Speed 6
ⓐ **Devouring Touch** (standard; at-will)
  Reach 2; +19 vs. Reflex; the target takes ongoing 15 damage (save ends).
↞ **Corpse Star's Grip** (minor; at-will)
  Close burst 5; +19 vs. Fortitude; the maw of Acamar pulls the target 3 squares.
↞ **Devouring Star** (standard; at-will)
  Close burst 3; +19 vs. Fortitude; the target takes ongoing 10 damage (save ends).
Destroyer of Life
  When an enemy adjacent to the maw of Acamar succeeds on a saving throw against ongoing damage, the ongoing damage is reduced by 5 instead of ending.
Life Devourer (immediate reaction, when a creature within 2 squares of the maw of Acamar spends a healing surge; at-will)
  The reach of *devouring touch* and the burst areas of *corpse star's grip* and *devouring star* increase by 2 until the end of the maw's next turn.
Alignment Chaotic evil   **Languages** telepathy 10
Str 20 (+12)   **Dex** 15 (+9)   **Wis** 19 (+11)
Con 17 (+10)   **Int** 11 (+7)   **Cha** 16 (+10)

HERALD OF HADAR LORE

Dungeoneering DC 18: A herald of Hadar is spawned by its namesake, a dying ember of a star. The herald feasts on life energy, channeling it back to its creator in an effort to avert its demise.

MAW OF ACAMAR

THE STAR ACAMAR IS A CORPSE STAR, a dead star of utter inky nothingness that devours other stars that draw too close. The maw of Acamar is that star's hunger made real, an avatar of devastation that eats everything in its path.

In battle, the maw of Acamar strides amid its foes, relying on the powerful magic that surges from its form to drag victims to their doom. Winds howl as Acamar draws the very air around the maw into itself. Creatures slain by the maw are ripped apart and dragged away to disappear into Acamar's endless darkness. The maws are deadlier still when encountered in numbers; they crowd around a foe and tear him in half as they pull him in several directions at once.

MAW OF ACAMAR LORE

Dungeoneering DC 18: A maw of Acamar enters the world when the dark influence of the star Acamar is at its peak. The maw wanders the world, pulling living creatures into its destructive void to feed Acamar, a dead star wracked by endless hunger.

SCION OF GIBBETH

GIBBETH IS A CURSED GREEN STAR, said to have at its core an utterly unknowable being. Warlocks and other arcane users say that Gibbeth shall show its face only at the end of the world, when the very glare of its eyes and the monstrous aspect of its being pushes all of creation into inescapable madness. The scion of Gibbeth is a terrible shard of that green star, a herald of Gibbeth's curse and a forerunner of what might come.

When the scion appears, no two observers can agree on its actual appearance. Some see a green-skinned, horned giant, while others report a red, spiderlike creature with a child's face or a serpentine monstrosity with dozens of gibbering mouths along its body. Sages maintain that this outer appearance is merely an aspect projected by the shard that dwells within the scion. The mental strain of seeing even a shadow of Gibbeth's essence is such that mortal minds must conjure knowable, though strange, images to contain it. Anyone who sees the scion's true form is doomed to madness.

Scion of Gibbeth	Level 17 Controller
Large aberrant humanoid	XP 1,600

Initiative +11   **Senses** Perception +11; darkvision
Aura of Revulsion aura 10; each creature within the aura cannot target the scion of Gibbeth with melee or ranged attacks unless the scion is the nearest enemy.
HP 163; **Bloodied** 81; see also *revelation of Gibbeth*
AC 31; **Fortitude** 29, **Reflex** 27, **Will** 29
Speed 6
⊕ **Slam** (standard; at-will)
   Reach 2; +22 vs. AC; 2d10 + 5 damage.
⊗ **Mind-Splintering Gaze** (standard; at-will) ✦ Charm, Gaze, Psychic
   Ranged 20; +21 vs. Will; 1d8 + 2 psychic damage, and the target is dominated (save ends).
⊗ **Gibbeth's Baleful Glare** (opportunity, when an enemy targets the scion of Gibbeth with a melee or ranged attack; at-will) ✦ Charm, Psychic
   Ranged 20; targets the triggering enemy; +21 vs. Will; 1d8 + 2 psychic damage, and the scion slides the target 2 squares.
⬅ **Revelation of Gibbeth** (when the scion of Gibbeth drops to 0 hit points) ✦ Charm
   Close burst 5; +21 vs. Will; the target is dazed and uses its standard action each turn to charge or to make a melee or ranged basic attack against its nearest ally (save ends).
Offering to Gibbeth (immediate reaction, when a creature within 2 squares of the scion of Gibbeth spends a healing surge; at-will)
   The scion gains a +2 bonus to attack rolls until the end of its next turn.
Alignment Chaotic evil   **Languages** telepathy 10
Str 22 (+14)   **Dex** 16 (+11)   **Wis** 17 (+11)
Con 19 (+12)   **Int** 11 (+8)   **Cha** 19 (+12)

SCION OF GIBBETH LORE

Dungeoneering DC 20: A scion of Gibbeth wanders the world seemingly at random. Prophets, the insane, and cultists are drawn to its presence. The scion typically lashes out at any living creature that draws near, but it tolerates these worshipers.

Dungeoneering DC 25: The scion of Gibbeth manifests in the world when Gibbeth is in conjunction with the star Allabar, a celestial object known as the Opener of the Way. Allabar wanders the sky in a pattern unlike that of any other star. It follows a seemingly random path, and when it draws near one of the baleful stars, that star's spawn appear in the world. The wandering star avoids only Acamar, because that object's hunger is so great that it would destroy even the star that would open its path to the world.

ENCOUNTER GROUPS

Their malevolence runs rampant, but star spawn are cunning and calculating enough to entertain alliances of convenience.

Level 13 Encounter (XP 4,200)
✦ 2 battle wight commanders (level 12 soldier, *MM* 262)
✦ 1 beholder eye of flame (level 13 elite artillery, *MM* 32)
✦ 1 herald of Hadar (level 15 brute)

Level 13 Encounter (XP 4,800)
✦ 2 hook horrors (level 13 soldier, *MM* 158)
✦ 1 maw of Acamar (level 15 controller)
✦ 2 mind flayer infiltrators (level 14 lurker, *MM* 188)

STEEL PREDATOR

Born of the machinations of Bane, steel predators are deadly planar creatures designed for war. Ranging through the Astral Sea and into the world, predators are relentless hunters, sometimes pursuing quarry for weeks and across planar boundaries. They delight in the consumption of the *residuum* in magic items, and so the more richly endowed the target, the farther they will pursue it.

Steel Predator	Level 20 Elite Soldier
Large immortal animate (living construct)	XP 5,600

Initiative +18   **Senses** Perception +16; darkvision
HP 388; **Bloodied** 194
AC 36; **Fortitude** 34, **Reflex** 32, **Will** 30
Saving Throws +2 (+4 against ongoing damage)
Speed 8
Action Points 1
⊕ **Bite** (standard; at-will)
  Reach 2; +27 vs. AC; 4d6 + 4 damage, and the target is marked until the end of the steel predator's next turn.
↯ **Snap Jaw** (standard; at-will)
  The steel predator makes a bite attack. On a hit, the target is also knocked prone, and the predator makes another bite attack against a different target.
↯ **Vicious Pounce** (standard; at-will)
  The steel predator charges and makes the following attack in place of a bite attack: +25 vs. Fortitude; 2d12 + 5 damage, and the target is pushed 1 square and knocked prone. The predator moves into the space vacated by the target.
⬅ **Resonating Roar** (standard; recharge ⚄ ⚅ or when the steel predator takes thunder or lightning damage) ✦ **Thunder**
  Close burst 3; +25 vs. Fortitude; 4d8 + 7 thunder damage, and the target is deafened and dazed (save ends both).
Shifting Steel (immediate reaction, when a creature adjacent to the steel predator shifts; at-will)
  The predator shifts into the space vacated by the triggering creature.
Alignment Evil   **Languages** Supernal
Skills Acrobatics +21, Athletics +21, Endurance +23, Stealth +21
| **Str** 22 (+16) | **Dex** 23 (+16) | **Wis** 23 (+16) |
| **Con** 26 (+18) | **Int** 15 (+12) | **Cha** 12 (+11) |

STEEL PREDATOR TACTICS

The steel predator stalks its prey patiently, entering combat only when it thinks it is assured of victory. It begins with a *vicious pounce*, then releases a *resonating roar* in the midst of its foes. While the steel predator waits for that power to recharge, it makes *snap jaw* attacks against the closest foes, using *shifting steel* to keep targets close.

STEEL PREDATOR LORE

Arcana or Religion DC 14: Created by Bane to track and slay the foes of the god of conquest, steel predators are relentless hunters that pursue their prey even across the planes. Thunder and lightning attacks made against a steel predator only increase the creature's power.

Arcana or Religion DC 22: Steel predators are agile, graceful beasts. These metallic felines are often led by teams of bladelings in Chernoggar, where they are most frequently found.

Arcana or Religion DC 27: Steel predators have a taste for magic items. Once they have slain a foe, they often consume the entire body, including both flesh and magical items.

Arcana or Religion DC 29: A steel predator's body contains *residuum*, which can be extracted upon its death. For this reason, many planar creatures hunt steel predators for profit and sport.

ENCOUNTER GROUPS

Steel predators can be found anywhere the servants of Bane do battle. They serve faithfully with other creatures working toward common goals, but can quickly turn on those that betray Bane's ideals.

Level 21 Encounter (XP 17,600)
✦ 2 steel predators (level 20 elite soldier)
✦ 2 marut castigators (level 21 skirmisher)

TIGER

TIGERS ARE POWERFUL AND CUNNING PREDATORS. A tiger looks for distracted prey on the periphery of a battle.

Tiger	Level 6 Skirmisher
Large natural beast	XP 250

Initiative +9   **Senses** Perception +10; low-light vision
HP 73; **Bloodied** 36
AC 20; **Fortitude** 19, **Reflex** 19, **Will** 17
Speed 8, climb 4
⊕ **Bite** (standard; at-will)
    +11 vs. AC; 1d6 + 4 damage, and ongoing 5 damage (save ends).
Feral Surge (minor; encounter)
    The tiger takes a move action.
Blur of Fur
    A tiger that moves 2 squares or more gains a +4 bonus to AC against opportunity attacks until the start of its next turn.
Charging Pounce
    When a tiger charges, its attack deals 1d8 extra damage, and the charge does not end its turn.

Alignment Unaligned	**Languages** –

Skills Acrobatics +12, Stealth +12

Str 18 (+7)	**Dex** 19 (+7)	**Wis** 15 (+5)
Con 17 (+6)	**Int** 2 (-1)	**Cha** 11 (+3)

TIGER TACTICS

A tiger uses its ability to continue moving after a *charging pounce* to set up future charges, relying on *feral surge* to move toward more vulnerable targets.

DIRE TIGER

A MASSIVE DIRE TIGER is a serious menace even in wildernesses filled with more fantastic monsters.

Dire Tiger	Level 8 Soldier
Large natural beast	XP 350

Initiative +8   **Senses** Perception +6; low-light vision
HP 89; **Bloodied** 44
AC 24; **Fortitude** 22, **Reflex** 19, **Will** 19
Speed 8, climb 4
⊕ **Bite** (standard; at-will)
    +15 vs. AC; 2d6 + 5 damage.
⸭ **Leaping Pounce** (immediate reaction, when the tiger's quarry is within 5 squares of the dire tiger and shifts; at-will)
    The dire tiger shifts to the nearest space adjacent to its quarry and makes a bite attack against it. While shifting, the tiger can move through enemy-occupied spaces.
Feral Surge (minor; encounter)
    The dire tiger takes a move action.
Hunter's Instinct (minor 1/round; at-will)
    The nearest enemy is designated as the dire tiger's quarry until the end of the encounter or until the tiger designates another quarry. The tiger's attacks deal 1d6 extra damage against its quarry.

Alignment Unaligned	**Languages** –

Skills Stealth +11

Str 20 (+9)	**Dex** 15 (+6)	**Wis** 15 (+6)
Con 17 (+7)	**Int** 2 (+0)	**Cha** 13 (+6)

DIRE TIGER TACTICS

Nature DC 8: Tigers are quick and agile hunters that are often found in rugged natural environments. They are often trained as guards by ogres.

Nature DC 14: Dire tigers live in dense forests or jungles. They target lone, weaker foes. If under the watchful eye of a dire tiger, it is best to stand your ground—they are known to leap at slight movements.

ENCOUNTER GROUPS

Tigers hunt alone, but they can be found in mated pairs, siblings, or with young (a single cub or pair of cubs). Tigers join in on others' combats to make a quick meal of the weak and the weary.

Level 7 Encounter (XP 1500)
✦ 1 macetail behemoth (level 7 soldier, *MM* 31)
✦ 2 ogre savages (level 8 brute, *MM* 199)
✦ 2 tigers (level 6 skirmisher)

Level 9 Encounter (XP 2250)
✦ 3 dire tigers (level 8 soldier)
✦ 1 weretiger (level 11 elite skirmisher)

TROGLODYTE

TROGLODYTES ARE TRIBAL CREATURES that dwell in the Underdark and raid communities at the edge of civilization. Highly territorial, troglodytes engage trespassers in combat without bothering to ask questions.

TROGLODYTE THRASHER

THIS PRIMITIVE SAVAGE lives to bathe itself in the blood of its foes. It cleaves through enemies, completely unaware of its own mortality.

Troglodyte Thrasher		Level 7 Brute
Medium natural humanoid (reptile)		XP 300

Initiative +5   **Senses** Perception +6; darkvision
Troglodyte Stench aura 1; each living enemy within the aura takes a -2 penalty to attack rolls.
HP 100; **Bloodied** 50
AC 19; **Fortitude** 19, **Reflex** 15, **Will** 17
Speed 5
⊕ **Claw** (standard; at-will)
   +10 vs. AC; 3d6 + 4 damage.
† **Tooth and Claw** (standard; at-will)
   +10 vs. AC; 1d6 + 4 damage. If this attack bloodies the target, the troglodyte thrasher makes a claw attack against the target as a free action. *Effect:* Make one more attack against the same target or a different one.
Alignment Chaotic evil   **Languages** Draconic
Str 18 (+7)   **Dex** 15 (+5)   **Wis** 16 (+6)
Con 20 (+8)   **Int** 4 (+0)   **Cha** 11 (+3)

TROGLODYTE THRASHER TACTICS

A troglodyte thrasher enjoys going after the biggest, toughest, or most physically dangerous-looking enemy. It tends to ignore ranged attackers, but attacks them if no other enemies remain. If a thrasher is hit by a melee attack, it usually focuses its attention on that attacker during its next turn.

TROGLODYTE THRASHER LORE

Dungeoneering or Nature DC 14: Although truly intelligent members of the troglodyte race do exist, the dimwitted hordes vastly outnumber them. Troglodyte thrashers posses only a beast's intellect. Other troglodytes keep thrashers in cages to prevent them from turning on each other or on their more intelligent cousins.

TROGLODYTE DEEPSCOURGE

THROUGH THE ALIEN ALCHEMY of their own bodies, troglodyte deepscourges learn to channel their awful stench into a multitude of different attacks against enemies.

Troglodyte Deepscourge	Level 9 Artillery (Leader)
Medium natural humanoid (reptile)	XP 400

Initiative +7   **Senses** Perception +4; darkvision
Dizzying Stench aura 10; each troglodyte within the aura gains an increase of 1 to the size of its *troglodyte stench* aura.
Troglodyte Stench aura 2; each living enemy within the aura takes a -2 penalty to attack rolls.
HP 78; **Bloodied** 39
AC 22; **Fortitude** 22, **Reflex** 21, **Will** 19
Speed 5
⊕ **Claw** (standard; at-will)
   +17 vs. AC; 1d4 + 5 damage.
↗ **Debilitating Ray** (standard; at-will) ✦ **Implement**
   Ranged 10; 1d8 + 4 damage, and if the target is within a *troglodyte stench* aura, it is weakened until the end of its next turn.
↤ **Blinding Stench** (immediate reaction, when hit by an attack; recharges when first bloodied)
   Close burst 2; targets nonreptiles; +13 vs. Fortitude; the target is blinded (save ends).
❋ **Rancid Cloud** (standard; recharge ⚄ ⚅)
   Area burst 2 within 10; targets nonreptiles; +13 vs. Fortitude; 2d6 + 5 damage, and the target is weakened until the end of the troglodyte deepscourge's next turn.
Alignment Chaotic evil   **Languages** Draconic
Skills Dungeoneering +9
Str 12 (+5)   **Dex** 16 (+7)   **Wis** 11 (+4)
Con 18 (+8)   **Int** 12 (+5)   **Cha** 13 (+5)
Equipment leather armor, staff

TROGLODYTE DEEPSCOURGE TACTICS

In combat, a deepscourge remains safely behind its brutish allies. If attacked, it uses *blinding stench* to incapacitate the enemy and cover its retreat. The deepscourge coordinates with its allies in combat, ordering other troglodytes into formations where their auras can have the most potency in conjunction with the deepscourge's *debilitating ray* and *dizzying stench*.

TROGLODYTE DEEPSCOURGE LORE

Dungeoneering or Nature DC 14: A troglodyte deepscourge often serves alongside a troglodyte curse chanter or in the curse chanter's stead as the leaders of a tribe. A deepscourge is a shaman for a troglodyte tribe. Troglodytes often rely on deepscourges for guidance in ritual as well as in combat.

TROGLODYTE TEMPLE CHAMPION

A SAVAGE SOCIETY DRAWS TROGLODYTES to worship brutal gods. It should be no surprise that their dark religions produce vicious champions.

Troglodyte Temple Champion		Level 9 Soldier
Medium natural humanoid (reptile)		XP 400

Initiative +9   **Senses** Perception +6; darkvision
Troglodyte Stench aura 1; each living enemy within the aura takes a -2 penalty to attack rolls.
HP 101; **Bloodied** 50
AC 25; **Fortitude** 23, **Reflex** 21, **Will** 20
Speed 5
⊕ **Flail** (standard; at-will) ✦ **Weapon**
    +16 vs. AC; 1d10 + 7 damage.
⊛ **Javelin** (standard; at-will) ✦ **Weapon**
    Ranged 10/20; +16 vs. AC; 1d6 + 6 damage.
‡ **Sweeping Trip** (standard; at-will) ✦ **Weapon**
    +14 vs. Reflex; 1d8 + 6 damage, and the target is knocked prone.
⟡ **Whirlwind Attack** (standard; encounter) ✦ **Weapon**
    Close burst 1; +16 vs. AC; 1d10 + 7 damage.
Alignment Chaotic evil   **Languages** Draconic
Skills Athletics +13, Endurance +14

Str 19 (+8)	**Dex** 17 (+7)	**Wis** 14 (+6)
Con 21 (+9)	**Int** 10 (+4)	**Cha** 12 (+5)

Equipment scale armor, flail, 2 javelins

TROGLODYTE TEMPLE CHAMPION TACTICS

Troglodyte temple champions are not subtle; they charge into combat as soon as possible, flinging javelins when unable to attack in melee. Temple champions use their *sweeping trip* attacks to stop opponents from escaping.

TROGLODYTE TEMPLE CHAMPION LORE

Dungeoneering or Nature DC 14: Hidden away deep underground are foul troglodyte temples dedicated to demons such as Demogorgon and deities such as Torog. The strongest troglodytes from nearby tribes rise to become temple champions.

Temple champions fight to the death with fanatical devotion; anyone taken alive by a temple champion is quickly sacrificed in a nearby temple.

Dungeoneering or Nature DC 19: Due to the comprehension and patience required of a temple champion, the strongest warriors are often the smartest as well. If temple champions leave their temples' boundaries, they often do so at the behest of their leaders and as the head of a larger force of less intelligent troglodytes.

ENCOUNTER GROUPS

Troglodytes often use drakes and other reptilian monsters to guard their lairs.

Level 7 Encounter (XP 1,600)
✦ 2 horned drakes (level 5 skirmisher)
✦ 1 troglodyte impaler (level 7 artillery, *MM* 252)
✦ 3 troglodyte thrashers (level 7 brute)

Level 10 Encounter (XP 2,650)
✦ 1 troglodyte curse chanter (level 8 controller, *MM* 252)
✦ 2 troglodyte deepscourges (level 9 artillery)
✦ 3 scytheclaw drakes (level 10 skirmisher)

Level 11 Encounter (XP 3,100)
✦ 1 balhannoth (level 13 elite lurker, *MM* 24)
✦ 2 troglodyte temple champions (level 9 soldier)
✦ 4 troglodyte warriors (level 12 minion, *MM* 252)

Level 12 Encounter (XP 3,750)
✦ 1 troglodyte curse chanter (level 8 controller, *MM* 252)
✦ 2 troglodyte deepscourges (level 9 artillery)
✦ 4 troglodyte thrashers (level 7 brute)
✦ 8 troglodyte warriors (level 12 minion, *MM* 252)

TROLL

These monstrous humanoids strike fear into their enemies with their strength and ravenous appetites.

ICE TROLL

ICE TROLLS ARE SKILLED ARMORERS and weaponsmiths that can be found in the frozen north, the Frostfell, and anywhere that supernatural cold persists.

Ice Troll	Level 10 Soldier
Large natural humanoid	XP 500

Initiative +9   **Senses** Perception +10
Emanating Cold aura 1; each enemy that starts its turn in the aura is slowed until the start of its next turn.
HP 109; **Bloodied** 54; see also *troll healing*
Regeneration 10
AC 26; **Fortitude** 23, **Reflex** 19, **Will** 17
Vulnerable acid or fire (if the ice troll takes acid or fire damage, its regeneration does not function until the end of its next turn)
Speed 8
ⓐ **Maul** (standard; at-will) ✦ **Weapon**
    Reach 2; +17 vs. AC; 2d6 + 6 damage.
✚ **Frenzied Strike** (free, when the ice troll's attack bloodies an enemy; at-will)
    The troll makes a maul attack.
Troll Healing ✦ **Healing**
    If the ice troll is reduced to 0 hit points by an attack that does not deal acid or fire damage, it falls prone and remains at 0 hit points until the start of its next turn, when it regains 10 hit points. If an attack deals acid or fire damage to the ice troll while it is at 0 hit points, it is destroyed.
Alignment Chaotic evil   **Languages** Giant
Skills Athletics +16, Endurance +15
Str 22 (+11)   **Dex** 15 (+7)   **Wis** 10 (+5)
Con 21 (+10)   **Int** 9 (+4)   **Cha** 8 (+4)
Equipment scale armor, maul

ICE TROLL TACTICS

An ice troll wades into combat and pounds its enemies with its powerful maul. It also knows full well the effect its aura has on creatures not accustomed to supernatural cold, and it positions itself to include as many of its foes as possible in the aura.

ICE TROLL LORE

Nature DC 16: Ice trolls inhabit the Frostfell, but they occasionally make their way into less frigid regions. Ice trolls are more intelligent than most other trolls, and they have learned to craft weapons. They prefer to use such weapons in combat instead of their claws.

BLADERAGER TROLL

A BLADERAGER TROLL IS THE RESULT of modification to a normal troll.

Bladerager Troll	Level 12 Brute
Large natural humanoid	XP 700

Initiative +10   **Senses** Perception +9
HP 151; **Bloodied** 75; see also *death burst*
Regeneration 10
AC 24; **Fortitude** 26, **Reflex** 24, **Will** 23
Vulnerable acid or fire (if the bladerager troll takes acid or fire damage, its regeneration does not function until the end of its next turn)
Speed 7
ⓐ **Claw** (standard; at-will)
    Reach 2; +15 vs. AC; 2d10 + 6 damage.
✚ **Bladerager Rend** (standard; recharge ⚄ ⚅)
    Reach 2; +15 vs. AC; 3d10 + 6 damage, and ongoing 5 damage (save ends).
◄ **Death Burst** (when the bladerager troll drops to 0 hit points)
    The troll explodes in a burst of shrapnel: close burst 2; +13 vs. Reflex; 2d6 + 5 damage.
Alignment Chaotic evil   **Languages** Giant
Skills Athletics +17, Endurance +16
Str 23 (+12)   **Dex** 18 (+10)   **Wis** 16 (+9)
Con 21 (+11)   **Int** 3 (+2)   **Cha** 10 (+6)

BLADERAGER TROLL TACTICS

A bladerager troll attacks the most physically menacing target, but quickly switches to the enemy that appears to be doing the most damage or hindering it the most. It doesn't employ concerted tactics beyond dealing as much damage to its enemies as possible.

BLADERAGER TROLL LORE

Nature DC 16: Bladerager trolls are barely sentient berserker trolls. They run at their foes, ripping them limb from limb and devouring the pieces. Bladeragers are created in violent rituals that bind weapons and metal shards with troll flesh. In constant pain, bladeragers survive because of their regenerative capabilities, but death breaks the binding magic in an explosion of metal and blood.

Nature DC 21: Duergar, drow, and mind flayers commonly capture trolls and enslave them. On the surface of the world, bladerager trolls can be found in the employ of oni and minotaurs. Some minotaur cabalists know the secret to binding magic weapons and armor into trolls, giving the trolls the properties of the metal items that cut their bodies. Such items can often be retrieved after the bladeragers' destructive deaths.

Troll Vinespeaker

Troll vinespeakers fight by calling upon an ancient magic of wild lands.

Troll Vinespeaker — **Level 14 Controller**
Large natural humanoid — XP 1,000

Initiative +10 **Senses** Perception +13
HP 142; **Bloodied** 71; see also *troll healing*
Regeneration 10
AC 28; **Fortitude** 26, **Reflex** 23, **Will** 21
Vulnerable acid or fire (if the troll vinespeaker takes acid or fire damage, its regeneration does not function until the end of its next turn)
Speed 8

Claw (standard; at-will)
Reach 2; +19 vs. AC; 2d6 + 7 damage.

Frenzied Strike (free, when the troll vinespeaker's attack bloodies an enemy; at-will)
The vinespeaker makes a claw attack.

Ray of Thorns (standard; at-will) ✦ **Implement**
Ranged 10; +18 vs. Reflex; 2d8 + 6 damage.

Chant of Power (standard; encounter) ✦ **Healing, Implement**
Close burst 5; targets allies; the target gains 10 temporary hit points and a +4 bonus to damage rolls while it has the temporary hit points.

Thorny Burst (standard; at-will) ✦ **Implement, Zone**
Area burst 1 within 10; +18 vs. Reflex; 1d10 + 6 damage, and the target is immobilized (save ends). The burst creates a zone of thorns and brambles that lasts until the end of the encounter. The zone is difficult terrain, and each creature that enters the zone or starts its turn there takes 1d8 damage.

Troll Healing ✦ **Healing**
If the troll vinespeaker is reduced to 0 hit points by an attack that does not deal acid or fire damage, it falls prone and remains at 0 hit points until the start of its next turn, when it regains 10 hit points. If an attack deals acid or fire damage to the vinespeaker while it is at 0 hit points, it is destroyed.

Alignment Chaotic evil **Languages** Common, Giant
Skills Athletics +16, Endurance +15

Str 18 (+11)	**Dex** 16 (+10)	**Wis** 12 (+8)
Con 22 (+13)	**Int** 16 (+10)	**Cha** 10 (+7)

Equipment mantle of thorny vines, gnarled staff

Troll Vinespeaker Tactics

Troll vinespeakers use *thorny burst* as much as possible, switching to *ray of thorns* only when a *thorny burst* would inhibit the movement of allies on the battlefield. They remain out of melee and allow others to do the hand-to-hand fighting.

Troll Vinespeaker Lore

Nature DC 18: The intelligent troll vinespeakers act as shamans and leaders in troll communities. They can be found among only the largest troll packs and war bands. Draping themselves in mantles of thorny vines, vinespeakers use a nature magic that gives the vines violent life.

Encounter Groups

Trolls work well with other creatures as long as the trolls' appetites are kept in check. Most trolls lack intelligence and are easy to manipulate.

Level 10 Encounter (XP 2,800)
- 2 ice trolls (level 10 soldier)
- 1 manticore (level 10 elite skirmisher, *MM* 184)
- 2 worg (level 9 brute, *MM* 265)

Level 12 Encounter (XP 3,800)
- 3 bladerager trolls (level 12 brute)
- 1 duergar blasphemer (level 14 controller)
- 1 duergar hellcaller (level 12 artillery)

Level 15 Encounter (XP 6,200)
- 1 destrachan far voice (level 15 artillery, *MM* 59)
- 1 troll vinespeaker (level 14 controller)
- 4 war trolls (level 14 soldier, *MM* 254)

(Top to bottom) bladerager troll and troll vinespeaker

WAYNE ENGLAND

Ambulatory carnivorous vines threaten wilderness dwellers and travelers, and are often as dangerous as any predatory animal. These vines are sometimes cultivated by dryads and vine horrors for use as guardians.

AMBUSH VINE

Ambush vines have voracious appetites, and find flesh to be particularly delectable. They hunt both above and below the ground, and can even snake through the water to strike at swimming prey.

Ambush Vine	Level 16 Elite Controller
Large fey beast (plant)	XP 1,400

Initiative +15 **Senses** Perception +15; tremorsense 20
HP 308; **Bloodied** 154; see also *rapid growth*
AC 30; **Fortitude** 28, **Reflex** 30, **Will** 25
Saving Throws +2
Speed 6 (forest walk), climb 6, burrow 6, swim 6
Action Points 1

⊕ **Poison Lash** (standard; at-will) ✦ **Poison**
  Reach 2; +20 vs. Reflex; 1d8 + 6 damage, and ongoing 5 poison damage (save ends).

↯ **Foot Snare** (minor; at-will)
  Reach 4; +20 vs. Fortitude; 1d8 + 6 damage, and the target is knocked prone.

⇐ **Lashing Vines** (standard; at-will) ✦ **Healing**
  Close burst 4; targets enemies; +20 vs. Reflex; 2d8 + 6 damage. If the target is immobilized, the attack deals 1d8 extra damage, and the ambush vine regains 5 hit points.

Rapid Growth (when first bloodied; encounter)
  The ambush vine spawns two ambush vine shoots in spaces within 4 squares of the ambush vine. The shoots act on the vine's initiative count, immediately after the vine.

Sprout Vine (minor; at-will)
  The ambush vine takes 10 damage and spawns an ambush vine shoot in a space within 4 squares of the vine. The shoot acts on the vine's initiative count, immediately after the vine.

Alignment Unaligned **Languages** –
Skills Athletics +18, Stealth +20 (+25 in undergrowth, trees, or swamp)
Str 21 (+13)	**Dex** 25 (+15)	**Wis** 15 (+10)
Con 18 (+12)	**Int** 2 (+4)	**Cha** 12 (+9)

AMBUSH VINE SHOOT

Ambush vine shoots are the immature form of the vine, and can be spawned by a parent ambush vine during combat.

Ambush Vine Shoot	Level 15 Minion Controller
Medium fey beast (plant)	XP 300

Initiative +14 **Senses** Perception +14; tremorsense 20
HP 1; a missed attack never damages a minion.
AC 29; **Fortitude** 27, **Reflex** 30, **Will** 23
Speed 6, burrow 6

⊕ **Wrapping Vines** (standard; at-will)
  Reach 2; +20 vs. Fortitude; 12 damage, and the target is restrained (save ends).

Enwrap
  Each enemy adjacent to an ambush vine shoot takes a -2 penalty to saving throws against immobilized and restrained.

Alignment Unaligned **Languages** –
Skills Stealth +19 (+24 in undergrowth, trees, or swamp)
Str 18 (+11)	**Dex** 25 (+14)	**Wis** 15 (+9)
Con 16 (+10)	**Int** 2 (+3)	**Cha** 12 (+8)

AMBUSH VINE LORE

Nature DC 20: Ambush vines infect vast wilderness areas in the Feywild. Although less common in the world, they often blight the deepest reaches of forests or swamps. They can swim through water, burrow through the earth, and climb through treetops to reach prey.

Nature DC 25: An ambush vine has unusual cunning for a plant. It often hides beneath the ground or attempts to blend in with other plants.

Nature DC 27: Occasionally, a blight of ambush vines becomes so vast that it encroaches on civilization. Some scholars speculate that widespread occurrences of ambush vines in the former eladrin empire of Cendriane contributed to its downfall.

BLOODTHORN VINE

DEADLY BLOODTHORN VINES CREEP through forests seeking the life fluids of other creatures to draw up through their hollow thorns.

Bloodthorn Vine	Level 2 Soldier
Medium natural beast (plant)	XP 125

Initiative +3   **Senses** Perception +3; blindsight 10
HP 41; **Bloodied** 20
AC 18; **Fortitude** 15, **Reflex** 12, **Will** 14
Speed 5 (forest walk)
⊕ **Striking Vine** (standard; at-will)
  +9 vs. AC; 1d8 + 5 damage.
✦ **Impaling Thorn** (standard; recharges when the bloodthorn vine doesn't have a creature grabbed) ✦ **Healing**
  The vine impales the target's flesh with a thorn: +9 vs. Fortitude; 1d8 + 4 damage, and the target is grabbed. *Sustain Standard:* The vine sustains the grab, the target takes 2d8 + 4 damage, and the vine regains 5 hit points.
Pulling Vines (minor; at-will)
  The bloodthorn vine shifts 1 square, pulling any creature grabbed by it into a space adjacent to it.
Alignment Unaligned   **Languages** —
Str 17 (+4)   **Dex** 10 (+1)   **Wis** 14 (+3)
Con 17 (+4)   **Int** 2 (-3)   **Cha** 6 (-1)

BLOODTHORN VINE LORE

Nature DC 10: A bloodthorn vine attacks by grabbing a foe and sucking its blood through a sharp, hollow thorn. When a bloodthorn vine feeds, its pale leaves turn the color of its victim's blood.

GREENVISE VINE

THE ENORMOUS GREENVISE VINES SLOWLY PROWL forests, snaring any creature unwary enough to come close.

Greenvise Vine	Level 7 Soldier
Large natural beast (plant)	XP 300

Initiative +3   **Senses** Perception +5; blindsight 10
HP 83; **Bloodied** 41
AC 23; **Fortitude** 21, **Reflex** 17, **Will** 19
Speed 4 (forest walk)
⊕ **Striking Vine** (standard; at-will)
  +14 vs. AC; 1d10 + 6 damage.
✦ **Ensnaring Vine** (standard; at-will)
  Reach 4; +10 vs. Reflex; 1d10 + 6 damage, and the target is grabbed.
✦ **Vise Bite** (minor; recharges when no creature is affected by this power)
  Targets a creature grabbed by the greenvise vine; +10 vs. Fortitude; 2d4 damage, and the target is restrained and takes ongoing 5 damage (save ends both).
Pulling Vines (minor; at-will)
  The greenvise vine shifts 1 square, pulling any creature grabbed by it into a space adjacent to it.
Alignment Unaligned   **Languages** —
Str 19 (+7)   **Dex** 10 (+3)   **Wis** 14 (+5)
Con 19 (+7)   **Int** 2 (-1)   **Cha** 6 (+1)

GREENVISE VINE LORE

Nature DC 14: Greenvise vines are slow, opportunistic eaters that feed on unwary animals, but they aren't averse to attacking larger prey.

ENCOUNTER GROUPS

Fey creatures sometimes cultivate predatory vines as guardians near their homes. Stirges have been known to lair near these plants, drawn by the prospect of finding easy prey among ensnared creatures.

Level 2 Encounter (XP 675)
✦ 3 bloodthorn vines (level 2 soldier)
✦ 3 stirges (level 1 lurker, *MM* 248)

Level 9 Encounter (XP 2,200)
✦ 2 greenvise vines (level 7 soldier)
✦ 1 spectral panther (level 9 lurker, *MM* 213)
✦ 3 quickling runners (level 9 skirmisher, *MM* 215)

Level 17 Encounter (XP 9,600)
✦ 1 ambush vine (level 16 elite controller)
✦ 1 lingerer fell incanter (level 18 elite artillery)
✦ 1 lingerer knight (level 16 elite soldier)

WARFORGED

WHETHER FRESH FROM THE CREATION FORGE or decades old, warforged can be much more than mere soldiers, but they are all creatures of war.

WARFORGED RESOUNDER

THE WARFORGED RESOUNDER brings the force of thunder to the maelstrom of combat, blasting foes from afar.

Warforged Resounder	Level 6 Artillery
Medium natural humanoid (living construct)	XP 250

Initiative +3 **Senses** Perception +5
HP 57; **Bloodied** 28
AC 19; **Fortitude** 16, **Reflex** 18, **Will** 18
Saving Throws +2 against ongoing damage
Speed 6

⊕ **Quarterstaff** (standard; at-will) ✦ **Weapon**
+10 vs. AC; 1d8 + 1 damage.

⨀ **Rumble Staff** (standard; encounter) ✦ **Force, Implement**
+11 vs. Fortitude; 2d6 + 4 force damage, and the target is pushed 1 square and knocked prone.

↗ **Collision Bolt** (standard; encounter) ✦ **Force, Implement**
Ranged 10; +11 vs. Fortitude; 1d6 + 4 force damage, and the warforged resounder makes a secondary attack against one or two targets within 3 squares of the primary target. *Secondary Attack:* +11 vs. Fortitude; 1d6 + 4 force damage, and the resounder slides the target 3 squares toward the primary target. *Effect:* After all attacks are resolved, any target hit by an attack is knocked prone if it is adjacent to another target.

↗ **Thunder Orb** (standard; at-will) ✦ **Implement, Thunder**
Ranged 10; +11 vs. Reflex; 2d6 + 4 thunder damage, and the warforger resounder pushes the target 2 squares.

✴ **Resounding Sphere** (standard; encounter) ✦ **Implement, Thunder**
Area burst 3 within 10; +10 vs. Reflex; 2d8 + 4 thunder damage, and the target is knocked prone. *Miss:* Half damage.

Warforged Resolve (minor; encounter) ✦ **Healing**
The warforged resounder gains 6 temporary hit points and can make a saving throw against an ongoing damage effect. If it uses this power while bloodied, it also regains 6 hit points.

Alignment Unaligned **Languages** Common
Skills Arcana +12, Nature +10
Str 12 (+4)	**Dex** 11 (+3)	**Wis** 15 (+5)
Con 15 (+5)	**Int** 18 (+7)	**Cha** 12 (+4)

Equipment robes, quarterstaff

WARFORGED RESOUNDER TACTICS

A warforged resounder prefers to open with *resounding sphere* against enemies not yet engaged in melee. It saves *collision bolt* for later use against enemies in close combat. The warforged resounder avoids melee with the help of *rumble staff*.

WARFORGED RESOUNDER LORE

Arcana or Nature DC 12: Ringing with the power of its creation, a warforged resounder focuses the echoes of its forging into deadly attacks.

WARFORGED SAVAGE

WARFORGED SAVAGES GIVE THEMSELVES OVER to rage in battle, becoming vicious, crazed killers.

Warforged Savage	Level 7 Brute
Medium natural humanoid (living construct)	XP 300

Initiative +5 **Senses** Perception +4
HP 98; **Bloodied** 49
AC 20; **Fortitude** 21, **Reflex** 18, **Will** 19
Saving Throws +2 against ongoing damage
Speed 6

⊕ **Scimitar** (standard; at-will) ✦ **Weapon**
+10 vs. AC; 1d8 + 6 damage (crit 1d8 + 14), and 4 damage to another enemy adjacent to the warforged savage.

⨀ **Wild Charge** (standard; recharges after the warforged savage hits two or more targets with a *savage sweep*) ✦ **Weapon**
The savage charges, gains a +3 bonus to AC during the charge, and makes the following attack in place of a melee basic attack: +11 vs. AC; 2d8 + 9 damage (crit 2d8 + 25).

← **Savage Sweep** (standard; recharge ⚄ ⚅) ✦ **Weapon**
Close burst 1; +10 vs. AC; 1d8 + 6 damage (crit 1d8 + 14). *Miss:* 4 damage.

Battlefield Tactics
A warforged savage gains a +1 bonus to melee attack rolls while an ally is adjacent to the target.

Savage Bloodlust
Whenever a warforged savage hits with a melee attack, it gains 4 temporary hit points.

Warforged Resolve (minor; encounter) ✦ **Healing**
The warforged savage gains 6 temporary hit points and can make a saving throw against an ongoing damage effect. If it uses this power while bloodied, it also regains 6 hit points.

Alignment Unaligned **Languages** Common
Skills Endurance +12, Intimidate +11
Str 20 (+8)	**Dex** 15 (+5)	**Wis** 12 (+4)
Con 18 (+7)	**Int** 10 (+3)	**Cha** 16 (+6)

Equipment hide armor, scimitar

WARFORGED SAVAGE TACTICS

At its first chance, the warforged savage makes a *wild charge*. It might even do so if already engaged, in order to attack several enemies with *savage sweep*. The warforged savage thereafter makes use of *savage sweep* whenever the attack recharges, in order to change its tactical position or to deal as much damage as possible.

WARFORGED SAVAGE LORE

Arcana or Nature DC 14: A warforged savage has far more emotion than most other warforged, but that emotion tends to be expressed as fury. Irritable and quick to draw blades, warforged savages make uncertain allies in peacetime and deadly foes during war.

(Left to right) warforged anvilpriest, warforged resounder, and warforged savage

WARFORGED ANVILPRIEST

A SOLDIERLY MINISTER, the warforged anvilpriest burns with the memories of its creation, and it carries that fire into battle.

Warforged Anvilpriest	Level 8 Controller (Leader)
Medium natural humanoid (living construct)	XP 350

Initiative +4   **Senses** Perception +8
HP 89; **Bloodied** 44
AC 22; **Fortitude** 20, **Reflex** 20, **Will** 21
Saving Throws +2 against ongoing damage
Speed 5

⊕ **Fiery Warhammer** (standard; at-will) ✦ **Fire, Weapon**
    +13 vs. AC; 1d10 + 4 damage plus 1d6 fire damage, and the target takes a -2 penalty to AC until the end of the warforged anvilpriest's next turn.

↓ **Heat of Battle** (standard; recharge ⚄ ⚅) ✦ **Fire, Weapon**
    +13 vs. AC; 1d10 + 4 damage plus 1d6 fire damage, and ongoing 5 fire damage until the target ends its turn in a space that isn't adjacent to the warforged anvilpriest.

⬅ **Mending Flash Fire** (standard; encounter) ✦ **Fire, Implement**
    Close burst 5; targets enemies; +11 vs. Reflex; 1d8 + 4 fire damage. *Effect:* The warforged anvilpriest and each ally within the burst gain 5 temporary hit points. Each warforged ally within the burst uses *warforged resolve* as an immediate reaction.

❇ **Blunted Mind** (standard; encounter) ✦ **Illusion, Implement, Psychic**
    Area burst 3 within 10; targets enemies; +11 vs. Will; 2d6 + 4 psychic damage, and the target takes a -2 penalty to attack rolls and a -4 penalty to damage rolls (save ends both). *Aftereffect:* The target takes a -2 penalty to damage rolls (save ends).

Warforged Resolve (minor; encounter) ✦ **Healing**
    The warforged anvilpriest gains 7 temporary hit points and can make a saving throw against an ongoing damage effect. If it uses this power while bloodied, it also regains 7 hit points.

Alignment Unaligned   **Languages** Common
Skills Heal +13, Religion +12
| **Str** 14 (+6) | **Dex** 10 (+4) | **Wis** 19 (+8) |
| **Con** 17 (+7) | **Int** 16 (+7) | **Cha** 12 (+5) |

Equipment chainmail, warhammer, holy symbol

WARFORGED ANVILPRIEST TACTICS

The warforged anvilpriest first targets enemies with *blunted mind*. It then wades in among its enemies to use its melee attacks, starting with *heat of battle*. The anvilpriest keeps an eye on its allies, using *mending flash fire* when one or more are bloodied.

WARFORGED ANVILPRIEST LORE

Arcana or Nature DC 14: Warforged anvilpriests use the still-hot flames of their creation, maintaining a link to that formative moment despite years of existence in the world. Although some are true clerics devoted to a deity, other anvilpriests care little for religion.

Arcana or Nature DC 19: Only a few anvilpriests fully live up to their name by venerating the creation forges. These strange and often crazed warforged present a threat to all who would keep them from the objects of their worship.

WARFORGED TITAN

MASSIVE WARFORGED TITANS thunder over the battlefield, swinging arms that end in immense weapons.

Warforged Titan	Level 19 Elite Soldier
Huge natural humanoid (living construct)	XP 4,800

Initiative +15   **Senses** Perception +13
HP 362; **Bloodied** 181
AC 35; **Fortitude** 35, **Reflex** 30, **Will** 30
Saving Throws +2 (+4 against ongoing damage)
Speed 8
Action Points 1
⊕ **Axe** (standard; at-will)
    Reach 3; +24 vs. AC; 2d10 + 9 damage, and 9 damage to one enemy adjacent to the target. *Effect:* The target is marked until the end of the warforged titan's next turn.
⊥ **Hammer** (minor 1/round; at-will)
    Reach 3; +24 vs. AC; 2d8 + 9 damage, the warforged titan slides the target 2 squares, and the target is knocked prone. *Miss:* 9 damage.
Unstoppable Charger
    A warforged titan can take additional actions after it resolves its charge attack.
Threatening Reach
    A warforged titan can make opportunity attacks against all enemies within its reach (3 squares).
Warforged Resolve (minor; encounter) ✦ **Healing**
    The warforged titan gains 12 temporary hit points and can make a saving throw against an ongoing damage effect. If it uses this power while bloodied, it also regains 12 hit points.
Alignment Unaligned   **Languages** Common
Str 28 (+18)   **Dex** 18 (+13)   **Wis** 18 (+13)
Con 21 (+14)   **Int** 5 (+6)   **Cha** 8 (+8)

WARFORGED TITAN TACTICS

A warforged titan charges into melee without hesitation. When possible, it makes a *hammer* attack to slide one enemy adjacent to another. The warforged titan then charges (or otherwise attacks) the enemy with the lightest armor with an axe attack, cleaving into both enemies.

WARFORGED TITAN LORE

Arcana or Nature DC 22: Among the first warforged created, warforged titans are barely sentient, with just enough intelligence to follow changing commands in the heat of battle.

Arcana or Nature DC 27: A warforged titan comprehends allegiance in simplistic terms. It often follows the commands of someone that has a symbol of the titan's creator, regardless of its creator's goals or how much time has passed since its creation.

ENCOUNTER GROUPS

Free warforged fight for a variety of causes—including their own.

Level 7 Encounter (XP 1,500)
✦ 1 warforged anvilpriest (level 8 controller)
✦ 1 warforged resounder (level 6 artillery)
✦ 3 warforged savages (level 7 brute)

Level 19 Encounter (XP 12,400)
✦ 1 cambion hellfire magus (level 18 artillery, MM 39)
✦ 1 steel predator (level 20 elite soldier)
✦ 1 warforged titan (level 19 elite soldier)

MARK TEDIN

WILL-O'-WISP

THESE CRUEL FEY CREATURES feed on powerful emotions such as horror, despair, and anguish.

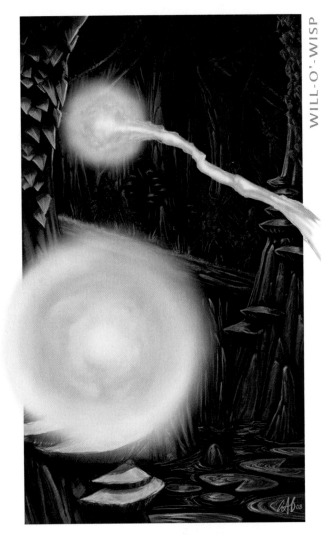

Will-o'-Wisp	Level 10 Lurker
Small fey magical beast	XP 500

Initiative +15 **Senses** Perception +11; low-light vision
HP 57; **Bloodied** 28
AC 22; **Fortitude** 19, **Reflex** 24, **Will** 22
Resist insubstantial
Speed fly 6 (hover; altitude limit 2)

⊕ **Glimmer Wisp** (standard; at-will) ✦ **Radiant**
Reach 2; +13 vs. Reflex; 2d6 + 6 radiant damage.

⨟ **Spirit Drain** (standard; usable only while illuminated; see *fey light*; encounter) ✦ **Healing, Psychic**
Reach 3; targets a bloodied creature; +12 vs. Fortitude; 2d8 + 3 psychic damage, and the target is weakened (save ends). The will-o'-wisp regains 14 hit points.

⬳ **Luring Glow** (standard; usable only while illuminated; see *fey light*; at-will)
Close burst 20; targets one creature that is not blinded; +13 vs. Will; the target is pulled 3 squares and dazed (save ends).

Blink Out (immediate reaction, when the will-o'-wisp is missed by an attack; at-will) ✦ **Teleportation**
The will-o'-wisp darkens and teleports 5 squares (see *fey light*).

Fey Light (free 1/round; at-will)
A will-o'-wisp illuminates or darkens its light. The will-o'-wisp's light is equivalent to that of a torch. The will-o'-wisp must be illuminated to attack. While darkened, the will-o'-wisp has concealment and can make a Stealth check to become hidden.

Alignment Evil	**Languages** Elven	
Skills Stealth +16		
Str 4 (+2)	**Dex** 22 (+11)	**Wis** 12 (+6)
Con 13 (+6)	**Int** 8 (+4)	**Cha** 18 (+9)

WILL-O'-WISP TACTICS

A will-o'-wisp prefers distracted prey. It uses *fey light* when it wishes to be seen, or to draw prey in with *luring glow*. As soon as it is aware of bloodied prey, it closes to employ *spirit drain*. It douses its *fey light* and uses Stealth to move to the bloodied target and attack with combat advantage.

WILL-O'-WISP LORE

Arcana DC 16: Will-o'-wisps lurk in marshlands, where mists and swamp lights provide hiding places. They gather near natural dangers, such as quicksand or other monsters. Will-o'-wisps use their lights to draw unwary travelers into peril.

Arcana DC 21: A will-o'-wisp can speak in a ghostly voice. As it speaks, the creature brightens and dims. Its actual body is a tiny orb of diaphanous material.

ENCOUNTER GROUPS

Fey creatures, undead, and predators of many kinds take advantage of will-o'-wisps as lures. Will-o'-wisps are attracted to the sounds of travel or battle.

Level 9 Encounter (XP 2,100)
✦ 2 spriggan powries (level 7 skirmisher)
✦ 2 spriggan thorns (level 6 soldier)
✦ 2 will-o'-wisps (level 10 lurker)

CHRISTOPHER BURDETT

WINTER WOLF

SLY HUNTERS AND FEROCIOUS COMBATANTS, winter wolves have an evil intelligence and powers of deadly cold.

Winter Wolf	Level 14 Skirmisher
Medium natural magical beast	XP 1,000

Initiative +14 **Senses** Perception +10; low-light vision
HP 141; **Bloodied** 70
AC 28; **Fortitude** 27, **Reflex** 26, **Will** 24
Resist 20 cold
Speed 8 (ice walk)

⊕ **Bite** (standard; at-will) ✦ **Cold**
+19 vs. AC; 1d10 + 6 damage plus 1d6 cold damage, or 2d10 + 6 damage plus 1d6 cold damage against a prone target.

† **Takedown** (standard; usable only when charging; at-will) ✦ **Cold**
+19 vs. AC; 2d10 + 6 damage plus 1d6 cold damage, and the target is knocked prone.

↞ **Freezing Breath** (standard; recharge ⚄ ⚅) ✦ **Cold**
Close blast 5; +17 vs. Reflex; 2d6 + 6 cold damage. *Miss:* Half damage.

Drag (minor; usable only while adjacent to a prone enemy; at-will)
The winter wolf shifts 1 square and pulls a prone target that is adjacent to it 1 square.

Alignment Evil **Languages** Common, Giant
| **Str** 23 (+13) | **Dex** 21 (+12) | **Wis** 17 (+10) |
| **Con** 21 (+12) | **Int** 9 (+6) | **Cha** 10 (+7) |

WINTER WOLF SNOWFANG

WINTER WOLF SNOWFANGS ARE PATIENT, elusive foes that like to toy with their victims.

Winter Wolf Snowfang	Level 16 Lurker
Medium natural magical beast	XP 1,400

Initiative +19 **Senses** Perception +12; low-light vision
HP 124; **Bloodied** 62
AC 30; **Fortitude** 28, **Reflex** 29, **Will** 26
Resist 20 cold
Speed 8 (ice walk)

⊕ **Bite** (standard; at-will) ✦ **Cold**
+21 vs. AC; 1d10 + 5 damage plus 1d8 cold damage.

↞ **Frigid Breath** (standard; recharge ⚄ ⚅) ✦ **Cold**
Close blast 5; +19 vs. Reflex; 2d8 + 7 cold damage, and ongoing 5 cold damage (save ends). *Miss:* Half damage.

Icy Rending ✦ **Cold**
The winter wolf snowfang deals 2d8 extra damage with its bite attack against any creature that is taking ongoing cold damage.

Snow Zephyr (immediate reaction, when an attack damages the winter wolf snowfang; at-will)
The winter wolf snowfang changes into a whirling zephyr of snow. It gains insubstantial and shifts its speed as a move action. While in this form, the wolf can use only its *frigid breath* attack. The wolf remains in this form until it uses *frigid breath* or until it chooses to resume its normal form as a minor action.

Alignment Evil **Languages** Common, Giant
Skills Stealth +20 (+25 in snow or ice)
| **Str** 21 (+13) | **Dex** 25 (+15) | **Wis** 18 (+12) |
| **Con** 22 (+14) | **Int** 10 (+8) | **Cha** 11 (+8) |

BEN WOOTTEN

WINTER WOLF SNOWFANG LORE

Nature DC 20: Snowfangs are clever and malicious killers that often serve more powerful monsters as sentries. In winter wolf packs, snowfangs sometimes wait in ambush while their packmates drive prey toward them.

RIME HOUND

RIME HOUNDS ARE GIFTS of powerful primordials of cold to their worshipers.

Rime Hound		Level 17 Elite Skirmisher
Huge elemental magical beast (earth, cold, mount)		XP 3,200
Initiative +16	Senses Perception +12; low-light vision	
HP 332; Bloodied 166		
AC 31; Fortitude 30, Reflex 29, Will 27		
Resist 20 cold		
Saving Throws +2		
Speed 8 (ice walk)		
Action Points 1		

⊕ **Bite** (standard; at-will) ✦ **Cold**
Reach 2; +22 vs. AC; 1d12 + 6 damage plus 1d6 cold damage, or 2d12 + 6 damage plus 1d6 cold damage against a prone target.

↯ **Ice Spikes** (immediate reaction, when an enemy misses the rime hound or a friendly rider of 17th level or higher with a melee attack; at-will) ✦ **Mount**
The icy spikes on the rime hound's body extend: targets the triggering enemy; +20 vs. Reflex; 1d12 + 6 damage plus 1d6 cold damage.

↯ **Takedown** (standard; usable only when charging; at-will) ✦ **Cold**
Reach 2; +20 vs. AC; 2d12 + 6 damage plus 1d6 cold damage, and the target is knocked prone.

↞ **Frost Storm** (standard; recharge ⚃ ⚅) ✦ **Cold, Zone**
Close burst 3; +20 vs. Fortitude; 2d8 + 6 cold damage. *Miss:* Half damage. *Effect:* The burst creates a zone of icy terrain that lasts until the end of the rime hound's next turn. The zone is difficult terrain.

Drag (minor; usable only when adjacent to a prone enemy; at-will)
The rime hound shifts 1 square, and pulls a prone target that is adjacent to it 1 square.

Alignment Evil	Languages Common, Giant	
Skills Intimidate +13		
Str 24 (+15)	Dex 22 (+14)	Wis 19 (+12)
Con 22 (+14)	Int 10 (+8)	Cha 10 (+8)

RIME HOUND LORE

Arcana DC 25: Certain primordials of cold are said to create rime hounds out of the cold heart of elemental blizzards. These enormous hounds work with frost giants as mounts, or hunt alongside frost titans and similar icy beings.

SON OF THE SPIRIT WOLF

A SON OF THE SPIRIT WOLF USES ITS ICY BREATH to keep its victim's allies away while it concentrates on biting and rending the hapless target to death.

Son of the Spirit Wolf		Level 26 Elite Skirmisher
Large elemental magical beast (cold)		XP 18,000
Initiative +23	Senses Perception +20; low-light vision	
Everfrost Coat (cold) aura 1; each enemy that enters the aura takes 10 cold damage. A creature that takes cold damage from *everfrost coat* cannot make opportunity attacks until the end of the son of the spirit wolf's next turn.		
HP 486; Bloodied 243		
AC 40; Fortitude 39, Reflex 37, Will 36		
Resist 30 cold		
Saving Throws +2		
Speed 8 (ice walk)		
Action Points 1		

⊕ **Bite** (standard; at-will) ✦ **Cold**
Reach 2; +31 vs. AC; 2d10 + 9 damage plus 1d10 cold damage, and the target is grabbed.

↯ **Terrible Rush** (free; usable only after the son of the spirit wolf makes a charge attack; encounter) ✦ **Cold**
Close burst 2; +29 vs. Fortitude; 2d10 cold damage, and the target is knocked prone.

↞ **Black Ice Breath** (standard; recharges when first bloodied) ✦ **Cold, Zone**
Close blast 5; +29 vs. Fortitude; 4d10 + 9 cold damage. *Miss:* Half damage. *Effect:* The blast creates a zone of ice that lasts until the son of the spirit wolf drops to 0 hit points. The zone is difficult terrain.

Rending Jaws (minor; recharge ⚄ ⚅)
Reach 2; targets a creature grabbed by the son of the spirit wolf; +32 vs. AC; 3d10 + 9 damage, and ongoing 10 damage (save ends). The grab ends, and the son of the spirit wolf then pushes the target 5 squares and knocks it prone.

Drag Away (move; at-will)
The son of the spirit wolf shifts 1 square or moves its speed and pulls a creature it has grabbed into a space adjacent to it. This movement does not end the grab.

Alignment Evil	Languages Common, Giant	
Skills Intimidate +21		
Str 30 (+23)	Dex 26 (+21)	Wis 25 (+20)
Con 27 (+21)	Int 11 (+13)	Cha 16 (+16)

SON OF THE SPIRIT WOLF LORE

Arcana DC 31: Sons of the spirit wolf are winter wolves descended from the primal spirit known as the great spirit wolf. Driven by insatiable hunger, they greedily devour any source of life they encounter. Only the most powerful of beings can hold sons of the spirit wolf in check.

ENCOUNTER GROUPS

Winter wolves mix well with humanoid denizens of colder climes, such as frost giants.

Level 14 Encounter (XP 5,000)
✦ 1 beholder eye of frost (level 14 elite artillery)
✦ 1 chillfire destroyer (level 14 brute)
✦ 2 winter wolves (level 14 skirmisher)

WITHERLING

Witherlings are undead creatures created by gnolls to serve as shock troops and raiders. Gnoll priests of Yeenoghu use a ritual to fuse the essence of a demon with the body of a foe slain in battle. The result is a shrunken, emaciated creature that has a ghoul's paralyzing touch and a demon's relentless frenzy.

WITHERLING

A witherling is the animated corpse of a small humanoid with the head of a hyena. It menaces its victims with claws made of sharpened gazelle horns, which are sticky with poison.

Witherling	Level 4 Skirmisher
Small natural animate (undead)	XP 175

Initiative +8   **Senses** Perception +2; low-light vision
HP 56; **Bloodied** 28
AC 18; **Fortitude** 16, **Reflex** 17, **Will** 15
Speed 8, climb 6
⊕ **Claw** (standard; at-will)
   +9 vs. AC; 1d6 + 2 damage, and the target is slowed (save ends).
‡ **Double Attack** (standard; usable only while bloodied; at-will)
   The witherling makes two claw attacks.
Combat Advantage
   A witherling deals 1d6 extra damage on attacks against any creature granting combat advantage to it.
Blood Dance (move; usable only while bloodied; at-will)
   The witherling shifts 2 squares.
Pack Attack
   A witherling's melee attacks deal 2 extra damage against any enemy that has two or more of the witherling's allies adjacent to it.
Sudden Leap (move; at-will)
   The witherling jumps 4 squares. During the jump, it gains a +5 bonus to AC against opportunity attacks, and any enemy that misses the witherling with an opportunity attack grants combat advantage to it until the end of the witherling's turn.

Alignment Evil	**Languages** Abyssal, Common	
Str 11 (+2)	**Dex** 19 (+6)	**Wis** 11 (+2)
Con 16 (+5)	**Int** 7 (+0)	**Cha** 12 (+3)

WITHERLING TACTICS

As befits undead creatures infused with the spirits of demons, witherlings use simple mob tactics to overwhelm their enemies. Gnolls use them as a screening force, sending them ahead of a gnoll pack to harass and slow the enemy, allowing pursuing gnolls to overrun their prey. When a witherling closes with a foe, it uses *sudden leap* in an effort to gain combat advantage. It then attacks the first foe to grant combat advantage to it.

WITHERLING DEATH SHRIEKER

A death shrieker is a larger, more ferocious form of witherling. Its blood-curdling shriek drains the life from its enemies while granting strength and vitality to its undead companions.

Witherling Death Shrieker	Level 5 Controller (Leader)
Medium natural animate (undead)	XP 200

Initiative +5   **Senses** Perception +4; low-light vision
HP 65; **Bloodied** 32
AC 19; **Fortitude** 17, **Reflex** 17, **Will** 16
Speed 6
⊕ **Claws** (standard; at-will)
   +10 vs. AC; 1d10 + 5 damage.
↞ **Death Shriek** (standard; recharge ⚄ ⚅) ✦ **Healing**
   Close blast 5; targets enemies; +9 vs. Fortitude; 2d6 + 4 damage, and any undead ally adjacent to the target regains 5 hit points. An undead ally can regain hit points only once per round in this way.
↞ **Thunder Shriek** (standard; at-will) ✦ **Thunder**
   Close blast 5; targets enemies; +9 vs. Fortitude; 1d6 + 4 thunder damage, and the witherling death shrieker pushes the target 2 squares.
Pack Attack
   A witherling death shrieker's melee attacks deal 2 extra damage against any enemy that has two or more of the death shrieker's allies adjacent to it.

Alignment Evil	**Languages** Abyssal, Common	
Str 12 (+3)	**Dex** 16 (+5)	**Wis** 15 (+4)
Con 17 (+5)	**Int** 11 (+2)	**Cha** 12 (+3)

WITHERLING DEATH SHRIEKER TACTICS

A death shrieker causes chaos and terror among its enemies with its devastating shrieks. Its *death shriek* allows it to hurt its enemies while helping its allies. It uses *thunder shriek* to create gaps in defensive lines for agile skirmishers to penetrate.

WITHERLING HORNED TERROR

A HORNED TERROR IS AN UNDEAD abomination created from the specially preserved corpse of a minotaur. Owing to Yeenoghu's long war against Baphomet, the gnolls have many opportunities to produce these horrors. Minotaurs loathe them, viewing these undead as a blasphemy against their kind.

Witherling Horned Terror	Level 8 Brute
Large natural animate (undead)	XP 350

Initiative +6   **Senses** Perception +6; low-light vision
HP 107; **Bloodied** 53
AC 19; **Fortitude** 22, **Reflex** 18, **Will** 18
Speed 7
⊕ **Claws** (standard; at-will)
   Reach 2; +11 vs. AC; 2d10 + 3 damage.
♦ **Horns** (standard; at-will)
   +9 vs. Fortitude; 2d6 + 5 damage, and the witherling horned terror pushes the target 2 squares.
♦ **Rampaging Charge** (standard; recharge ⚄ ⚅)
   The witherling horned terror charges and makes the following attack in place of a melee basic attack: +11 vs. AC; 2d6 + 5 damage. *Effect:* Make a secondary attack against a different target. *Secondary Attack:* Reach 2; +11 vs. AC; 2d6 + 5 damage. *Effect:* Make the same attack (without charging) two more times against different targets.
Pack Attack
   A witherling horned terror's melee attacks deal 2 extra damage against any enemy that has two or more of the horned terror's allies adjacent to it.

Alignment Evil	**Languages** Abyssal, Common	
Str 22 (+10)	**Dex** 15 (+6)	**Wis** 15 (+6)
Con 17 (+7)	**Int** 6 (+2)	**Cha** 11 (+4)

WITHERLING HORNED TERROR TACTICS

A horned terror is as direct and unsubtle a warrior as it was in life. It uses *rampaging charge* as often as it can, even provoking opportunity attacks in order to run down as many foes as possible.

WITHERLING RABBLE

WHEN GNOLLS OR NECROMANCERS create witherlings, the process sometimes goes awry. The magic instead creates witherling rabble, inferior forms of the creatures.

Witherling Rabble	Level 9 Minion Skirmisher
Small natural animate (undead)	XP 100

Initiative +10   **Senses** Perception +4; low-light vision
HP 1; a missed attack never damages a minion.
AC 23; **Fortitude** 21, **Reflex** 22, **Will** 20
Speed 8, climb 6
⊕ **Claw** (standard; at-will)
   +14 vs. AC; 9 damage.
Combat Advantage
   A witherling rabble deals 2 extra damage on attacks against any creature granting combat advantage to it.
Pack Attack
   A witherling rabble's melee attacks deal 2 extra damage against any enemy that has two or more of the rabble's allies adjacent to it.
Sudden Leap (move; at-will)
   The witherling rabble jumps 4 squares. During the jump, it gains a +5 bonus to AC against opportunity attacks, and any enemy that misses the rabble with an opportunity attack grants combat advantage to it until the end of the rabble's turn.

Alignment Evil	**Languages** Abyssal, Common	
Str 11 (+4)	**Dex** 19 (+8)	**Wis** 11 (+4)
Con 16 (+7)	**Int** 7 (+2)	**Cha** 12 (+5)

WITHERLING LORE

Religion DC 14: Yeenoghu recently imparted to the gnolls the knowledge of the blasphemous process used to create witherlings. A war between Yeenoghu and Orcus is brewing, and the witherlings are but one of several new weapons that the Prince of Gnolls has given to his children.

ENCOUNTER GROUPS

Witherlings were first made by gnolls, but the secret of their creation has spread to necromancers of other races.

Level 6 Encounter (XP 1,300)
✦ 2 deathpledged gnolls (level 5 brute)
✦ 1 gnoll huntmaster (level 5 artillery, *MM* 132)
✦ 4 witherlings (level 4 skirmisher)

Level 8 Encounter (XP 1,800)
✦ 2 cambion hellswords (level 8 brute, *MM* 39)
✦ 1 fang of Yeenoghu (level 7 skirmisher)
✦ 8 witherling rabble (level 9 minion skirmisher)

WOOD WOAD

WOOD WOADS SEEK VENGEANCE for each tree that falls to the axe. A creature that intrudes into a forest protected by wood woads is held responsible for the actions of all previous intruders.

Wood Woad	Level 8 Soldier
Medium fey humanoid (plant)	XP 350

Initiative +5   **Senses** Perception +12
HP 92; **Bloodied** 46
AC 23; **Fortitude** 21, **Reflex** 18, **Will** 21
Speed 5

ⓐ **Club** (standard; at-will) ✦ **Weapon**
+16 vs. AC; 1d8 + 6 damage.

✟ **Nature's Judgment** (standard; recharge ⚅⚅) ✦ **Healing, Reliable, Weapon**
+16 vs. AC; 2d8 + 6 damage, and the target is immobilized and takes ongoing 5 damage (save ends both). When the target takes the ongoing damage, the fey enemy or plant enemy nearest to the target regains an equal number of hit points.

⬳ **Nature's Mystery** (minor; encounter) ✦ **Charm**
Close burst 2; targets one creature; no attack roll; the target takes a -2 penalty to attack rolls, all defenses, and saving throws (save ends). In addition, the target takes a -5 penalty to saving throws against this effect unless it succeeds on a DC 20 Nature check (a free action on the target's turn).

Alignment Unaligned   **Languages** Common, Elven
Skills Intimidate +11
Str 18 (+8)   **Dex** 9 (+3)   **Wis** 16 (+7)
Con 20 (+9)   **Int** 10 (+4)   **Cha** 10 (+4)
Equipment small wooden shield, club

WOOD WOAD TACTICS

A wood woad uses *nature's judgment* as soon as it can, preferring to target an enemy that relies on speed or mobility rather than an enemy that wishes to hold a position. It stays near allies in order to defend them.

WOOD WOAD LORE

Nature DC 14: Those who have extensive knowledge of nature, such as rangers, druids, and wardens, can usually overcome a wood woad's magic more easily than those who are not wise in the ways of the woods.

Nature DC 19: Wood woads and dryads share a common heritage. Dryads are sometimes at peace, comforted by the presence of their trees, but wood woads are constantly enraged by slain forests.

ENCOUNTER GROUPS

Wood woads gladly ally with other creatures that share their drive to protect the natural world. Centaurs and dryads fight alongside them. Clever fey creatures, particularly gnomes and eladrin, sometimes trick wood woads into allying with them by creating a link between the fey's goal and the wood woads' desires.

Level 8 encounter (XP 1,800)
✦ 2 dryads (level 9 skirmisher, *MM* 96)
✦ 1 vine horror spellfiend (level 7 artillery, *MM* 260)
✦ 2 wood woads (level 8 soldier)

Level 9 encounter (XP 2,150)
✦ 1 gnome entropist (level 8 artillery)
✦ 1 satyr piper (level 8 controller, *MM* 228)
✦ 1 shambling mound (level 9 brute, *MM* 232)
✦ 3 wood woads (level 8 soldier)

XORN

BIZARRE SCAVENGERS originally from the Elemental Chaos, xorns now inhabit the world's deep subterranean tunnels and remote mountain caverns.

XORN

Xorns move through solid rock like fish through water, seeking out rare metals and gems to devour.

Xorn		Level 9 Skirmisher
Medium elemental magical beast (earth)		XP 400
Initiative +8	**Senses** Perception +7; all-around vision, darkvision	
HP 102; **Bloodied** 51		
AC 23; **Fortitude** 24, **Reflex** 19, **Will** 20		
Speed 5, burrow 5; see also *earth glide*		
⊕ **Claw** (standard; at-will)		
+14 vs. AC; 1d6 + 5 damage.		
⸭ **Triple Strike** (standard; at-will)		
The xorn makes three claw attacks, each against a different target.		
⸭ **Earthy Maw** (standard; at-will)		
+14 vs. AC; 2d6 + 5 damage.		
Earth Glide		
A xorn can burrow through solid stone as if it were loose earth.		
Retreat (immediate reaction, when the xorn is missed by a melee attack; at-will)		
The xorn burrows its speed.		
Submerge (minor; at-will)		
The xorn sinks partially under the ground and gains a +2 bonus to AC until it moves.		
Alignment Unaligned	**Languages** Common, Primordial	
Str 20 (+9)	**Dex** 15 (+6)	**Wis** 17 (+7)
Con 22 (+10)	**Int** 12 (+5)	**Cha** 12 (+5)

DIAMONDHIDE XORN

In the deep recesses of the Elemental Chaos and in stony realms across the planes, diamondhide xorns glide through the earth in search of the rarest minerals. The armored skin of a diamondhide xorn glitters with the remnants of minerals it has ingested.

Diamondhide Xorn		Level 16 Skirmisher
Large elemental magical beast (earth)		XP 1,400
Initiative +13	**Senses** Perception +12; all-around vision, darkvision	
HP 160; **Bloodied** 80		
AC 29; **Fortitude** 29, **Reflex** 25, **Will** 26		
Speed 5, burrow 5; see also *earth glide*		
⊕ **Claw** (standard; at-will)		
Reach 2; +21 vs. AC; 1d8 + 7 damage.		
⸭ **Triple Strike** (standard; at-will)		
The diamondhide xorn makes three claw attacks, each against a different target.		
⸭ **Earthy Maw** (standard; at-will)		
+21 vs. AC; 2d8 + 7 damage.		
⸭ **Undermine** (standard; recharge ⚄ ⚅)		
The diamondhide xorn burrows its speed and attacks one nonflying enemy whose space it passes under: +19 vs. Reflex; 4d8 + 7 damage, and the target is restrained (save ends).		
Earth Glide		
A diamondhide xorn can burrow through solid stone as if it were loose earth.		
Retreat (immediate reaction, when missed by a melee attack; at-will)		
The diamondhide xorn burrows its speed.		
Submerge (minor; at-will)		
The diamondhide xorn sinks partially under the ground and gains a +2 bonus to AC until it moves.		
Alignment Unaligned	**Languages** Common, Primordial	
Str 22 (+14)	**Dex** 17 (+11)	**Wis** 19 (+12)
Con 24 (+15)	**Int** 13 (+9)	**Cha** 13 (+9)

XORN LORE

Dungeoneering DC 23: Xorns are creatures from the Elemental Chaos that feed on metal and minerals. Their appetite for rare gemstones makes them open to bargaining. However, they have been known to engage in diplomacy while using the time to set up ambushes.

ENCOUNTER GROUPS

Xorns bargain their services across the planes in exchange for precious metals and gemstones. They can be found aiding the mining or smelting operations of duergar or fire giants, and sometimes allied with galeb duhrs or other creatures of elemental earth.

Level 10 Encounter (XP 2,400)
✦ 1 duergar fleshtearer (level 11 lurker)
✦ 4 duergar shock troopers (level 6 brute)
✦ 2 xorns (level 9 skirmisher)

GLOSSARY

This glossary defines game terms used in this book. The glossary supersedes previous sources and incorporates clarifications and new rules.

aberrant [origin]: Aberrant creatures are native to or shaped by the Far Realm.

acid [keyword]: A damage type.

aftereffect: An aftereffect automatically occurs after another effect ends. In a power description, an "Aftereffect" entry follows the effect it applies to.

A target is sometimes subject to an aftereffect after a save. If that save occurs when the target is rolling multiple saving throws, the aftereffect takes effect after the target has rolled all of them.

air [keyword]: An air creature is strongly connected to the element of air.

all-around vision: Enemies can't gain combat advantage by flanking a creature that has all-around vision.

altitude limit: If a creature has a specified altitude limit, the creature crashes at the end of its turn if it is flying higher than that limit. See also **fly speed**.

angel [keyword]: Angels are immortal creatures native to the Astral Sea. They don't need to breathe, eat, or sleep.

animate [type]: Animate creatures are given life through magic. They don't need to breathe, eat, or sleep.

aquatic [keyword]: Aquatic creatures can breathe underwater. In aquatic combat, an aquatic creature gains a +2 bonus to attack rolls against nonaquatic creatures. See also "Aquatic Combat," *Dungeon Master's Guide*, page 45.

aura: An aura is a continuous effect that emanates from a creature. The aura affects each square within line of effect and within a specified range of that creature's space. The aura does not affect that creature, unless otherwise noted, and is unaffected by terrain or environmental phenomena.

A creature can deactivate or reactivate its aura as a minor action. If the creature dies, the aura ends immediately.

If auras overlap and impose penalties to the same roll or game statistic, a creature affected by the overlapping auras is subject to the worst penalty; the penalties are not cumulative. Similarly, a creature in the overlapping area takes damage only from the aura that deals the most damage, regardless of damage type.

beast [type]: Beasts are either ordinary animals or creatures akin to them. They behave instinctively.

blind [keyword]: A blind creature relies on special senses, such as blindsight or tremorsense, to see within a specified range, beyond which the creature can't see. The creature is immune to gaze attacks and cannot be blinded.

blindsight: A creature that has blindsight can clearly see creatures or objects within a specified range and within line of effect, even if they are invisible or obscured. The creature otherwise relies on its normal vision.

burrow speed: A creature that has a burrow speed can move through loose earth at a specified speed, and the creature can move through solid stone at half that speed. The creature can't shift or charge while burrowing.

change shape: A creature that has the polymorph power *change shape* can assume the form of another creature. The power specifies the type and size of that form. The new form lasts until it is changed or until the creature dies.

The creature retains its statistics in its new form. Its clothing, armor, and other possessions do not change with the new form.

If the creature can use *change shape* to assume the form of an individual, the creature must have seen that individual. Other creatures can make an Insight check (opposed by the creature's Bluff check with a +20 bonus) to discern that the form is a disguise. See also **polymorph**.

charm [keyword]: A charm power controls or influences a subject's actions.

climb speed: A creature that has a climb speed moves on vertical surfaces at that speed without making Athletics checks to climb. While climbing, the creature ignores difficult terrain and doesn't grant combat advantage because of climbing.

clumsy: Some creatures are clumsy while using a specific movement mode (noted next to that mode in the creature's "Speed" entry), and others are clumsy while on the ground (noted next to the creature's speed). While a creature is clumsy, it takes a –4 penalty to attack rolls and all defenses.

cold [keyword]: A damage type. A creature that has this keyword is at least partially composed of ice.

conjuration [keyword]: A conjuration power creates a conjuration, which is an object or a creature of magical energy. A conjuration occupies no squares, is unaffected by the environment, does not need to be supported by a solid surface, cannot be attacked or physically affected, and ends immediately when its creator dies.

If a conjuration can be attacked or physically affected, it uses its creator's defenses. Unless an attack specifically targets conjurations, only the attack's damage (not including ongoing damage) affects the conjuration. If a conjuration can attack, its creator makes the attack, determining line of sight normally but determining line of effect from the conjuration.

If the power that creates a conjuration includes the ability to move it, the conjuration is considered a movable conjuration. A movable conjuration ends at the end of its creator's turn if the creator is not within range of at least 1 square it's in (using the power's range) or if the creator doesn't have line of effect to at least 1 square it's in. A conjuration can't be moved through a solid obstacle.

construct [keyword]: Constructs are not living creatures, so effects that specifically target living creatures do not work against them. They don't need to breathe, eat, or sleep.

darkvision: A creature that has darkvision can see in dim light and darkness without penalty.

demon [keyword]: Demons are chaotic evil elemental creatures native to the Abyss. They don't need to sleep.

devil [keyword]: Devils are evil immortal creatures native to the Nine Hells. They don't need to sleep.

disease [keyword]: Some powers expose a target to a disease. If a creature is exposed to a disease one or more times during an encounter, it makes one saving throw at the end of the encounter to determine if it contracts the disease. If the saving throw fails, the target is infected. See also "Disease," *Dungeon Master's Guide*, page 49.

dragon [keyword]: Dragons are reptilian creatures. Most of them have wings as well as a breath weapon.

earth [keyword]: An earth creature is strongly connected to the element of earth.

earth walk: A type of terrain walk. A creature that has earth walk ignores difficult terrain that is rubble, uneven stone, or an earthen construction.

elemental [origin]: Elemental creatures are native to the Elemental Chaos.

extra damage: Many powers and other effects grant the ability to deal extra damage. Extra damage is always in addition to other damage. This means an attack that deals no damage can't deal extra damage.

fear [keyword]: A fear power inspires fright.

fey [origin]: Fey creatures are native to the Feywild.

fire [keyword]: A damage type. A fire creature is strongly connected to the element of fire.

fly speed: A creature that has a fly speed can fly a number of squares up to that speed as a move action. To remain in the air, the creature must move at least 2 squares during its turn, or it crashes at the end of its turn. While flying, the creature can't shift or make opportunity attacks, and it crashes if it's knocked prone. See also "Flying," *Dungeon Master's Guide*, page 47.

force [keyword]: A damage type.

forest walk: A type of terrain walk. A creature that has forest walk ignores difficult terrain that is part of a tree, underbrush, or some other forest growth.

gaze [keyword]: A type of attack. Blind or blinded creatures are immune to gaze attacks, and a creature cannot make a gaze attack while blinded.

giant [keyword]: Giants are Large or larger humanoid creatures.

grabbed: Being grabbed means a creature is immobilized. Unless otherwise noted, a grab lasts until the end of the grabber's next turn, and the grabber can sustain the grab as a minor action and end it as a free action. Certain circumstances end a grab: if the grabber is affected by a condition that prevents it from taking opportunity actions, if either the grabber or the creature it's grabbing moves far enough away that the grabbed creature is no longer in the grabber's reach, or if the grabbed creature escapes. See also "Escape" and "Grab," *Player's Handbook*, pages 288 and 290.

half damage: When a power or another effect deals half damage, apply all modifiers to the damage, including resistances and vulnerabilities, and then divide the damage in half.

healing [keyword]: A healing power restores hit points.

hidden: When a creature is hidden from an enemy, the creature is silent and invisible to that enemy. A creature normally uses the Stealth skill to become hidden.

homunculus [keyword]: Homunculi are animate constructs tasked with guarding a creature, an area, or an object.

hover: If a creature can hover, it can remain in the air without moving during its turn. It can also shift and make opportunity attacks while flying. See also **fly speed**.

humanoid [type]: Humanoid creatures vary greatly in how much they resemble humans. Most are bipedal. They include humans as well as monstrous humanoids such as yuan-ti.

ice walk: A type of terrain walk. A creature that has ice walk ignores difficult terrain that is ice or snow.

illusion [keyword]: An illusion power deceives the mind or the senses.

immortal [origin]: Immortal creatures are native to the Astral Sea. Unless they are killed, they live forever.

immune: A creature that is immune to a damage type (such as cold or fire), a condition (such as dazed or petrified), or another specific effect (such as disease or forced movement) is not affected by it. A creature that is immune to charm, fear, illusion, poison, or sleep is not affected by the nondamaging effects of a power that has that keyword. A creature that is immune to gaze is not affected by powers that have that keyword.

implement: The implement keyword identifies a power that can be used through an implement. A monster's statistics block notes the implements it uses. See also "Adding Equipment," *Dungeon Master's Guide*, page 174.

insubstantial: When a creature is insubstantial, it takes half damage from any damage source, including ongoing damage. Some creatures are inherently insubstantial, which is noted in their "Resist" entries. See also **half damage**.

lightning [keyword]: A damage type.

living construct [keyword]: Unlike other constructs, living constructs are living creatures.

low-light vision: A creature that has low-light vision can see in dim light without penalty.

magical beast [type]: Magical beasts resemble beasts but often behave like people.

marked: When a creature marks a target, that target takes a –2 penalty to attack rolls for any attack that doesn't include the creature as a target. A creature can be subject to only one mark at a time, and a new mark supersedes an old one.

maximum altitude: See **altitude limit**.

minion: A minion is destroyed when it takes any damage. If a minion is missed by an attack that deals damage on a miss, the minion doesn't take that damage.

mount [keyword]: A creature that has the mount keyword has at least one mount power. A mount power is usable only when the creature's rider has the Mounted Combat feat. See also "Mounted Combat," *Dungeon Master's Guide*, page 46.

natural [origin]: Natural creatures are native to the natural world.

necrotic [keyword]: A damage type.

ooze [keyword]: Oozes are amorphous creatures. When an ooze squeezes, it can move at full speed (rather than half speed), it doesn't take the –5 penalty to attack rolls, and it doesn't grant combat advantage because of squeezing.

overland flight: Overland flight works like a fly speed with one exception: A creature can take a move action to use overland flight only if it has taken no actions that turn, except free actions or move actions using overland flight. The creature can then take only those actions until the start of its next turn. See also **fly speed**.

phasing: While phasing, a creature ignores difficult terrain and can move through obstacles and other creatures, but it must end its movement in an unoccupied space.

plant [keyword]: Plant creatures are composed of vegetable matter. They don't need to sleep.

poison [keyword]: A damage and effect type.

polymorph [keyword]: Polymorph powers change a target's physical form. If a target is affected by more than one polymorph power, only the most recent one has any effect. The other powers' effects remain on the target and their durations expire as normal, but those effects don't apply. However, when the most recent effect ends, the next most recent one that is still active applies to the target. If the target dies, polymorph effects end on it immediately.

If a polymorph effect reduces a target's space, the target doesn't provoke opportunity attacks for leaving squares as it shrinks. If a polymorph effect makes a target too large to fit in the available space, the effect fails against the target, but the target is stunned (save ends).

psychic [keyword]: A damage type.

radiant [keyword]: A damage type.

reliable [keyword]: If a creature misses every target when using a reliable power, the use of that power isn't expended.

reptile [keyword]: Reptiles are cold-blooded creatures that have scaly skin.

resist: A creature that has resistance takes less damage from a specific damage type. For example, a creature that has resist 10 fire takes 10 less damage whenever it takes fire damage.

Resistance doesn't reduce damage unless the target has resistance to each type of damage from the attack, and then only the weakest of the resistances applies. For example, a creature that has resist 10 lightning and resist 5 thunder that takes 15 lightning and thunder damage takes 10 damage because the resistance value to the combined damage types is limited by the lesser of the two resistances.

shadow [origin]: Shadow creatures are native to the Shadowfell.

shapechanger [keyword]: Shapechangers, such as doppelgangers, have the ability to alter their form, whether freely or into specific forms.

sleep [keyword]: Sleep powers knock creatures unconscious.

spider [keyword]: Spider creatures include spiders as well as creatures that have spiderlike features: eight legs, web spinning, and the like.

spider climb: A creature that can spider climb can use its climb speed to move across overhanging horizontal surfaces (such as ceilings) without making Athletics checks. See also **climb speed**.

swamp walk: A type of terrain walk. A creature that has swamp walk ignores difficult terrain that is mud or shallow water.

swarm [keyword]: A swarm is composed of multiple creatures but functions as a single creature. A swarm can occupy the same space as another creature, and an enemy can enter a swarm's space, which is difficult terrain. A swarm cannot be pulled, pushed, or slid by melee or ranged attacks.

A swarm can squeeze through any opening large enough for even one of its constituent creatures. For example, a swarm of bats can squeeze through any opening large enough for one of the bats to squeeze through.

swim speed: A creature that has a swim speed moves through water at that speed without making Athletics checks to swim.

telepathy: A creature that has telepathy can communicate telepathically with any other creature that has a language. The other creature must be within line of effect and within a specified range. Telepathy allows for two-way communication.

teleportation [keyword]: A teleportation power transports creatures or objects instantaneously from one location to another. A creature that uses a teleportation power must have line of sight to the destination space, but neither that creature nor the target being teleported needs line of effect to that space. The destination must be a space that the target can occupy without squeezing.

The target being teleported disappears and instantaneously appears in the destination space. The movement doesn't provoke opportunity attacks and is unhindered by intervening creatures, objects, or terrain.

Being immobilized or restrained doesn't prevent a creature from teleporting. If a creature teleports away from a physical restraint, a monster's grasp, or some other immobilizing effect that is located in a specific space, the creature is no longer immobilized or restrained. Otherwise, the creature teleports but is still immobilized or restrained when it reaches the destination space.

threatening reach: A creature that has threatening reach can make an opportunity attack against any enemy within its reach that provokes an opportunity attack.

thunder [keyword]: A damage type.

tremorsense: A creature that has tremorsense can clearly see creatures or objects within a specified range, even if they are invisible, obscured, or outside line of effect, but they and the creature must be in contact with the ground or the same substance, such as water or a web. The creature otherwise relies on its normal vision.

truesight: A creature that has truesight can see invisible creatures and objects within a specified range as long as they are also within line of sight.

tunneling: A creature that has tunneling leaves tunnels behind it as it burrows. The creature, as well as smaller creatures, can move through these tunnels without any reduction in speed. Creatures of the same size as the tunneling creature must squeeze through these tunnels, and larger creatures cannot move through them at all. See also **burrow speed**.

undead [keyword]: Undead are not living creatures, so effects that specifically target living creatures do not work against them. They don't need to breathe or sleep.

variable resistance: A creature that has variable resistance can activate it a specified number of times per encounter as a free action. When the creature activates variable resistance, it chooses a damage type: acid, cold, fire, lightning, or thunder. (The creature can't choose a damage type to which it is vulnerable.) Until the end of the encounter, the creature gains a specified amount of resistance to that damage type. This resistance replaces any resistance the creature already had against that damage type. If a creature can activate variable resistance more than once per encounter, the creature can resist only one damage type at a time using variable resistance. See also **resist**.

vulnerable: A creature that is vulnerable to a specified damage type usually takes a specific amount of extra damage when it takes damage of that type, or it suffers a specific effect. For example, a creature that has vulnerable 10 radiant takes 10 extra radiant damage when an attack deals radiant damage to it or when it takes ongoing radiant damage.

water [keyword]: A water creature is strongly connected to the element of water.

weapon [keyword]: The weapon keyword identifies a power that is used with a weapon, which can be an unarmed strike. A monster's statistics block notes the weapons it uses. Monster attacks don't use proficiency bonuses. See also "Adding Equipment," *Dungeon Master's Guide*, page 174.

zone [keyword]: A zone power creates a zone, a magical area that lasts for a round or more. A zone is formed by an area of effect and fills each square in the area that is within line of effect of the origin square. A zone is unaffected by the environment, cannot be attacked or physically affected, and ends immediately when its creator dies.

If the power that creates a zone includes the ability to move it, the zone is considered a movable zone. A movable zone ends at the end of its creator's turn if the creator is not within range of at least 1 square of it (using the power's range) or if the creator doesn't have line of effect to at least 1 square of it. A zone can't be moved through a solid obstacle.

If zones overlap and impose penalties to the same roll or game statistic, a creature affected by the overlapping zones is subject to the worst penalty; the penalties are not cumulative. Similarly, a creature in the overlapping area takes damage only from the zone that deals the most damage, regardless of damage type.

RACIAL TRAITS

As in the *Monster Manual*, a few of the monsters in *Monster Manual 2* have racial traits and powers similar to those of the races presented in the *Player's Handbook* and *Player's Handbook 2*.

These traits and powers are most useful to Dungeon Masters interested in creating detailed non-player characters (NPCs). The information can also be used as guidelines for creating player character (PC) versions of these creatures. Be aware that the traits and powers that follow are more in line with monster powers than with player character powers—actual PC versions of any of the races published later would likely be slightly different.

As a DM, you should carefully consider which, if any, of the monster races you wish to include as PC options in your campaign.

BULLYWUG

Average Height: 5′ 4″ - 6′ 0″
Average Weight: 150-240 lb.

Ability Scores: +2 Constitution, +2 Dexterity
Size: Medium
Speed: 6 squares (swamp walk)
Vision: Normal

Languages: Common, Primordial
Skill Bonuses: +2 Athletics
Rancid Air (Poison) aura 2: Any enemy that spends a healing surge within the aura is weakened until the end of its next turn.

DUERGAR

Average Height: 4′ 2″ - 4′ 8″
Average Weight: 160-220 lb.

Ability Scores: +2 Constitution, +2 Wisdom
Size: Medium
Speed: 6 squares
Vision: Darkvision

Languages: Common, Deep Speech, Dwarven
Skill Bonuses: +2 Dungeoneering
Infernal Quills: You can use *infernal quills* as an encounter power.

Infernal Quills — Duergar Racial Power

You tense and send the quills projecting from your body into the gaps in your foe's armor.

Encounter ✦ Poison
Minor Action — Ranged 3
Target: One creature
Attack: Constitution + 2 vs. AC
  Level 11: Constitution + 4 vs. AC
  Level 21: Constitution + 6 vs. AC
Hit: 1d8 + Constitution modifier damage, and the target takes a -2 penalty to attack rolls and ongoing 2 poison damage (save ends both).
  Level 11: 2d8 + Constitution modifier damage, and the target takes a -2 penalty to attack rolls and ongoing 5 poison damage (save ends both).
  Level 21: 3d8 + Constitution modifier damage, and the target takes a -2 penalty to attack rolls and ongoing 8 poison damage (save ends both).

KENKU

Average Height: 5′ 0″ - 5′ 6″
Average Weight: 110-150 lb.

Ability Scores: +2 Dexterity, +2 Charisma
Size: Medium
Speed: 6 squares
Vision: Low-light

Languages: Common
Skill Bonuses: +2 Bluff, +2 Stealth
Flock Effect: You gain a +3 bonus to attack rolls against a creature you are flanking instead of the normal +2 bonus, and you grant a +3 bonus to attack rolls or skill checks when aiding another instead of the normal +2 bonus.
Mimicry: You can mimic sounds and voices. A successful Insight check opposed by your Bluff check allows a listener to determine that the effect is faked.

MONSTERS BY LEVEL

Every monster in the book appears on this list, which is sorted alphabetically by level and monster role. Monster leaders are indicated with an (L).

Monster	Level and Role	Page
Fell Taint Pulsar	1 Artillery	104
Ankheg Broodling	1 Minion Brute	11
Bullywug Mucker	1 Brute	28
Goblin Acolyte of Maglubiyet	1 Controller	131
Blood Hawk	1 Skirmisher	142
Fell Taint Lasher	1 Soldier	104
Poisonscale Magus (Lizardfolk)	2 Artillery	156
Centipede Swarm	2 Brute	33
Dretch (Demon)	2 Brute	54
Poisonscale Savage (Lizardfolk)	2 Brute	156
Fell Taint Thought Eater	2 Controller	104
Bullywug Twitcher	2 Skirmisher	28
Gray Ooze	2 Skirmisher	173
Hive Warrior (Ant)	2 Skirmisher	12
Stonefist Defender (Homunculus)	2 Skirmisher	143
Bloodthorn Vine	2 Soldier	205
Poisonscale Slitherer (Lizardfolk)	2 Soldier	156
Bullywug Mud Lord	3 Artillery	29
Bullywug Croaker	3 Minion Brute	28
Myconid Rotpriest	3 Brute (L)	164
Ankheg	3 Elite Lurker	11
Poisonscale Collector (Lizardfolk)	3 Lurker	156
Dust Devil (Elemental)	3 Skirmisher	99
Kenku Ruffian	3 Minion Skirmisher	152
Kenku Warrior	3 Skirmisher	152
Skeletal Steed	3 Skirmisher	183
Hive Soldier (Ant)	3 Soldier	12
Infernal Armor Animus (Devil)	3 Minion Soldier	66
Lolthbound Goblin	3 Soldier	131
Poisonscale Myrmidon (Lizardfolk)	3 Soldier	157
Arbalester (Homunculus)	4 Artillery	143
Storm Shard	4 Artillery	34
Barghest Savager	4 Brute	20
Mud Lasher (Elemental)	4 Brute	100
Fell Taint Warp Wender	4 Controller	105
Krenshar	4 Controller	155
Myconid Sovereign	4 Controller (L)	164
Umbral Sprite Swarm	4 Controller	194
Dimensional Marauder	4 Lurker	69
Duergar Scout	4 Lurker	92
Green Slime (Ooze)	4 Lurker	173
Kenku Sneak	4 Lurker	153
Centipede Scuttler	4 Skirmisher	33
Winged Drone (Ant)	4 Skirmisher	12
Witherling	4 Skirmisher	212
Bloodseeker Drake	4 Soldier	88
Duergar Guard	4 Soldier	92
Kenku Ringleader	4 Soldier (L)	152
Myconid Guard	4 Soldier	164
Beholder Gauth	5 Elite Artillery	24
Eladrin Arcane Archer	5 Artillery	96
Kenku Wing Mage	5 Artillery	153
Runespiral Demon	5 Artillery	60
Deathpledged Gnoll	5 Brute	126
Krenshar Blood Slayer	5 Brute	155
Duergar Theurge	5 Controller	93
Hive Queen (Ant)	5 Elite Controller (L)	13

Monster	Level and Role	Page
Human Noble	5 Controller (L)	148
Witherling Death Shrieker	5 Controller	212
Gnome Mistwalker	5 Lurker	128
Young Iron Dragon	5 Solo Lurker	84
Cockatrice	5 Skirmisher	36
Gnaw Demon	5 Skirmisher	54
Half-Orc Hunter	5 Skirmisher	140
Horned Drake	5 Skirmisher	88
Kenku Assassin	5 Elite Skirmisher	154
Flamespiker (Elemental)	5 Soldier	99
Rupture Demon	5 Minion Soldier	60
Warforged Resounder	6 Artillery	206
Duergar Shock Trooper	6 Brute	93
Wereboar (Lycanthrope)	6 Brute	158
Half-Orc Death Mage	6 Controller	140
Hobgoblin Fleshcarver	6 Elite Controller	132
Geonid (Elemental)	6 Lurker	99
Abyssal Marauder (Demogorgon)	6 Skirmisher	48
Bugbear Wardancer (Goblin)	6 Skirmisher	130
Half-Elf Bandit Captain	6 Skirmisher (L)	138
Human Javelin Dancer	6 Skirmisher	147
Rust Monster	6 Skirmisher	178
Tiger	6 Skirmisher	199
Young Copper Dragon	6 Solo Skirmisher	78
Spriggan Thorn	6 Soldier	192
Goliath Sunspeaker	7 Artillery	136
Gnoll Gorger	7 Brute	127
Half-Orc Scarthane	7 Brute	141
Shrieking Cultist of Demogorgon	7 Brute	50
Troglodyte Thrasher	7 Brute	200
Warforged Savage	7 Brute	206
Barghest Battle Lord	7 Controller	20
Half-Elf Con Artist	7 Controller	138
Human Hexer	7 Controller	146
Bloodseep Demon	7 Skirmisher (L)	53
Fang of Yeenoghu (Gnoll)	7 Skirmisher (L)	126
Frost Hawk	7 Skirmisher	142
Genasi Skyspy	7 Skirmisher	117
Human Knife Fighter	7 Elite Skirmisher	147
Shardstorm Vortex (Elemental)	7 Skirmisher	101
Spriggan Powrie	7 Skirmisher	192
Bonecrusher Skeleton	7 Soldier	183
Greenvise Vine	7 Soldier	205
Human Cavalier	7 Soldier (L)	144
Oni Devourer	7 Soldier	170
Young Adamantine Dragon	7 Solo Soldier	75
Death Shard (Chaos Shard)	8 Artillery	34
Direguard Deathbringer	8 Elite Artillery (L)	70
Doom Flayer (Demogorgon)	8 Artillery	49
Gnome Entropist	8 Artillery	128
Spriggan Witherer	8 Artillery (L)	193
Black Pudding (Ooze)	8 Elite Brute	172
Black Pudding Spawn (Ooze)	8 Minion Brute	172
Human Slaver	8 Brute	149
Spriggan Giantsoul	8 Brute	192
Witherling Horned Terror	8 Brute	213
Young Silver Dragon	8 Solo Brute	86
Berserker Prelate of Demogorgon	8 Controller (L)	48
Genasi Hydromancer	8 Controller	117
Warforged Anvilpriest	8 Controller (L)	207
Darkmantle Enveloper	8 Lurker	41
Neldrazu (Demon)	8 Lurker	56
Phase Spider	8 Skirmisher	190
Behir Bolter Whelp	8 Solo Soldier	22
Dire Tiger	8 Soldier	199
Wood Woad	8 Soldier	214

ABOUT THE DESIGNERS

ROB HEINSOO led the design of the 4th Edition D&D® Roleplaying Game. His 4th Edition design credits include *Martial Power*™ and the *FORGOTTEN REALMS*® Player's Guide. His other game designs include *Three-Dragon Ante*™ and DUNGEONS & DRAGONS *Inn Fighting*™.

EYTAN BERNSTEIN is a freelance RPG designer hailing from New York City. His many previous credits for Wizards of the Coast include *Adventurer's Vault*™, *Open Grave: Secrets of the Undead*™ and *Arcane Power*™.

GREG BILSLAND is a game editor and designer at Wizards of the Coast. His writing credits include the *FORGOTTEN REALMS*® Player's Guide, *Divine Power*™, and several *D&D Insider*™ articles.

JESSE DECKER works as Director of Organized Play Operations at Wizards of the Coast. He's been working on D&D professionally for more than a decade, and still needs more monsters to put in his campaign.

N. ERIC HEATH has been making up stories, creatures, and worlds for decades. Although Eric keeps his stuff in Seattle, he is more likely to be found in various fantasy realms.

PETER LEE works as a game designer for Wizards of the Coast, where he splits his time between RPG design and leading the design for D&D® Miniatures.

CHRIS SIMS works as a game designer and web specialist for Wizards of the Coast. His recent credits include the 4th Edition *Monster Manual*® and *Dungeon Master's Guide*®, as well as the *FORGOTTEN REALMS*® Player's Guide.

OWEN K.C. STEPHENS is a freelance RPG writer whose recent work for Wizards of the Coast includes *Adventurer's Vault*™, *Dragon Magic*™, *Scum and Villainy*, and *The Force Unleashed Campaign Guide*.

LEVEL UP YOUR GAME.

Bring more to the gaming table, and make every session even better — D&D® accessories are an indispensable addition to any game. Pick 'em up at the same place you got this boo

Dungeon Master's Screen
Conceal your secrets without blocking your view. Quick reference to common tables helps you keep your game moving.

D&D™ Dungeon Tiles
Define dungeons and add details to every encounter quickly and easily, and help your game come to life.

D&D® Miniatures
Know where everyone, and every thing, is at all times to keep your combats under control.

Character Record Sheets
Keep up with your character and use Power Cards to stay out of the books and in the fight.

D&D™ Premium
Everyone needs dice. And need more than others. Ke in a D&D logo-embroidere

DUNGEON & DRAGON